IT F
Study Guide
Second Edition

IT Project+™
Study Guide
Second Edition

William Heldman
Lona Cram

San Francisco • London

SYBEX

Associate Publisher: Neil Edde
Acquisitions Editor: Elizabeth Hurley Peterson
Developmental Editor: Heather O'Connor
Production Editor: Elizabeth Campbell
Technical Editors: Claudia Baca, Warren Wyrostek
Copyeditor: Cheryl Hauser
Compositor and Graphic Illustrator: Happenstance Type-O-Rama
CD Coordinator: Dan Mummert
CD Technician: Kevin Ly
Proofreaders: Rachel Gunn, Laurie O'Connell, Nancy Riddiough
Indexer: Nancy Guenther
Book Designers: Bill Gibson and Judy Fung
Cover Designer: Archer Design
Cover Illustrator/Photographer: Photodisc and Victor Arre

Copyright © 2004 SYBEX Inc., 1151 Marina Village Parkway, Alameda, CA 94501. World rights reserved. No part of this publication may be stored in a retrieval system, transmitted, or reproduced in any way, including but not limited to photocopy, photograph, magnetic, or other record, without the prior agreement and written permission of the publisher.

First edition copyright © 2002 SYBEX Inc.

Library of Congress Card Number: 2003115674

ISBN: 0-7821-4318-0

SYBEX and the SYBEX logo are either registered trademarks or trademarks of SYBEX Inc. in the United States and/or other countries.

Screen reproductions produced with FullShot 99. FullShot 99 © 1991-1999 Inbit Incorporated. All rights reserved.

FullShot is a trademark of Inbit Incorporated.

The CD interface was created using Macromedia Director, COPYRIGHT 1994, 1997-1999 Macromedia Inc. For more information on Macromedia and Macromedia Director, visit http://www.macromedia.com.

Sybex is an independent entity from CompTIA and is not affiliated with CompTIA in any manner. Neither CompTIA nor Sybex warrants that use of this publication will ensure passing the relevant exam. IT Project+ is either a registered trademark or trademark of CompTIA in the United States and/or other countries.

TRADEMARKS: SYBEX has attempted throughout this book to distinguish proprietary trademarks from descriptive terms by following the capitalization style used by the manufacturer.

The author and publisher have made their best efforts to prepare this book, and the content is based upon final release software whenever possible. Portions of the manuscript may be based upon pre-release versions supplied by software manufacturer(s). The author and the publisher make no representation or warranties of any kind with regard to the completeness or accuracy of the contents herein and accept no liability of any kind including but not limited to performance, merchantability, fitness for any particular purpose, or any losses or damages of any kind caused or alleged to be caused directly or indirectly from this book.

Manufactured in the United States of America

10 9 8 7 6 5 4 3 2 1

SYBEX

To Our Valued Readers:

Thank you for looking to Sybex for your IT Project+ exam prep needs. We at Sybex are proud of our reputation for providing certification candidates with the practical knowledge and skills needed to succeed in the highly competitive IT marketplace. Certification candidates have come to rely on Sybex for accurate and accessible instruction on today's crucial technologies and business skills. For the second year in a row, readers such as yourself voted Sybex as winner of the "Best Study Guides" category in the 2003 CertCities Readers Choice Awards.

Just as CompTIA is committed to establishing measurable standards for certifying individuals with project management responsibilities in the field of IT, Sybex is committed to providing those individuals with the knowledge needed to meet those standards.

The authors and editors have worked hard to ensure that the new edition of the IT Project+ Study Guide you hold in your hands is comprehensive, in-depth, and pedagogically sound. We're confident that this book will exceed the demanding standards of the certification marketplace and help you, the IT Project+ certification candidate, succeed in your endeavors.

As always, your feedback is important to us. Please send comments, questions, or suggestions to support@sybex.com. At Sybex we're continually striving to meet the needs of individuals preparing for certification exams.

Good luck in pursuit of your IT Project+ certification!

Neil Edde
Associate Publisher—Certification
Sybex, Inc.

Software License Agreement: Terms and Conditions

The media and/or any online materials accompanying this book that are available now or in the future contain programs and/or text files (the "Software") to be used in connection with the book. SYBEX hereby grants to you a license to use the Software, subject to the terms that follow. Your purchase, acceptance, or use of the Software will constitute your acceptance of such terms.

The Software compilation is the property of SYBEX unless otherwise indicated and is protected by copyright to SYBEX or other copyright owner(s) as indicated in the media files (the "Owner(s)"). You are hereby granted a single-user license to use the Software for your personal, noncommercial use only. You may not reproduce, sell, distribute, publish, circulate, or commercially exploit the Software, or any portion thereof, without the written consent of SYBEX and the specific copyright owner(s) of any component software included on this media.

In the event that the Software or components include specific license requirements or end-user agreements, statements of condition, disclaimers, limitations or warranties ("End-User License"), those End-User Licenses supersede the terms and conditions herein as to that particular Software component. Your purchase, acceptance, or use of the Software will constitute your acceptance of such End-User Licenses.

By purchase, use or acceptance of the Software you further agree to comply with all export laws and regulations of the United States as such laws and regulations may exist from time to time.

Software Support

Components of the supplemental Software and any offers associated with them may be supported by the specific Owner(s) of that material, but they are not supported by SYBEX. Information regarding any available support may be obtained from the Owner(s) using the information provided in the appropriate read.me files or listed elsewhere on the media.

Should the manufacturer(s) or other Owner(s) cease to offer support or decline to honor any offer, SYBEX bears no responsibility. This notice concerning support for the Software is provided for your information only. SYBEX is not the agent or principal of the Owner(s), and SYBEX is in no way responsible for providing any support for the Software, nor is it liable or responsible for any support provided, or not provided, by the Owner(s).

Warranty

SYBEX warrants the enclosed media to be free of physical defects for a period of ninety (90) days after purchase. The Software is not available from SYBEX in any other form or media than that enclosed herein or posted to www.sybex.com. If you discover a defect in the media during this warranty period, you may obtain a replacement of identical format at no charge by sending the defective media, postage prepaid, with proof of purchase to:

SYBEX Inc.
Product Support Department
1151 Marina Village Parkway
Alameda, CA 94501
Web: http://www.sybex.com

After the 90-day period, you can obtain replacement media of identical format by sending us the defective disk, proof of purchase, and a check or money order for $10, payable to SYBEX.

Disclaimer

SYBEX makes no warranty or representation, either expressed or implied, with respect to the Software or its contents, quality, performance, merchantability, or fitness for a particular purpose. In no event will SYBEX, its distributors, or dealers be liable to you or any other party for direct, indirect, special, incidental, consequential, or other damages arising out of the use of or inability to use the Software or its contents even if advised of the possibility of such damage. In the event that the Software includes an online update feature, SYBEX further disclaims any obligation to provide this feature for any specific duration other than the initial posting.

The exclusion of implied warranties is not permitted by some states. Therefore, the above exclusion may not apply to you. This warranty provides you with specific legal rights; there may be other rights that you may have that vary from state to state. The pricing of the book with the Software by SYBEX reflects the allocation of risk and limitations on liability contained in this agreement of Terms and Conditions.

Shareware Distribution

This Software may contain various programs that are distributed as shareware. Copyright laws apply to both shareware and ordinary commercial software, and the copyright Owner(s) retains all rights. If you try a shareware program and continue using it, you are expected to register it. Individual programs differ on details of trial periods, registration, and payment. Please observe the requirements stated in appropriate files.

Copy Protection

The Software in whole or in part may or may not be copy-protected or encrypted. However, in all cases, reselling or redistributing these files without authorization is expressly forbidden except as specifically provided for by the Owner(s) therein.

To Kimmie
—Bill Heldman

To Michael, who always supports me in everything I do.
—Lona Cram

Acknowledgments

I'd like to acknowledge my co-author, Lona Cram; copyeditor Cheryl Hauser, and also Elizabeth Hurley Peterson, Elizabeth Campbell, and Heather O'Connor; our tech-editors Claudia Baca and Warren Wyrostek; and the rest of the staff at Sybex for creating such a wonderful work environment in which to create books.

I'd also like to acknowledge you, the reader, hungry for more knowledge about IT projects. You are on a good path to finding out more about the ever-increasing world of project management.

Also, I'd like to acknowledge that it is the Lord who gives talent and to thank Him for that ability.
—Bill Heldman

I could not have done this without the support and help of everyone at Sybex who dedicated their efforts to helping a new author be successful. Thanks first to Elizabeth Hurley Peterson for her idea to add a PMP perspective to this book and to guide me through the process of writing a study guide. Heather O'Connor, thank you for all the time you spent providing feedback on my initial submissions and for answering all my numerous questions. Elizabeth Campbell, you always kept me up to date as to what to expect next and when, which was critical to balancing my time and schedule. And to all of the staff that worked behind the scenes to create the figures and design the layout, thanks for all of your hard work.

Thanks to the technical editors, Claudia Baca and Warren Wyrostek. Claudia, you are a walking PMBOK, and Warren you always caught anything that was not clear or needed further explanation. Cheryl Hauser, your detailed copyedits of every chapter assured that my content was consistent and grammatically correct.

I would like to thank my co-author Bill Heldman, for stepping up to the challenge of creating material that applied the project management discipline to the real world challenges faced by IT Project Managers.

Finally, I would like to thank my family for supporting me in this effort, even though that meant watching me spend evenings, weekends, and even a couple of holidays working at my computer rather than spending time with them. Michael, I have always been an over-achiever, and you have always stepped up to the plate to do whatever it took to allow me to be successful.
—Lona Cram

Contents at a Glance

Introduction   *xvii*

Assessment Test   *xl*

Chapter	**1**	IT Project Management Overview	1
Chapter	**2**	Project Initiation	31
Chapter	**3**	Scope Planning	69
Chapter	**4**	Schedule Planning	103
Chapter	**5**	Cost Planning	133
Chapter	**6**	Other Planning Processes	165
Chapter	**7**	Comprehensive Project Plan	207
Chapter	**8**	Project Execution	231
Chapter	**9**	Project Control	275
Chapter	**10**	Project Closure	321
Appendix	**A**	Systems Development Life Cycle	343
Appendix	**B**	Standard IT Project Documents	353
Glossary			363

Index   *381*

Contents

Introduction	*xvii*
Assessment Test	*xl*

Chapter 1   IT Project Management Overview   1

Defining a Project	2
Defining an IT Project	3
Common Job Roles for the IT Project Manager	6
Communication among the Various IT Job Roles	9
Defining Project Management	9
The *Guide to the PMBOK*	9
Project Management Knowledge Areas	10
General Management Skills	10
Leadership	11
Communication	11
Problem Solving	12
Negotiation	13
Organization and Time Management	13
Project Processes	14
Initiation Processes	14
Planning Processes	15
Executing Processes	15
Controlling Processes	15
Closing Processes	15
Project Life Cycles	16
IT Project Life Cycles	16
IT Project Milestones and Checkpoints	19
Organizational Structure Impacts	19
Functional Organization	19
Matrix Organization	21
Projectized Organization	21
Summary	22
Exam Essentials	22
Key Terms	23
Review Questions	25
Answers to Review Questions	29

Chapter 2   Project Initiation   31

Receiving a Project Request	33
High-Level Requirements	34
Vendor Bids	37

Documenting the Requirements		38
Project Selection		40
Selection Techniques		41
Project Selection Criteria		41
Project Stakeholders		43
Project Sponsor		44
Other Project Stakeholders		44
Who Are Your IT Project Stakeholders?		46
Stakeholder Matrix		51
Project Charter		51
Project Description		52
Project Team		52
Goals and Objectives		53
Business Case		53
Formal Approval		54
Summary		58
Exam Essentials		59
Key Terms		60
Review Questions		61
Answers to Review Questions		66
Chapter 3	**Scope Planning**	**69**
Scope Overview		71
Project Scope Statement		72
Scope Management Plan		77
The Work Breakdown Structure (WBS)		79
Evaluating Your IT Project Scope		85
Size of the IT Shop		85
Definition of the Project Deliverables		86
Working with Your Business Clients		87
Success Criteria Tough to Define		88
Sidebar Systems and Undisclosed Process Elements		88
"Mini-Project" Consultant/Vendor Relationships		88
Senior Project Technician Quits or Leaves		89
Project Goes across IT Shops		90
Testing Elements Need Good Definition		90
Summary		95
Exam Essentials		95
Key Terms		96
Review Questions		97
Answers to Review Questions		101
Chapter 4	**Schedule Planning**	**103**
Activity Definition		104
Activity Sequence		105

		Types of Dependencies	106
		Task Dependency Relationships	106
		Creating a Network Diagram	107
		Activity Duration Estimates	108
		Defining Duration	108
		Estimating Techniques	109
		Schedule Development	110
		Schedule Development Techniques	110
		Milestones	115
		Schedule Baseline	116
		Juggling Project Time in the Real World	116
		Summary	122
		Exam Essentials	122
		Key Terms	123
		Review Questions	124
		Answers to Review Questions	130
Chapter	**5**	**Cost Planning**	**133**
		Resource Planning	134
		Types of Resources	135
		Defining Resource Requirements	137
		Cost Estimating	141
		Cost Estimating Techniques	142
		Estimating Tips	145
		Cost Budgeting	148
		Creating Your Budget	149
		Cost Baseline	151
		Budget Targets	151
		Using Project Management Software	154
		Summary	155
		Exam Essentials	155
		Key Terms	156
		Review Questions	157
		Answers to Review Questions	162
Chapter	**6**	**Other Planning Processes**	**165**
		Human Resources Planning	166
		Organizational Planning	166
		Staff Acquisition	172
		Quality Planning	176
		Quality Planning Tools and Techniques	176
		Quality Management Plan	179
		Risk Planning	181

		Risk Identification	181
		Risk Analysis	182
		Risk Response	184
	Communications Planning		185
		Communications Strategy	186
		Communicating with Project Team Members	188
		Engaging Stakeholders	188
	Procurement Planning		190
		Make or Buy Analysis	190
		Types of Contracts	191
		Statement of Work	192
		Vendor Solicitation	192
		Vendor Selection Criteria	193
	Summary		197
	Exam Essentials		197
	Key Terms		198
	Review Questions		199
	Answers to Review Questions		204
Chapter 7	**Comprehensive Project Plan**		**207**
	What Is a Project Plan?		208
	Project Plan Components		209
		Administrative Components	210
		Planning Components	210
		Templates and Checklists	213
		References	213
		Appendix	213
	Putting It All Together		214
		Organizing and Writing the Plan	214
		Updating the Plan	215
		Reviewing the Plan	216
		Closing Out the Planning Phase	216
	Summary		221
	Exam Essentials		222
	Key Terms		222
	Review Questions		223
	Answers to Review Questions		228
Chapter 8	**Project Execution**		**231**
	Team Development		233
		Building and Managing a Cohesive Team	234
		Training	239
		Rewards and Recognition	239
	Other Stakeholder Relationships		241

		Relationship Management with the Client	241
		Managing a Wavering Sponsor	242
		Relationships with Functional Managers	243
		Perform According to Plan	244
		Collect Data	244
		Progress Against Baselines	246
		Information Distribution	248
		Project Team Meetings	248
		Status Reports	250
		Project Reviews	250
		Vendor Contract Administration	253
		Progress Reporting	253
		Managing Vendor Disagreements	253
		Vendor Delays	256
		Vendor Payment Process	256
		Dealing with Vendors	257
		Summary	261
		Exam Essentials	262
		Key Terms	263
		Review Questions	264
		Answers to Review Questions	272
Chapter	**9**	**Project Control**	**275**
		Integrated Change Control	278
		Scope Change Control	279
		Schedule Control	280
		Cost Control	281
		Other Plan Changes	282
		Quality Control	283
		Inspection (Testing)	284
		Other Quality Control Tools and Techniques	285
		Quality Control Actions	287
		Documentation Quality	288
		IT Quality Control	290
		Standards	290
		Setting Up Your Environmental Processes	292
		Risk Monitoring and Control	293
		Monitoring Risk Response Results	293
		Performance Reporting	296
		Performance Reporting Tools and Techniques	297
		Driving Stakeholder Action	302
		Summary	306
		Exam Essentials	307
		Key Terms	308
		Review Questions	309

		Answers to Review Questions	317
Chapter	10	**Project Closure**	**321**
		Types of Closure	322
		Contract Closeout	323
		Administrative Closure	323
		Project Archive	324
		Formal Acceptance	324
		Comprehensive Review (Lessons Learned)	325
		Project Turnover	329
		Release of Team Members	331
		Summary	332
		Exam Essentials	333
		Key Terms	333
		Review Questions	334
		Answers to Review Questions	340
Appendix	A	**Systems Development Life Cycle**	**343**
		Planning	345
		Analysis	345
		Design	347
		Implementation	348
		Operations and Support	349
		Comparing the *Guide to the PMBOK*'s Process Groups with the SDLC Phases	350
Appendix	B	**Standard IT Project Documents**	**353**
		Initial Project Proposal Analysis Template	354
		Customer Information	354
		Success Information	355
		Business Impact	355
		Issue Notification	355
		Risk Identification and Assessment	356
		Basic Risk Identification Template	356
		Risk Assessment	358
		Vested Interest Breakdown	359
		Human Resources Considerations	360
		Human Resources Assessment	360
		Skills Inventory Worksheet	361
		Responsibility Assignment Document	362
Glossary			**363**
Index			*381*

Introduction

Have you ever sat back and wondered how the pyramids were built? Or the Eiffel Tower? Or the Golden Gate Bridge? How did someone have the organizational skills to put all those people together and create such magnificent structures? Coming forward to recent times—how is Microsoft capable of putting together the literally *millions* of lines of code that become Windows Server 2003 or Windows XP? The answer to all of these: project management.

The CompTIA IT Project+ will test your knowledge of the extraordinarily large world of IT project management. The basics of project management are simple and elegant, but there are many different opinions about how project management should be done. Some project management experts suggest project management methodologies that are rigorous, others more casual ones. It's left up to you to decide which you'll use and how you'll use them.

Fortunately, the IT Project+ test wasn't written with any one project management methodology in mind. Instead, it's written from the perspective of understanding good project management principles and techniques—something that all project management methodologies embrace. That being said, this second edition of the CompTIA IT Project+ Study Guide reflects CompTIA's commitment to the Project Management Institute (PMI) and its associated project management practices. These project management practices are detailed in PMI's standards document, *A Guide to the Project Management Body of Knowledge (Guide to the PMBOK)*. The four domains measured in CompTIA's 2003 version of the IT Project+ exam map to the five process groups that are the foundation of the *Guide to the PMBOK*: Initiating, Planning, Executing, Controlling, and Closing.

In *IT Project+ Study Guide*, you'll find plenty of discussion of these project management concepts, such as requirements definition; the concept, charter, and scope documents; the project planning process itself; risk assessment and management; and closing out the project. Also, you'll find that the exam quizzes you on categories that are hard to objectively test on, such as team building and people management, and we give you the skinny on these as well. Additionally, you'll find that this study guide is a good starter for your journey to the "Holy Grail" of project management certifications, the Project Management Professional (PMP) certification as offered through PMI.

If you have a modicum of practical, hands-on project management experience from your work background, you'll find that the test is much more project management–oriented than IT-oriented. We've included more IT-centric material than you'll see on the test. We did this because there's an interesting quagmire in the project management industry today. Almost all new projects, regardless of their nature, use information systems in one way or another. So you'll find that your project management career will always involve some sort of IT—and IT presents many interesting twists in the road, in terms of project tasks. For example, suppose that you work for a large manufacturing concern. In the past, the machinery that ran the manufacturing line didn't have any semblance of electronics or IT gear in it, anywhere. But today, manufacturing gear is full of electronics, along with servers and software that run the various manufacturing components. Manufacturing segments may even include lasers and robotics. Regardless of your background, it is likely some segment of IT software and hardware directly affects your business.

Where should you go beyond taking your IT Project+ test? If you haven't already, and you find that you're interested in all things project management, you should enroll in a good university-level class that takes you through the heavier stages of project management. This book and this test only touch the surface of what's really out there. You'll find that there is so much more to learn that you could make a career out of managing projects. After all, that's what a project manager does, isn't it?

> *Don't* just study the questions and answers in this book; the questions on the actual exam will be different from the practice ones included in the book and on the CD-ROM. The exam is designed to test your knowledge of a concept or objective, so use this book to learn the objective *behind* the question.

What Is the IT Project+ Certification?

CompTIA is a pretty cool outfit because its mission is to create tests and certifications that aren't company specific. For example, you can take a server test that deals with the elements of servers and server operation, but doesn't ask you specifics about, say, Dell, HP, IBM, or Compaq. CompTIA got its start with what is now almost a standard in the industry, the A+ exam—a test designed to quiz you on your understanding of the guts of a PC and its associated connection to a network. But there are other tests as well: Network+, Linux+, and others.

Why Become IT Project+ Certified?

With IT Project+, CompTIA has given people who are affiliated with the IT industry the capability of proving their project management prowess. You'll find that this test will help you fill in some blanks you may have had regarding project management. You'll also find, if you're like us, that it whets your appetite for more information about project management. This exam and subsequent certification make a nice addition to any IT person's certification repertoire, and it is a great starting place for those interested in project management but not necessarily in heavy-duty IT.

Here are some reasons to consider the IT Project+ test and this study guide:

Demonstrates Proof of Professional Achievement   You can put IT Project+ beside your name on your business cards, proving passed a test that shows you know something about project management. You'll also get a certificate of achievement from CompTIA that you can frame, as well as a wallet card certifying you as IT Project+.

Increases Your Marketability   With a certification in IT project management, you may find that some positions open up to you a little easier than they did before. You should augment any IT career with a technical understanding relative to your interests (servers, databases, networks, software development, etc.), but the IT Project+ certification takes you a step beyond. It says that you understand not only the tech talk behind an IT project, you also understand how the project should go together.

Provides Opportunity for Advancement You may find that your IT Project+ certification is just what you need to get that next step up the ladder. People who study hard and pass certification tests prove, if nothing else, that they have the tenacity to get through a difficult subject and to prove their understanding by testing out on the subject.

Provides a Prerequisite for Advanced Project Management Training Above all else, if you're considering a project management career, the IT Project+ exam is a great way to start. It uses an agnostic technique that doesn't preach about any one project management methodology and thus gives you a background on what project management is really all about, not simply what one company or organization thinks it's about. You'll find that the dialog on the Web is *tremendous* regarding this subject, and there are lots of experts—some of whom disagree with one another! To find your own way in the project management world, start by getting a handle on the basics of IT without any predilection toward one methodology or another.

Raises Customer Confidence Because It Raises *Your* Confidence Customers who know you're certified in project management and who hear you speak and act with confidence are more confident in the company you represent. If you're able, for example, to identify and describe the four categories of risks to prepare for in a project, you might well validate to your customer that you know what you're talking about. Being able to talk intelligently about project management techniques has worked for us, and we are sure it will for you too.

How to Become IT Project+ Certified

Simply go to the CompTIA website (www.comptia.com) to visit the list of testing sites where the exam is currently conducted. We took ours at a VUE center (U.S. telephone number, 1-877-551-PLUS), but you can also take your test at Prometric (1-877-287-6872). The test has a varying range of prices for members of CompTIA ($155 for 1-50 members, $134 for 51-250 and $108 for 250+). The exam fee for nonmembers is $207. See the website for more details.

> **NOTE** Prices are subject to change at anytime. Please visit CompTIA's website for the most up-to-date pricing information at http://www.comptia.org. Note that the prices quoted are for the United States. Prices may vary for other countries.

You're allowed 90 minutes to take the test and a minimum score of 63 percent is required to pass. There are 84 questions on the test, which are simple multiple choice.

You'll need a driver's license and one other form of ID (doesn't have to have a picture on it, but must have a signature). No calculators, computers, cell phones, or other electronic devices are allowed. You'll be notified of your grade as soon as you finish the test.

You cannot take this test online.

> **NOTE** In addition to reading the book, you might consider visiting the major project management websites: www.gantthead.com, www.techrepublic.com, www.4pm.com, and www.pmi.org.

Who Should Buy This Book?

You should buy this book if you're interested in project management and want to see what it's all about. Your IT background doesn't have to be very in-depth to take the IT Project+ test. Project managers aren't typically subject matter experts in the IT area they're working in; they utilize the people around them who *are* experts to get the job done. Project management is about putting the right people (with the right attitudes) together in order to achieve the project's objectives—to create its deliverables.

We would advise you to not be afraid of this test. If you've never taken a certification test before (we've taken dozens), you'll find that this is a very pleasant way to get your feet wet. The test isn't complicated or riddled with trick questions—just good old meat-and-potatoes questions about the basics of project management. We find that CompTIA creates an excellent test and is able to thoroughly test an individual on a given subject.

This book will also be a good basic IT primer for those who are immersed in conventional project management but who have now entered into the arena of IT projects.

How to Use This Book and CD

We've included several testing features, found in both the book and on the CD-ROM bound at the back of the book. At the beginning of the book (right after this introduction, in fact) is an assessment test that you can use to check your readiness for the actual exam. Take this exam before you start reading the book; it will help you determine the areas you may need to brush up on. The answers to the assessment test appear on a separate page after the last question of the test. Each answer also includes an explanation and a note telling you in which chapter this material appears.

To test your knowledge as you progress through the book, there are review questions at the end of each chapter. As you finish each chapter, answer the review questions and then check your work—the correct answers appear on the page following the last review question. You can reread the section that deals with each question you got wrong to ensure that you get the correct answer the next time you are tested on the material.

> **NOTE** Every question on the IT Project+ exam will be multiple choice. We used this question format for this study guide to ensure that you were tested as comprehensively as possible.

In addition to the assessment test and chapter review questions, you'll find two bonus exams on the book's companion CD-ROM. Take these exams just as if you were actually taking the exams (i.e., without any reference material). When you have finished the first exam, move on to solidify your test-taking skills with the second exam.

Also on the CD, you'll also find over 150 flashcard questions for on-the-go review. Download them right onto your Palm OS device for quick and convenient reviewing.

Additionally, if you are going to travel but still need to study for the IT Project+ exam, and you have a laptop with a CD-ROM drive, you can take this entire book with you just by taking the CD. This book is in PDF (Adobe Acrobat) format so it can be easily read on any computer.

Tips for Taking the IT Project+ Exam

Here are some general tips for taking your exam successfully:

- Bring two forms of ID with you. One must be a photo ID, such as a driver's license. The other can be a major credit card or a passport. Both forms must have a signature.
- Arrive early at the exam center so you can relax and review your study materials, particularly tables and lists of exam-related information.
- Read the questions carefully. Don't be tempted to jump to an early conclusion. Make sure you know exactly what the question is asking.
- Don't leave any unanswered questions. Unanswered questions are scored against you.
- There will be questions with multiple correct responses. When there is more than one correct answer, a message at the bottom of the screen will prompt you to "Choose all that apply." Be sure to read the messages displayed.
- When answering multiple-choice questions you're not sure about, use a process of elimination to get rid of the obviously incorrect questions first. This will improve your odds if you need to make an educated guess.
- For the latest pricing on the exam and updates to the registration procedures, refer to the CompTIA site at www.comptia.com.

The Exam Objectives

Behind every computer industry exam, you can be sure to find exam objectives—the broad topics in which the exam developers want to ensure your competency. Exam objectives are subject to change at any time without prior notice and at CompTIA's sole discretion. This study guide includes, at the start of each chapter, the test objectives covered in that chapter. But please visit the Certification page of CompTIA's website (www.comptia.com) for the most current listing of IT Project+ exam objectives.

> **WARNING** Be careful about the test objectives (for any test, not just CompTIA's). Our experience has been that exam objectives are sometimes hastily written and might contain misspellings and grammar errors, or might be missing information that would help you study for the test. Additionally, they might be out of order. Read the objectives carefully to make sure you understand what the objective authors were really getting at.

The IT Project+ exam will test you on four domains, or topics and each domain is worth a certain percentage of the exam. Following is a breakdown of the domains and their representation in the exam.

Domain	% of Examination
1.0) IT Project Initiation and Scope Definition	20%
2.0) IT Project Planning	30%
3.0) IT Project Execution, Control and Coordination	43%
4.0) IT Project Closure, Acceptance and Support	7%
Total	100%

You can find information on each exam objective of the IT Project+ exam in the *IT Project+ Study Guide*. Each is represented in the following table along with the chapter where the objective is covered.

IT Project+ Study Guide

Exam: PKO-002

OBJECTIVE	CHAPTER
Domain 1.0 IT Project Initiation and Scope Definition	

This domain requires that the candidate possess the knowledge to:
    Identify stakeholder objectives for an IT project and prepare a high- level scope statement the correctly defines the work required to achieve those objectives.
    Define high-level business and technical requirements, outcomes, criteria for success, stakeholders' low-level needs and expectations including boundaries for project budget, duration, and risk
    Identify the project roles of stakeholders including project manager, project sponsor, and project team members.
    Secure stakeholder/client consensus and obtain approval of the project charter and preliminary scope documents.

OBJECTIVE	CHAPTER
1.1: Given a vague or poorly-worded customer request or business need, determine the appropriate course of action in order to handle various business-and project-related issues such as:	2
Understand a business case scenario and create a proposal, and/or analyze an RFP and create a project proposal.	2
Generate and refine a preliminary project concept definition or statement of work.	2
Informally determine the business need and feasibility of the project.	2
Identify project sponsors who will help obtain resources.	2
Understand the concept of cost-benefit analysis to justify the project.	2
Obtain formal approval by the project sponsor.	2
Confirm management support.	2
1.2: Given a set of criteria which outlines an enterprise's minimal requirements for a project charter, together with stakeholder input, synthesize a project charter Including:	2
Project title and description.	2
Project manager.	2
Key roles and responsibilities.	2
Project objectives and success criteria.	2
High-level cost benefit analysis.	2

OBJECTIVE	CHAPTER
Business case/ mission.	2
Product/deliverable description, performance criteria and enhancement opportunities.	2
High-level risk assessment.	2
Consensus building.	2
1.3: Identify strategies for building consensus among project stakeholders. Select an appropriate course of action involving negotiation or interviewing strategies, meetings, memos, etc.	2
1.4: Recognize and explain the need to obtain formal approval (sign-off) by the project sponsor(s) and confirm other relevant management support to consume organization resources as the project charter is refined and expanded.	2
1.5: Given a scope definition scenario, demonstrate awareness of the need to secure written confirmation of customer expectations in the following areas:	3
The background of the project (e.g., a problem/opportunity statement, strategic alignment with organizational goals and other initiatives, why the project is being initiated at this time, etc.).	3
The deliverable from the project (i.e. what the product will look like, be able to do, who will use it, etc.).	3
The strategy for creating the deliverable.	3
Targeted completion date and rationale behind that date.	3
Budget dollars available and basis upon which that budget was determined.	3
Areas of risks which the project client is not willing to accept.	3
The priority of this project as it relates to all the other projects being done within the organization.	3
The sponsor of the project (i.e., who will provide direction and decisions).	3
Any predetermined tools or resources.	3
Assumptions that resources will be available as needed.	3
1.6: Given a project initiation document (a project charter or contract), including a confirmed high-level scope definition and project justification, demonstrate the ability to identify and define the following elements:	3, 5
The stakeholders, including the primary project client, the ultimate end users and any other impacted parties (internal or external to the organization), their roles and special needs.	3
An all-inclusive set of requirements presented in specific, definitive terms which include: Differentiation of mandatory versus optional requirements; Success criteria upon which the deliverable will be measured; Completion criteria (for example: what needs to be delivered; such as a fully tested system or a system after being live for three months); Requirements that are excluded from the project.	3

OBJECTIVE	CHAPTER
Targeted completion date including: Relative to a specific target date; Expressed as a 1) specific date i.e. mm/dd/yyyy; 2) range of dates; 3) specific quarter and year (3rd quarter, 2000); The consequences if that date is not met; A milestone chart including any phase reviews, if appropriate.	3
Anticipated budget, including any or all of the following: Plus or minus tolerance; Contingency funds and/or any management reviews, if negotiated; The consequence if that budget is not met.	5
Which of the above three criteria — for example, technical performance (quality), completion date (schedule) or anticipated budget — is the highest priority to the project client.	3
All assumptions made relative to completion date, budget and priorities.	3
1.7: Given a project initiation document (a project charter or contract), including the client's highest priority between quality, time, and budget, estimate any or all of the following:	3
The potential impact of satisfying the client's highest priority at the expense of the other two.	3
The impact of the project on business operations.	3
Worse case scenario targeted completion date, budget, and quality-level.	3
Your confidence level in the projected completion date, budget, and prospects for a high quality deliverable.	3
1.8: Given a project charter or contract, including a statement of work (SOW), recognize and explain the need to investigate specific industry regulations requirements and contractual/legal considerations for their impact on the project scope definition and project plan.	2
1.9: Given a proposed scope definition and based on the scope components, assess the feasibility of the project and the viability of a given project component against a pre-determined list of constraints, including:	3, 6
A clearly defined project end date.	3
A clearly defined set of monetary resources or allocation.	3
A clearly defined set of product requirements based on a thorough decomposition of the system's hardware and software components.	3
Clearly defined completion criteria.	3
Clearly defined priorities.	3
The relative priority of cost, schedule, and scope.	3
Project ownership.	3
Mandated tools, personnel, and other resources.	3
The requirement that scope will change only per change control.	3
Vendor terms and conditions.	3
Company terms and conditions.	3

OBJECTIVE	CHAPTER
A "best practices" life cycle for this type of project.	3
Required reviews of deliverables by stakeholders and approvals by sponsors.	3
RFP procedures, selection criteria, evaluation criteria and standards.	6
1.10: Recognize and explain the need to obtain formal approval (sign-off) by the project sponsor(s) and confirm other relevant management support to consume organizational resources as the project scope statement is being developed.	3
1.11: Given an incomplete project scope definition, complete or rewrite the definition to: 1) reflect all necessary scope components, or 2) explicitly state which is included in the project and which is not included. Necessary components include:	3
Project size.	3
Project cost.	3
Projected schedule and window of opportunity.	3
Stakeholders, their roles and authorities.	3
The project manager's role and authority.	3
Completion criteria.	3
Methodologies to be followed.	3
The scope change control process.	3
Mandated tools, personnel, and other resources.	3
Industry or government regulations that apply.	3
1.12: Identify the following as possible elements of a final project scope definition and the circumstances in which they would be appropriate: A requirements change control process, including: how to request a change, how to analyze the impact of the change, and how to obtain approval for the additional funds and/or time to implement the change.	3
1.13: Recognize and explain the need to build management buy-in and approval into the structure of the project, and describe strategies for doing so, including:	2
Involving management in up-front definitions of project concept and charter.	2
Involving management in defining and approving project scope.	2
Involving management in reviewing and approving all key project deliverables as they evolve, providing a role for management as a spokesperson-advocate for the project, for team member participation, and for the deliverables.	2
1.14: Recognize the need to obtain consensus of stakeholders and to obtain buy-in from the team to proceed to the planning stage of the project given a high level estimate of scope, schedule, budget, and resources.	3

OBJECTIVE	CHAPTER
1.15: Recognize the need to conduct a review meeting as the project transitions from the initiation phase to the planning phase. The review would include an assessment of key items.	2
Completion of the project initiation documentation.	2
Viability of the business case.	2
Achievement of the stakeholder consensus.	2

Domain 2.0 Project Strategy Development and Preliminary Planning Objective

This domain requires the knowledge and skills to:
- Define in adequate depth the project deliverable(s)/product(s) and associated requirements.
- Create a work breakdown structure (WBS)..
- Identify a project strategy and life-cycle.
- Create a schedule.
- Create a list of required resources.
- Perform project cost estimation and create a budget.
- Perform risk analysis and create a risk management plan.
- Create a communication management plan.
- Create a quality management plan.
- Organize a comprehensive, detailed project plan.
- Validate stakeholder expectations.
- Establish change control over the project plan and develop procedures for updating and/or changing the plan.
- Close out the planning phase.

OBJECTIVE	CHAPTER
2.1: Demonstrate knowledge of the typical IT Project life cycle and its application to IT projects, including:	1
Phases (requirements, design, build/unit test, integration test, deploy)	1
The reasons for the phases.	1
The common deliverables from the phases.	1
Target phase transition dates.	1
2.2: Given an approved project charter, high level scope documents, and schedule/budget objectives, demonstrate the ability to create a project management plan that illustrates the following:	7
Understanding of the roles of stakeholders, what reporting information each needs, and when it is needed.	7
Understanding the risks incurred by not including key participants during the planning process.	7

OBJECTIVE	CHAPTER
Knowledge of how to establish a project tracking mechanism.	7
Awareness that a training plan may be necessary.	7
Awareness that a procurement plan may be necessary.	7
2.3: Demonstrate understanding of the following estimating concepts, techniques, and issues:	5
The concept of bottom up cost estimates, their purpose, and the conditions under which they are necessary.	5
Standard estimating techniques that can be used to solicit initial financial budget inputs based on mutually agreeable high level requirements.	5
2.4: Given a team-building scenario, including a scope definition and work breakdown structure (WBS), identify selection criteria for particular team members. Demonstrate the ability to ask interview questions that will assist the team selection process. Assume project organization includes:	6, 7
Business.	6
Leadership.	6
Administration.	6
Technical.	6
Stakeholders.	6
2.5: Identify methods for resolving disagreements among team members when evaluating the suitability of deliverables at each point in their evolution.	8
2.6: Given a project description/overview and a list of the project business and technical requirements, do the following:	3
Decide if the project is defined well enough to achieve a measurable outcome and metrics for success.	3
Determine if the requirements include the necessary range of inputs (assumptions, expectations, technical issues, industry issues, etc.) in order to validate the input given and gaps related to scope.	3
Distinguish any input provided which do not relate to the project at hand in order to achieve greater focus.	3
Recognize whether the list of requirements is complete, accurate, and valid enough to move on to the planning step.	3
Given a situation where the project outcomes are not possible to verify.	3
Recognize the role which poorly detailed requirements, assumptions, and expectations play.	3
Identify the high level value of the project to sponsors and users of the outcome.	3
Describe the role of project value and its importance to individual and team effectiveness.	3

OBJECTIVE	CHAPTER
2.7: Describe the goals of a useful project requirements review with the client (e.g., verify mutual understanding of client's product delivery, product performance, and budget requirements, etc.) and describe when it is important to have such reviews.	2, 3
2.8: Given the client's approved project requirements and the input of stakeholders, decompose these requirements into business, functional and technical requirements while maintaining trace ability within strict configuration control.	2, 3
2.9: Given a project planning scenario, demonstrate an understanding of and the ability to develop a phase-oriented WBS with high detail for an early phase and with low detail for later phases by:	3
Identifying elements (phases) likely to require iterative planning.	3
Explicitly deciding to provide for iteration in the project plan (e.g., scope approval, plan approval, project design, final deliverable turnover, etc.).	3
2.10: Given a scenario involving tasks, resources (fixed or variable), and dependencies for a multi-phase IT project, demonstrate knowledge of the standards for creating a workable WBS by:	3
Recognizing and explaining the need to creatively visualize all deliverables (interim and finished).	3
Thoroughly decomposing the system into all potential hardware and software components.	3
2.11: Recognize and explain the need to obtain:	3
Consensus among all stakeholders regarding project deliverables and other elements of the WBS.	3
Formal approval (sign-off) of project sponsor(s) regarding project deliverables and other elements of the WBS.	3
2.12: Given a project scenario with many phases and activities:	4, 5
Set realistic, measurable milestones.	4
Demonstrate understanding that measurable targets are required in order to determine if the project is proceeding on time and within budget.	5
2.13: Given a set of specific milestones and their descriptions, specify entry and exit criteria for each.	4
2.14: Demonstrate the ability to create an activity cost estimate Given:	5
An activity scope of work.	5
Required resources.	5
Level of effort.	5
Resource availability.	5
Resource rate.	5

OBJECTIVE	CHAPTER
2.15: Demonstrate the ability to create an activity time estimate (in units of time) given:	4, 5
An activity scope of work.	4
Required resources.	4
Level of effort.	5
Resource availability.	4
2.16: Recognize and explain the difference between a project cost estimate, effort estimate, and time estimate.	5
2.17: Identify and list the components needed to generate a workable project schedule. Demonstrate the ability to create appropriate project schedules, which meet the approved project start and finish dates, given the following information:	4
A detailed list of project deliverables (both interim and finished).	4
A detailed estimate of project tasks.	4
A list of activities and phases.	4
A detailed estimate of the time and resources required to complete all project tasks.	4
Information about the preferences of the project team regarding schedule formats.	4
2.18: Given a scenario with necessary project documents, and given enterprise holiday and individual resource calendars, demonstrate the ability to develop a project schedule by doing the following:	4
Define and sequence project tasks, activities, and phases which are needed to bring about the completion of given interim or finished project deliverables.	4
Estimate durations for project tasks, activities, and phases.	4
Estimate work effort for project tasks and assignments.	4
Specify resources required for the completion of each phase.	4
Identification of the project critical path.	4
2.19: Demonstrate the ability to identify project team organization roles and responsibilities required for the execution of the project including:	6
The role of the customer (sponsor) of the project as it relates to the project manager's role.	6
The major skills required in the project team.	6
The type of team structure; e.g., part-time matrix, full-time matrix.	6
Confirm the roll of the project manager including any of the following: Responsibilities, accountabilities; Authority; formal and informal; Percentage of time available to this project; Performance appraisal process relative to this project.	6

OBJECTIVE	CHAPTER
2.20: Demonstrate the ability to assign resources to the schedule by:	5
Creating a list of resources needed and their availabilities.	5
Assigning responsibilities to tasks.	5
2.21: Given a project scope, timeline, cost, project team, and dependencies, demonstrate the ability to:	5
Create and manage a high level (top down) budget based on assumptions/estimates.	5
Identify and budget the level, cost, and duration of resources and dependencies (internal and external).	5
Create and manage a detailed bottom up budget, containing actual/scheduled expenses.	5
Identify, implement, and budget all project trade-offs, while understanding the implications, and impacts of the trade-offs.	5
Install and maintain systems for tracking budgetary expenses against the plan based on the existing enterprise systems.	5
Align the budget with the spending plan of the organization.	5
2.22: Demonstrate an understanding of the components of a project quality management plan (e.g., measured quality checkpoints, assignments for architectural control, systems test, and unit tests, user sign-off, etc.).	6
2.23: Demonstrate the skills to develop a quality plan that assures:	6
Awareness of the need to develop a test plan and defect tracking procedure which ensures that appropriate testing steps and defect resolution and documentation steps occur during the project life cycle.	6
A configuration management exists that ensures: Phase deliverables are reviewed and inspected for completion, defects are removed, and issues are resolved prior to acceptance; Documented sufficiency criteria exist for the exiting of each phase; A change control process exists for all technical environments; A requirements management process exists; Formal customer acceptance and sign-off is obtained at appropriate points.	6
2.24: Demonstrate the ability to perform risk assessment and mitigation (given a scenario including the appropriate project documentation):	6
Identify and prioritize the most important risks that will impact the project.	6
Evaluate the severity of the risks to successful completion of the project.	6
Identify risks contained on a project's critical path and identify procedures to reduce potential impacts on schedule.	6
2.25: Demonstrate the ability to create a project communication plan that clearly indicates what needs to be communicated during a project, to whom, when, and how (using formal, informal approaches).	6

OBJECTIVE	CHAPTER
2.26: Identify the components/documents of an adequate project plan and explain the function of each. Components include:	7
Table of contents.	7
Overview/Executive summary.	7
Sponsors.	7
Team members.	7
Requirements.	7
Scheduled tasks (WBS).	7
Expected resources.	7
Environmental issues.	7
Business and technical requirements.	7
Implementation plans.	7
Support plans.	7
Training plans.	7
Document (plan) location and revision control.	7
2.27: Identify the steps involved in organizing a comprehensive project plan and using it to close out the planning phase of a project, including:	7
Assembling all project planning elements (estimates of deliverables, time, costs, etc.).	7
Create an outline or table of contents for the comprehensive project plan.	7
Review the outline of the comprehensive project plan with sponsor and key stakeholders, obtaining feedback and concurrence, and revising as needed.	7
Writing the comprehensive project plan by integrating all planning elements according to the outline and creating a full document with transitions, introductions, graphics, exhibits, appendices, etc., as appropriate.	7
Circulating the comprehensive project plan to all stakeholders.	7
Obtaining top management support of the comprehensive project plan by making certain it reflects their concerns and that they have had an opportunity to provide input.	7
Conducting a formal review of the comprehensive project plan in which stakeholders have an opportunity to provide feedback.	7
Adjusting the comprehensive project plan based on stakeholder feedback.	7
Obtaining formal approval (sign-off) of the comprehensive project plan by sponsor(s).	7
2.28: Demonstrate knowledge of how to set performance baselines for:	7
Project scope and deliverable performance requirements.	7
Schedule.	7

OBJECTIVE	CHAPTER
Budget.	7
Resources.	7
2.29: Demonstrate knowledge of the need to create change management procedures for the project plan.	7
2.30: Be able to identify project performance indicators that will be used to monitor and control performance during execution.	7
2.31: Be able to secure staffing commitments and resolve staffing issues.	6
2.32: Recognize the need to conduct a review meeting as the project transitions from the planning phase to the execution/control/coordination phase. The review would include an assessment of the following:	7
Completion of the project planning documentation.	7
Resolution of all planning issues.	7
Continued viability of the business case.	7
Alignment of stakeholder expectations with the plan.	7

Domain 3.0 IT Project Execution, Control, and Coordination

This domain requires the candidate to demonstrate knowledge and skills in:
- Project monitoring, tracking and performance reporting.
- Interpreting project performance indicators and identifying variances from plan.
- Taking corrective action.
- Updating the plan and re-planning by project phase.
- Issue tracking and issue resolution.
- Risk tracking and risk removal/mitigation.
- Change control.
- Quality management.
- Team management, coordination and communication.
- Resource management.

OBJECTIVE	CHAPTER
3.1: Identify the following as tasks that should be accomplished on a weekly basis in the course of tracking an "up and running" project. Explain the rationale for performing these tasks and explain how to adapt these tasks to different situations such as:	8, 9
Check the project's scope status to determine "in scope" versus "out of scope" status of project elements.	8
Check the evolution and status of project deliverables.	8
Check the project schedule.	8

OBJECTIVE	CHAPTER
Analyze variances (deviations from plan) by comparing "estimated" to "actual" resource time expenditures, dollar expenditures, milestones and elapsed duration of activities.	9
Handle scope changes if needed.	9
List, track, and try to resolve open issues.	8
Report project status.	8
Look for opportunities to and "push" for close out of activities and sign-off of deliverables.	8
Decide whether it is appropriate to continue the project. Discontinue the project if appropriate.	9
3.2: Given a scenario with set project performance indicators, demonstrate the ability to recognize when performance problems are occurring on the project and determine if/when corrective action/recovery needs to occur.	9
3.3: Given a scenario with updates/changes made to the project plan demonstrate the need to check for impact On:	9
The project critical path/schedule/WBS.	9
Project performance indicators.	9
Resource availability.	9
Budget.	9
Risks.	9
Project objectives.	9
3.4: Given a scenario involving a project with a schedule delay, choose an appropriate course of action.	9
3.5: Given an approved project and a status report scenario containing a significant variance from plan (e.g., excessive overtime, purchased items more expensive than anticipated, etc.), do the following:	9
Clearly identify the reasons for the variance.	9
Determine the impact on schedule and budget and the effect on stakeholders.	9
Determine if scope creep is occurring.	9
Identify options for corrective action.	9
Identify options for absorbing part or all of the increase in the overall budget (if any).	9
Identify stakeholders who must be notified or must give approval to a change of schedule or budget and develop a plan for advising them of the change, the rationale for the change, and the consequences if not approved.	9

Exam Objectives **xxxv**

OBJECTIVE	CHAPTER
3.6: Given a scenario in which a vendor requests a two-week delay in delivering its product, explain how to do the following:	8
Negotiate a lesser delay by identifying things the vendor might do to improve its schedule.	8
Clearly identify the impact of the negotiated delivery on the project scope and critical path.	8
Present this impact to the appropriate stakeholders.	8
3.7: Given a scenario in which there is a disagreement between a vendor and your project team, identify methods for resolving the problem.	8
3.8: Identify issues to consider when trying to rebuild active project support from a wavering executive (e.g., the need to identify the source of doubts, interpersonal communications skills that might be employed, the need to act without creating negative impact, the need to identify and utilize various allies and influences, etc.). Given a scenario involving a wavering executive, choose an appropriate course of action.	8
3.9: Identify issues to consider when trying to obtain approval of a changed project plan that is still within expected budget, but has a schedule that extends outside of the original baseline end date.	9
3.10: Define and explain Estimate to Complete (ETC), Estimate at Complete (EAC), and Budget at Complete (BAC).	9
3.11: Demonstrate the ability to track the financial performance of a project, given the financial management baseline and data on the actual performance of the project. Demonstrate:	8, 9
The need to identify and understand proposed changes from plan.	8
The need to be able to justify and sell the changes.	9
The need for alternative courses of action if the plan isn't accepted.	9
3.12: Given an approved project plan and a specific scope deviation (for example: design change, schedule or cost change, etc.), demonstrate your ability to:	9
Identify the cause(s).	9
Prepare a status report for the user identifying problems and corrective action.	9
Determine the impact of the deviation on the scope of the project.	9
Quantify the deviation in terms of time, cost, and resource.	9
Distinguish between variances which will affect the budget and duration and those that will not.	9
Determine and quantify at least one possible alternative solution that has less impact but requires some scope compromise.	9

OBJECTIVE	CHAPTER
Distinguish between variances that should be elevated to the sponsor and those that should be handled by the project manager and team.	9
Develop a plan to gain stakeholder approval.	9
Use a change order.	9
3.13: Identify and justify the following conditions for initiating a change control process:	9
Resource chances.	9
Schedule changes.	9
Cost changes.	9
Requirements changes (or changes in expectations).	9
Infrastructure changes.	9
As a response to scope creep.	9
3.14: Given scenarios involving requests for changes from sponsors, team members, or third parties, recognize and explain how to prevent scope creep.	9
3.15: Recognize and explain the importance of communicating significant proposed changes in project scope, and their impacts to management, and getting management review and formal approval.	9
3.16: Identify and explain strategies and requirements for maintaining qualified deliverables, given a large project with many team members at multiple locations (e.g., communication standards, work standards, etc.).	9
3.17: Recognize and explain the importance of testing in situations where tasks are being performed both by project team members and by third parties.	9
3.18: Identify and explain strategies and requirements for assuring quality during the turnover phase (e.g., user docs, user training, helpdesk training, support structure, etc.)	9
3.19: Identify and explain strategies and requirements for assuring quality of deliverables and meeting sufficiency standards during each phase.	9
3.20: Recognize the need and explain the importance of controlling changes on the configuration of the project deliverable.	9
3.21: Recognize the relevance of the organization's Quality Policy to project quality.	6
3.22: Identify effective strategies for providing timely performance feedback to team members.	8
3.23: Demonstrate an understanding of how to effectively manage disgruntled team members so that team performance is not adversely affected.	9

OBJECTIVE	CHAPTER
3.24: Demonstrate an understanding of how to recognize individual team member performance issues and to identify effective strategies for corrective action.	9
3.25: Given an initial high level scope, budget, and resource allocation, demonstrate understanding of the need to investigate the aspects of the project that could be modified to improve outcomes (i.e., find out what is negotiable, prepare to negotiate). Provide evidence of the following competencies:	8, 9
Recognize that individual project team member's needs must be addressed to the extent that project activities can be modified without significant impact on final scope, budget, quality, or schedule.	8
The ability to evaluate alternatives to a scope change request that stakeholders may find acceptable.	9
The ability to recognize which aspects (schedule, budget, quality) of the project are most important to the stakeholders and be able to propose trade-offs during the project that can be made to meet or exceed those aspects.	9
The ability to identify all of the individuals and groups with which you will need to negotiate during the life if the project (sponsors, vendors, users, internal and external service organizations, other project teams, project team members, finance/accounting, etc.)	8, 9
3.26: Given a project scenario, demonstrate the ability to resolve a resource availability (staffing) issue requiring escalation to the project sponsor and senior level stakeholders.	8
3.27: Given a project scenario during the implementation phases, demonstrate the understanding of the need to organize and effectively run meetings.	8
3.28: Given a project team meeting scenario in which a decision must be made with imperfect information, demonstrate the knowledge of problem solving techniques to help the team through a decision making process.	8
3.29: Given a project team meeting scenario, demonstrate the awareness of the need to provide direction and clarify work instructions to team members.	8
3.30: Given a project team meeting scenario under a situation whereby the project is behind plan, demonstrate the awareness of the need to:	8
Identify an accountable team member.	8
Clarify the root cause of the problem causing the delay.	8
Develop a strategy for corrective action.	8
Implement the corrective action strategy.	8

OBJECTIVE	CHAPTER
Follow up to check on results.	8
3.31: Given a project scenario in which intra-team communication is inadequate, demonstrate the ability to improve communication to an appropriate level.	8
3.32: Given a project team meeting scenario, demonstrate the knowledge to review an issue log with team members and secure closure of issues.	9
3.33: Demonstrate the ability to prioritize issues by severity and impact on quality.	9
3.34: Demonstrate understanding of how to determine if/when planned risks have materialized and how to implement planned risk mitigation and removal strategies.	9
3.35: Demonstrate the ability to prioritize risks by severity and impact on quality.	9
3.36: Demonstrate the ability to remove/mitigate a project risk.	6
3.37: Demonstrate an understanding of how to report to the project sponsor that a project is in jeopardy and how to report corrective action strategies that are underway.	8
3.38: Demonstrate understanding of how to determine when a project should be prematurely terminated.	9
3.39: Recognize potential organizational and political barriers inhibiting an effective working relationship between the IT organization and the client/ business organization.	8
3.40: Demonstrate an understanding of the following methods to develop and maintain an effective working relationship during projects between the IT organization and the client/ business organization:	8
Frequent communication.	8
Team building.	8
Managing by fact.	8
Issue management and problem solving.	8
Timely decision making.	8
Importance of written communication.	8
Gaining consensus.	8
Managing expectations.	8

OBJECTIVE	CHAPTER
Domain 4.0 Project Closure, Acceptance and Support	
4.1: Recognize and explain the value of conducting a comprehensive review process that identifies the lessons learned and evaluates the planning, organizing, directing, controlling, execution, and budget phases of the project, identifying both the positive and negative aspects in a written report.	10
4.2: Recognize the need to plan to transfer the project deliverable to support and maintenance and to budget for these resources including help desk.	10
4.3: Recognize the need for acceptance testing (user acceptance testing, factory acceptance testing, site acceptance testing) of the project deliverable.	9
4.4: Recognize the need to obtain formal customer sign-off of the project deliverable and hand-off to the customer, including:	10
Close out meeting with customer/sign-off to statement of work.	10
Begin support/maintenance.	10
Change control to additional scope.	10
Formally turn over deliverable to the customer.	10
4.5: Recognize the need to complete project documentation, secure approvals, and archive/store appropriately.	10
4.6: Recognize the need to close out contracts and sign-off for vendors.	10

Assessment Test

1. How many ways can a project be declared final?
   A. 1
   B. 2
   C. 3
   D. 4
   E. 5

2. Select all the *Guide to the PMBOK* project management process groups.
   A. Activating
   B. Initiation
   C. Requirements gathering
   D. Planning
   E. Executing
   F. Scheduling
   G. Controlling
   H. Budgeting
   I. Closing
   J. Ending

3. In what ways would not having thorough requirements identification, documentation, and metrics adversely impact your project? (Select all that apply.)
   A. Scope may arbitrarily enlarge.
   B. Can't tell who the customer is.
   C. Don't know what deliverables to develop.
   D. Can't tell when the project is complete.
   E. Can't tell when the project is successful.
   F. Sponsors may back out.

4. The _____ _____ is the component that authorizes the project to begin.
   A. Customer request
   B. Concept document
   C. Project charter
   D. Project sponsor

5. When should you seek recommendations from the sponsor to either kill a project or come up with alternative strategies? (Select all that apply.)
   A. Costs far outreach the budgeted amount the project was originally given.
   B. An activity is insurmountable.
   C. The elapsed time used for one or more tasks far outreaches time estimates.
   D. The enthusiasm of the project sponsor wanes.

6. You're the project manager for a small project that is in the Closing phase. You prepare closure documents and take them to the project sponsor for sign-off. She tells you that the documents are not needed because the project is so small. What should you tell her?
   A. OK, sorry to bother you.
   B. You are the one who needs to sign off on the documents showing that the project is officially closed.
   C. I can have a stakeholder sign in your place.
   D. I'll just go ahead and sign them instead.

7. The _____ _____ is the document that defines the height and breadth of the project.
   A. Project concept
   B. Project scope
   C. Project charter
   D. Project plan

8. A _____ _____ estimate is one predicated on assumptions and initial estimates.
   A. Top down
   B. Bottom up
   C. Cost center
   D. Capital expense

9. Which of these can convey that you've achieved the completion of an interim deliverable?
   A. Completion criteria
   B. Milestone
   C. Gantt chart
   D. Project sign-off document

10. What will be the outcome of the work breakdown structure (WBS)?

   A. Phase

   B. Task

   C. Deliverable

   D. Activity

11. Of these, which one thing is a customer responsible for in the project development process?

   A. Review of project deliverables

   B. Sign-off of scope document

   C. Development of project schedule

   D. Prioritization of project steps

12. You're the project manager of a project in which the scope has expanded. What steps must you take to acknowledge the expansion? (Select all that apply.)

   A. Modify the project charter.

   B. Modify the project concept definition document.

   C. Obtain a new sign-off on the project charter.

   D. Obtain a new sign-off on the project concept definition document.

13. When taking over an incomplete project, what item should be of most interest to the new project manager?

   A. Project concept document

   B. Project charter

   C. Project scope document

   D. Project plan

14. In the IT world, which of these statements about a project manager is the most true?

   A. The project manager doesn't have to have any IT background.

   B. The project manager should have a minimum of IT background.

   C. The project manager should be moderately IT oriented.

   D. The project manager should be heavily IT oriented.

15. In the project management world, what entity is responsible for signing the project charter?

   A. Customer

   B. Project sponsor

   C. Stakeholder

   D. Project manager

16. Select the component that belongs in the Controlling process group of the project, not the Planning process group.
   A. Risk definition
   B. Risk quantification
   C. Risk response development
   D. Risk control

17. What signals the end of the Planning phase?
   A. The project team begins to execute the tasks in the project plan.
   B. The project scope document is formally signed.
   C. The hardware and software comes in.
   D. The project plan document is formally signed.
   E. Upper management frees up the money for the project budget.

18. When developing the requirements for the project, what might you consider for each requirement?
   A. Provide a place for project sponsor sign-off.
   B. Provide a place for customer sign-off.
   C. Link each with a specific customer need.
   D. Link each with a separate project step.
   E. Provide metrics by which you can assess the requirement.

19. Two different sets of "criteria" might be alluded to in the project scope document. What are the names of these specialized project monitoring criteria? (Select two.)
   A. Budget
   B. Project
   C. Completion
   D. Deliverable
   E. Success

20. A well-written change control process should include which of the following components? (Select all that apply.)
   A. The type of change requested
   B. The amount of time the change will take to implement
   C. The cost of the change
   D. How to obtain approval for additional funds and/or time
   E. The stages at which changes are accepted

21. Given the standard IT project, which cost estimating technique would be the most beneficial?
    A. Top down
    B. Unit
    C. Parametric
    D. Bottom up
    E. Linear regression
    F. Indexing

22. What is the best way to prevent scope creep?
    A. Make sure the requirements are thoroughly defined before the project begins.
    B. Put a proviso in the charter that no additions to the project will be allowed once it's under way.
    C. Alert the sponsor that you will not be taking any change requests after the project starts.
    D. On your project intranet site, supply a button, labeled "Nice To Have," that the user can check for changes that aren't really necessary.

23. Which of the following is NOT a true statement about cost estimating?
    A. Cost estimates are provided by team members.
    B. Cost estimates make up the project budget.
    C. Cost estimates have a quality factor built into them.
    D. You should average all cost estimates.

24. What project elements may benefit from management input?
    A. Review of project deliverables
    B. Sign-off of scope document
    C. Development of project schedule
    D. Prioritization of project steps

25. Who is responsible for assembling the project's team members?
    A. Project sponsor
    B. Project stakeholders
    C. Project customer
    D. Project manager

26. Milestones that occur between phases typically have? (Select all that apply.)
   A. Predecessors
   B. Exit Criteria
   C. Successors
   D. Entry criteria
   E. Activity sequences

27. _____ are the elements that might have a direct impact on the length of the project scope.
   A. Challenges
   B. Possibilities
   C. Opportunities
   D. Capabilities
   E. Constraints

28. The output of scope definition is the:
   A. Scope document
   B. Work Breakdown Structure
   C. Project charter
   D. Project plan

29. What are the two types of charts that you might utilize in a typical project management plan to denote the project's tasks?
   A. Gantt
   B. GERTT
   C. Network Diagram
   D. AVERT
   E. Critical Path

30. What are the three areas of estimation that you'll be interested in when preparing your project schedule?
   A. Materials
   B. Time
   C. Person-hours
   D. Skill levels

31. When would you use your negotiation skills on a project that's well under way? (Select all that apply.)

   A. You want a certain set of individuals on your project team.

   B. You're running a high-level project in which you could augment the outcome by adjusting certain tasks.

   C. You want a raise.

   D. You're attempting to get better hardware for the same money.

32. Suppose that a corporate organizational change occurs that affects your team. Who should handle the communication of this news, and how soon should it be communicated?

   A. Project sponsor, immediately

   B. Project sponsor, not immediately urgent

   C. Project manager, immediately

   D. Project manager, not immediately urgent

33. At a minimum, how many reviews will your project plan go through?

   A. 1

   B. 2

   C. 3

   D. 4

   E. 5

34. What analysis should you perform to see whether the proposed scope change request should be elevated to the sponsor and stakeholders or can stay within the confines of the project manager and the project team?

   A. Index

   B. Deviation

   C. Portion

   D. Variance

35. In which process do you compare budgeted costs versus actual?

   A. Capacity analysis

   B. Metrics measurement

   C. Variance analysis

   D. Status measurement

36. It's recommended that any given milestone should have, along with its description, these two components.
    A. Success criteria
    B. Entry criteria
    C. Completion criteria
    D. Exit criteria
    E. Deliverable criteria

37. When you want to compare the ratio of budgeted versus actual hours or dollars spent on a task, which type of financial variable will you use?
    A. Index
    B. Cost
    C. Portion
    D. Variance

38. What are the three basic types of changes that someone might bring to a project, changes that may represent deviations in scope?
    A. Design change
    B. Schedule change
    C. Monitoring change
    D. Cost change
    E. Methodology change

39. When is it your job as project manager to also manage the people who are your team members?
    A. Only when authorized to do so by stakeholders
    B. Only when authorized to do so by the team member's regular supervisor
    C. Always
    D. Never

40. What are some team member issues that you will have to get involved in as a people manager? (Select all that apply.)
    A. Team member reports to you that another team member is performing substandard work.
    B. Stakeholders come to you requesting a schedule change.
    C. Top performer is slacking off.
    D. Management rumor mill is saying layoffs are in the offing.

41. In what process do you determine whether there is enough money in the budget or if there are enough hours left to complete the project?

   A. Earned value analysis

   B. Earned income proration

   C. Estimated portion analysis

   D. Estimated profitability analysis

42. What are some team dynamics that might come into play as your project unfolds? (Select all that apply.)

   A. One team member works longer hours than the others.

   B. One or more team members has to leave the team.

   C. Team isn't focused—it's going in divergent ways.

   D. Team is fragmented along the lines of special interests.

43. How many outflows are there from the Closing phase?

   A. 1

   B. 2

   C. 3

   D. 4

44. What is one important step that new project managers might overlook when faced with a possible scope deviation?

   A. Telling the customer no

   B. Determining an alternative solution

   C. Alerting vendors

   D. Complaining to the sponsor

45. Select the three most common project constraints.

   A. Schedule (Time)

   B. Budget (Cost)

   C. Priorities

   D. Quality

46. What resources are released once the project has been closed? (Select all that apply.)

   A. Hardware

   B. Human resources

   C. Vendor

   D. Contractual

   E. Customer

47. A diagram that's used in quality control by examining the 80/20 rule is called a _____ ___ _____.
    A. Resource diagram
    B. Quality model
    C. Pareto diagram
    D. Gantt chart
    E. PERT chart

48. From the list below, select the four common techniques used in developing a cohesive project team:
    A. Forming
    B. Worming
    C. Storming
    D. Alarming
    E. Quoruming
    F. Norming
    G. Warning
    H. Performing

49. What is the methodology arising out of systems analysis and design efforts—a grouping of phases that closely parallels the *Guide to the PMBOK* process groups.
    A. SDLC
    B. ADLC
    C. SADL
    D. PMDL

50. In project management, the process of taking high-level project requirements and boiling them down into the tasks that will generate the deliverables is called:
    A. Analysis
    B. Decomposition
    C. Entity-relationship diagramming
    D. Task focus

Answers to Assessment Test

1. **D.** A project can be declared complete because its deliverables have been created, or because the success and completion criteria have been met. A project can also be canceled, or the resources just wind up being depleted requiring cancellation. For more information, see Chapter 10.

2. **B, D, E, G, I.** You can remember the old poison antidote, syrup of IPECaC (leaving out the "a"), to assist you with this. Initiation, Planning, Executing, Controlling, and Closing are the five distinct project management process groups . For more information, please see Chapter 1.

3. **A, C, D, E.** By not providing adequate requirements formulation, you might have a rough feel for what deliverables you're providing, but you certainly couldn't absolutely pinpoint them. You won't be able to tell when the project's complete or when it's successful, and as a result, the scope might enlarge without your being aware of it. You'll probably be able to tell who the customer is. For more information, please see Chapter 3.

4. **C.** Signing the project charter authorizes the project work to go forward. For more information, please see Chapter 2.

5. **A, B, C.** When the project's costs exceeds its budget, you have to go to the sponsor and get input on what to do next. When the elapsed time taken for one or more tasks far outreaches your initial time estimates or you find that project activity is insurmountable, it's time to visit with the stakeholders and project sponsor to see if you need an extension, not to kill the project. If the sponsor loses interest, it's time to talk with the sponsor, not necessarily to pull the plug on the project. For more information, see Chapter 8.

6. **B.** The sponsor is the one who must sign off on completion of the project, whether successful or unsuccessful. Just as the sponsor is authorized to expend resources to bring forth the project's deliverables, so the sponsor must also close down the project and thus release the resources. For more information, see Chapter 10.

7. **B.** The project scope document details the various components that will go into the project to make it happen. The project scope document includes things like the enumeration of the deliverables, the end product that's expected, the risks associated with the project, the budget and any spare funds that may be available to augment the budget, rules and regulations that may impact the project, and so on. For more information, please see Chapters 3 and 6.

8. **A.** A top down estimate is one in which you're allocated money in which to complete a project. Because of this you'll have to rely on estimates and assumptions in order to apportion the money in each area in which you require it. For more information, see Chapter 5.

9. **B.** One of the uses for a milestone is to signal that you've completed one of the deliverables that are to be obtained from the project. For more information, please see Chapter 4.

10. **C.** The outcome of your WBS will be the project's deliverables! For more information, see Chapter 7.

11. A. A more formal approach to the sign-off of the deliverables is a project phase called acceptance testing, where users actually test out the new software to make sure it works correctly and that it does what they need it to do. For more information, please see Chapter 2.

12. A, C. Anytime there's a significant expansion or modification to the project, the project charter must be modified and the project sponsor must sign off anew on it. For more information, please see Chapter 7.

13. C. The project's scope document should be of most interest to the new project manager. First, if the project scope doesn't match the concept document and charter, the project manager has a problem. Second, the scope denotes the amount of work involved in the project and, if inaccurate, may result in project overruns both in budget and resource terms as well as schedule. For more information, please see Chapter 3.

14. A. In an ideal project management world, the IT project manager isn't any different than the project manager that's building a bridge, sinking an oil well, or mapping the Amazon. Wonderful communications skills are the biggest asset any project manager can have. In most IT environments, you'll have experts in the various areas that you need for the project. For more information, please see Chapter 1.

15. B. The project sponsor signs the project charter. For more information, please see Chapter 2.

16. D. You go through a full-bodied risk assessment process while you're in the Planning phase of the project. You define risks associated with each requirement, try to quantify their impact on the requirement, and prepare a response for each risk. You control risks as they appear when you're in the Controlling phase of your project. For more information, please see Chapter 6 and 8.

17. D. After the sponsor has formally signed the project plan, you've finished the Planning stage and now move into Executing. For more information, see Chapter 7.

18. E. While it's good to boil the requirements down to separate project steps, that's not always possible. However, you should always strive to word the requirements in such a way that you can assess their success and completeness by some metric. Sponsors and customers don't need to sign off on individual requirements. For more information, please see Chapter 4.

19. C, E. You should think about including both the success criteria and the completion criteria in your project scope document. Success criteria are the things that you'd expect to occur in order to be able to declare the project a success. Completion criteria are the items that must be accomplished to complete the project. For more information, please see Chapter 4.

20. A, D, E. The amount of time and money a change will require are *outcomes* of a change control process, not inputs to the process. For more information, please see Chapter 9.

21. D. The bottom up cost estimating method is recommended for most IT projects that do not result in a product or service that your company will be reselling. The reason for this is that you're managing the project from a pure "what's it gonna cost?" methodology, rather than "how much can we expect to make per unit?" perspective. A bottom up estimate is the most precise because you begin your estimating at the smallest of tasks and work your way up. For more information, see Chapter 5.

22. A. The best way to avoid scope creep as much as possible (you're never going to totally avoid it) is to make sure the project's requirements have been thoroughly fleshed out before the project starts. For more information, see Chapters 2 and 3.

23. B. Cost estimates do not make up the project budget; they act as an *input* to the budget. Cost estimates are provided by the team members who will be performing the task they're estimating. For more information, see Chapter 5.

24. A. In order to facilitate management buy in to a given project, one of the options to consider is to allow management to review and approve project deliverables. For more information, please see Chapter 2.

25. D. The project manager assembles the team members for the project. The project manager may certainly have input from the sponsor, stakeholders, or customers, but it is the project manager who decides what the formation of the team should be. For more information, please see Chapter 1.

26. B, D. There are some project life cycle methodologies that also use milestones to mark the end of one project phase and the beginning of the next. Generally milestones between phases have exit or entrance criteria. For example, consider a standard system development cycle in which you perform rigorous testing. A milestone for moving from a test phase to a deployment phase could have a list of specific test scenarios that must be successfully completed before the testing phase is complete. This is the exit criterion that must be met before the test phase is considered complete. For more information, see Chapter 4.

27. E. There is a long list of things that can be considered constraints—elements that could potentially lengthen the scope of the project. Corporate priorities, suitable members for the project team, and budget restrictions are a few. For more information, please see Chapter 3.

28. B. The output of scope definition is the Work Breakdown Structure (WBS). The WBS is a deliverables-oriented hierarchy that defines all of the project work. Each level has more detail than the previous level. For more information see Chapter 3.

29. A, C. Most projects will utilize a Gantt chart—basically a grouping of task blocks put together to reflect the time that each task is going to take relative to a calendar, along with any precursors or successors the task may have. If you were to take some sticky notes and stick them on a flip chart, writing on each note the task, the date it starts, the date it ends, the duration it'll take, along with all precursors and successors, you'd essentially have a network diagram. Network diagrams are capable of showing interrelationships between tasks that a Gantt chart cannot. You'll use network diagrams on very large projects, whereas most small- to medium-sized projects will work fine with Gantt charts. For more information, see Chapter 4.

30. A, B, C. You're interested in what you'll use, who'll do the work, and how much the effort will cost, both in terms of materials and time. For more information, see Chapter 5.

31. B. Think of the phrase "well under way" as code in the IT Project+ test that means the project is in the Executing/Controlling phases. In high-level projects that have a lot at stake and are under very high visibility, you could use your negotiation skills with the stakeholders and sponsors to try to slim down some of the requirements so as to bring the project in sooner, using less budget, or with greater quality. For more information, see Chapter 8.

32. A. The project sponsor has authority to spread the news first. He will give you further information and instructions as to the impact on your team. For more information, see Chapter 8.

33. B. You'll write your project plan then submit to the stakeholders for their review. After you make the recommended changes, you'll then submit it to the sponsor for review. If there are no additional changes the sponsor will sign off on the finalized project plan. For more information, see Chapters 2 and 3.

34. D. You should run a variance analysis on the proposed deviation from scope. You do this by estimating the amount of time the additional tasks the deviation requires and the additional costs. You then compare this to tasks that you've already planned and more or less fit the tasks involved with the deviation. If you can't find a fit, then the tasks represent additions to the scope. You run the variances to see how far over you would be if the new work was added in, and you then have a good feel for how far out of scope the deviation will take you. For more information, see Chapter 9.

35. C. Variance analysis consists of measuring the predicted cost of resource time, dollar expenditures, and elapsed duration of activities, then comparing these to the actual values. For more information, see Chapter 9.

36. B, D. A milestone consists of a description, entry criteria, and exit criteria. These criteria detail how you know when you've entered an area of the project that has resulted in a milestone and how to exit this milestone to the next section of the project. For more information, see Chapter 4.

37. A. There are two indexes associated with earned value analysis: cost performance index (CPI), the budgeted monetary cost of a task versus the actual, and schedule performance index (SPI), the budgeted hours for a task versus actual. For more information, see Chapter 9.

38. A, B, D. A scope deviation can represent itself in the form of a change in the design of the project, a schedule change (typically a reduction in schedule), or a budget change of some kind. Of these, the design change may have the most far-reaching ramifications in terms of scope alteration. For more information, see Chapter 8.

39. C. As a project manager, your team members are under your leadership until the project's over. However, in IT projects, you're often working with people from other business organizations (at least for part of the time) to help with the project. Because these people have a regular supervisor who's responsible for keeping track of their performance and time, you're working in what we called a "matrixed environment," using matrix management. You track part of their time and performance, and their regular supervisor does the same. Sounds easy, but it's very difficult to do in the real world. Politics, personality issues, and other elements get in the way. For more information, see Chapters 1 and 8.

40. A, C. You'll be directly involved with team members when you find that one of your better workers is, for some reason, not getting her work done as before. You'll also wind up using your people management skills when someone else comes to you to report that another team member isn't working as well as they should be. You have to deal with stakeholders requesting a schedule change before it ever gets to the individual team member level. And you shouldn't pay attention to the gossip mill. For more information, see Chapter 8.

liv Answers to Assessment Test

41. A. The process of examining financial variables to determine where you're at in a project is called earned value analysis. For more information, see Chapter 9.

42. C, D. When a team loses its focus, it also loses its sharpness and the project begins to go in different directions. Likewise, when teams split out into special interest groups or cliques, the project suffers as well. In either case, it's up to you as project manager to manage these very real people situations. For more information, see Chapter 8.

43. B. You'll create closure documentation that includes items such as lessons learned and the sign-off for the closure. You'll also release the resources of the project. For more information, see Chapter 10.

44. B. When faced with the possibility of a serious scope deviation, the project manager should determine whether there are alternatives that, while compromising the scope, may not have as much impact as the proposed deviation. For more information, see Chapters 8 and 9.

45. A, B, D. Time (schedule), budget, and quality maintain a delicate seesaw balance with one another, and it is important that project managers keep a close eye on the three. For more information, please see Chapter 5.

46. A, B, D. You would release resources that were allocated for the project. That would include hardware, human resources, contractors, software, and other such resources. Vendors, while a resource, are released as they supply the things that you're purchasing—they're not released at closure time. The customer isn't a resource that's released. For more information, see Chapter 10.

47. C. A Pareto diagram is used to rank the importance of a problem based on its frequency of occurrence over time. This diagram is based on the Pareto principle, which is more commonly referred to as the 80/20 rule. Applying the principle to quality control, it says that the majority of the project defects are caused by a small set of problems. A Pareto diagram helps to isolate what the major problems are, so that you can take action that will have the greatest impact. A bar graph is used to display problems in decreasing order of occurrence so that priorities for improvement can be established. For more information, see Chapter 9.

48. A, C, F, H. Well-known in general management and project management circles, the concept of developing a high-quality team involves (a) forming—the process team members go through to become established; (b) storming—the struggle for control, power, and influence; (c) norming—the process of the team settling into a routine as the project proceeds; and (d) performing—when the team is cohesive and able to produce. For more information, see Chapter 8.

49. A. A systems development life cycle (SDLC—also sometimes referred to as software development life cycle) most commonly denotes five distinct phases: planning, analysis, design, implementation, and operations and support. These phases loosely align with the *Guide to the PMBOK* process groups. It's important to understand that IT specialists may have had training in SDLC, but not in *Guide to the PMBOK*. There is a potential for a difference of opinion between the way that "SDLCers" think things should be handled versus a PMP. By understanding how the two map to one another, smart project managers can avert unneeded project tension. For more information, see Chapter 1.

50. B. Decomposition is the process of analyzing the requirements of the project in such a way that you reduce the requirements down to the steps and tasks needed to produce them. For more information, see Chapter 2.

Chapter 1

IT Project Management Overview

THE COMPTIA IT PROJECT+ EXAM TOPICS COVERED IN THIS CHAPTER INCLUDE:

✓ 2.1 Demonstrate knowledge of the typical IT project life cycle and its application to IT projects.

Your decision to take the CompTIA IT Project+ exam is an important step in your IT career. Certification is becoming more important for project managers, and many employers look for evidence of formal education as well as real life experience from job applicants. This book is designed to provide you with the necessary concepts to prepare for the exam. Much of the information here will be based on the knowledge areas documented in *A Guide to the Project Management Body of Knowledge (Guide to the PMBOK)* published by the Project Management Institute (PMI). We will include tips on how to prepare for the exam, as well as examples and real world IT scenarios to illustrate the concepts.

This chapter will provide you with a high level overview of project management and how it fits into the bigger scheme of an IT operation.

Defining a Project

What makes a new assignment a project? How do you know if you are working on a project? What distinguishes a project from an ongoing operational activity? Both new project managers and team members frequently ask these questions. Projects involve a team of people, but so does day-to-day business. Projects and ongoing operations often fight for the same limited resources. They both involve following a plan or a process with consequences for actions taken. So what is so special about a project?

A *project* is a *temporary* work effort that delivers an *exclusive* product or service. A project always has a designated start and finish—thus it is temporary. A project has clearly defined and measurable goals, which are used to determine project completion and success. A project brings about a *unique* product *or* service—something that has not existed in the organization heretofore.

> **TIP** The word "service" is tricky in this definition because, obviously, there is a difference between ongoing service (operations) and a one-time or specified period of time service (project). Providing janitorial services on contract is *operations;* providing contract JAVA coders for 18 months to work on an IT project (providing programming services) is a *project*.

Another project management term you may have heard is program. A *program* is a grouping of related projects, that are managed together in some sort of harmonized fashion. Programs are often used in the defense industry or large government contracts. From an IT perspective, a large customer support application can be set up as a program, with separate projects representing billing, sales, and repair.

Let's take a closer look at the criteria that defines a project.

A project is typically undertaken to meet a specific business objective. It involves doing something new, which means that the end result should be a unique product or service. These products may be marketed to external clients, or they may be used internally.

A project is always temporary. In addition to a unique end result, it has a defined start and a defined finish. Projects can vary in length from a few weeks to several years, depending on the complexity of the product, but they are not an ongoing set of daily activities.

A project must begin with a clear goal and stakeholders. A project starts when the goal is clearly defined and the appropriate stakeholders have provided approval. A project ends when those goals have been met. A project can also end by being canceled if it is determined that the goal can no longer be met.

With this information under our belts, let's take a look at some IT scenarios to determine whether they are projects or an ongoing operations.

Defining an IT Project

The activities associated with an IT project cross the entire genre of things typically categorized as projects, whether large or small. The reason is in almost every project, some component of IT must be included in the project plan.

For example, if you were building a submarine, you'd need to provide a datacenter, servers, infrastructure wiring, and many other IT elements associated with the project. If your project was to create a manufacturing facility, again, you would need to consider how computers and IT fall into such an effort.

Setting up a vineyard and winery? Again, the scientific basis behind today's wineries is completely enveloped in the things that IT can offer—any great winery would also have a great facility for ascertaining when those grapes are precisely ready for the crush.

You would probably agree that you could come up with very few projects that do not in some way involve aspects of IT.

So What *Is* an IT Project?

While an IT project can and should closely follow the regimen of the project management guidelines PMI set, how closely you follow that regimen, of course, depends on the complexity of the project before you. All of the characteristics of any well-managed project, no matter how large or small, are embodied within the *Guide to the PMBOK*. The size and complexity of the project will dictate the level of detail that you go to in order to bring about the project's deliverables.

Let's take a minute to discuss some of the different IT projects you may find before you.

Software Development

When working on a software development project, not only must you follow high-quality project management techniques, but also be conscious of the *software development methodology* that you use. You will learn the project phases specific to software development later in this chapter.

Infrastructure—Old or New

When we say *infrastructure*, generally we're talking about the cabling, wide area network (WAN) connectivity, and routing/switching plant. In many cases the infrastructure also includes the telephone wiring and switching infrastructure as well.

You might, for example, be moving into a new building with virtually no infrastructure—your project *is* to come up with the design and deployment of that infrastructure. Or, you may have projects in which you rewire the building, upgrade the switches and routers, or upgrade the WAN connectivity you have between sites. All of these kinds of projects involve the infrastructure.

The primary room where most of the cabling terminates, typically called the *datacenter* (see the following), is usually referred to as the *Main Data Facility (MDF)*. Wiring then flows from the MDF to switchgear and routers in other closets within your campus or building. These other closets are called *Intermediate Data Facilities (IDF)*. A building may have many IDF closets spread throughout but generally speaking there is only one MDF per building.

Datacenter Creation/Improvements

The datacenter is the place where the servers, mid-range computers, mainframes, large tape-backup devices, and telephony equipment such as Post Branch Exchanges (PBXs — telephone switchgear) live. The WAN connections coming into a building, be they T1 Frame Relay, Asynchronous Transfer Mode (ATM — a WAN protocol), Integrated Services Digital Networks (ISDN — a telecommunications protocol), or other are demarcated at the datacenter (MDF) location. As a general rule, the datacenter and *demarcation* location (or "demark") are usually one and the same, though some companies may have a demark at a different spot in the building than the datacenter. In any event, you should think about a datacenter as the place where the hub of your computing business gets done.

Datacenters include elements such as a raised floor (for air-conditioning airflow under the servers as opposed to above), commercial quality power- and air-conditioning units, security systems for secure entry into the datacenter, uninterruptible power supplies (UPS), and often a power generator in the event that the power fails to the datacenter.

A datacenter project might involve installing a datacenter in a new building, replacing old power- or air-conditioning equipment, adding server racks to accommodate new servers, or upgrading the power distribution units (PDUs) that provide breakers and power for different systems. Note that a datacenter project isn't necessarily about servers—it's about the place where you're *keeping* the servers.

Server/System Deployment

With the exception of regular file servers, which store user files, you will seldom deploy servers without planning on some sort of system for running on them. For example, you might have a large database system that you need to deploy. Or you might have a *Commercial Off The Shelf (COTS)* program that your company purchased to fulfill a business requirement and it needs a place to run. Or, you might have a combination of some code that your company's software development shop wrote, coupled with a database and other systems in the enterprise. A deployment that relies on the components of several disparate systems is called an *integrated system* and requires careful dexterity on the part of the project manager so that all the parts work together harmoniously.

It's not unreasonable to expect that your telephony systems might need to interact with a server system. For example, perhaps you have a project to install some call-routing software that handles call-center traffic, making sure that customer calls are answered as quickly as possible.

Generally speaking, most system deployments are going to require, at a minimum, server(s), the network operating system (NOS) to run on them, any required software applications, network connections, and testing. A system may be deployed across several campuses, greatly increasing the complexity and requirements of the project.

Storage Area Network (SAN)

Another unique IT project is the installation of a *Storage Area Network (SAN)*. This installation is specialized and may involve fiber-channel switches, fiber-optic cabling, big SAN arrays, WAN connectivity, and so forth. To set up a moderately sized SAN you're facing a fairly complex project that's going to consume several months of your project team's time. A big SAN installation is one in which you're very likely to require contract assistance from the manufacturer for deployment.

Enterprise Resource Planning (ERP)

The largest and most complex of IT projects centers on the installation of *Enterprise Resource Planning (ERP)* software such as that offered by SAP, Siebel, PeopleSoft, Oracle, Great Plains, Lawson, or other ERP manufacturers. ERP software is designed to handle most of an enterprise's business computing needs from human resources to accounting and payroll and even manufacturing. As a result, the systems can be complex and esoteric in nature, requiring significant contract expertise to deploy.

ERP rollouts generally require massive server power, coupled with large-scale enterprise databases such as Oracle or Microsoft SQL Server. Additionally, because an ERP rollout can create diversity of roles—including the implementation of a portal—no one individual can know it all about the deployment. Many different business functions must be involved, requiring the participation of several different managers and stakeholders, encompassing the notion of *matrix management* of a project.

> **NOTE** When we talk about matrix management—the notion that you're deriving workers from various departments and thus you and their supervisor must jointly manage their time—you should keep in mind that an ERP rollout probably represents most fully the notion of matrix management within the realm of IT projects.

Automated Systems

Some systems can be migrated from a manual process to a more automated approach. Think of an assembly line where cars are built. In the early days of automobile production, people assembled cars by hand. Today, robots do much of the welding and assembly of the components of the cars.

The same is true of many systems within industry; electronic pharmaceutical delivery systems count pills and put them in bottles, freeing pharmacists to do other things, for example. An IT project in which you're going to replace a formerly manual process with an automated one will require robust understanding of the business function that you're augmenting and may include plenty of training.

IT Project Considerations

IT projects rely on expertise, process, and communication in order to be successful. For all IT projects you put together the necessary hardware and software components, utilizing expertise in each area in order to make things work. Think about a building engineer responsible for managing a project to erect a high-rise building. The engineer doesn't necessarily have to understand how the hundreds of sinks and toilets in the building operate, but the engineer must understand that they are connected to a big piping system. So it is with your IT project—you may not understand absolutely every nuance of the system you're putting together, but you're far better off if you can put in context how all the pieces interoperate.

The key to understanding IT projects is to think about the process of getting from point A to point B and the highway that got you there. How does, for example, an Internet user navigate a screen that in turn communicates with a database? By moving through servers and security processes over cabling, routing, and switching components. All of these elements, whether germane to your particular project or not, are part of the end-to-end process that you must consider.

Finally, it's important that IT project teams are highly communicative. You can't afford to have a rogue programmer miscommunicate the way that he or she designed the system, for example. When you have live business personnel testing it (called a *pilot test*), you don't want to run into any programming surprises.

Common Job Roles for the IT Project Manager

IT project managers have a difficult job. They must fit into a variety of molds in order to fully comprehend the project and to bring it in on time and under budget. Following are some of the hats that an IT project manager wears:

Project manager (PM) As the *project manager (PM)* it is your primary responsibility to formulate the project team, develop and assign tasks, and manage the project in such a way that the deliverables are built and deployed on time, with the required quality, and within budget.

Business analyst (BA) While the business unit may donate a Subject Matter Expert (SME) or two to help you flesh out the project's requirements, as the *business analyst (BA)* you must have some understanding of what the business entity does. You must have a robust comprehension of the various departments in your company, the job functions of each department, the constraints and obstacles that for each job, the type of people who work in the business unit, how they're managed, and the impact that they have on meeting corporate objectives. You must, in essence, be a corporate department SME of sorts, well able to describe all of the departments (at least the major ones) in your organization.

Systems analyst (SA) In larger projects, the *systems analyst (SA)* function may well wind up being handled by another person, but you still must have a solid grasp of systems analysis and design techniques (see sidebar "Understanding SDLC, Systems Analysis, and Business Processes"). In smaller projects, the SA is also the BA.

Negotiator Not only do you have to negotiate with business unit heads, you must also negotiate with contractors, vendors, and other business unit managers who need to supply you with elements that you require.

Budget analyst As a *budget analyst*, you also have to keep track of the project's budget. Generally you're given a specific pot of money with which to accomplish your goals and you will have some heavy explaining to do if you go over budget.

Legal analyst IT PMs must also understand the legal, ethical, and regulatory ramifications of their projects. This subject has become much more important since the advent of Sarbanes-Oxley document retention mandates, among others.

Technologist IT PMs, while not necessarily heavily technological, must have a modicum of understanding of most things having to do with IT. You can't be in the middle of a meeting with the network manager, for example, and not know the difference between a switch and a router. All the network manager will have to do is step up to a whiteboard and draw a few diagrams and you'll be completely snowed! It's key that you familiarize yourself with all elements of IT related to your project, at least at a conversational level. This is a large thing to say and we're certainly not mandating that you be an expert in all things IT—it's not possible even if you're in IT—but you should be clear in your communications when you're confronted with a term or concept you don't understand to try to gain some clarity on the subject.

Visionary and strategist This function is tightly coupled with technologist. You have to read up on the latest trends in IT. For example, you may not want to recommend a fat client/server system when browser-based technologies are all the rage and your new system would benefit from a thin client. That being said, you also don't want to put your project out on the "bleeding edge" utilizing unproven new technology.

Communicator The most important job of all is to be a precise and thorough communicator. You'll translate statements from one group to another. You'll keep people abreast of the project's status. You'll be in front of important people telling them what the project is about—seeking their buy in. You'll communicate with vendors and contractors. You'll have regular meetings with your project team. You must have highly developed oral and written communications skills, the most important of which is *listening*.

Time manager IT PMs must keep their finger on the pulse of all of the project's activities and when there is a task slow-down, find out why. The PM has the clock running against him or her.

Team builder The IT PM must able to manage a highly diversified team of people with significantly different skill sets in order to achieve the project goals. You'll have project teams that have programmers, networking professionals, server administrators, security analysts, web page designers, and a potential host of other technological folks on your team. Getting these people to relate to one another and to work as a well-oiled team can be very challenging.

Clearly, the IT PM has a broad role, one that is crucial and sometimes unpopular. It's vital that IT PMs understand the "20-60-20" rule of management. Twenty percent of the people are going to dislike you no matter what you do or don't do. Sixty percent are neutral about you and have no opinion one way or the other. The remaining 20 percent think you're the greatest thing since sliced bread and would swim across the ocean for you. As an IT PM you're going to hear a wide variety of opinions, dissension, arguments, persuasion, and other kinds of communication. Some of the decisions you make and things you do will not be popular, at least with one or another group of people. But you can't live in the popularity contest world. You have to operate within the context of producing the finest-quality deliverables possible within the budget and time constraints you've been given.

> **Understanding SDLC, Systems Analysis, and Business Processes**
>
> While the IT Project+ test doesn't test you on your knowledge of the *software development life cycle (SDLC)*, when you're working with software development teams you're going to have to make sure that you have a solid understanding of it. It'll be of great benefit to you to understand how SDLC maps to the PMI process groups so that you manage your project according to solid project management standards, while being able to recognize what SDLC phase your software development is in at any given time. The two do not precisely correlate, but they are similar enough that you'll be able to precisely manage your project and keep your coders happy at the same time.
>
> We strongly suggest that you consider taking a course in systems analysis and design so that you fully augment your understanding of project management with the essential design elements of a technological system. In a systems analysis and design class you'll learn how *Data Flow Diagrams (DFDs)*, context diagrams, *Entity Relationship Diagrams (ERDs)*, and other outputs will assist you in rapidly deploying a fully functional, robust system that meets your customer's needs.
>
> It's also important to note that in the initial business request and requirement-gathering phases of your project, you *do not* try to apply any given technology as a solution to the request. Instead, your focus should be on the *business process*. If you understand the order of flows that users go through to accomplish their tasks, you'll find that the technology will logically evolve. If you're heavily technological, you might have a tendency to think in terms of how a given software or hardware solution from a well-known company will meet the business need. But you should reverse that and first think of the business need, then try to apply various technological alternatives to the process that you've discovered.
>
> Finally, by paying attention to the business process first, you may find areas where the process can be changed in some way to simplify it, or reduce the complexity of the technologies you're going to introduce. This is called *business process re-engineering (BPR)* and is often the first thing a systems analyst will recommend prior to applying any technology.
>
> While developers know about and understand the SDLC, they don't get it when it comes to project management. So, the trick is to translate where you are in the SDLC into the PMI process groups so that you can manage the project utilizing consistent methodologies that have been highly refined and are well understood.

Communication among the Various IT Job Roles

As an IT PM, you'll deal with a wide variety of people. When speaking with executives, you'll have to relate to them on their level so you put on your negotiator or your "businessperson" hat, in order to get your point across. Likewise, when you talk to a software developer, you will rely on your technical skills. With the executive, you probably won't use heavily technical language or computer acronyms. With the software developer, he or she probably won't have much tolerance for listening to budget dialog. The point is that you put on the appropriate hat for the person that you're dealing with. So the IT PM must get into the habit of being able to switch communication hats very quickly in order to accurately convey the message.

Try to make your language as clear as possible for the person you're dealing with. Avoid acronyms unless they're likely to be well-understood by the person or group you're talking to.

> **NOTE** The IT Project+ exam doesn't actually test you directly on these elements, but you'll find a certain indirect flavor in the questions regarding the different hats that the IT PM wears. When a question tells you, for example, that you are speaking with the project sponsor, think about that individual differently than you would a technical team member and see if it doesn't make a difference in the answer you'd give.

Defining Project Management

You are now equipped to identify a project and have a better idea of what types of IT projects you will be managing. But what exactly is project management? You may have already heard a lot of different answers to that question. To eliminate any confusion, we define project management and associated terms according to the standards set by the *Project Management Institute (PMI)*. PMI is the leading professional project management association, with over 100,000 members in over 125 countries worldwide. PMI is a leader in the development of project management standards, which are listed in what is called the *Guide to the PMBOK*.

The *Guide to the PMBOK*

Project management's standards are documented in *A Guide to the Project Management Body of Knowledge (Guide to the PMBOK)*. PMI also manages a very rigorous certification program, the Project Management Professional (PMP) certification. The *Guide to the PMBOK* is the basis for the exam portion of the PMP certification. If you continue in a career in project management, you may move on to the PMP certification. The material you have studied to prepare for the IT Project+ exam is an excellent foundation on which to build your project management knowledge. PMI members were involved in the revision of the IT Project+ exam, and the questions on the exam are consistent with the *Guide to the PMBOK* standards.

The *Guide to the PMBOK* defines *project management* as "the application of knowledge, skills, tools, and techniques to project activities to meet project requirements."

The project manager (PM) is the person who oversees all of the work identified to complete the project and applies a variety of tools and techniques. Successfully managing a project involves dealing with competing needs for your resources, obtaining adequate budget dollars, identifying risks, managing to the project requirements, interacting with stakeholders, staying on schedule, and ensuring a quality product. Sounds a little overwhelming at times, doesn't it? *Guide to the PMBOK* categorizes each of these into nine knowledge areas. Let look at these in more detail.

Later in this chapter we will look at the five process groups that cover these knowledge areas.

Project Management Knowledge Areas

Successful project management is dependent on the use of key processes. These processes must cover the core knowledge areas critical to project management. The *Guide to the PMBOK* defines the nine *Project Management Knowledge Areas* as:

- Scope Management
- Time Management
- Cost Management
- Quality Management
- Human Resources Management
- Communications Management
- Risk Management
- Procurement Management
- Integration Management

As you move through subsequent chapters, we will cover these items in more detail. These areas make up the total realm of project management, and *Guide to the PMBOK* threads each of these knowledge areas into a series of process groups, which will be discussed later in this chapter. These knowledge areas may not have equal importance in your specific IT job area. For example, if you do not have outside contracts for your project, Procurement Management may not apply. The IT Project+ exam has a strong focus on the knowledge areas that are part of the planning processes and the project execution processes.

General Management Skills

Project managers possess many skill sets that are unique to running a project. Successful project managers also possess general management skills, sometimes referred to as soft skills. These are skills that any good manager uses on a daily basis to manage resources and meet goals. You probably already use some of these skills in your day-to-day work activities. General management encompasses many skill areas including:

- Leadership
- Oral communication
- Written communication
- Listening
- Organization
- Time management
- Planning
- Problem solving
- Consensus building
- Conflict resolution
- Negotiation
- Team building

A project manager looks at the big picture and interacts with a broad spectrum of stakeholders. Good management skills are as critical to the success of a project as the correct technical skills.

In the following sections, we are going to take a look at a few key general management skills and how they apply to project management. We will also examine how these fundamental skills translate into your industry.

Leadership

A project manager needs to be a good leader. A project team comes together for the life of the project, which can sometimes only be a few months. Team members will have very different skill sets and project experience. IT projects commonly have both technical team members and representatives from other areas, such as marketing, sales, customer service, or training. Team members may not have worked together in the past. To add even more complexity, team members may roll on and off the project at different times.

The project manager is accountable for sharing the strategic vision that created the project and providing overall direction to the team members. A good project manager knows how to align and motivate diverse people with varying backgrounds and experience.

Communication

Successful project managers will tell you that they spent a great deal of time communicating. Even the most detailed project schedule can fail without proper communication.

Project managers must develop a communication strategy that includes the following critical components:

- WHAT you want to communicate
- AUDIENCE to receive the communication

- MEDIUM used for communication
- MONITOR outcome of communication

Keeping these components in mind and developing a comprehensive communication plan up front will prevent misunderstanding and conflict as the project progresses.

Problem Solving

Projects always have problems. Some are just more serious than others. Project managers must use problem-solving techniques throughout the life of the project.

Real World Scenario

Negotiating with the Business Unit

You're working on a software development project for a business unit in your company. You've gotten past the initial project request steps and you're now in the process of honing in on the details of the requirements for the project.

You require subject matter expertise from the business unit in order to more fully understand and appreciate the business processes that your software is going to automate.

You set up a meeting with the director of the business unit. At the meeting you ask her two things. First, you want to know if you can use someone from the business unit to assist you in understanding the business process flows. You make it clear that the assigned individual must be an SME in the business process. Second, you ask if you can have this individual full-time for a minimum of two weeks. You suggest the name of someone whom you think will perform very adequately as a business SME.

The director is shocked that you require so much time from one of her people. She asks you to more thoroughly explain your need. You explain to her that in order for you to develop software that fully meets the business need, you must understand the flows that are involved in the business process. Further, you describe the process of generating a data flow diagram (DFD), a block diagram that shows, at a very high nontechnical level, the process as you see it, noting that you'll need the SME to validate the DFD.

After some bantering back and forth, the two of you come to an agreement that you can have a week and a half of someone's time and that you'll use not one but two different business SMEs, splitting their efforts accordingly so that neither one has to fully dedicate their time to the business flow discovery process. The director stresses repeatedly to you that her people are so busy, she is being very generous in letting you have them at all.

You agree to the specifications, thank her for her time, and get to work figuring out the best questions to ask the SMEs in order to complete the business flow discovery process in as efficient and timely a manner as possible.

The key to problem solving is to recognize that a potential problem exists. Early recognition of warning signs will simplify the process. Pay close attention not only to your project team's formal progress reports, but also to what team members say and do.

If you do identify a potential problem area, take the time to clearly identify the problem. A vaguely stated problem may drive the wrong solution.

Once a problem is clearly and concisely identified, the project manager works with the appropriate project team members to brainstorm alternatives. These alternatives can now be evaluated and a solution chosen. A project manager monitors the implementation of the solution to ensure that the problem is resolved.

Negotiation

A project manager is involved in negotiating throughout the life of the project. Negotiation is the process of obtaining mutually acceptable agreements with individuals or groups.

Depending on the type of organizational structure, you may start the project by negotiating with functional managers regarding assignment of resources. Project team members may negotiate specific job assignments. Project stakeholders may change the project objectives, which drives negotiations regarding the schedule, the budget, or both. As you execute the project, change requests often involve complex negotiations, as various organizations propose conflicting requests.

If your project includes deliverables from an outside vendor, you will be involved in negotiating a contract. This area is specialized and may involve representatives from a legal or procurement department.

Organization and Time Management

A project manager oversees all aspects of the work involved to meet the project goals. The ongoing responsibilities of a typical project manager include tracking schedule and budget updates, conducting regular team meetings, reviewing team member reports, tracking vendor progress, communicating with stakeholders, meeting individually with team members, preparing formal presentations, and managing change requests.

Meetings consume valuable project time. Effective meetings do not just happen; they result from good planning. Whether you conduct a formal team meeting or an individual session, you should define the purpose of the meeting and develop an agenda of the topics to be discussed or covered. Time allocation for each item is critical to keep a meeting within the allotted time.

Clear documentation is critical to project success, and it must be available for immediate use. Without an efficient system for maintaining documentation, a project manager will waste precious time searching for the latest version of the schedule.

An excellent way to learn organization and time management techniques is to spend time with an experienced project manager willing to act as a mentor.

Project Processes

As we discussed earlier, PMI defines project management as a series of processes that are executed to apply knowledge, skills, tools, and techniques to project activities to meet project requirements. These processes have been organized into five groups.

The process groups are tightly linked, as the outputs from one group are the inputs to another group. Figure 1.1 shows the links between the groups. The process groups may overlap. You may begin planning the project before all of the initiation activities are complete.

FIGURE 1.1 PMI Process Groups

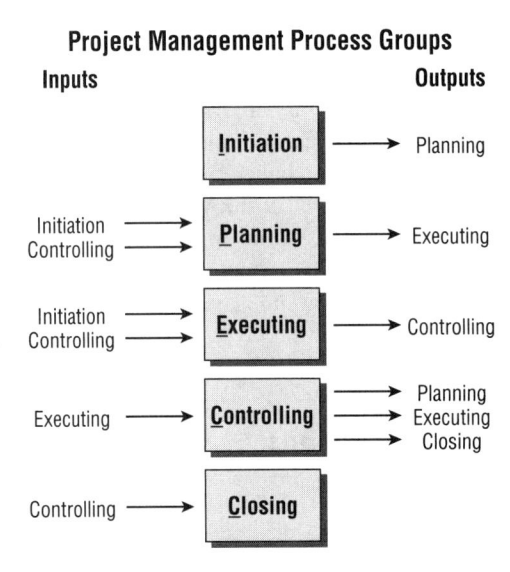

Project Management Process Groups

Inputs		Outputs
	Initiation →	Planning
Initiation → Controlling →	Planning →	Executing
Initiation → Controlling →	Executing →	Controlling
Executing →	Controlling →	Planning, Executing, Closing
Controlling →	Closing	

As we discuss each group, notice the correlation between the process groups and the domains covered in the CompTIA IT Project+ exam. The process groups are the foundation of project management. You need to understand each group and how it contributes to the completion of the project.

Initiation Processes

Initiation processes include all of the activities that lead up to the authorization to start the project. These activities include such items as business need identification, high-level requirement definition, and cost justification. Because the Initiation process is an integral part of Domain 1.0 on the IT Project+ objective blueprint, we will take a more detailed look at the initiation process in Chapter 2, "Project Initiation."

Planning Processes

Planning processes are where the project goals and objectives are refined and broken down into manageable pieces of work. Project managers create time and cost estimates, and determine resource requirements for each activity.

Several other critical areas of managing a project require up-front planning. These areas include communication, risk, quality, and procurement.

> **Note:** The Planning process group, which is included in both Domains 1.0 and 2.0 of the exam, is undoubtedly one of the most critical stages of managing a project. For that reason Planning will be covered in detail in Chapters 3–7.

Executing Processes

Executing processes are where the work to complete the project is done. The project manager must coordinate all the project team members as well as other resources assigned to the project.

Executing processes include the actual execution of the project plan, team development, quality assurance, and information distribution. We will examine this more closely in Chapter 8, "Project Execution."

Controlling Processes

Controlling processes are the activities that monitor the progress of the project to identify any variances from the project plan. Requests for changes to the project scope are included in this process. This area is also where any corrective action will be taken.

Other areas of the Controlling process group are cost control, quality control, performance reporting, and risk control. In Chapter 9, we will spend considerable time discussing the various methods for monitoring progress, specifically change control and quality control.

Closing Processes

The closing processes drive the formal acceptance of the project work and provide a means to fold the product into the ongoing organization structure.

Closing processes include sign-off, archive of project documents, turn over to a maintenance group, release of project team members, and review of lessons learned. Although some of these activities may seem fairly straightforward, several areas deserve close attention. Chapter 10, "Project Closure," will explore the last stages of an IT project and how they can differ from other projects.

Project Life Cycles

Every project has a number of phases to mark the beginning, middle, and end of the project. The *project life cycle* is the composition of these multiple phases, which can be laid out on a timeline. In an ideal world, all deliverables from one phase would be complete and approved prior to the start of the next phase. In reality, the various phases of a life cycle can overlap. The term for starting one phase prior to the completion of a previous phase is *fast tracking*. This is normally done to shorten the project schedule.

Project life cycles vary widely between different industries and to some degree even within an organization. Although project life cycles are diverse, you will find several key elements. A project life cycle should depict at the highest level the deliverables for each phase and the category of resources involved. A life cycle should also depict how the project will be folded into the operational business on completion.

Now let's take a look at some examples of typical life cycles of IT projects.

IT Project Life Cycles

Every IT project has a life cycle and a series of phases. The *software development life cycle (SDLC)* closely parallels project management process groups with its five phases: planning, analysis, design, implementation, and operation and support. The following is a closer look at each of these phases.

Systems Planning

The *systems planning phase* begins with a formal request to IT for a system that will solve a problem, or provide an upgrade or improvement to an existing system. The formal request is called a *systems request* and embodies the problem and business processes that need to be addressed within the given system.

A systems request has two potential outcomes: a *preliminary investigation* and a *feasibility study* (depending on the size of the system). The preliminary investigation basically maps to the preliminary requirement-gathering process that you go through when you're in the Initiation process group of project management. From this preliminary investigation you may derive a feasibility study that denotes the cost-benefits associated with the request as well as recommendations that drill down into the various factors involved, such as operational, time, economic, or technical conditions.

But systems planning goes beyond the notion of "we've got a system we'd like for you to build." It also gets into the idea of how that system fits into the overall corporate scheme of things—does the system enhance the corporate vision and goals?

Additionally (and more subtly), good systems planning may well point back to the need for a change in business processes in order to more closely accommodate the stated desired results. Sometimes automation and technology can't (or shouldn't) solve a problem, when a change in the way that a business process is currently being done will do nicely.

Systems Analysis

You've solidified a feasible *system request* and you're planning on going forward. The *systems analysis* segment is the next logical step in your progression. In this phase you develop a logical model of the system by diagramming the logical flows of the data. You'll map out what the requirements are for the new system.

> **NOTE** Some good system analysis techniques (but beyond the scope of this book) include data flow diagrams (DFDs) and use case scenarios and entity relationship diagrams (ERDs) that illustrate the various inflows and outflows of the system, in addition to the anticipated way that people will interact with it.

If you understand the goals of the business manager that is requesting the system and you couple that with the logical flows that you derive for the system by going through a business process analysis, you can make your job much easier in diagramming, at a high level, how the proposed new system will operate. A visual representation of the basic business flows will also help others understand how the system parts interoperate and help nontechnical people understand how you think about their business process.

In the analysis phase you begin to knock out what it is—the nuts and bolts—that this system consists of. Through your previous analysis process, including interviewing various stakeholders, performing fact-finding analysis, and formulating solid objective ideas about what the system should be comprised of and what it should do, you can build various enterprise models that include the data objects themselves. You also can understand the various process and data models that are involved. Also, fleshing out a prototype at this point will prove to be a worthwhile effort because prototypes give stakeholders a way to visualize the new system.

The systems planning and analysis phases roughly correlate to the Initiation and Planning process groups, which we'll discuss in more detail in Chapter 2.

The final outcome of the systems analysis phase is called a *systems requirements document*. The document spells out what you heard the business representatives say that they wanted in the new system. You got here by going through a variety of processes including interviewing various experts in the business process, sitting with them to watch how they go about their work, questioning the manager, and other such methods. The document is about the business for the business. Like a da Vinci charcoal drawing intending to help the artist understand what it was he was going to paint, the business requirements doc will help you derive your new system.

Systems Design

In the *systems design* phase you denote all the components that will be included in your IT project, including all of the inputs (such as data flowing into the system or keyboard input by a data-entry clerk), outputs (such as screen displays or reports), and processes involved. Additionally, at design time you flesh out the various controls required, whether automated or manual, that will contribute to the system's successful operation. If you're working on a project in which code has to be written, you'll draw out the architecture that the application(s) will use in a document, called the *system design specification (SDS)*, a detailed document that allows the project team members to exactly build the desired system. The SDS illustrates exactly how programmers are to create the system.

If the system doesn't require software development, but does require database or infrastructure creation or enhancement, it's key that all stakeholders, from management to end users, understand what you've designed and how you imagine it will work, and that technicians be able to build the desired system. If you're using a Commercial Off The Shelf (COTS) program, you'll design its integration into the system that you're building.

Note too that other elements such as infrastructure additions or renovations, cabling upgrades, WAN connectivity (including wireless), new types of computing such as PDAs, telephony integration, and a host of other things may be included in the design of your system. Just because your system primarily uses software does not mean that the underlying components don't need to be addressed and freshened as well.

Systems Implementation

In the *systems implementation* phase of the IT project life cycle, the system is constructed. Whether that means that programmers write programs, you purchase COTS programs, or you come up with some in-between system that uses elements from both worlds, you'll want to deliver a completely functional and fully documented system.

This phase includes such elements as the conversion of old data to new tables, training the users, testing, and migrating to the new system. You'll also prepare a write-up called the *systems evaluation* to provide an earmark as to how well the system performs relative to your stipulations in the system design specification.

Systems Operation and Support

Mapping somewhat to the Closing process group, which we'll discuss in just a moment, the *systems operation and support* phase means that you put the system into routine operation, and provide a method whereby the system can be supported if there is trouble. However, the operation and support phase goes beyond Closing in that it calls for elements such as change management where you have maintenance or enhancements that need to be performed and you provide for some modicum of scalability in the system, should it need to be added to later.

You need to know two other things as a manager of projects in the IT project life cycle: setting milestones and checkpoints. Let's discuss this further.

Project Concept Documentation

Let us mention here another type of document that you might want to consider when you're meshing two management methodologies together (i.e., project management and the SDLC): the Project Concept Document. At initial requirements-gathering time, the systems analyst will generate a document that contains the high-level requirements she discovered upon examining the customer request. This document could act as a starting point in the project planning process as well. A systems analyst may not be a project manager, or may be—it depends on the way your company is laid out and the complexity of the project before you. But we know that good quality systems analysis and design leads to high-efficiency systems, especially when built under a well-developed project management paradigm. A starting-point document for both players—the project concept document—is an ideal way to flesh out the skeleton of the project and get the two parties talking.

Note that the systems analyst will go on to develop some very elaborate flows out of her initial requirements—the project manager must be in lockstep with the elements being worked out.

IT Project Milestones and Checkpoints

Any good SDLC process should include the milestones on which you see the project pivoting. For example, perhaps a significant milestone for an e-commerce project would be the purchase, acquisition, installation, configuration, and deployment of the web servers that will be used for the system. A very discreet set of tasks are needed in order to accomplish this milestone. At its accomplishment, in the systems design world, we'd step back and ask project stakeholders such as the managers and technicians to give us a go/no-go decision regarding whether the project should move forward.

Additionally, in between milestones, good projects include several checkpoints along the way that reveal whether we're on time and within budget in our project. A prudent number of checkpoints (not too many to be burdensome) can reveal the pulse of the project at any given point.

Organizational Structure Impacts

The structure of your organization has a great impact on many aspects of project management, including the authority of the project manager and the process to assign resources.

Project managers can often become frustrated by what appear to be roadblocks in moving the project forward. It many cases the root issue is the organizational structure and how it operates. You must understand how your project fits within the organization in order to know the correct approach to resolving issues.

Functional Organization

The classic organization structure is the *functional organization*, as shown in Figure 1.2. In this structure, the staff is organized along departmental lines, such as IT, marketing, sales, network, public relations, customer support, and legal. Each person within a department has a clearly identified superior.

A project that is approved within a functional organization often has silos of work that are completed independently within each department. These silos may even be managed as separate projects.

The typical characteristics of a functional organization are limited authority for the project manager, part-time rather than full-time project resources, and an issue resolution process that must go up the departmental chain of command and laterally to other departments.

FIGURE 1.2 The Functional Organization

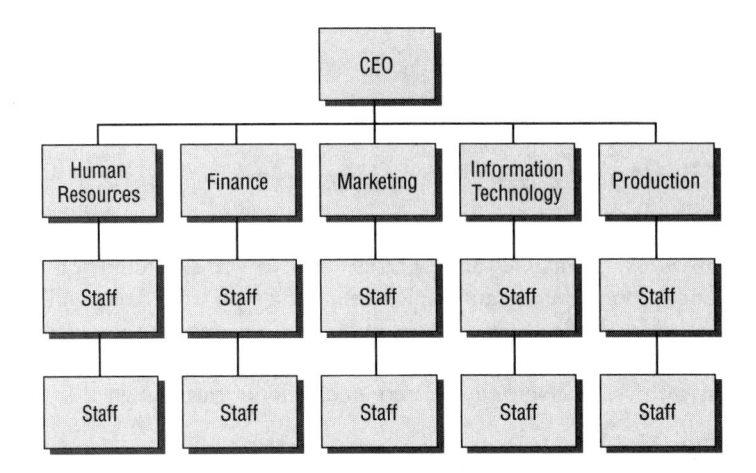

Project managers in functional organizations are often frustrated, because they are held accountable for the results of the project, but they have no means of holding team members accountable for project deliverables. The functional manager controls a team member's salary, bonus, and job rating. You may see some functional organizations that allow project managers input into team member compensation and rating, but the amount of weight it carries may not always be in proportion to the time spent on the project.

A project manager in a functional organization will benefit greatly from developing a good relationship with the functional managers. These managers can greatly influence the success of the project. Often they are asked to provide more resources to projects than they have available or qualified people. Working with the functional manager to resolve these issues is critical.

FIGURE 1.3 The Matrix Organization

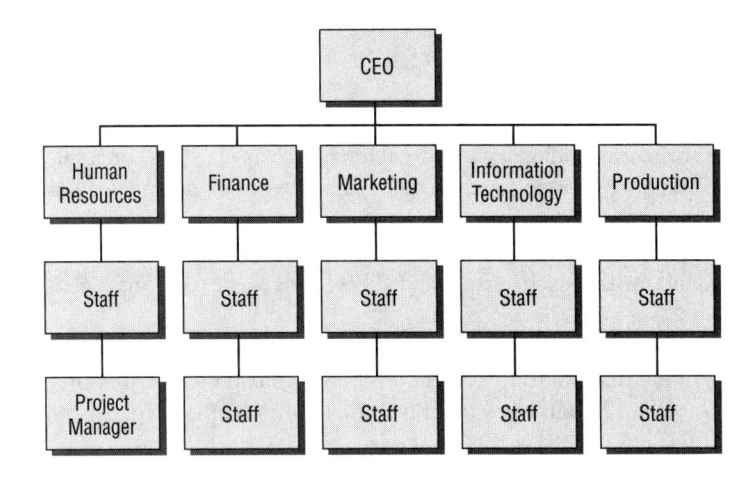

Matrix Organization

Another common organizational structure is the *matrix organization*, which is depicted in Figure 1.3. Matrix organizations typically are organized along departmental lines, like a functional organization, but resources assigned to a project are accountable to the project manager for all work associated with the project.. The project manager is often a peer of the functional staff managers. The project team members have two or more bosses; their functional manager and the project manager(s) they are reporting to.

The typical characteristics of a matrix organization are low to moderate authority for the project manager, a mix of full-time and part-time project resources, and better interdepartmental communication. There are both weak and strong matrix organizations: the stronger the matrix, the more authority for the project manager.

Project managers in a matrix organization need to be very clear with both the project team members and their respective functional managers which results the team member is accountable for to the project manager and which are accountable to the functional manager. The team member should only be accountable to one person for a given result to avoid conflicting direction. Another trouble area in a matrix organization is how thin resources may be spread. If you have a resource assigned 50 percent to your project, it should be reflected in the work assigned by the functional manager or other projects to which the team member has been assigned. Addressing resource issues up front will prevent problems down the road.

Projectized Organization

The last type of organization structure we are going to discuss is the *projectized organization*, which is depicted in Figure 1.4. This organization is far less common in our experience than the other two. In this type of an organization, most of the work is project work, and the company is organized by projects.

FIGURE 1.4 The Projectized Organization

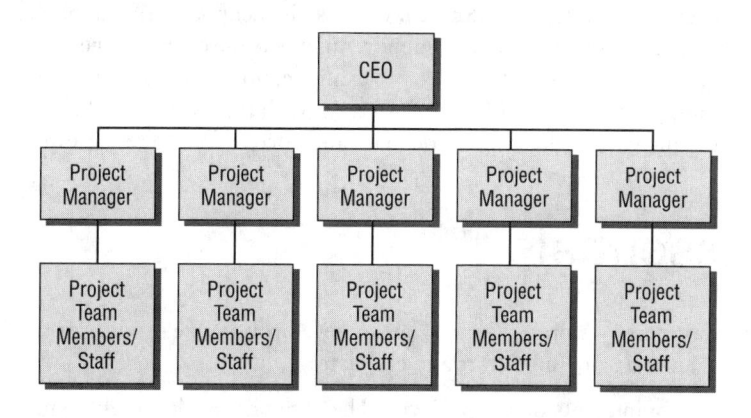

The typical characteristics of a projectized organization are a high level of authority for the project manager, full-time project resources, and a dedicated project support staff.

Project managers in a projectized organization are responsible for all decisions regarding the project. Team members are usually colocated, which enhances communication and efficiency.

The big drawback of a projectized organization is the how to handle staffing as one project ends. There may not always be a new project waiting for resources. The timing of increasing or decreasing resources can become very complex.

Summary

A project is a group of activities that produces a unique product or service with a measurable goal. It has a defined start and finish. Project management is the application of tools and techniques to organize the project activities to successfully meet the project goal. A project manager manages these activities.

A project manager needs not only technical knowledge of the product or service being produced by the project, but also a wide range of general management skills. Key general management skills include leadership, communication, problem solving, negotiation, organization, and time management.

Projects have life cycles that are composed of multiple phases. Applying tools and techniques from process groups completes these phases. The five process groups defined by the *Guide to the PMBOK* are Initiation, Planning, Executing, Controlling, and Closing. The type of organizational structure impacts how projects are managed and staffed. The primary structures are functional, matrix, and projectized. The traditional departmental hierarchy in a functional organization provides the project manager with the least authority. The other end of the spectrum is the projectized organization, where resources are organized around projects, and the project manager has the authority to take action and make decisions regarding the project. The matrix organization is a middle ground between the functional and the projectized organization.

The Systems Development Life Cycle (SDLC), with its distinct phases of Planning, Analysis, Design, Implementation and Operations and Support augments the overall project planning elements. In a new software development project, for example, not only would you utilize high-quality project planning principles, but you'd mesh them with the elements of SDLC so you're assured that the system you're delivering is adequate and correct for the requestors.

Exam Essentials

Be able to define a project.   A project is an effort to develop a unique product or service. The effort is temporary and has a definite start and end date.

Know the four main components of any project.   They are phases, deliverables, people, and constraints.

Be able to name the three primary constraints. You'll encounter the time, quality, and costs (budget) constraints in any project. You should be able to understand the TQB equilibrium is one of the keys to solid project management.

Understand the five basic phases of any project. They are Initiation, Planning, Executing, Controlling, and Closing.

Be able to identify the difference between a project and ongoing operational work. A project is a temporary endeavor to create a unique product or service. Operational work is ongoing.

Name the three types of organization structure. Organizations can either be functional, matrix, or projectized.

Be able to define the role of a project manager. A project manager is the person who leads the project team and oversees all of the work required to complete the project.

Understand what skills are needed to manage a project beyond technical knowledge of the product. General management skills are important, as the project manager must interact with the sponsor, the project team members, and other key stakeholders. Key general management skills include leadership, communication, problem solving, negotiation, organization, and time management.

Key Terms

Before you take the exam, be certain you are familiar with the following terms:

A Guide to the Project Management Body of Knowledge (Guide to the PMBOK)	pilot test
budget analyst	preliminary investigation
business analyst (BA)	program
business process re-engineering (BPR)	project
Commercial Off The Shelf (COTS)	project life cycle
data flow diagram (DFD)	project management
	Project Management Institute (PMI)
Datacenter	Project Management Knowledge Areas
Demarcation	project manager (PM)
Enterprise Resource Planning (ERP)	projectized organization
Entity Relationship Diagrams (ERDs)	software development life cycle (SDLC)
fast tracking	Storage Area Network (SAN)

feasibility study

functional organization

Infrastructure

integrated system

Intermediate Data Facilities (IDF)

Main Data Facility (MDF)

matrix management

matrix organization

system design specification (SDS)

system request

systems analysis

systems analyst (SA)

systems design

systems implementation

systems operation and support

Systems Planning phase

Review Questions

1. How is a project is defined?
   A. A group of interrelated activities performed over an unspecified period of time
   B. A repeatable process
   C. A temporary endeavor undertaken to create a unique product or service
   D. All of the above

2. What organization is recognized worldwide for setting project management standards?
   A. PMC
   B. PMI
   C. PMP
   D. CompTIA

3. What is the term for a group of related projects managed in a coordinated fashion?
   A. Life cycle
   B. Phase
   C. Process group
   D. Program

4. Which of the following is NOT one of the PMBOK Knowledge Areas?
   A. Quality
   B. Time
   C. Negotiation
   D. Cost

5. Which of the following is NOT a general management skill?
   A. Programming
   B. Communications
   C. Leadership
   D. Problem Solving

6. What are Initiation, Planning, Executing, Controlling, and Closing?
   A. Life cycles
   B. Process groups
   C. Management skills
   D. All of the above

7. The sales director comes to you with a request for a new order entry system. What project process group are you in?

   A. Planning
   B. Executing
   C. Initiating
   D. Controlling

8. You have moved into the Planning phase before the initiating phase is formally approved. This is an example of

   A. Scope creep
   B. Poor management
   C. Fast tracking
   D. Problem solving

9. A project manager has the most authority under which organizational structure?

   A. Projectized
   B. Functional
   C. Weak matrix
   D. None of the above

10. You are assigned to install a software upgrade to the customer support servers. Why would this not be considered a project?

    A. You already know how to install a software upgrade.
    B. It does not create a unique product or service.
    C. It is not temporary.
    D. All of the above

11. Which items represent milestones? (Select all that apply.)

    A. Assembling of team members
    B. Key software module finished
    C. Servers procured and shipped
    D. Sponsors sign off on requirements

12. Frederico, the director of the marketing department, has approached you with an idea for a project. What is your next step in getting the project going?

    A. Business-case analysis
    B. Project concept document
    C. Project charter
    D. Stakeholder determination

13. You've been given an idea for a project by a customer. After some preliminary business-case analysis, you've developed a project concept document and submitted it to the customer for review. The customer has some minor changes she'd like to make to the way you've analyzed the project. Where do the changes need to be made?

    A. Project concept document revision

    B. First draft of the project charter

    C. Project charter scope change

    D. Not necessary to note changes

14. In terms of resource loss, who has the most at risk with any given project?

    A. Customer

    B. Stakeholders

    C. Project sponsor

    D. Project manager

15. Given no preset corporate criteria for a project charter, what are some of the minimum requirements you'd want to put into a charter? (Select all that apply.)

    A. Projected costs

    B. Milestones

    C. Business case

    D. Deadlines

    E. Project manager

16. When is a project concept document required? (Select all that apply.)

    A. Always

    B. Always if required by the company as a part of their project management standards

    C. For large projects

    D. For projects that will be reviewed by a central committee

    E. Never

17. A person who's in charge of working through the design process in a computerized system is called:

    A. Project manager

    B. Systems analyst

    C. Business analyst

    D. Chief architect

18. Your boss approaches you to develop a project plan to install an upgrade to some existing server software. You tell your boss that this activity doesn't really qualify as a project. When he asks why, what reasons do you give him? (Select all that apply.)

    A. This activity doesn't create a unique product or service.

    B. This activity isn't temporary.

    C. This activity can't be broken out into phases.

    D. This activity doesn't have any constraints associated with it.

19. Some of your project team members are driving you crazy! They're not adhering to the project's schedule, and they're falling way behind. You need to jump-start them. What phase of the project are you in?

    A. Initiation

    B. Planning

    C. Executing

    D. Controlling

    E. Closing

20. Suppose that you're a project manager working on a software development project. You are working hand-in-hand with a systems analyst. Which person is it who actually makes the decisions about the project—the requirements, scope, etc?

    A. Project manager

    B. Systems analyst

    C. Project manager with input from systems analyst

    D. Systems analyst with input from project manager

Answers to Review Questions

1. **C.** A project creates a unique product or service and has a defined start and finish.

2. **B.** The Project Management Institute (PMI) is the leading professional project management association with over 100,000 members worldwide.

3. **D.** A program is a group of related projects that can benefit from coordinated management.

4. **C.** The nine PMBOK Knowledge Areas are Scope, Time, Cost, Quality, Human Resources, Communications, Risk, Procurement, and Integration.

5. **A.** General management skills are the skills required of any manager to be successful at achieving goals. They include leadership, communications, problem solving, negotiation, and time management. Programming is a skill set specific to an IT organization.

6. **B.** The five process groups are Initiation, Planning, Executing, Controlling, and Closing

7. **C.** Discussions of a client's high-level requirements are part of the Initiation process group.

8. **C.** The overlapping of project phases is called fast tracking.

9. **A.** A projectized organization is designed around project work, and resources are assigned to projects. The project manager makes decisions affecting the project work.

10. **B.** The work you are undertaking does not create a unique product or service. It is part of the ongoing operational maintenance.

11. **B.** The procuring and shipment of servers is a budget and time constraint item, not a milestone. The placing of a server into duty might represent a milestone, however. The assembling of team members and sponsors signing off on requirements don't represent milestones, but functional aspects of formulating the project plan and scope document, respectively.

12. **A.** As a project manager, you start by running through a business-case analysis so that you can validate what the customer is requesting and whether or not the project is viable. A combination of people can help you with this analysis—technical people who understand the technology that can make the project happen, as well as people in the line of business (in this case, marketing) who understand the nuances of what's desired from a business perspective. You could certainly formulate a project concept document even if the project isn't viable, just so that everyone knows what was studied and what determinations were made. In larger projects with more esoteric inputs and outputs, you might ask for a feasibility study from a contractor.

13. **A.** Before writing the project charter, it's important to make sure you've clearly stated the business case within the project concept document. Since the customer has said to you "This is *almost* correct, but I have these things I'd like to change," now is the time for you to update the project concept document before putting it in the charter. The charter is a document that shouldn't really be altered unless there are heavily mitigating circumstances.

14. C. The project sponsor is the one who authorizes the project and approves the use of the resources necessary to accomplish the project's goals. From a resource perspective, the project sponsor is the one with the most to lose. You might lose your job if the project goes very poorly, the customer won't get the refinements he or she asked for, and the stakeholders will be disappointed, but it's the project sponsor who'll have to answer for the waste of time, money, and resources. It's the project sponsor who will be in the hot seat when others above him or her are asking the hard questions about how he or she's going to go about fixing a broken and costly project.

15. C, E. The project charter contains the name of the project manager and the business case for the project (as well as the name of the project sponsor). The other things listed are a part of the actual project plan—a different document than the project charter.

16. B, C. If a corporation has no rule regarding project concept documents, then you don't need to write one. However, for large projects these documents are a must-have because they set up the written dialog between the project manager and the customer and provide a paper path that can be backtracked in case the project goes awry.

17. B. A systems analyst is one who understands the Systems Development Life Cycle (SDLC) phases (and quite possibly *does not* understand anything about formal project management processes as denoted in PMI). She has had training in developing systems by working through the requirements for a given system and then boiling them down into procedures that developers can work from. She uses five distinct phases: Planning, Analysis, Design, Implementation and Operations and Support for the system.

18. A. Certainly, upgrading server software is a temporary phenomenon; however, what you're doing isn't creating anything unique, therefore you really don't have a project on your hands. That being said, it would be no big deal to whip up a quick mini-project plan that details the steps required to systematically come up with a successful upgrade. Upgrading server software can be really scary.

19. D. The controlling phase happens when you've launched the project and you're underway. Now, as project manager, you segue into the role of having to keep people motivated and moving forward.

20. C. Think of it as similar to an engineer who designs an automobile and a project manager who gets all of the processes rolling to actually manufacture that automobile. The systems analyst is going to formally work out all of the necessary details to get the software developed. In larger shops, she may (either informally or formally) don two hats: systems analyst and project manager, but the processes are very distinct. In larger shops, the project manager has under her a systems analyst (or two or more) doing the systems design work, and then feeding the project manager with (some of) the input necessary to get the deliverables manufactured and out the door.

Chapter 2

Project Initiation

THE COMPTIA IT PROJECT+ EXAM TOPICS COVERED IN THIS CHAPTER INCLUDE:

- ✓ 1.1 Given a vague or poorly worded customer request or business need, determine the appropriate course of action in order to handle various business- and project-related issues.

- ✓ 1.2 Given a set of criteria that outlines an enterprise's minimal requirements for a project charter, together with stakeholder input, synthesize a project charter.

- ✓ 1.3 Identify strategies for building consensus among project stakeholders. Select an appropriate course of action involving negotiation or interviewing strategies, meetings, memos, etc.

- ✓ 1.4 Recognize and explain the need to obtain formal approval (sign-off) by the project sponsor(s) and confirm other relevant management support to consume organization resources as the project charter is refined and expanded.

- ✓ 1.8 Given a project charter or contract including a statement of work (SOW) recognize and explain the need to investigate specific industry regulation requirements and contractual/legal considerations for their impact on the project scope definition and project plan.

- ✓ 1.13 Recognize and explain the need to build management buy in and approval into the structure of the project, and describe strategies for doing so.

- ✓ 1.15 Recognize the need to conduct a review meeting as the project transitions from the initiation phase to the planning phase. The review should include an assessment of key items.

- ✓ 2.7 Describe the goals of useful project requirements, review with the client (e.g., verify mutual understanding of client's product delivery, product performance, and budget requirements, etc.) and describe when it is important to have such reviews.
- ✓ 2.8 Given the client's approved project requirements and the input of stakeholders, decompose these requirements into functional, business, and technical requirements while maintaining trace ability within strict configuration control.

The Initiation process group is the first of the five process groups that PMI lays out in the *Guide to the PMBOK*. Initiation covers the receipt of a request through the authorization to start a project. This process can be formal or informal, depending on the organization.

Initiation includes reviewing a customer request with the client to refine and clarify measurable deliverables and to develop a high-level requirements document.

A project selection process or criteria may be used to determine project approval. In this chapter we will discuss the most common methods used for project selection: cost-benefit analysis, scoring models, financial analysis, and expert judgment.

You will learn about project stakeholders: the people with a vested interest in the outcome of the project, including one of the most important stakeholders: the project sponsor.

The end result of the Initiation process is a project charter and the formal assignment of a project manager.

This chapter marks the start of an ongoing IT case study that will be used to demonstrate the application of these process groups.

Receiving a Project Request

Initiation is the formal authorization of a project and is the only process in the Initiation process group.

Before you can initiate a project, you need to have a request. A number of events can drive a new project request. These requests fall into one of the following categories:

- New product development to meet a market demand
- Internal business need, such as a new invoice system
- External customer request
- New technology
- Legal requirement
- Social need, such as infrastructure in a developing country

The manner in which a project request is received can vary widely in different organizations. Requests may come from inside your corporation or from external customers. Your IT organization may have business analysts who are assigned to work with various departments and proactively document departmental requests. The company may have regular interdepartmental meetings to discuss future IT projects. The person from another department making a request for an IT project is often referred to as the client or the customer. We have found that some organizations use the term customer only to refer to people external to the company, while others use customer to refer to the source of either internal or external requests. You need to be aware if there is any distinction in those terms at your company. A customer (either internal or external) may take a project request directly to your VP or CIO.

Regardless of who initiates a request or the event that triggers a request, the organization must review the request and make a decision on a course of action. Even though an initial request may not be detailed, you need to get enough information to adequately evaluate the request. As project manager, you need to meet with the requestor to clarify and further define the request, identify the functional and technical requirements, and document the high-level requirements.

High-Level Requirements

To clarify any project request, you need to develop what the *Guide to the PMBOK* refers to as a *product description*. In IT projects, a product description is often referred to as *high-level requirements*.

The high-level requirements explain the major characteristics of the product and describe the relationship between the business need and the product requested. In order to develop high-level requirements, you need to understand the problem or business need that generated the project request, and the functions you are providing or supporting.

Before you jump into completing your high-level requirements, you need to make sure the problem or need that generated the project request is clearly defined and understood. If the problem is unclear, the solution may be off target. You also need to understand the different categories of requirements and the importance of obtaining both functional requirements and technical requirements.

Defining the Problem

Have you ever been on a project where people are working furiously to meet a deadline, but no one appears to know why the work is being done? Then halfway through the project everything changes or worse yet, the whole thing gets canceled? If this sounds familiar, it may be that a solution was being developed without clarifying the problem. A project can get off to a bad start if the project manager does not take the time to clearly define the problem or need generating the project request.

The customer request may be nebulous and loosely worded. Your job as project manager is to figure out what the customer really means. You need to investigate the customer request and communicate your understanding of the request. This may result in the creation of a project concept document, which represents your first attempt at restating the customer request to demonstrate understanding of the project.

Problems also arise when project requests are proposed in the form of a solution. It is not uncommon, especially in the IT world, for clients to come to you with a very specific request. A client has already identified the solution required to satisfy the request. You may be thinking that is great news, because there is no need to tie up your calendar with a lot of meetings. The problem is, your client may not be asking for the right solution. As a project manager, you need to make sure that the problem has been identified before the solution is proposed.

Let's say that you get a request for a new billing system, which would be a pretty major undertaking. The first thing you should do is meet with the person making the request to get more information. Why does she need a new billing system? What functionality is the current billing system not providing? What business need or opportunity does she believe this new system will solve? These kinds of questions will help you to understand what is behind the new billing system request. If your client is concerned about the number of customer calls related to general billing questions, the best solution might not be a new billing system, but rather a clearer explanation of the charges or a bill insert explaining each line item on the bill. If she is interested in a new look and feel for the bill, you may be dealing with requirements that range from reformatting the current bill data to using a different paper to print bills. Numerous business needs may cause your client to want a "new billing system," but many of them may have nothing to do with developing an entirely new application. That is why a good project manager asks questions to uncover what is behind a request. Lack of up-front clarification and problem definition has been the downfall of numerous IT projects. Do not assume that a customer-requested solution is always the best solution until you understand the business need. Clearly defining the problem up front will give you and the client a better starting point for identifying the functional and technical requirements.

Requirement Categories

Once you have a clear idea of the problem behind your client's request, you must also understand what the client's requirements/objectives/expectations for the project outcome are. You need to identify three types of requirements: functional, business, and technical requirements.

Functional Requirements

Remember from Chapter 1 that a project produces a unique product. *Functional requirements* define what the product of the project will do. Functional requirements focus on how the end user will interact with the product. The requirements for a client whose business need is a new bill format are going to be very different than the requirements of a client who wants to introduce a new product or feature. This why it is so important to have the problem defined before you start looking at specific requirements. Knowing the problem will assist you in asking the right questions to identify the client requirements. For a new bill format, you need to know how the client wants the bill to appear. What are the categories of charges and credits? For a new product or feature, you will need very different data. Will this be a one-time fee or a recurring rate or both? If there is a monthly fee, is it a fixed rate or does it vary by usage? Are there discount periods? Is there a contract period or a penalty for breaking the contract?

Applications being used internally are an area where you should use extra caution in defining the requirements. Your client may assume things will work in a certain fashion without explicitly stating that assumption as a requirement. Let's use a new order entry system for sales consultants as our example. Your client has told you that the system needs to display product availability, generate sales reports, and include a help feature. Although these may sound like good requirements, they are missing some critical data. What drives the product availability? How will the sales reports be generated? What information is included in the help feature? By asking these questions you come up with the following requirements:

- The system will display product availability by wire center.
- The user can generate sales reports online in real time.
- Each product will include a help feature that provides detailed information on the cost, benefits, and usage of the product.

Although functional requirements can be stated in more general terms than technical requirements, as a project manager, you must ask questions to drive out ambiguity. If your client requirement states that a new sales system must be easy for the sales consultants to use, do you know what that means? If the answer is no, you do not have a clear requirement, and you need to define what "easy to use" means to the client. It could be the flow of the screens, built-in help, or other criteria. The client needs to clarify the meaning so the requirement defines the functionality that will make the system easy to use. If you are not sure whether you have a clearly defined requirement, ask yourself how you would create a test scenario to validate the requirement. If there is no way to validate that the requirement has been met, you need to get more data.

Business Requirements

An organization's *business requirements* are the big picture results of fulfilling a project. Business results can be anything from a planned increased revenue to a decrease in overall spending. They can even mean that an organization plans to downsize as a result of a project's outcome.

Technical Requirements

Technical requirements, also known as non-functional requirements, are the product characteristics that are needed so that the product can perform the functional requirements. You can think of technical requirements as the things that happen behind the scenes to meet the client's request.

There are many categories of technical requirements, and the need to include a specific type varies based on the product being developed. Some of the more common technical requirements include usability requirements, maintainability requirements, legal requirements, performance requirements, operational requirements, and security requirements.

If you work in a regulated industry, make sure you address the question of whether any specific government- or industry-related regulations impact the design or delivery of your product. Regulatory noncompliance is a serious offense and correcting infractions can be both time consuming and costly.

Industry or corporate standards may also impact your technical requirements if you are developing an application with interfaces to existing systems. The application interface may require a specific programming language or methodology. These restrictions need to be documented in the requirements, as they may impact activity duration or cost estimates that are completed in later planning processes.

Examples of technical requirements for an IT project are:

- System response time can be no greater than 5 seconds.
- The system must be available Monday through Saturday from 7 AM to 7 PM.
- The system must run on both PCs and Macs.

Your client may be more prepared to discuss the functional requirements than the technical requirements. You need to be prepared with a list of standard questions. For a new customer service application you can ask for data such as the number of concurrent users, hours of operation, hardware platform, peak busy times, and other elements of the product that could impact the design and development of the new system. If your company has a requirements template or checklist, use it in your meetings with the client group.

> ### Real World Scenario
>
> **Assessing the Impact of Regulations and Requirements**
>
> Projects often have legislative, regulatory, or other third-party restrictions imposed upon their processes or outputs. For example, suppose that you are managing a project that will create a new IT system for a funds management company, one that's in the business of managing individual stock portfolios. You can imagine that this company is heavily regulated by the Securities and Exchange Commission (SEC) and that your new system, in turn, will encounter several regulatory guidelines that you must follow. Especially pertinent will be the security aspect of your new system. You must be able to assure the SEC and your shareholders that the system is hack-proof.
>
> It's important that a project manager be able to not only recognize the need to investigate specific industry regulations and requirements, but also to communicate this need and its associated impact on the project scope and project plan to the stakeholders. Here are a few examples of the many external considerations you need to account for:
>
> **Legal and regulatory conditions** Know the statutes covering the type of activity your deliverable involves. If you collect information about customers, are you complying with privacy laws? Do you know which types of encryption can be exported legally? Also, you may face government reporting and documentation requirements or public disclosure rules.
>
> **Licensing terms** Suppose that part of your project requires that developers write some code according to a Microsoft application programming interface (API). You need to be well aware of the licensing ramifications associated with using a Microsoft API. Trademark, copyright, and intellectual property issues all enter into this category.
>
> **Industry standards** Your project may utilize various interfaces between systems. Is there some standard that governs such things? For example, Microsoft uses the Web-Based Enterprise Management (WBEM) standards to move management data from one place to another. You will need to find out how your new system can use the Windows Management Instrumentation (WMI) interface to provide support for a heterogeneous system that you're developing. Theoretically, you would need to determine what, if any, specific methodologies or approved coding practices should be used in the implementation of your project.
>
> Considerations such as these will help you refine the scope of the project, thus producing a more accurate project timeline.

Vendor Bids

Occasionally, project initiation depends on the receipt of bids from outside vendors. This situation occurs if the project request involves a new technology that requires outside expertise or if it is known up front that the project timeline cannot be completed internally.

If your project or a key component of your project is going to be completed outside your organization, you may be involved in writing or providing input for a *Request For Proposal (RFP)*. An RFP is a document that is sent out to of vendors requesting them to provide a proposal on providing a product or service.

Once a vendor is selected, a *statement of work (SOW)* is completed. The SOW is a description of what product or service the vendor will provide under the terms of the contract agreed to with the selected vendor.

The use of an outside vendor involves unique considerations that would not apply to an internally developed project. The contract is a legal document that needs to be taken into consideration as you move forward to complete the project scope and the overall project plan.

RFPs, SOWs, and contracts are part of Procurement Planning, which will be covered in more detail in Chapter 6, "Additional Planning Processes."

Documenting the Requirements

Once you have clarified what problem your client is trying to solve and defined the functional, business, and technical requirements, you are ready to start documenting the requirements and complete the product description.

The high-level requirements document is part of the formal request for project approval. It is also the basis for defining the project scope, estimating the cost of the project, identifying the resources required, and developing the schedule. The high-level requirements should contain the following information:

Problem Statement:

What issue or problem generated this request?

What is the specific business need that the client wants to address?

Objectives:

How do you define project success?

What is the end result?

What are the deliverables leading to the end result?

What are the goals?

How are the goals measured?

Strategic Value:

How does this product fit the strategic vision of the corporation?

Is there a link to other proposed or ongoing projects?

Requirements:

What work functions are required?

Are there interfaces to existing systems?

What are the performance criteria?

What are the support requirements?

Timing:

When does the customer need the project completed?

Are there market windows involved?

Are there significant business expenses to be incurred if the project is not complete?

Is there an impact to corporate revenue if the project is delayed?

Historical Data:

Have there been similar projects in the past?

Were they successful?

Can pieces of previous projects be reused for this project?

Clearly defined high-level requirements with measurable objectives and good supporting data regarding strategic value, timing, and relevant historical information on similar projects is critical to project approval as well as ongoing communications regarding the project.

Decomposing Requirements

Objective 2.8 of the CompTIA exam specifications talks about the ability to *decompose*, or break down, the initial project requirements, as approved by the stakeholders and passed down to the project manager into functional, business, and technical requirements. This means you take the requirements initially given to you and try to boil out the different facets that will make these requirements come about. Then you make a determination as to whether the requirement is functional, business, or technical in nature. Additionally, "maintaining trace ability within strict configuration control", as alluded to in the objective, means that you're careful to make sure that the requirements you've decomposed continue to match the type of requirement you noted in the first place and you do not allow the requirement to morph into something else. Let's try an example:

Stakeholder Requirement: Users throughout the company's *fifty-three campuses* will be able to connect to a *centralized database system via browser* in order to *manage sales and inventory information*. You and the stakeholders have agreed upon this *high-level* requirement and you are now ready to decompose this complex requirement into its baser elements.

> **Decomposition** To decompose the stakeholder requirement, we'll pick out the main elements and determine the types of requirements these entail.
>
> **Fifty-three campuses** This element of the stakeholder requirement is a business requirement because the company has fifty-three campuses and you're *required* to have all of them connect to a central database.
>
> **Centralized database** This element is a technical requirement. You'll use a single centrally located database for all transaction activity.
>
> **Via browser** This is a functional requirement. The stipulation is that all users will use a browser to connect to the system. (A very right and proper standard and requirement in today's complex network topographies, we might add.)
>
> **In order to manage sales and inventory information** This is also a functional requirement. You might confuse this as a business requirement, but in actuality you're saying here that the users are functionally going to do something with the system—they're going to manage sales and inventory information.
>
> Noting these elements, it is now within your obligation to make sure as you go forward and boil the requirements down even further into the tasks, dependencies, milestones, and resources required, and that you do not violate the spirit of each of these requirements. If, for example, a business unit came to you and said: "We don't want to connect to a centralized system because our network connection is very slow. This will just serve to slow it down further!" You might be tempted to raise a huge red flag and say "Wait a minute!" But in reality, this business unit has pointed out a fundamental issue that has to be examined for factualness and rectified if true. It does not alter the initial high-level requirement that started the project in the first place.

> **NOTE** A number of the elements described in this table will also be included in your scope statement, which will be discussed in Chapter 3, "Scope Planning."

Project Selection

We received a project request and defined and documented the high-level requirements, so it must be time to actually start working on the project—right? A little wishful thinking perhaps, because our project still needs to be approved. The good news is that it is time to move on to the final hurdle to get our project authorized: project selection.

Multiple projects compete for limited budget dollars and human resources. No organization we are familiar with has ever been in a position to complete all the requests for projects that it receives. The organization evaluates project requests to determine which projects will be approved to receive funding and resources. In some instances the client is the sole approver, but often approval is required at a cross-functional or executive level.

An organization can use a number of techniques to select new projects. You need to understand the basic concepts of these techniques, so that you understand how the project selection process works and are prepared to present the appropriate data for your project.

Selection Techniques

Project selection is used to determine which proposed projects are approved to move forward. It usually includes the allocation of high-level funding. Project selection may take place using formal documented guidelines, or it may be informal, requiring only the approval of a certain level of management.

Typically, a high-level board or committee will do project selection. This committee may be cross-functional in nature and accountable for corporatewide project selection, or selection can be done on a departmental basis. A committee at the corporate level is composed of representatives from all corporate departments such as IT, sales, marketing, networking, and customer service. In other companies, an internal IT committee may review and select all IT projects.

Complex projects, especially those involving new technology or a major business process change, may be required to undergo an additional step called a *feasibility study* prior to review by the project selection committee. This is a more detailed look at the request than what is normally required at initiation. All aspects of the request, including profitability, marketability, risks, and alternatives will be evaluated, typically by people not associated with the project request.

Project Selection Criteria

A project selection committee uses a set of criteria to evaluate and select proposed projects. The selection method needs to be applied consistently across all projects to assure the company is making the best decision in terms of strategic fit as well as the best use of limited resources. The exact criteria varies, but selection methods usually involve a combination of decision models and expert judgment.

Decision Models

A *decision model* is a formal method of project selection that helps managers make the best use of limited budgets and human resources. Requests for projects can span a large spectrum of needs, and it can be difficult to determine a priority without a means of comparison. Is an online order entry application for the sales team more important than the addition of online help for the customer support team? To the impacted departments, each project is probably viewed as a number one priority. The problem is there may not be adequate budget or staffing to complete both requests, and a decision must be made to approve one request and deny the other. Unless you can make an "apples to apples" comparison of the two requests, the decision will be very subjective. A decision model uses a fixed set of criteria agreed on by the project selection committee to evaluate the project requests. By using the same model to evaluate each project request, the selection committee has a common ground on which to compare the projects and make the most objective decision. You can use a variety of decision models, and they range from a basic ranking matrix to elaborate mathematical models.

There are two primary categories of decision models: benefit measurement methods and constrained optimization models.

Benefit Measurement Methods

Benefit measurement methods provide a means to compare the benefits obtained from project requests by evaluating them using the same criteria. Benefit measurement methods are the most commonly used of the two categories of decision models. Three common benefit measurement methods are cost-benefit analysis, scoring model, and economic model.

A *cost-benefit analysis* calculates the cost, projected savings, and projected revenue of a project. This model is a good choice if the project selection decision is based on how quickly the project investment will be recouped from either decreased expenses or increased revenue. The weakness of using just a cost-benefit analysis is that it does not account for other important factors like strategic value. The project that pays for itself in the shortest time is not necessarily the project that is most critical to the organization.

A *scoring model* has a predefined list of criteria against which each project is rated. Each criterion is given both a scoring range and weighting factor. The weighting factor accounts for the difference in importance of the various criteria. Scoring models can include financial data, as well as items such as market value, organizational expertise to complete the project, innovation, and fit with corporate culture. Scoring models have a combination of objective and subjective criteria. The final score for an individual project request is obtained by calculating the rating and weighting factor of each criteria. Some companies have a minimum standard for the scoring model. If this minimum standard is not obtained, the project will be eliminated from the selection process. A benefit of the scoring model is that you can place a heavier weight on a criterion that is of more importance. Using a high weighting factor for innovation may produce an outcome where a project with a two-year time frame to pay back the cost of the project may be selected over a project that will recoup all costs in six months. The weakness of a scoring model is that the ranking it produces is only as valuable as the criteria and weighting system the ranking is based on. The development of a good scoring model is a complex process that requires a lot of interdepartmental input at the executive level.

An *economic model* is a series of financial calculations that provide data on the overall financials of the project. A whole book can be dedicated to financial evaluation, so we will give you a brief overview of some of the common terms you may encounter when using an economic model: discounted cash flow, net present value, and internal rate of return.

Discounted Cash Flow (DCF) *Discounted cash flow (DCF)* compares cash inflows and outflows over the life of the investment. It uses the concept of opportunity cost in discounting the cash flows. There are several measurement methods associated with DCF.

Net Present Value (NPV) *Net present value (NPV)* is the discounted value of future cash flows associated with a business activity. NPV measures increase in wealth and assumes that cash inflows are re-invested as capital. It is a measure of marginal return.

Internal Rate of Return (IRR) *Internal rate of return* measures the rate of return earned on money committed to a capital investment. IRR states the profitability of an investment as an average percent over the life of the investment.

Constrained Optimization Models

Constrained optimization models are mathematical models, some of which are very complex and require specially trained resources. They are typically used in very complex projects and require a detailed understanding of statistics and other mathematical concepts. Further discussion of these models is beyond the scope of this book.

Expert Judgment

Expertise may be sought regarding the requested product. A project sponsor, key stakeholders, other departments, consultants, or industry groups can provide this expertise.

Expert judgment can be used in conjunction with one of the decision models. We have frequently seen a combination of decision models and expert judgment used if the top project request rankings obtained from a decision model are very close to each other.

Companies with an informal project selection process may use only expert judgment to make project selection decisions. Although using only expert judgment can simplify the data required to complete project selection, there are dangers in relying on this one technique. It is not likely that the project selection committee members will all be authorities on each of the proposed projects. Without access to comparative data, a project approval decision may be made based solely on who has the best slide presentation or who is the best salesperson.

Political influence can also be part of the expert judgment. An executive with a great deal of influence may convince the selection committee to approve a particular project.

Project Stakeholders

The refinement of high-level requirements and the project selection process is where you will first interact with a very important group of people: stakeholders. You have probably seen or heard references to project stakeholders. But what exactly is a stakeholder and why is it important to identify all your key stakeholders?

A *stakeholder* is a person who is either actively involved in the project or is impacted by the project. Stakeholders have something to gain or lose, and you need to meet their expectations. Stakeholders may be interested and involved with the project at different phases.

Some stakeholders may not support your project. A project that creates a major impact on operational procedures may be viewed as a threat. Change can be a frightening proposition. Projects that result in a more efficient business operation may cause a staff reduction. Fear of job loss may cause certain people or organizations to work against a project.

Dealing with your stakeholders is where you will put to use many of the general management skills we discussed in Chapter 1. Individual stakeholders may have very different priorities regarding your project, and you will do a great deal of negotiating with your stakeholder group. Building consensus among a group with diverse viewpoints starts with up-front negotiation during Project Initiation and continues with ongoing communication throughout the life of the project. In Chapter 6 we will discuss Communications Planning in detail, including how you define and implement a communications plan geared to the needs of individual stakeholders.

Set up individual meetings or interviews early on in the project to get to know your stakeholders and understand their perspectives and concerns about the project. These people will not go away, and if you ignore some of your stakeholders, the issues they raise will become more difficult to resolve.

Project Sponsor

The project sponsor is a special type of stakeholder. Although projects have multiple stakeholders, whom we will discuss shortly, there is (or should be) only one project sponsor.

The *sponsor* is the person who champions the project throughout the organization. The sponsor acts as an advisor to the project manager. The project manager keeps the project sponsor informed of current project status, including conflicts or potential risks. The project sponsor typically has the following accountabilities:

- Provide or obtain financial resources.
- Analyze key stakeholders.
- Negotiate support from key stakeholders.
- Monitor delivery of major milestones.
- Run interference and remove roadblocks.
- Provide political coaching to the project manager.

> **NOTE** From time to time you might hear a reference to a person called the *project champion*. The project champion is generally a technical person aligned with the project for the purpose of supporting the project. She is not necessarily one who has a lot of power, but is one who understands the goals of the project and can help you keep the project moving forward.

Other Project Stakeholders

A complete list of stakeholders varies by project and by organization. The larger and more complex your project is, the more stakeholders you will have. Sometimes you will have far more "stakeholders" than you want or need, especially on high-profile projects. I recommend that you define who you think the other stakeholders are on the project and review the list with your project sponsor. He or she is often in a better position to identify what we refer to as "political" stakeholders—influential people in the organization who have expressed a desire to be involved in this project, without a direct or obvious connection. You do not want to ignore these people just because their role is not obvious, and your sponsor can assist you in identifying the needs of these stakeholders.

Some stakeholders are more obvious and much easier to identify. In addition to the project sponsor, the following are generic stakeholders you should find on most projects:

Project manager   We have already talked about the project manager in detail. This is the person responsible for managing the work associated with the project.

Project team members   These are the experts who will be performing the work associated with the project. Depending on your organizational structure, these people may report directly to the project manager, matrix report to the project manager, or simply be provided by another department. Project team members may be assigned to the project either full-time or part-time. Most projects have a combination of dedicated and part-time resources. If you have part-time resources, you need to understand the other obligations of these team members to make sure they are not being over allocated.

Your project team may include only people from other IT groups, or it may include other departments such procurement, legal, public relations, marketing, sales, and customer service.

Functional managers   If your resources are supplied by another organization, the functional managers who assign those resources are critical stakeholders. Normally multiple projects compete for the same resource pool. You need to establish a good relationship with your functional managers. Documented agreements on the amount of time a resource will be available to the project as well as the deliverables the resource is accountable for will prevent future misunderstandings. You should obtain up-front agreement as to your input in such areas as appraisal, salary increase, and bonus opportunity.

The functional manager is the decision maker in these areas. If you approach functional managers with these questions up front, there will be much greater clarity as to your role and your authority.

Customer/Client   The *customer* is the recipient of the product or service created by the project. In some organizations this stakeholder may also be referred to as the client. A customer is often a group or an organization rather than a single person. A customer can be internal to the company, as would be the case if you were on a project to install a server system for the sales organization. An example of external customers is the people who purchase a new feature.

End user   The term *end user* denotes the person who directly uses the product produced by the project. This term is often seen in IT projects to distinguish between the organization purchasing the output of the project and the group who will use it on a daily basis. As an example, the sales department may be viewed as the customer for an online order entry system, while the frontline sales consultants are the end users of this system.

End users may participate at some level in requirements review or functional testing of the product.

As you can see from even this generic list, your stakeholders represent a wide range of functional areas and very diverse wants and needs relative to your project. To keep track of everyone, you may want to develop a stakeholder matrix.

Who Are Your IT Project Stakeholders?

Typically your IT stakeholders will come from the corporate business unit(s) requesting the project. Because IT touches virtually every facet of an organization's business, it's very likely that as time goes on you'll encounter a variety of projects from all or a combination of the business units that your particular IT shop supports. You're likely to encounter three classes of IT projects that will affect specific groups of stakeholders: single business unit projects, multiple business unit projects, or enterprise projects. Let's talk about each of these in more detail.

Single Business Unit Project

In a single business unit project, you might be approached by a representative from, say, marketing or sales, for example, to help design and build a system that meets a specific business requirement.

Often in such situations you're presented with a system that the business unit is currently using but is not satisfied with. In a lot of cases, business unit stakeholders have already done some research into what they want and have some recommendations to offer for COTS applications that they think will meet their needs. As a project manager you should scrutinize the software very carefully because it may not meet the scalability requirements that larger shops have. Additionally, if the software being put forward is from another firm that wrote a custom application but is willing to "loan their code" you need to be doubly careful to make sure that the application being considered is solid, reliable, and, most important, supportable by your IT shop.

In some cases, the business unit has no idea about any other software applications that are available to meet a business objective or solve a business problem and they're coming to you to formulate a project that fulfills the goal. You're afforded much more leeway in a situation such as this. Generally speaking, COTS applications are so plentiful today that you will probably be successful finding a fairly close match to what the business unit is asking for. However, some instances may require that a new software application be written to custom specifications. It is up to you as the project manager wearing a systems analysis hat (or vice versa) to make the best educated decision about the proper approach to the solution.

Multiple Business Unit Project

Sometimes two or more business units can make use of a system in order to meet business objectives or solve a business problem. Document imaging and management systems (DMS) are an example of this. In a *multiple business unit project*, you might be approached by two or more business units that have determined that they collectively have enough capital funding to "go in together" on a DMS that they can all use.

Now your task has gotten more difficult because you have a variety of stakeholders involved, all with different agendas, but similar interests. Gaining consensus in such stakeholder environments will be the most important item of the day.

Additionally, you'll be forced to understand each business unit's logical flows in order to make collective sense out of the system that you design and build. One business unit, for example, may not require quality control procedures for incoming documents, for example, because they're already quality checked by the sender due to some regulation or another. But another participating business unit does have a quality control step that they need to continue to maintain. Solving for such stakeholder irregularities makes for interesting project management issues.

Enterprise Project

Another interesting project is one that impacts the entire enterprise. What we mean by the word *enterprise* is the complete array of business units—everyone in the company or division is affected.

You may not be aware of it, but you've probably been a part of or at least interacted in some way with an *enterprise project*. Two distinct examples come to mind: your organization's email system and its corporate intranet. All persons interact with each of these enterprise systems, and yet at most probably one group of IT people is involved with each respective system's maintenance.

> **Real World Scenario**
>
> **The Shared DMS**
>
> Marvin works as an IT specialist for a business unit in a company. His business unit managers have voiced a need for a DMS in order to scan in old documents and archive them in some DMS software. Any new documents will be electronically submitted and automatically populated into the DMS software.
>
> Another business unit with similar needs has gotten wind of the project and approached Marvin's managers. Together the managers of both business units have agreed to partner to procure and implement the new system. The other business unit does not have an IT department, so they'll be relying on Marvin to assist with their implementation. They will be assisting by providing some funding for the project.
>
> Marvin is not the owner of the datacenter, where the new DMS servers will be housed. This function is handled by the central IT shop (called "Ops") responsible for enterprise operations. He will manage the software on the servers, but Ops will be responsible for maintaining the server hardware and the database on the system.
>
> In this case Marvin has a very complex stakeholder environment. Ops and the other business unit are both stakeholders in the efforts that Marvin's business unit is making. Success or failure can be had at the hand of any of these stakeholders. If, for example, the second business unit drops their funding, then the project is in jeopardy. If Ops cannot or will not manage the server, the primary business unit will have to find some other workaround, potentially resulting in increased project costs or duration or both. Ops must rely on Marvin's training in the new DMS software in order to make sure that users can reliably utilize the system.

Enterprise projects bring interesting stakeholder issues. Who are your stakeholders in enterprise systems? Generally, everyone will use the system. So you have to look at representatives from each group as your key stakeholders, or conversely, at certain select groups as the primary stakeholder for the system. For example, when considering a new email system, your corporate records manager; that is, the person or group responsible for setting down document retention policies, will be a very important stakeholder in any decisions you make about the retention of email items. In a new corporate intranet project, all users will be stakeholders, but most likely the content providers for each business unit will be the key stakeholder for the project.

IT Project Team Members

The IT project team has several stakeholders in various positions. The IT project team is different than a team you're assembling for a construction project. Construction workers work within their own areas of expertise (a plumber doesn't necessarily care, or have to care, what the electrician is doing, for example). But in an IT team, you have individuals who have specialized in their respective areas of IT and who may well have a clue, perhaps a substantial one, about the other team member's functions. A software developer has to be fairly database savvy, for example, because he or she will be working extensively with writing data taken from user input screens to a database somewhere. *Database administrators (DBAs)* must be extremely knowledgeable about the things software developers do, plus they need to understand how servers work and also how users connect to databases across the network wire. Server administrators must understand that their servers are there to support business functions—that the underlying *network operating system (NOS)* isn't the sum total of what the server's about. And woven through it all are systems analysts, business analysts, business subject matter experts, and others who are participating together to bring in the project's deliverables.

Following is a list of the kinds of people you might expect to join you on any given IT project team, depending on the deliverables you're trying to produce:

Software developers   Software developers are often called on to work on IT projects. This category of team member may also include folks who specialize in writing programs that run on application servers such as JBOSS, Microsoft BizTalk, or BEA WebLogic; user-interface developers; firmware coders who write software that works inside hardware devices; database stored procedure developers; and Internet/intranet developers and specialized module developers (for things such as printer and communications modules).

Server administrators   These team members are responsible for bringing up the servers (whether Intel-, mid- or mainframe-based) that will house your project.

Database administrators (DBAs)   DBAs are responsible for creating the database schema (structure) and associated requirements, plus planning out the backup and recovery methodologies for the data. DBA work includes the concept of reducing the table structures to their lowest operable form, a process called *normalization*.

Internetworking specialists   Internetworking specialists are the folks who handle the routers, switches, LAN cabling, and WAN connections.

Telephony specialists The people who manage the company's telephone equipment and operations are telephony specialists. It's amazing how many systems today interoperate with telephony. Think of a telephone-based menu system, called *Interactive Voice Response (IVR)*, realizing that a software developer had to write that code that intercepts the incoming call, provides a menuing system for the user to pick from, then routes the call back out to the appropriate party. The IVR software runs on a server but is connected to the telephony backbone.

Systems analysts Systems analysts (SAs) are people trained and skilled in IT subjects, but who operate at the functional level of taking the system requirements and boiling them down to a system design specification that the system developers can use to build the project. SAs today use very cool software such as the offerings from Rational that help them quickly and accurately model the system from business flows.

Business analysts Often one and the same as the system analyst, business analysts (BAs) are able to work at the high level of the business unit in order to understand their needs but are also able to interface with the IT folks to help them understand what it is the business unit really wants. BAs can be IT-savvy folks who come from the business unit, or business-savvy people who are in the IT shop.

System architects System architects have a very technical level of knowledge about systems and are able to draft out the "blueprint" of the proposed system. Sometimes the system analyst can be the architect; other times, a developer or perhaps even the project manager is in charge of architecture. However, in larger systems, it is not unusual for project managers to use the assistance of an actual system architect.

Budget analyst Especially in very large projects, a budget analyst is required to keep track of the project's budget and associated expenses.

Security analyst The security analyst is a new, yet indispensable character on most systems project teams. The security analyst is the person who makes sure that all security aspects are ironed out. Security is a unique specialty and really requires, especially in mid- to large-sized projects, someone who has a firm background and understanding of the subject.

Technical writers In larger projects a technical writer is put in charge of writing all of the documentation (with the exception of the comments directly entered into the code) for the project. This includes training documents as well as user manuals, help-desk "cheat sheets" and other documentation.

All of these people must be able to understand technical jargon and acronyms, and be able to fully function and get along with one another. It's important that these people feel a sense of freedom to be able to question something that's being done and to work closely with one another in making sure that the right decisions are being made going forward. There is little room for superstars or "Lone Rangers" (those who prefer to work alone and not associated with project teams) in efforts such as these. The project team must consist of a group of people who understand the project's goals and who come together with a cohesive purpose. Otherwise chaos will occur.

Additionally, people on project teams must be great self-starters, able to work on their tasks with little guidance apart from the system design specification. System project teams are usually not a good place for a beginner to start out because you need folks who have some basis of experience for what they're being asked to create.

As the project manager of a technical project team you must realize that you'll be working with a wide variety of personality types and you'll have to somehow manage the psychology of process accordingly. While you need to have a firm grasp on all of the technological ramifications of the deliverables being created, you must also understand team dynamics and how humans interact with one another in high-stress settings. You should be prepared to handle grievances, to mediate arguments, to gather around a whiteboard and draw out a logical function so all stakeholders understand it, to communicate in one person's lingo what the other person is trying to say, and so forth. Clear, concise and adequate communications are essential in IT project management.

Real World Scenario

Matching the Project Charter to the Project Team

By writing a good quality project description, you'll probably have a fairly clear idea of exactly the kinds of people you'll need on your team before you even start assembling the team. Take, for example, the project description in the sidebar, "IT Project Descriptions":

"IT will create a set of computer programs and databases that will allow the vehicle service department to track all warranty work performed on any given vehicle. The system will be intranet-based and accessible via browser from any computer in the environment. The database will contain fields to house all relevant pieces of information for warranty work performed by the department. Reports will be generated that can be electronically shipped to the vehicle manufacturer for reimbursement. Drop-downs using lookup tables will be provided on the user interface wherever possible to minimize data entry time and incorrect data entry. Consistency checking will be performed on key fields that require double-checking of the data (such as VIN)."

Clearly you can tell from this short description that you're probably going to need at least one web programmer. You don't know yet whether you'll opt for Java, C#, or some other Internet programming language—that's not important just yet. You also know that you're going to need at least one DBA because there are databases to be created. You'll doubtless need the assistance of a server administrator to assist you in placing the databases and software that you'll develop. You'll also need a good BA to help you understand the business processes and translate them into the computer programs.

As you drill into the project a little more, you'll discover how many of each you need, but for now you've at least identified the relevant technology people.

Stakeholder Matrix

If you have a large project with multiple stakeholders, it may be appropriate to create a stakeholder matrix to help you keep track of everyone. A stakeholder matrix should include a list of the stakeholders with the following information on each one:

- Role on the project
- Needs from the project
- Involvement on the project
- Level of influence over the project

This matrix can be a useful tool to review during project execution, as conflicts arise. It can help the project manager understand and deal with various behaviors. It is of particular value if your project has some of the political stakeholders I mentioned earlier.

Since project stakeholders can move on and off the project at different times, it is very important that the project manager reviews the project charter and the project plan as stakeholders become involved in the project.

Project Charter

The result of the Initiation planning process is the *project charter*. This document provides formal approval for the project to begin and authorizes the project manager to apply resources to the project. This is a major milestone, as the charter is the first official document of your approved project. All that hard work in the Initiation process has finally paid off.

The person or group approving the project issues the project charter. If your organization has a formal project selection committee, it may define who issues the project charter. This is typically someone in upper management, but this will vary between companies or departments. It may or may not be the project sponsor.

The charter is the project blueprint; similar to the blueprint you develop if you build a new home. The finished product will look a whole lot different, but at least you now have a map to help you get started.

Organizational standards drive the specific format of a project charter and the information it contains. As a project manager, you always want to determine if there is a template or required format to follow. At a minimum, your charter should contain a description of the project, the business need that created the project, and formal approval for the project to begin. If your project was involved in a formal selection process, you will have more data and can develop a project charter that contains the project description, project team information, goals and objectives, high-level business case, and formal approval.

Let's discuss the components of a charter in more detail.

> ### Real World Scenario
>
> **IT Project Descriptions**
>
> An IT project description needs to be a quick-read paragraph that encapsulates and describes in a few sentences what the project's product will do. It documents the key characteristics of the product or service that you're going to create as well as the work required to deliver the project.
>
> The following are some examples of IT project descriptions:
>
> - IT will create a set of computer programs and databases that will allow the vehicle service department to track all warranty work performed on any given vehicle. The system will be intranet-based and accessible via browser from any computer in the environment. The database will contain fields to house all relevant pieces of information for warranty work performed by the department. Reports will be generated that can be electronically shipped to the vehicle manufacturer for reimbursement. Drop-downs using lookup tables will be provided on the user interface wherever possible to minimize data entry time and incorrect data entry. Consistency checking will be performed on key fields that require double-checking of the data (such as VIN).
>
> - IT will assemble a bar-code system so that two assembly-line employees can scan all parts coming off of the line and enter them into a database tracking system. The system will consist of two PCs connected to the network and the company's ERP system. The assembly-line technicians will affix a bar code to the item, scan it, then key in pertinent data relative to the item. The data will be subsequently posted to the ERP's equipment inventory catalog for use by parts persons in the field.

Project Description

The *project description* documents the key characteristics of the product or service that will be created by the project and the work required to deliver the product. The description in the charter will be high level and more detail will be added when you develop the project scope statement, which is discussed in Chapter 3. The project description documents the relationship between the product being created and the business need that drove the project to be requested. This description needs to contain enough detail to be the foundation for the scope planning process that will be the next step.

Project Team

The project charter should formally identify the project manager and his or her authority. Detailing the project manager's authority in writing early on will prevent misunderstandings or issues down the road. Authority areas to document include personnel management and budget authority.

- Does the project manager have hiring and firing authority over team members?

- Does the project manager have input into the appraisals or salary reviews of team members?
- Is the project manager authorized to spend the project budget?
- Are there any limits on the dollar amount that can be spent without sponsor or other executive approval?

All known project team members can be listed. A charter does not normally list project team members by name, but lists the category of resources required. Job titles such as Business Analyst, Systems Analyst, Programmer, and Tester can be listed. Charters for cross-functional projects should also list known team members from other departments such as a Product Manager, Marketing Communications Manager, Training Developer, or Contract Specialist.

Goals and Objectives

The charter documents the high-level goals and objectives of the project. The project charter is the first communications document to explain what the project is all about.

A charter needs to include a clear statement as to what end result the project will produce and how success will be measured. Goals and objectives must be clear and stated in such a manner that the end result can be measured against the objective. Instead of stating, "Install a fast customer record retrieval system," a goal should state a measurable outcome like "Retrieve customer records in an average of 5 seconds."

Working with the client to document quantifiable and measurable goals is key to the project success. It puts the client, the sponsor, key stakeholders, the project manager, and team members on the same page. Fuzzy objectives with no measurement create vastly different perspectives as to what constitutes project success.

Business Case

Approval of the project charter also marks the initial approval for project funding. The amount of funding initially approved for the project is linked to the business case. A *business case* formally documents components of the project assessment generated by the project selection process. It includes a description of the analysis method and the results.

A business case is typically a stand-alone document that is initially created at a very high level with multiple iterations over the course of the project. Details to the business case are added at various points in the project planning process. Many organizations have business case templates, with some of the sections completed at the time of project selection.

A business case summary in the project charter may include high-level costs, benefits, and payback period estimates.

Costs All costs estimated at the time of project approval should be listed. These costs include estimates for materials, equipment, and human resources. The estimates in a project charter are very high-level estimates based on costs of similar projects or estimates from experts familiar with the type of work involved.

In a typical IT project, there are both capital and expense costs. Capital costs would include the purchase of new equipment such as servers or workstations. Expense costs include items like salaries, travel, and training.

Benefits   A key benefit is revenue. Revenue is the cash flow generated by providing a billable good or service to an external customer. Not all projects generate revenue, but for those projects that will be sold to external customers, this is a critical component. The early revenue estimates are provided by the marketing organization based on a target price and a forecast of sales.

Revenue is a benefit that can be quantified and measured. A new product may be projected to bring in $2M in revenue during the first year of product launch.

Other benefits, such as increased customer satisfaction, may be more difficult to quantify. Benefits that cannot be easily quantified in dollars are sometimes referred to as soft benefits.

Payback period   The payback period identifies when the project will pay for itself. For a revenue-generating project, this can be a timeline of the project costs compared to project revenue.

There can also be a payback period on a project that does not generate revenue. A new call handling system with menu options may drive efficiencies in a call center operation that will allow the center to grow without adding additional staff. This cost avoidance figure can be used to calculate when the system will pay for itself.

Formal Approval

The project charter should be signed by the executive with the authority to move the process forward. This person could be the project sponsor, the project client, or a representative of the project selection committee. The key is making sure the person signing the charter is at the appropriate level within the company to authorize the project.

This sign-off provides the project manager with the authority to move forward with the work required to complete the project. This approval may be required prior to the release of purchase orders or the formal commitment of functional managers to provide resources to support the project.

Issuing the project charter moves the project from the initiation phase into the planning phase. Regardless of who actually signs the project charter, now is the time to make sure you have buy-in from your stakeholder group. All of the stakeholders need to receive a copy of the charter. It is also a good idea to schedule a meeting to review the charter, review next steps, and answer any questions or concerns. To eliminate any future disagreements regarding the outcome of the meeting, all key points and any decisions made should be documented in a memo sent to all the stakeholders. Issues that are dealt with as soon as they surface are easier to resolve. Ignoring concerns or not keeping stakeholders in the loop can create escalations to higher management and start your project off on the wrong foot. The support of management is critical and the best way to maintain this support is through ongoing communications. Maintaining consensus among stakeholders is a key part of the project manager's responsibility throughout the life cycle of the project.

IT Chain of Command

When considering the overall project, especially in context of the charter and the associated names of people in that charter who are able to authorize the resources necessary to enact the project, it will be beneficial for you to understand who's in the IT chain of command so that you know who is capable of doling out this authorization. While most IT shops are somewhat small-ish (i.e., just a few members in each specialty group—servers, programming, etc.) these groups can be broken out among various managers who each have their own budget, and who can call the shots for the employees under them. For example, your project might call for a telephony person, who reports to the telecommunications department, of which there are four or five employees and who have a manager over them who is responsible for their day-to-day operations. This person is one who must appear on the charter because he has the ability to authorize the use of the resources you require. Ditto for programmers, who probably come from a different group, with a different manager. You can't schedule a telecommunications person using the authorization of the programming manager because she doesn't manage the telecom folks! So it's prudent to understand the chain of command that's involved with any given technological project.

The IT chain of command can vary widely depending on the size and spread of the organization you're working for. Generally speaking, however, there will always be a supervisor or manager of the software development, network operations, server administration, telephony, security, Internet/intranet, architecture, and database teams.

Typically, these supervisors/managers report to a director-level individual or perhaps even the chief technology officer (CTO) or chief information officer (CIO) (the so-called C-band executives) of the company. This, of course, depends on the company's size. See Figure 2.1 for an example of the IT reporting hierarchy.

In Figure 2.1 you'll see a department called the *project management office (PMO)*. Some (not all) enterprises have realized that many endeavors benefit from a professional project manager overseeing the project—whether the project is technical in nature or not. So the idea of a PMO was formed—a centralized location for all project managers, staffed and managed by project professionals, and capable of taking on any project in the organization.

FIGURE 2.1 The IT reporting hierarchy

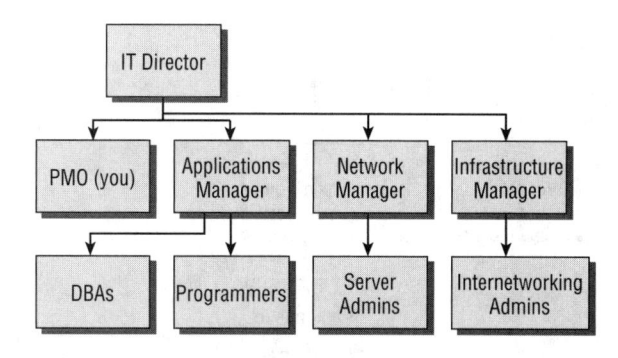

The Frustrations of Hierarchy

Because the charter speaks to the *types* of people who will be required to complete the project (note that we may not necessarily know the names of the people at this point in time, but we *do know* that we need a certain class of individual) understanding the chain of command makes your job easier when it comes to understanding who's got to sign off on who's joining the project. You can't, for example, stipulate that you need a programmer but not list the head of the programming department as one of the persons who must authorize the usage of his or her resources.

Here's the problem with a chain-of-command hierarchy in a standard IT shop: The director of applications development's goals may not be the same as the director of operations. Your job as a member of the project management office (PMO) is to try to get these two on the same page with respect to your project—to see that the outcome of this project is of paramount importance and that the two must agree on this. But that's not always the case. So you wind up doing a lot of resource allocation planning, working with the leaders of each unit in order to come up with convenient windows of time when the people you need are going to be available. You don't usually have the luxury of a manager telling you "You can have my best programmer for as long as you need him or her!"

Another similar, only worse, problem arises when the directors of these various units don't report to the same individual, as shown in Figure 2.2.

Now you've got an issue where you not only need to coordinate resources across various managers but also across executive leaders. While the executive might say "Sure, you can use so-and-so!" the manager may not be so wild about the idea. Or vice versa.

Still more confusing is the hierarchy in which the business unit has some IT staff and you also have some IT folks who are going to work on the project. This is similar to the CIO/CTO model shown in Figure 2.2 except that the business unit's objectives may be quite different than the objectives of executives who are committed to IT. You may well find that you get an initial commitment from the business unit director to use a staff IT person, but that permission is yanked back at the last minute due to other pressing issues. Or you might find that your assigned staff person is a yo-yo, being pulled constantly off of the project in order to put out business unit IT fires.

FIGURE 2.2 Business units not associated with the IT hierarchy

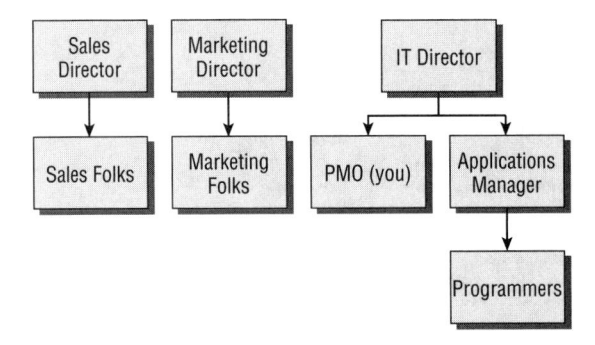

Unfortunately, there is no really good way to manage such complicated scheduling issues, apart from doing your best to anticipate problems up front and then planning into your project enough leeway to handle such issues. Business unit leaders need to understand that a commitment to an important IT project means that the staff you need are available to you at the time you need them and they cannot be used for other work!

Case Study: Chaptal Wineries Email and Intranet Systems

This case study will follow you through the remainder of the book. It's designed to be complicated enough to require the use of all of the project management components we talk about, using information from each chapter you read.

You work for a mid-sized winery—Chaptal (named for the process of adding sugar to wine to increase its alcohol level—chaptalization)—in the Sonoma county region of California. Business has been very, very good! Wine is hot, hot, hot all over the country and your wine maker, Rachel Ranee, has gained in stature and favor throughout the major wine circles.

The owner of the winery, Kim Cox, has decided to set up shop in other interesting parts of the world: Chile, southeastern Australia, and western France. She has established strong partnerships in these areas and is now ready to connect the three sites together into one network so that she can keep track of the daily activities of each new winery. The prospective new wineries are as follows:

France LaCroix is in the Bordeaux region of France. Chaptal's partner is Guillaume Fourche, a long-time Bordeaux *negociant*, one who buys wine from the various smaller wine merchants to blend into interesting *cuvees* that are then bottled and sold. Kim wants to set up an international distributorship with this man, utilizing Rachel's wine-making skills to seriously kick up the quality of the wines that LaCroix distributes.

Chile Metor Sanchez in the Aconcagua Valley has been making wonderful Chilean red wines for several years now. Metor Sanchez is interested in branching out internationally and understands that a partnership such as one through Chaptal would be beneficial for both wineries.

Southeastern Australia In Adelaide, Australia, a new renegade winery has sprung up. Roo Wines, headed up by a young new upstart wine maker, Jason Jay, holds Kim in a spell with the luscious dark Shiraz wines that they release.

Kim has entered into financial agreements and working partnerships that allow her to own a stake in each of the wine company's output, while allowing them to retain their original look and feel. The people who work for each entity will ultimately report to Kim, but each endeavor is free to continue doing what it does best. Kim has committed to not creatively interfere.

As the head of IT for Chaptal, you've been with the winery since it had one little fileserver on which Kim kept the spreadsheets for the various accounts and Rachel kept track of the residual sugar readings of the grapes.

> Today Kim has told you that she wants you to install an email server in each of the other three locations, connecting them so that everyone can quickly communicate with one another. She also wants an intranet site set up so that the new wine releases can be easily pre-released to all sites for comment and approval.
>
> Having just recently passed the CompTIA IT Project+ test, you understand that there are some basic elements you need to capture in this first meeting:
>
> **Basic Requirements** You have two requirements that you must fulfill:
>
> 1. Set up an email system between the four sites.
> 2. Set up an intranet.
>
> **Stakeholders** Clearly, Kim is the project sponsor, but who will be the stakeholders? In addition to Kim there are three primary stakeholders:
>
> 1. Guillaume Fourche
> 2. Metor Sanchez
> 3. Jason Jay
>
> But in addition to this list, various staff members will benefit from the new changes. Also, the support entities that assist in the production of the various wines will be stakeholders as well.

Summary

Initiation is the formal authorization for the project to move forward. It starts with the identification of a problem, a business need, or a requirement that in turn sparks a project request. Events that trigger a project request are market demand, internal business need, legal requirement, new technology, external customer request, technological change, and social need.

The initial project request needs to be clarified to create high-level requirements, or the product description. High-level requirements and associated cost estimates are presented during a project selection process. This stage may be formal or informal, and may be done on a corporate basis or departmentally.

Project selection techniques involve the use of decision models, such as a cost-benefit analysis and expert judgment, to allocate limited resources to the most critical projects.

Project stakeholders are people who are involved in the project or people who will be impacted by the result of the project. Some project stakeholders you will likely encounter, besides yourself as the project manager, include team members, functional managers, customers (both internal and external), and end users. A project sponsor is a stakeholder who will promote the project and is available to mentor the project team as applicable.

The output from the Initiation process is the project charter. This contains the signature of the person or persons who have the authority to move the project forward. This document will be the basis for more detailed project planning. It should contain the project description, information on the project team, measurable objectives, and a high-level business case.

Exam Essentials

Be able to define the Initiation process. Initiation authorizes the project to move forward.

Be able to describe the events that drive new projects. Market demand, internal business need, legal requirement, new technology, external customer request, technological change, and social need are events that drive new projects.

Understand the three categories of requirements. Functional requirements define how the user will interact with the system. Business requirements are the big picture of what the business wants from the system. Technical requirements define what the system does to meet the business and functional requirements.

Be able to identify the most common project selection methods. The most common project selection methods are decision models such as benefit measurement or constrained optimization and expert judgment.

Be able to define a project stakeholder and list stakeholders common to most projects. A stakeholder is a person who is either actively involved in the project or is impacted by the project. Stakeholders include the sponsor, the project manager, project team members, functional managers, the customer, and end users.

Be able to describe a project charter and list the key components. A project charter provides formal approval for the project to begin and authorizes the project manager to apply resources to the project. The key components are the product description, the project team, goals and objectives, business case, and approval.

Understand the basic makeup of a project team upon reading the project charter project description. You need to quickly recognize the types of IT people you'll require for a given IT project such as programmers, network people, or telecommunications folks.

Key Terms

Before you take the exam, be certain you are familiar with the following terms:

benefit measurement methods

business case

business requirements

constrained optimization models

cost-benefit analysis

customer

database administrators (DBAs)

decision model

decompose

discounted cash flow (DCF)

economic model

end user

enterprise

enterprise project

expert judgment

feasibility study

functional requirements

high-level requirements

initiation

Interactive Voice Response (IVR),

internal rate of return

multiple business unit project

net present value (NPV)

network operating system (NOS)

normalization

product description

project champion

project charter

project description

project management office (PMO)

project selection

Request For Proposal (RFP)

scoring model

sponsor

stakeholder

statement of work (SOW)

Technical requirements

Review Questions

1. The process of project Initiation includes which task?
   A. Assigning work to project team members
   B. Sequencing project activities
   C. Approving a project and authorizing work to begin
   D. Coordinating resources to complete the project work

2. You receive a request from customer service to develop a desktop management system for the customer support staff. What type of project request is this?
   A. Internal business need
   B. Market demand
   C. Legal requirement
   D. Technological advance

3. Project stakeholders have which of the following characteristics?
   A. Actively involved in the project.
   B. Will be impacted by the project.
   C. Have something to gain or lose from the project product.
   D. All of the above.

4. The project sponsor has which of the following attributes?
   A. The person who initially makes the project request.
   B. The CIO.
   C. The person who champions the project throughout the organization.
   D. The project selection committee.

5. Which of the following would be responsibilities of the project sponsor?
   A. Provides or obtains financial resources
   B. Monitors delivery of major milestones
   C. Runs interference and remove roadblocks
   D. All of the above

6. Which of the following is NOT a component of a high-level requirements document or product description?
   A. Testing scenarios
   B. Historical data
   C. Technical requirements
   D. Problem statement

7. Which of these is NOT an example of a project selection method?
   A. Cost-benefit analysis
   B. Expert judgment
   C. Top-down estimating
   D. Scoring model

8. Which stakeholder provides the employees to do the project work?
   A. Project manager
   B. Functional manager
   C. Customer
   D. Sponsor

9. Which of the following is true of the project charter?
   A. Describes the project schedule
   B. Contains cost estimates for each task
   C. Authorizes the start of the project work
   D. Lists the responsibilities of the project selection committee

10. You receive a confusing request from the marketing department to develop a new billing system. What is the first step you should take?
    A. You meet with the marketing person to identify the reason for the request.
    B. You assemble a team of programmers.
    C. You submit a request to the project selection committee.
    D. You request the finance department to do a cost-benefit analysis.

11. Jane is a person affiliated with your project who has very sophisticated technical expertise. She's quite enamored with the project and serves to provide enthusiasm, critiques, energy, communication, and motivation for your project. What is Jane's role?
    A. Project sponsor
    B. Project champion
    C. Project team member
    D. Business analyst

12. You've been presented with a project in which you're going to develop a client/server application. Your company's collections department will equip their field personnel with tablet PCs that will wirelessly connect with the server and database. The manager of the collections department brought the request forward. You work for the PMO and are managed by the director of administrative services. The IT department is managed by the director of IT. The telecommunications segments, including wireless, are managed by the director of telecommunications. Who is the project sponsor?

    A. Manager of Collections

    B. Director of Administrative Services

    C. Director of IT

    D. Director of Telecommunications

    E. All of the above

    F. None of the above

    G. Not enough information

13. Identify the items that should NOT be included in a project charter. (Select all that apply.)

    A. Anticipated budget

    B. Project objectives and success criteria

    C. High-level cost-benefit analysis

    D. Hardware needed

    E. Business case/mission

    F. Project description

    G. Project objectives and success criteria

    H. Project title and description

14. Part of the work you're going to do will require a written document from an outside vendor indicating the type of work that needs to be done and the steps necessary to do them, along with the cost. What is this document called?

    A. SOW

    B. RFP

    C. RFI

    D. RFQ

64 Chapter 2 · Project Initiation

15. You're undertaking a brand-new project in which users will connect to an application running on a server and post information to a database. At first glance, what kinds of IT people do you think you'll need? (Select all that apply.)

    A. Database administrator
    B. Application developer
    C. Telecommunications specialist
    D. Server administrator
    E. Graphic designer

16. Which of these will a project sponsor have to take into account when considering your project? (Select all that apply.)

    A. The priority of your project as it relates to others
    B. The human resources available for the project
    C. The technology that will be used to create the deliverables
    D. The budget dollars that are available
    E. The equipment that will be required

17. From the options below, select the option that best demonstrates the functional requirements of a project (Select all that apply).

    A. System will display a final invoice.
    B. System will calculate business workdays, taking into account corporate holidays.
    C. System will be accessed through the corporate intranet.
    D. System will display in 1024 × 768 pixels.

18. From the options below, select the option that is NOT contained in a high-level requirements description.

    A. Problem statement
    B. Objectives
    C. Strategic value
    D. Persons involved
    E. Requirements
    F. Timing
    G. Historical data

19. You've prepared a charter for a brand-new project. Who will formally sign the project charter? (Select all that apply.)

　A. Project client

　B. Project sponsor

　C. Chief stakeholder

　D. Representative of the project selection committee

　E. Project sponsor, chief stakeholder, and client combined

　F. Chief executive officer

20. At what stage should the project sponsor get involved in the project?

　A. Customer contact with project manager

　B. Development of project concept document

　C. Development of project charter

　D. Revision of project charter

　E. Approval of the project charter

Answers to Review Questions

1. C. Project Initiation is the formal acceptance of the project and authorizes the project manager to start the project work. Assigning work to team members and sequencing activities are part of the Project Planning process group. Coordinating resources to complete the project will be discussed in Project Execution.

2. A. A request to support a process change from another department is an internal business need. A market demand is a request that is driven by the need for the organization to stay competitive. A legal requirement is a change that is mandated by a government agency or regulatory body. A technological advance is a request to use or develop technology that was not previously available.

3. D. Project stakeholders such as the project team members can be very involved in the project. Stakeholders impacted by the project include the functional managers providing the resources and the client. End users are an example of stakeholders who may have something to gain or lose from the project.

4. C. The project sponsor communicates the project purpose throughout the organization and acts as an advisor to the project manager. The project request can be initiated anywhere in the organization. The project sponsor could be a member of the project selection committee, but typically he or she would not participate in the selection of a sponsored project.

5. D. A project sponsor is responsible for obtaining financial resources for the project, monitoring the progress of the project, and handling escalations from the project manager.

6. A. A high-level requirements documents contains the problem statement, objectives, strategic value, functional and technical requirements, timing, and historical data. Testing scenarios would not be created at this point in the project.

7. C. Cost-benefit analysis, expert judgment, and scoring are all project selection techniques. Top-down estimating is a type of cost estimating.

8. B. The functional manager provides the employees performing the work of the project. The project manager is accountable for overseeing the work required to complete the project. The customer is the person or group that is the recipient of the product or service created by the project. The project sponsor champions the project throughout the organization and acts as an advisor to the project manager.

9. C. The project charter formally approves the project and authorizes work to begin. The project schedule and cost estimates are developed later in the planning process.

10. A. You must clarify the request to determine exactly what the marketing person needs. You need to understand the problem that needs to be addressed, so that you can define the high-level requirements. A cost-benefit analysis might be done following requirements definition if that is part of the project selection criteria. You would not start any programming work until after the project had been approved and further work had been done in the planning process.

11. B. The project champion is generally a technical person aligned with the project for the purpose of supporting the project. She is not necessarily one who has a lot of power, but is one who understands the goals of the project and can help you keep the project moving forward.

12. G.   The project sponsor is an individual who is authorized to expend the resources necessary to bring about the deliverables of the project. That means that either (1) this individual has authority over all the others (such as an executive in charge of a large segment of the organization) and can therefore authorize the resources necessary from each department or (2) a consensus has been reached about who is going to be the project sponsor and that person will act as though he or she does indeed have all the necessary resources. This latter option, of course, requires that the managers dialog with one another and come to terms with the resources required and the length of time they'll be needed. So, in the question above, we really don't have enough information to make a good decision about who should be the project sponsor yet.

13. A, D.   In addition to the including your name as project manager, you'll also denote the project title and description, key roles and responsibilities, project objectives and success criteria, high-level cost-benefit analysis, business-case/mission, project deliverable description, performance criteria and enhancement opportunities, and a high-level risk assessment. The anticipated budget happens in the scope document (which we'll discuss in Chapter 3) and the hardware needed will show up in the project plan itself.

14. A.   The statement of work (SOW) is a document that indicates what a company will do for you and the associated charges. Requests for Information, Proposal and Quote (RFI, RFP, and RFQ, respectively) are documents that you send out prior to project WBS initiation in order to get an idea of what vendors can offer, what their costs are, and so forth. The "R" documents are requests for information and thus high-level whereas the SOW is a document that tells you exactly how something is going to be worked.

15. A, B, D.   You will for sure need to have someone who can handle the database, someone to program the application code, and someone who can manage the server for you. Whether you need a graphic designer will depend on how jazzy you want the application interface to be—that information may flesh out later. You probably don't need a telecommunications specialist for this project.

16. A, B, D.   The project sponsor will be concerned with the priority of the project as it relates to others that may be in the loop, and the resources, both budgetary and human, that will be available. It's you and your team's job to determine the equipment and technology that's required and put that in the project plan.

17. A, C.   Functional requirements talk about how the user will interact with the system. Functional requirements refer to how the user will interact with the system (via browser, thin-client, wireless connection, etc.). Functional requirements also refer to the notion of usability—which screen pops up next after a transaction, how a user will be notified that the transaction has been successful, etc. Technical requirements are behind-the-scenes characteristics and refer to the hardware, programming, software and other technical underpinnings that will provide the backbone for the system. Note that there is a very fine line between a technical requirement and a functional requirement—the basic difference sitting with the idea of how the user interacts with the system. If you're thinking from a user's perspective, you're generally describing a functional requirement, if you're thinking about servers or code, you're in the technical camp.

18. D.   High-level requirements have several specifications that you might want to consider. The persons involved do not need to be mentioned at this juncture.

19. A, B, D. The project sponsor, project client, or a representative of the project selection committee (if you have one) can sign the project charter—effectively authorizing the project. The Chief Executive Officer (CEO) doesn't need to be the signer of a project charter for which she is not the sponsor. However, high-level projects probably deserve occasional CEO executive progress updates. The combination (letter E.) implies that all folks have to sign the charter. This isn't the case—but it is important that someone significant to the project sees and signs the charter. In some cases a project selection committee is utilized in the corporate world and it is a representative from this body that would sign the charter. Otherwise, the client or the sponsor could sign the charter. It's vital that all agree to the contents of the charter.

20. E. It's not necessary to get the sponsor involved when you're in the early stages of business analysis and formulating a solid project concept document. A well-written project concept will, in fact, often "sell" the sponsor on the need for the project. However, at project charter signing time, and any time after that when the charter needs to be amended, the sponsor gets involved.

Chapter 3

Scope Planning

THE COMPTIA IT PROJECT+ EXAM TOPICS COVERED IN THIS CHAPTER INCLUDE:

- ✓ 1.5 Given a scope definition scenario, demonstrate awareness of the need to secure written confirmation of customer expectations in key areas.
- ✓ 1.6 Given a project initiation document (a project charter or contract), including a confirmed high-level scope definition and project justification, demonstrate the ability to identify and define key elements.
- ✓ 1.7 Given a project initiation document (a project charter or contract), including the client's highest priority between quality, time, and budget, estimate a number of elements.
- ✓ 1.9 Given a proposed scope definition and based on the scope components, assess the feasibility of the project and the viability of a given project component against a predetermined list of constraints.
- ✓ 1.10 Recognize and explain the need to obtain formal approval (sign-off) by the project sponsor(s) and confirm other relevant management support to consume organizational resources as the project scope statement is being developed.
- ✓ 1.11 Given an incomplete project scope definition, complete or rewrite the definition to (1) reflect all necessary scope components or (2) explicitly state which is included in the project and which is not.
- ✓ 1.12 Identify possible elements of a final project scope definition and the circumstances in which they would be appropriate.
- ✓ 1.14 Recognize the need to obtain consensus of stakeholders and to obtain buy in from the team to proceed to the planning stage of the project given a high-level estimate of scope, schedule, budget, and resources.

- ✓ 2.6 Given a project description/overview and a list of the project business and technical requirements, perform key tasks to ensure project success.

- ✓ 2.7 Describe the goals of a useful project requirements review with the client (e.g., verify mutual understanding of client's product delivery, product performance, and budget requirements, etc.) and describe when it is important to have such reviews.

- ✓ 2.8 Given the client's approved project requirements and the input of stakeholders, decompose these requirements into business and functional requirements while maintaining trace ability within strict configuration control.

- ✓ 2.9 Given a project planning scenario, demonstrate an understanding of and the ability to develop a phase-oriented WBS with high detail for an early phase and with low detail for later phases.

- ✓ 2.10 Given a scenario involving tasks, resources (fixed or variable), and dependencies for a multiphase IT project, demonstrate knowledge of the standards for creating a workable WBS.

- ✓ 2.11 Recognize and explain the need to obtain consensus and formal approval (sign-off).

Now that we have covered the initiation process and have an approved project charter, it is time to talk about project planning. Planning can be one of the most overlooked areas of project management. Once a project is approved, everyone just wants to run off and start working. As a project manager, you may even find that your organization does not support taking the time to do planning. If you have ever had an executive call you to task for wasting valuable time planning when there is work to be done, you know what we are talking about.

A good understanding of the planning processes will prepare you to communicate within your organization about the benefits of taking time up front to define all aspects of managing a project before the work actually starts. Starting with this chapter and continuing through Chapter 7, "Creating a Comprehensive Project Plan," we will cover all the aspects of project planning. Our first planning topic is project scope.

Project scope is defined as the size of the work involved to complete the project. As a project manager, you need to be aware of what is included in the project as well as what is excluded. Scope planning will assist you in getting your arms around a project and setting the boundaries for what is included in the project.

You need to define and document three scope components to complete scope planning: the scope statement, scope management plan, and work breakdown structure (WBS). The scope statement provides a common understanding of the project by documenting the project objectives and deliverables. The scope management plan documents the procedures that you will use to manage any proposed changes to the project scope throughout the life of the project. The final component of scope is the work breakdown structure, which breaks the project deliverables down into smaller activities from which you can estimate task durations, assign resources, and estimate costs.

Scope Overview

Imagine trying to work on a project without knowing your expectations, limitations, or the nature of what you're producing. Would you even be able to begin a project without knowing these things? Luckily, in the project management business, there are rules and processes that help project managers define the limits of a project.

Scope puts boundaries around your project. Scope is like putting a fence around your property. The fence is a clear definition of where your property starts and where it ends. It is clear to anyone looking at your property what is included and what is excluded. Scope planning serves this same purpose for a project.

The project *scope* is the work that is done to deliver the product or service. Although this sounds simple and straightforward, a poorly defined scope can lead to missed deadlines, cost overruns, and unhappy clients. Good scope planning helps ensure that all of the work required to complete the project is agreed on and clearly documented.

Scope planning builds on and adds detail to the outputs you have created for the project charter. Scope planning is the starting point for defining the activities required to deliver the product requirements that were discussed in Chapter 2.

Depending on the detail of work completed for project initiation, scope planning may also include a more detailed analysis of the product, a cost/benefit analysis, and a look at alternative solutions. You may find that some of the work required for scope planning has already been completed during the initiation process. If that is the case, congratulations, as you are now ahead of the game.

The processes to define the scope planning elements are iterative, do not always occur in sequence, and can overlap. Regardless of the sequence, scope planning produces a scope statement, a scope management plan, and a work breakdown structure. Let's take a look at what is required to complete each of these.

> **Note:** It's important to understand that PMI's *A Guide to the PMBOK* defines *scope definition* as the process of breaking down the major deliverables from a scope statement to create the WBS. For the purposes of the CompTIA objectives and exam, scope definition is used in a much broader sense to cover several scope planning elements including the scope statement and the scope management plan.

Project Scope Statement

Have you ever received a bid to do remodeling work on your house? A remodeling bid typically includes a description of the work to be done, a list of the major deliverables, estimates for time and cost, and any assumptions and constraints. A contractor tells you in writing that he will remodel your bathroom (description) by replacing the countertops, flooring, and tile (deliverables) in six weeks at a cost of $4,550. The bid assumes no change to the existing bathroom fixtures and a stated grade of countertops and tile. The start of the project will be constrained by whether the chosen tile is in stock or must be special ordered. The bid documents the agreement between the contractor and the homeowner as to the scope of the remodeling work.

A project scope statement serves a similar purpose to the remodel bid. A project *scope statement* documents the agreement between the project manager and the stakeholders as to what is included in the delivery of the project. It is the foundation for defining the activities required to complete the project, and it will be used as a baseline to manage change requests to the project. Any major deliverable, feature or function, that is not documented in the scope statement is considered a change. Typically, the scope statement includes a project justification, product description, major deliverables, success criteria, time and cost estimates, assumptions, and constraints.

Let's take a closer look at what is included in each of these.

Project Justification

In the *project justification* portion of your scope statement, you must state the reason the project is being undertaken and document the business need that the project will address. You want to be clear what is driving the project request. Is the project creating a new product for external customers? Is the project developing a new system for an internal organization? Is this a legal mandate? The project justification identifies the source of the project request.

It is very important that any legal requirement behind the project request be documented in this section. This alerts anyone reading the scope statement that this is not an optional project.

Product Description

In your *product description*, briefly describe the features or function of the product. The description is what makes the product *unique*. (Remember that uniqueness of the product is part of the definition of a project.) You need to be as precise as you can using all of the data you have available. It may be appropriate to include not only the features or functions the product includes, but features or functions it does not include, if doing so will add clarity to your description. You can use your existing product description from the project charter and make changes or refinements based on any additional information you have obtained.

> By listing both included and excluded features, a product description narrows and clarifies the technical work that is required to produce this product—and keeps customers from coming back at product creation time to ask you for more for goodies to be added.

Major Deliverables

In the *major deliverables* section of the scope statement, you will list the summary level achievements that make up the delivery of the product. It can be easy to get hung up on just the end result when you are listing the major deliverables. When you are putting together the deliverables section, make sure that you focus on the entire project. Your end result may be a new software application for the company's sales agents, but there are other deliverables besides the application itself. Do not overlook key areas such as user documentation, user training, or help-desk training, to name a few. If you include at least one deliverable from each organization represented on the project team, it will show the big picture of what is involved in completing this project.

Success Criteria

Under *success criteria* in the scope statement you will define the measurable business results the product is expected to produce. This section is where you address items such as an increase to corporate revenue, a higher productivity rate, compliance with regulatory procedures, or reduced staffing needs. This section is very important as a tool for evaluating the project after it is complete. This is the section the stakeholders can reference to compare the actual business impacts of the project with the projected impacts. You want to define the success criteria so that each one can be measured. Criteria such as "become an industry leader" or "provide world class service" may sound good, but aren't measurable. It is much better to state a sales figure, a revenue figure, or a customer waiting interval that can be measured and compared to that same data collected prior to the completion of the project. The idea behind success criteria is to supply metrics by which people can gauge whether or not the project was successful.

Completion Criteria

Completion criteria denotes what needs to be delivered. For example, you may stipulate in your scope documentation that the system will be fully functional at delivery time. Or, you may choose to stipulate that the project will be considered complete after a 3-month period of testing to make sure that all components are working correctly.

Time and Cost Estimates

In the time and cost estimate portion of the scope statement, you'll provide an estimate of the time it will take to complete all of the work and the current high-level estimates for the cost of the project. These will be *order of magnitude* estimates based on actual duration and cost of similar projects or the judgment of someone familiar with the work involved in the project. These do not have to be precise estimates. A high-level estimate may also use ranges for either time or cost, in some cases including a worst case, best case, and most likely scenario.

> **NOTE** Estimates made during scope planning may be stated in different ways depending on the estimating method used. An estimate made strictly from the actual time and cost of a similar project is stated: "Based on the results of Project XYZ, it is estimated that New Project MAL will take three months to complete and cost $350,000." An estimate for the same project based on using ranges is stated: "New Project MAL will take between one and six months to complete at a cost of $100,000 to $500,000. The most likely scenario is four months at a cost of $400,000."

The time estimate for a new product created by market demand may also be defined based on the window of opportunity to market the product.

Target Completion

You may be asked to provide an estimated or target date for project completion. You really do not have enough data at this point to make a precise estimate. If you are forced to provide an estimated date in the scope statement, use either a month or a quarter, such as July 2004 or third quarter of 2004 instead of a specific date. When providing a target completion date, always include an assumed start date; otherwise, if the project starts later than anticipated, your six-month estimate may become three months.

Level of Confidence

Project estimates may include a caveat regarding the level of confidence the project manager has in the accuracy of the estimates. Estimates made during scope planning are based on very little detail, so don't say you are 90 percent confident just because that is what your client or your sponsor wants to hear. Cost estimates made during scope planning are commonly as much as 75 percent off the actual budget figures. We will talk more about the different types of cost estimates and the typical range of accuracy for each estimate in Chapter 5, "Cost Planning."

Assumptions

In the assumptions section of the scope statement, you'll document the beliefs the team shares regarding the project. An *assumption* is an action, a condition, or event that is believed to be true. The problem with assumptions is that they may not be common among all project team members or stakeholders. You may think something is obvious, but if it is not written down, chances are other players will have a different opinion. Assumptions must be shared, agreed on, and documented.

A key area to review in defining assumptions with your team is to discuss and document both what is included and what is excluded from the project. This is a good way to further clarify and bound the project scope. If you are developing software for a new desktop support system, you may assume that the software will be deployed on the existing computers at the client site. The client may assume that new workstations are part of the project. You will need to document in the assumptions section that the software will be deployed on existing workstations.

Constraints

The last part of your scope statement is the constraints list. A *constraint* is a restriction that will impact the outcome of the project. There are two types of constraints. The first are the constraints that apply to all projects. Every project faces potential constraints in time, budget, scope, or quality. From the start of the project at least one of these areas is limited. If you are developing software to support a new product with a very short market window, time will be your big constraint. If you have a fixed budget, money will be your constraint. If both time and money are constrained, quality may suffer. A predefined budget or a mandated finish date needs to be factored in to any discussion of project scope. Scope will be impacted if both time and budget are constrained. As the project progresses and scope changes are requested, scope may become a constraint that drives changes to time, cost, or quality.

> **NOTE** You may have heard the term *triple constraint* bandied about by project managers. Some project management books reference only three constraints: time, cost, and quality. Although you may still see the phrase triple constraint used in project management, be advised that most project managers think about project scope as a fourth constraint.

The second type of constraint is that specific to a project. These constraints may involve the schedule or previous commitments of human resources you need or the availability of a test system.

The push and pull of project constraints is an issue the project manager must deal with throughout the project life cycle. If a constraint is placed on time, cost, scope, or quality during up-front planning, now is the time to communicate with your stakeholder team regarding the impact of constraints. The project manager needs to have an understanding as to how the client prioritizes these constraints and be able to communicate possible scenarios that might occur as the project moves forward. As an example, if cost is cast in concrete during the planning phase, the client may have to give up functionality and scale down the scope of the project once more definitive cost estimates have been made. As you can see, the scope statement contains a lot of important project information. Let's take a look at a sample scope statement to help you put all the pieces together.

> ### Real World Scenario
>
> **Sample Project Scope Statement**
>
> Imagine you are a project manager for a wireless telecommunications carrier in charge of a project for a new consumer product called Voice Activated Dialing (VAD). The product is critical to the corporate strategy to become one of the top three carriers in the markets where your company offers wireless service. Using your high-level requirements, the project charter, and input from various team members and stakeholders, you are ready to create your project scope statement.
>
> Here is what your project scope statement might look like.
>
> **Project Justification:** Market research and customer feedback indicate that a demand for Voice Activated Dialing (VAD) has increased 40 percent over the past three months. One of our competitors has already announced a launch date for this product, and two others are expected to follow within the next two months.
> Our market share growth is expected to decline by 20 percent if we do not add VAD as part of our product mix.
>
> **Product Description:** The product features included in Voice Activated Dialing are dialing by speaking a phone number or name into the phone and the ability to create address book entries from a website. Voice Activated Dialing does not include the ability to add/edit/delete address book entries over the phone or an interface to personal information managers.
>
> **Major deliverables:**
>
> - Product requirements defined
> - System requirements defined
> - System requirements developed
> - Sales training developed
> - Customer service training developed
> - System enhancements implemented
> - 3,000 Sales consultants trained
> - 500 Customer service technicians trained
> - Marketing communication plans executed in all markets
> - VAD available in all markets
>
> **Success Criteria:** The launch of VAD will generate $2.5 million in incremental annual revenue for the corporation.
> The additional training required for sales consultants to be knowledgeable in offering the VAD product will increase the total sales consultant training package time by no more than two hours.

Time and Cost Estimates: VAD must be completed within six months for the company to be a viable player in this market.

The development and launch of VAD is estimated to cost $750,000. This includes all IT work, sales consultant training, customer brochures, and the marketing campaign. This is a high-level estimate based on the schedule and cost of a similar new product. Estimates will be refined as more detailed data is available.

Assumptions: IT has resources to implement system changes within the six-month time frame we need to start offering VAD.
Fifteen percent of our customers will add VAD to their current service option. Product will have a 15 percent take rate. VAD will be priced at $4.95/month.

Constraints: Billing releases are only done on a quarterly basis. The enhancement to bill for VAD must be scheduled within those parameters.
The window to obtain a share of the VAD market is six months.

As you can see, a lot of very important information is included in the project scope statement. From reading the VAD sample scope statement, you know the strategic value of the product, the features included and excluded in the product, the anticipated revenue the product will generate, and the aggressive schedule that must be met. This document can be used to give a clear and concise overview of the project to clients, team members, and other key stakeholders.

Review and Consensus

Once you have completed the scope statement, hold a review session with your entire project team to make sure that everyone is in agreement and there are no unresolved issues. Individual team members may have worked on specific sections of the scope statement, and a formal team review of the entire document will confirm that everyone is on the same page and prevent later misunderstandings of the project scope. Once the project team has resolved any outstanding issues, present the scope statement to all of the stakeholders and obtain approval from the project sponsor and the client. Other approvals may be required depending on the policies of your organization.

If any changes are made to the scope statement during the review with the client and the sponsor, you will need a follow-up meeting with the project team to cover the changes and discuss the impact on the project. One of your most important duties as project manager is to keep your team informed. We will talk a lot more about how to communicate with your project team in Chapter 6, "Additional Planning Processes."

With our approved scope statement in hand, we are now ready to create a scope management plan.

Scope Management Plan

Now that you have an approved scope statement, the real work begins. You may have heard horror stories from other project managers. How do you keep this "thing" from growing out of control and choking any chance you may have to successfully complete the project? You need to master that dreaded demon that has plagued every project manager—*scope creep*. Scope creep is the term commonly used to describe all those minor changes or small additions that just seem to happen out of nowhere, until suddenly you are not managing the same project anymore. The solution, of course, is having a plan.

The *scope management plan* documents how you will manage changes to the scope. Project scope change is inevitable with the majority of projects. The key to dealing with scope change is how you handle it. In our experience, you save yourself a lot of pain during project execution if you take the time at the start of the project to define the basics of how the team will handle requests for any changes to the defined scope.

If the project team defines the basic scope management framework early in the planning process, each team member has a point of reference to communicate with clients and stakeholders who may come to them with something they forgot to mention when the scope statement was approved. Everyone involved in the project needs to understand that the rules set up at project implementation time need to be followed to make a request to change the scope of any project. Without a documented plan, you will soon find that interested parties are talking to team members and changes are happening. The team members will, understandably, want to try to accommodate the client's needs. But without analysis of the impact these changes, adding 10 or 20 "minor" code changes may put your schedule or your budget in jeopardy.

Key items to consider when you are developing a scope management plan include:

Stability of the scope You probably have some indication at this point in the project as to how stable the scope is based on the work you have already done to define requirements, prepare and review the project charter, and define the scope statement. If you found major disagreement between stakeholders or gaps in the product description, you have a high probability for scope instability.

Impact of scope changes If you are constrained with a dictated finish date, any scope change can be critical. Adding to the scope of the project may also impact the budget. Do you have available resources to add to the project to complete the additional work? What is the process for securing additional funding?

Scope change process One of the primary reasons a project gets out of control is the lack of a documented process for scope changes. Clients and stakeholders will go directly to team members and before you know it, people will be working on deliverables that were never included in the scope statement.

Your scope change process needs at a minimum:

- A standard form to submit the request. Information required on a scope change request includes a description of the change, the reason for the change, and the originator of the request.
- An analysis of the impact of the request on the scope, budget, schedule, and quality of the project. The results of the analysis can be added to the form used to submit the request, so that all pertinent data in is one location.

- An approval process to accept or reject requests. This can range from ad hoc meetings called as scope changes are received to a formal change review board that meets on a regular basis.
- A communication plan to keep stakeholders informed of the status of requests.
- A method to incorporate approved changes into the project plan.

The implementation of your scope management plan will be discussed further in Chapter 9, "Project Control."

> **TIP** You can see why project managers are so interested in making sure they've established the scope of the project as best as they can before any work starts. Generally speaking, if you've done due diligence and tightly defined the scope of the project, with the exception of very minor changes, most new requests for changes on an IT project should be considered for "Version 2" of the product and included in a brand new project after the first one concludes.

The Work Breakdown Structure (WBS)

The final element of scope planning is the *work breakdown structure (WBS)*, where the project team starts decomposing the project deliverables. *Decomposition* is the process of breaking down the high-level deliverables into smaller, manageable components from which you can do time estimates, resource assignments, and cost estimates. The WBS is a deliverables-oriented hierarchy that defines all of the project work. Each level has more detail than the previous level.

A WBS is one of the fundamental building blocks of project planning. It will be used as an input to numerous other planning processes. It is the basis for estimating activity duration, assigning resources to activities, estimating work effort, and creating a budget. Because the WBS is a graphical representation, it can be a better vehicle for communicating the project scope than the charter or scope statement. It also contains more detail to further clarify the magnitude of the project deliverables.

The WBS acts to put boundaries around the project. Any work not defined in the WBS is considered outside the scope of the project. A WBS is a tool that can be used to keep customers, team members, and stakeholders focused on what is included in the project scope.

Like a blueprint used to build a building, the WBS is the document that will be used to build your project's product.

It is important that the project team devote adequate time to develop the WBS. Development of the WBS should focus on all aspects of the project and all impacted areas of the business.

The team may go through several iterations to complete the WBS. Once the team concurs that the WBS is complete, review sessions are scheduled with the client, the sponsor, and key stakeholders to examine and approve the WBS.

Organizing the WBS

The quality of your WBS depends on having the right players involved in the development. Provide adequate notice when you schedule a WBS session. Involve as many project team members or functional representatives as possible. Project team members may not be named at this point, but you'll probably have a good idea of the various groups or departments that will be involved based on the list of project objectives and deliverables. Work with functional managers or if necessary your sponsor to get representation from each group. A WBS is not something that should be developed in a vacuum. A WBS developed in isolation by the project manager frequently misses key components of the project. It is also more difficult to get buy in on something people had no input on.

A WBS is typically created using either a tree structure diagram or an outline form. A tree structure is the best method to use with a project team. The structure can be created on a white board or easel paper using sticky notes to write the tasks. This allows for tasks to be moved around as you work though the process. Figure 3.1 is an example of a template that can be used to create a WBS.

FIGURE 3.1 WBS Template

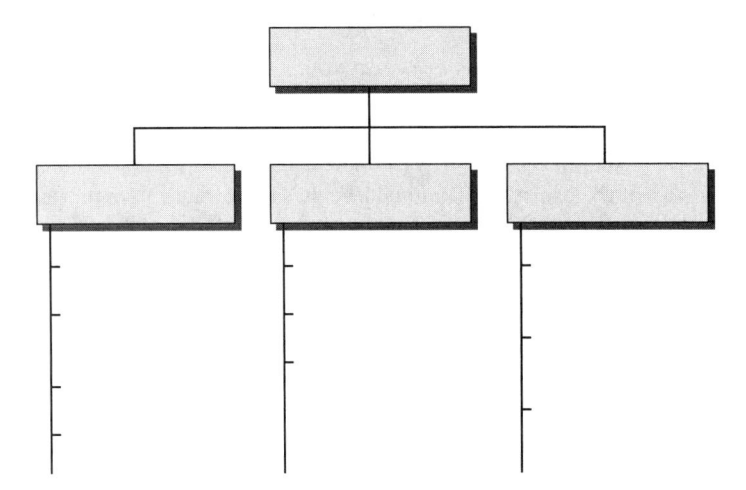

The space you reserve to conduct the WBS development needs to be adequate to allow all participants to see the work in progress. You need to encourage brainstorming. You can always remove or move activities as you work through the process or when you do subsequent reviews.

Make sure that all of the participants have reviewed all previous documentation like the charter and scope statement. Have copies of these documents available as reference. They will be your starting point for creating the WBS as well as a reference if there are questions.

Decomposing Major Deliverables

Decomposition, the breaking down of the project deliverables into smaller components, can be a challenge. Let's take a closer look at this tree diagram and how to work your way through the creation of a meaningful WBS.

The highest level of the WBS tree diagram encompasses the entire project. This level is referred to as level 1. The next level, level 2, relates to the high-level project deliverables defined in your scope statement. This level usually takes the form of listing the deliverables themselves. We have also seen this level show the phases of the project life cycle, the departments involved in the project, or a geographical focus. There is not one correct way to create a WBS, but the method you choose must be a logical way to break things down for your particular project.

Take for instance a simple home improvement project such as painting a porch. Figure 3.2 shows a few of the project deliverables for painting the porch. You'll notice that level 1 is the porch-painting project itself, and level 2 demonstrates the deliverables needed to paint the porch.

Project Planning Using the Tree Structure

You can begin brainstorming a WBS by utilizing the tree diagram and a bunch of sticky notes on a white board.

Recently we had to move 2,000 users from various places around the city into one centralized location—a brand new 11-story building. Each of these groups of users had a different function in life, with different managers and move timelines. Imagine the complexity of making sure that you move all the users' computers into this new building at different times and making sure that everything works. Now imagine that you're trying to figure out all the obstacles and tasks even before the building is complete—you're trying to get an advance feel for what's involved.

Our project managers started this effort by getting various stakeholders into a room and then, as ideas were voiced, writing them down on sticky notes and pasting them to a white board. Another person began to arrange the notes into some sort of logical order. One stakeholder, for example, might cry out "Make sure all monitors work!" while another would say "We need our email to work when we come in on Monday." Each of these sticky notes had something to do with powering up the machine and validating that it was connected to the network.

In time, as we fleshed out various components of the project, the white board looked just like a tree with yellow leaves all over it!

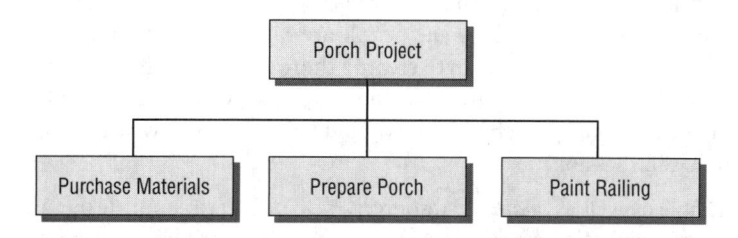

FIGURE 3.2 Starting a WBS

```
              Porch Project
       ┌───────────┼───────────┐
  Purchase      Prepare       Paint
  Materials     Porch         Railing
```

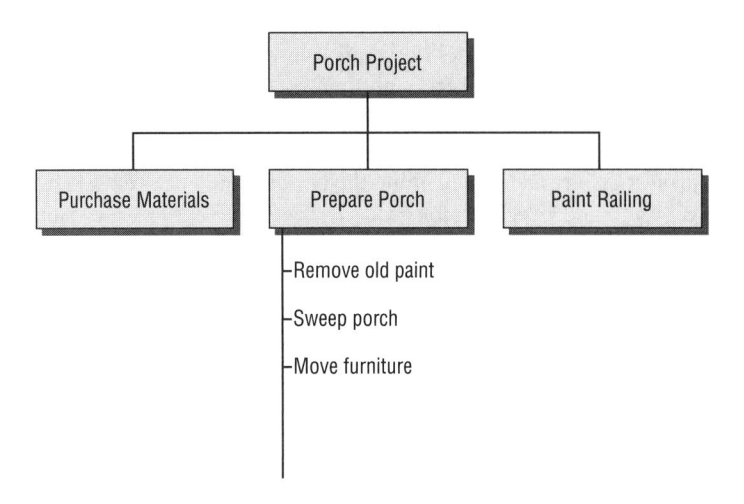

FIGURE 3.3 Decomposing a Major Deliverable

```
                    Porch Project
                         |
       ┌─────────────────┼─────────────────┐
  Purchase Materials  Prepare Porch    Paint Railing
                         |
                    ─Remove old paint
                    ─Sweep porch
                    ─Move furniture
```

As Figure 3.2 illustrates, you should always work through level 2 before moving down to the next level of decomposition. This method will help you make sure you encompass all of the project goals.

Each subsequent level should be a breakdown of the previous level. In our porch-painting example, we have taken Prepare Porch and decomposed it as shown in Figure 3.3.

The process continues until a task does not need to be subdivided again. You need to get to a level of detail that generates manageable activities, but do not go down to a level of detail that you cannot track and control. PMI's *A Guide to the PMBOK* refers to the lowest level of the WBS as a *work package*. The work package is just how far down you need to go to decompose the deliverables.

Guidelines for Creating a WBS

Getting started creating a WBS can sometimes seem overwhelming. we've found that a lot of people who struggle with this process are actually taking on more work than they should. Once you start breaking down your deliverables into activities, there is a temptation to immediately put the activities in order (called *sequencing* the activities) or estimate the length of an activity so you can just get people started on the work. Unfortunately, this type of behavior usually leads to a situation where key deliverables are missed or task sequences are incorrect because many tasks were not defined. The clock is ticking and people are working hard, but not necessarily on the right things, because time was not taken to create a thorough WBS. Although there is no one "right" way to complete a WBS, there are some tips on pitfalls you can avoid to help you be more successful. Here are some guidelines that we find helpful to review with project teams before diving into a WBS session.

Recruit knowledgeable as well as *available* resources. Do not try to complete the WBS yourself in the interest of saving time. If you are not an expert on the deliverables, you will miss key elements. You also want the team members to do the work so that they buy into what has been created. Involving knowledgeable team members in the creation of a WBS is far more effective at communicating what the project is all about than handing someone a completed WBS. If there are team members who will be involved in the project but who cannot participate in the session, make arrangements to get input from a representative at a separate session. Ideally, you want everyone in the same room, but if that is not possible make sure you get the input in some other fashion.

Work though all items at level 2 before you go down to the next level. You should be confident that the entire work of the project is represented at the high level. If you are completing the WBS as a team exercise, you will need to control the tendency the team may have to start decomposition immediately once a deliverable has been put up on the board. This is a natural inclination, once people see a deliverable, to start thinking of what it will encompass. As a project manager, you need to take control of the situation and remind the team to not decompose anything until all of the high-level deliverables have been identified. Otherwise you may end up putting tasks under a deliverable that are not really a part of that deliverable or worse yet miss a key component of the project. Keep referring the team back to the scope statement until everyone is confident that your high-level deliverables are covered. Then you can start decomposing.

Each item in a lower level is a component of the level above. Completion of all of the items in the lower level should mean completion of the higher level. As a checkpoint, you should always review the items at the lower level and ask the team if completion of those items will result in the task at the next higher level. If the answer to this question is no, than you have not identified all of the lower level tasks.

List all activities and continue to break them down to component parts. Make sure you get to a level where the team feels comfortable that resources can be assigned and estimates can be completed. Sequencing, assigning resources, and estimating are all separate activities that you will complete after the WBS is complete. We have seen many teams waste time doing separate tasks such as sequencing the activities while creating the WBS. These teams managed to break down the activities, but at the same time they got hung up with the sequence, which is not the goal of the WBS.

Do not create a To Do list. You should not decompose activities any further than to a level where they can be easily assigned, estimated, and produce a meaningful deliverable. Since the WBS will become the foundation for the project schedule, do not break down beyond a level that you can control. If you create a series of very short sequential tasks, you are expected to manage all of those tasks.

Let's take a look at the Purchase Materials deliverable for our porch project. Under Purchase Materials you could have just listed all the items you need to buy: sandpaper, sealer, paint, brushes, etc. But if you included your shopping list in your WBS, you would not have actually listed the activities that make the purchase complete. The items that you need to purchase to complete the porch project are only one of the activities associated with "Purchase Materials." Your shopping list is referenced on the WBS by the activity "Make a List," as shown in the completed Porch Project WBS in Figure 3.4.

Use the appropriate number of levels for each leg. Each major objective will have a different level of decomposition to get to the point where you can do estimating and resource scheduling.

84 Chapter 3 · Scope Planning

It is not uncommon for one leg to have three levels and another to have seven levels. You should be concerned about getting to a manageable activity, not on balancing the WBS. If you try to force an even number of levels across all deliverables, you will end up with some legs that are not broken down in adequate detail and others that end up listing all the steps to complete a simple task.

Create a numeric identifier for each item on the WBS. This is very similar to the format used for a numeric outline. Start at the left of the WBS and work across. Your major deliverables are 1.0, 2.0, 3.0, etc. As you move down a level, increment the second number. The level under deliverable 1.0 is labeled 1.1,1.2,1.3,1.4, etc. Figure 3.5 shows numeric identifiers added to the WBS we created earlier for the porch project.

FIGURE 3.4 Porch Project WBS

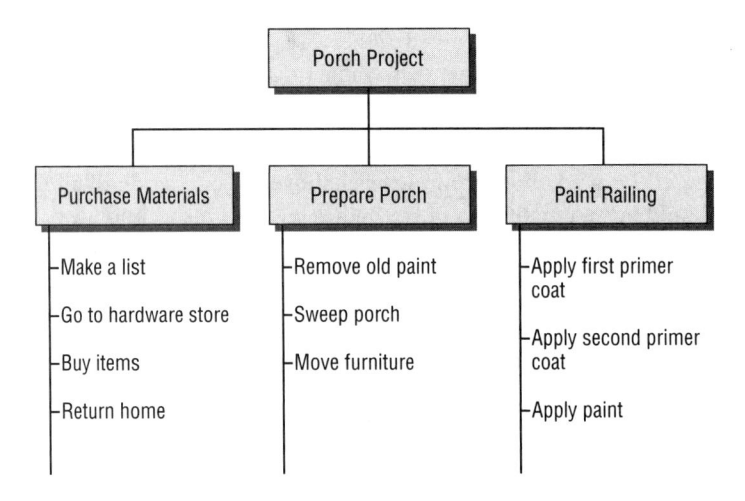

```
                        Porch Project
         ┌──────────────────┼──────────────────┐
   Purchase Materials   Prepare Porch       Paint Railing
   ─Make a list         ─Remove old paint   ─Apply first primer
   ─Go to hardware store ─Sweep porch         coat
   ─Buy items           ─Move furniture     ─Apply second primer
   ─Return home                               coat
                                            ─Apply paint
```

FIGURE 3.5 WBS with Numeric Identifiers

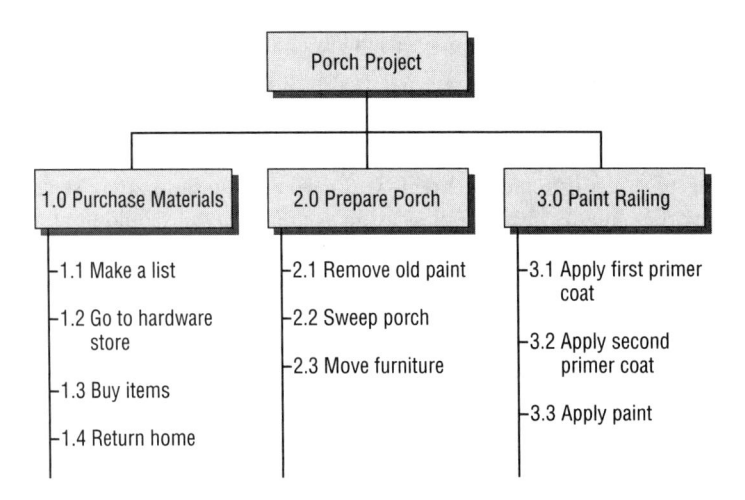

```
                        Porch Project
         ┌──────────────────┼──────────────────┐
   1.0 Purchase Materials  2.0 Prepare Porch   3.0 Paint Railing
   ─1.1 Make a list        ─2.1 Remove old paint  ─3.1 Apply first primer
   ─1.2 Go to hardware     ─2.2 Sweep porch         coat
       store               ─2.3 Move furniture   ─3.2 Apply second
   ─1.3 Buy items                                   primer coat
   ─1.4 Return home                             ─3.3 Apply paint
```

Benefits of the WBS

The WBS is often listed as one of the most important components of a successful project. As you will see in later chapters, the WBS is an input to numerous project management processes. In our experience as a project managers, we have also found it invaluable in many other ways.

The WBS is an excellent tool for team building and team communication. With a graphic representation of the major project deliverables and the underlying activities, team members can see the project big picture and how their portion fits in. The direct link between a given activity and a major project deliverable can also help clarify the impact of an individual team member. As new resources are added to the project, the WBS can be used to bring these new team members up to speed.

A good WBS can be turned into a template for future projects. Software development projects frequently have a similar life cycle, and what was done on a previous project can be used as a starting point for a new project. This allows the team to take an existing structure and customize it to fit the new project. This is also an excellent way for teams to look at areas of the project they may not have thought about on their own.

The picture of the project scope the WBS provides is an excellent tool for communicating with clients and stakeholders. People do not always comprehend the magnitude of a project until they see the diagram of the project objectives and the activities required to reach those objectives. It also is an excellent tool to use when discussing staffing requirements or budgets. It clearly shows what work is included in the project. If something is not covered in the project objectives and supporting activities, it is not part of the project.

A detailed WBS will not only prevent critical work from being overlooked, it will also help control change. If the project team has a clear picture of the project objectives and the map to reach these objectives, they are less likely to go down a path unrelated to the project scope. We do not mean to imply that a WBS will prevent change; there are always changes during the project life cycle. But a WBS will clarify that a request is a change and not part of the original project scope.

Evaluating Your IT Project Scope

The scope of projects that IT project managers undertake should never deviate very far from the established deadline set down in the WBS. Yet there are elements within an IT shop that unexpectedly surface, serving to slip the scope far from its original moorings.

IT shops run into interesting twists and nuances that will very definitely impact the project scope and that may be beyond ordinary scope assessment and planning. Let's examine some things that you'd want to think about when evaluating the scope of your IT project.

Size of the IT Shop

The size of an IT shop has a very direct impact on a project's scope. If you have a shop of only a handful of people, all of whom are constantly engaged on one project or another, then it's understandable that the scope of new projects depends highly on people's schedules. A major constraint is the limitation you have with human resources. Project priority comes into play in smaller shops as well. Suppose, for example, that all of your folks are working on a project when suddenly you're presented with a new project that's of much higher importance to the organization. What do you do—drop everything you're working on and begin on the new project or wait until you finish the first? It's a tough call to make—one that small shops are frequently faced with. If adequate assumption gathering hasn't been built into the first project (i.e., "we assume that the project might be interrupted by more important work") then you may be faced with a huge dilemma, one that impacts the scope, time, and cost (probably quality too, because it's tough for people to come back from a newer project and begin working on the old one without getting their sea legs back).

More importantly, IT shops that aren't heavily staffed might have a hard time simply maintaining the balance of the day's work, let alone take on new projects. And yet, in the interest of making sure that you meet your customer's needs (your end users are your customers, right?) you might be tempted to take on projects that you think you can effectively manage. In such situations, the server administrator also might be the one who manages the databases and so forth.

IT projects in minimally staffed environments such as the above often suffer from not having well-formed requirements and a well-developed WBS, never mind the rest of the support documentation.

For projects that have to be developed by folks in small or understaffed IT shops, it'll be key that you concentrate on making sure that the requirements are fully understood, that the WBS is very succinctly spelled out, and that your plan project fits within the confines of the schedules that the IT shop workers follow. In other words, you can't expect that a new Oracle database server project will be brought online in just a few days' time by people who are busy running around with their hair on fire most of each working day. That is, unless you expect them to bring up the server during the night (which is precisely what some administrators do—they're just too slammed during the day to finish projects).

> Communication with your business customers in such situations is very important—you have to be sure that you communicate to stakeholders why the project can't be completed in the blink of an eye. Customers might suggest that some of the work be outsourced in the interest of time. But this recommendation (i.e., to bring in a vendor or consultant to help) might be met with some disfavor by the IT folks. The reasons for this are myriad. If the idea of outsourcing is acceptable to all concerned you should be quite sensitive to the way that you present the idea.

Definition of the Project Deliverables

Usually it's easier to define the deliverables of an IT project with obvious requirement outcomes. For example, suppose that you've met with a business unit manager who wants a new software application written to meet a specific need. After some requirement-gathering efforts, you have a pretty firm idea of what the software's supposed to do. In talking with the folks in your IT shop you determine that the majority of your servers are Windows Server 2003, that the database of choice is Microsoft SQL Server 2000, and that there is plenty of room and hardware beef on which to host your application. From there the deliverables are pretty straightforward—you just figure out how the program will be delivered to the user (thin-client? thick?), settle on a programming environment, and away you go.

But defining the deliverables when the outcome of the project is more esoteric can be challenging. For example, suppose that you have a project in which you're going to replace your current help-desk software system with one that's more robust. What are the deliverables? Well, they might include a new server or servers and certainly the new software. But other deliverables will *also* include conversion of the old help-desk database data to the new database, training the users how to use the new system, creating new custom reports that match reports you had in the old, and so forth.

It's like skeet shooting: it's easy to see that red clay disk when it's flying across blue sky, much more difficult to spot it when it's traversing the landscape. You have to think of all of the deliverables that a project is going to produce—some of which aren't immediately obvious. As we mentioned earlier, for example, training stakeholders and creating support documentation are two of the deliverables you're likely to overlook if you don't really examine the complete output of your project.

Working with Your Business Clients

IT shops exist to serve the needs of the business unit end users. To that extent, an IT shop doesn't really have ownership in the organization's business processes and instead must rely on the input and expertise of the business unit to make a successful project. In other words you *serve* the business unit but you're not necessarily a part of it.

There are all sorts of things that fall out of this relationship that you might spot as adversely affecting the scope of your project. For one, consider the business unit director that loses interest in the project halfway through. Since the director is one of the project sponsors, how can you possibly proceed and satisfactorily complete the effort without her dedication?

Also, consider a business unit that's too busy to lend you an SME to help make sure that the deliverables actually match the unit's business needs. It's very difficult to simply assume that you know what your business unit needs when you don't have reliable input from those who actually do the day-to-day work. Many projects get done this way and they produce poor results.

What about the business unit that does all of its own research for a new COTS application, finds one that they think will work, then asks you at the last minute (almost as an afterthought) to implement the new program? The business unit stakeholders' idea of the project's scope might very well be a whole lot different than your own!

You might handle these elements by putting them in the assumptions section of your scope statement. For example, "It is assumed that marketing will lend the project team one full-time business representative for the first 30 percent of the project."

Success Criteria Tough to Define

Suppose that you are working on a new Internet-based e-commerce software application. One of the requirements of the application is that it must be guaranteed to be highly secure—that transactions taking place on the system are well-secured and not privy to hacking.

How on earth do you evaluate such a requirement in order to provide evidence that the system is safe? Furthermore, what happens when, well into the system's creation, the operating system manufacturer reveals that there are known security gaps in the code and affected systems must be patched? How will this news affect the operation of the system you've just created? Will the patching in some way affect your system's operation?

Like the items in the annual performance appraisal and report that your boss gives you every year, sometimes it's tough to put metrics to a subjective outcome. But you should try to pinpoint tangible reasons for *why* you're doing the project—what your customers hope to accomplish by creating the deliverables.

Sidebar Systems and Undisclosed Process Elements

Perhaps the most devastating scope killers arise out of the belief that you've completely uncovered the business processes only to find that your business end users are keeping track of some elements in their office automation software or, worse, they don't disclose all of their business processes because they either didn't think of them at the time you interviewed them, or they deliberately withheld some elements.

The first of these problems is what we call *sidebar systems*, meaning that users keep track of some things by using a spreadsheet or "mini-database" program, and then use that information to work with the primary system. For example, suppose that you have an old mainframe-based program that's been in use for 30 years. Its functionality isn't up to par with what the users require (and hasn't been for years), so sidebar systems have been developed to overcome the system's shortfalls. At requirement-gathering, business-process-discovery time, users just don't reveal that these sidebar systems are in use—they probably don't even connect the dots—and as a result your system winds up missing some key functionality.

Alternately, users might not fully disclose all of the process elements involved in a business transaction for whatever reason. In some cases, a user might just be forgetful about all of the processes he or she goes through in order to successfully conclude a transaction. But sadly, in some instances, a user might be (subconsciously?) trying to sabotage the new effort. This sounds paranoid, but it actually happens. You can imagine the consequences when you get far down the implementation road only to discover that some pretty important process has been left out!

"Mini-Project" Consultant/Vendor Relationships

In projects that are smaller in scope, your relationship with a vendor or contractor may not be as important to them as ones with bigger budgets. While the vendor or consultant is certainly very anxious to assist you, they may have another project on the hook that has the ability to demand instantaneous use of their time, resulting in you being left high and dry waiting for them to return. This, of course, shoots your planned scope out into the stratosphere while you wait on the contractor to come back to finish something.

> ### Real World Scenario
>
> **The Sidebar System That Killed Your Scope**
>
> You're the applications development manager for your company's IT department. You've recently been presented with a request from one of your business units to automate a function of theirs that currently takes a lot of time and person-hours to accomplish.
>
> You assign a systems analyst to the project. She begins the business analysis methodology by working with users to identify the business processes involved and trying to firmly nail down the requirements of the project. She comes back with her standard well-drafted documentation, including DFDs that show the logical flow of the current process.
>
> Everything looks great and you begin to go forward with your project. Halfway into the development of the system code, after going back to the stakeholders for routine communications updates, you find that little elements here and there are missing—almost as though your systems analyst didn't fully perform her usual thorough discovery.
>
> Upon re-interviewing some of the people that she initially sat with, you find a variety of sidebar systems that they evidently didn't bring up at the first interview. One man, for example, keeps a little Excel file listing of computations that he has done toward accomplishing the business function. These things are extremely valuable pieces of information that really should be included somehow in the new system. Another person keeps sticky notes on her desk blotter as she goes through the process. You realize that these step-monitoring activities actually are quite important for the new program and yet you had no knowledge of them when you began.
>
> Now you must go back to the design drawing board and add in these fundamental processes.

Delivery of parts is another issue that can dramatically affect the scope of your project without you being able to adequately spot it at scope-development time. For example, we recently completed a large Storage Area Network/Network Attached Storage (SAN/NAS) project. A simple element such as the rails for a server rack held up completion of an important project phase for almost a month! The vendor sent the wrong rails (ordered through a third-party provider) and was very slow in correcting the order. Finally, just to get a set of rails installed we wound up borrowing a set of the correct rails from another IT unit just so we could bring closure to this phase of the project.

Senior Project Technician Quits or Leaves

Suppose that you laid down your WBS tasks relying heavily on one of your more senior people. Further, suppose that the person moves on to greener pastures. What then? Do you have a less capable junior person to take his or her place? Recall that some IT teams aren't very big. What if you don't have anyone to take his or her place until someone's hired? Voila! The scope juts out like a cowlick on a kindergartner!

Again, in your assumptions statement, you'd note that you assume a certain caliber of individuals will be available.

Project Goes across IT Shops

Perhaps you work for an organization that has several different IT shops that serve different business units. For example, maybe the manufacturing segment of your company is so big that it has its own IT arm. Ditto for the legal department. You handle the rest. Suppose that you have a project in which everyone in the company will use the primary deliverable—for example, an electronic timesheet system that's going to be hosted through the company's intranet. You need the assistance and buy in from the other IT shops so that you appropriately meet the needs of the end users who will use the system. The manufacturing arm, for instance, is the only unit that has 24/7/365 workers, so their timesheet posting will be quite different from others.

In such instances, project management takes on a political diplomat flavor in which you work hard to garner buy in and cooperation from entities that don't necessarily have to play along (unless the CEO says "make go!").

Understandably, in a situation such as this, the scope is very much shaped by the priorities that each IT shop has weighed against the importance of the project. You might get Joe the graphics designer from marketing for 15 percent of his time per week, for example.

Testing Elements Need Good Definition

Lots of different IT projects require that you go through some testing elements to verify that the deliverables meet the requirements. Software development, for example, requires that you perform extensive testing to make sure that you're pushing out code that meets the user's needs as stipulated in the project requirements documentation. There are three forms of testing to be concerned with:

Unit Testing — This test involves the technician performing tests on his or her modules or elements that are going to be included in the overall package of deliverables. For example, a server administrator might get done burning a server, then go through a litany of tests to make sure that it's working as it's supposed to. A programmer, after completing her module, might run through a variety of tests to validate that the module is performing as expected. When you think unit testing, think *singular*—that is, usually a single person testing a single element. While this isn't a hard and fast rule, it gives you the flavor of what unit testing is all about.

Integration Testing — When you perform integration testing, you're testing a bunch of elements that are combined together to form a whole. For example, perhaps you've got several servers that are now burned and that will work together in an array of load-balanced Web servers. Integration testing would test these servers *as a whole*, rather than in distinct units. A programming team might test several modules that, when combined together, form a complete program element. For example, one programmer may have coded the print module, another the calculational elements, another the reporting. When they're combined, they should accurately calculate some figures, create a report, and print it out successfully. Integration testing would prove that this is so.

Case Study: Chaptal Wineries Email and Intranet Systems

Life is tough for you. You've been forced to fly to Bordeaux to meet with Monsieur Fourche so that you can discuss the email server and intranet sites. You really needed to visit each site so that you could understand what the physical connectivity elements are like. For example, you need to get a picture of where the server could actually be placed. Additionally, you also need to understand what the telecommunications picture is like—what wide area network prices are for, say, a T1 circuit (called an "E1" in Europe), what the provision times are for such connectivity, and where the demarcation point will be at the Fourche site.

You have to do the same things for Senior Sanchez' location and the Roo wines site.

On returning, you create a scope document containing the following elements:

Business Need   The president of Chaptal Wines, Kim Cox, has requested that the three new offshore acquisitions be connected to share email and calendar information as well as vino-vital information such as residual sugar (RS) and other viticultural data, vintage charts, wine blends, regulatory updates, and so forth. Two systems are required: an email system that connects all four sites together and a system that runs an intranet site.

Deliverables Description   The deliverables will consist of the installation of a server or servers at each site. The servers will connect together via wide area networking technology. Email software will be installed on each server in such a way that all sites belong to a single email organization. Users will utilize conventional email software to keep their email and calendars online. Additionally, an intranet site will be created on a Chaptal winery server and key users in each of the offshore sites will be trained how to post important data to the intranet so that all employees have complete data at their fingertips.

Major Deliverables   The deliverables include the following elements:

1. Installation of high-quality server gear at each site. Server gear will all be from the same vendor and each server will be identically equipped.
2. Installation of internationally well-known email software.
3. Wide area networking connectivity between sites.
4. Installation of appropriate internetworking gear such as routers and firewalls at each site.
5. Creation of an intranet site.
6. Training and documentation.

Success Criteria   Your success criteria includes the following:

1. Server gear will be installed at each site, baselined, and certified 100 percent functional.
2. Email software will be installed on each site server, site connections with the other site servers validated, and languages installed 100 percent.

3. Connectivity between sites installed and baselined by a telecommunications company.

4. ISP for each site will be determined and contracted.

5. Routers installed and router tables built. Firewalls installed, configured, and baselined. Administrator will be able to ping each site server within the network and send a test email to each site server. Port sniff will show ports 20 and 21 (FTP), 25 (SMTP), 80 (HTTP), and 443 (HTTPS) open, all others closed.

6. Intranet site created and all initial elements requested by the business made operational.

7. Users will be trained and documentation provided and maintained.

8. Users in all sites will be able to send email to one another 100 percent of the time and access viti-vital information 100 percent of the time.

Assumptions You have the following assumptions:

1. No variance in the behavior of like hardware.

2. Telecommunications companies in each nation will have reasonable wide area network setup request procedures and installation timelines.

3. Average T1/E1 cost is assumed to be $350/month U.S. dollars.

4. Intranet development time is assumed to be 60 person days (30 working days, 2 persons)

5. All sites will provide reasonable access for installers and a secure, climate-controlled, power-conditioned room for the electronic gear.

6. Routers will use Open Shortest Path First (OSPF) routing protocol.

7. Contractual help will be used for configuration of the routers.

Constraints Your constraints for the email server and intranet sites are:

1. Language barriers

2. Availability of people at any given site to be able to help with setup due to problems with the winemaking efforts

3. Harvest and crush seasons

Work Breakdown Structure (WBS) Finally, this list represents your WBS:

1. 1.0 Hardware procurement—Chaptal administrator

    1.10 Purchase servers and network operating system (NOS) licenses

    1.20 Purchase internetworking gear

2. 2.0 Wide area network telecommunications connection procurement—Chaptal administrator working with site business managers

    2.10 Provision an E1 connection with French telco

    2.20 Provision a T1 connection with So. Australian telco

    2.30 Provision a T1 connection with Chile telco

    2.40 Provision a T1 connection with California telco

3. 3.0 Internetworking gear installation—installed by contractor

    3.10 Contractor installs router and switches at French site, configures, baselines, and tests.

    3.20 Contractor installs router and switches at So. Australian site, configures, baselines, and tests.

    3.30 Contractor installs router and switches at Chile site, configures, baselines, and tests.

    3.40 Contractor installs router and switches at California site, configures, baselines, and tests.

4. 4.0 Server installation—installed by Chaptal administrator

    4.10 Install server at French site. Baseline and test.

    4.20 Install server at So. Australian site. Baseline and test.

    4.30 Install server at Chile site. Baseline and test.

    4.40 Install server at California site. Baseline and test.

5. 5.0 Email software installationInstalled by Chaptal administrator

    5.10 Install email software on French server. Baseline and validate the software is working correctly.

    5.20 Install email software on So. Australian server. Baseline and validate the software is working correctly.

    5.30 Install email software on Chile server. Baseline and validate the software is working correctly.

    5.40 Install email software on California server. Baseline and validate the software is working correctly.

6. 6.0 Intranet development—contractor

    6.10 Develop intranet pages

    6.20 Test intranet

7. 7.0 Training of users—Chaptal administrator

    7.10 Train French users on the use of email.

    7.20 Train French users on the use of intranet.

    7.30 Train So. Australian users on the use of email.

    7.40 Train So. Australian users on the use of intranet.

    7.50 Train Chilean users on the use of email.

    7.60 Train Chilean users on the use of intranet.

    7.70 Train California users on the use of email.

    7.80 Train California users on the use of intranet.

8. 8.0 Unit, integration, and user acceptance testing

    8.10 Unit testing

    8.20 Integration testing

    8.30 User Acceptance Testing (UAT)

We've also included part of what the tree structure diagram might look like for this case study as well. (See below.)

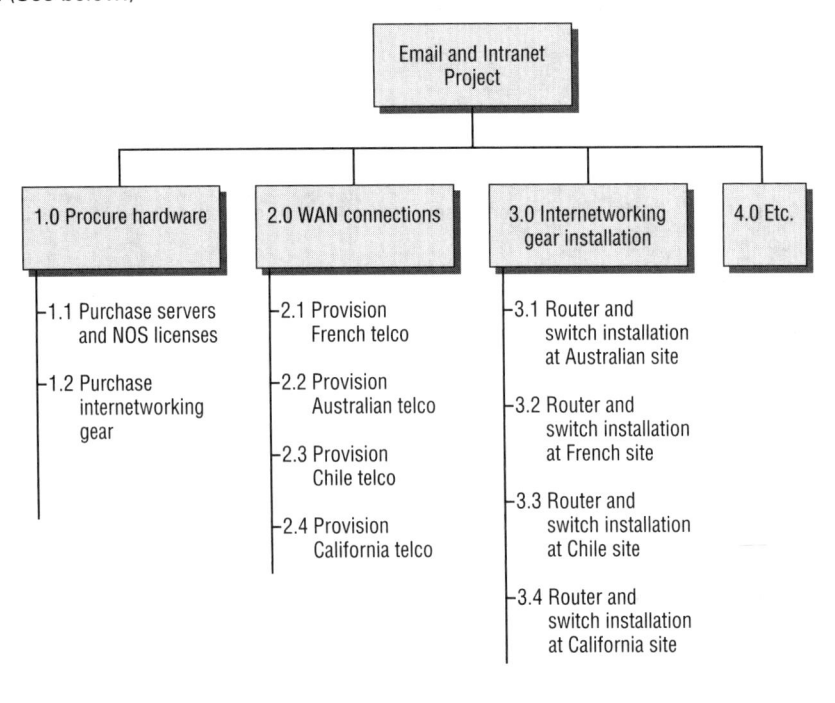

```
                        Email and Intranet
                             Project
          ┌──────────────┬────────────────┬──────────────┐
    1.0 Procure      2.0 WAN         3.0 Internetworking   4.0 Etc.
      hardware      connections       gear installation
    │                │                │
    ├─1.1 Purchase   ├─2.1 Provision  ├─3.1 Router and
    │   servers     │    French telco │    switch installation
    │   and NOS     │                 │    at Australian site
    │   licenses    ├─2.2 Provision   │
    │               │    Australian   ├─3.2 Router and
    ├─1.2 Purchase  │    telco        │    switch installation
    │   internet-   │                 │    at French site
    │   working     ├─2.3 Provision   │
    │   gear        │    Chile telco  ├─3.3 Router and
    │               │                 │    switch installation
    │               └─2.4 Provision   │    at Chile site
    │                    California   │
    │                    telco        └─3.4 Router and
    │                                      switch installation
    │                                      at California site
```

User Acceptance Testing (UAT) — The final element of testing happens when designated users are brought in to give the system a test drive. This is also probably the most revealing of all the testing phases you'll go through because it points out how well the team has done its job, in terms of the way that the users interact with the system. Be prepared for brutally honest assessments of your product.

At any step in the testing, if things don't work correctly the folks working on the problem must, of course, correct it. Significant testing errors will undoubtedly result in out-of-scope scenarios in which you're burning time and money trying to solve a problem. This is why project managers really harp on the idea of pairing the correct person for a task—so that you're sure the task gets done within the estimate that he or she provided.

Summary

Scope planning uses the output of the initiation process, the project charter, to create the scope statement and the scope management plan. The project scope statement is the basis for many of the other planning processes. It is also the basis for setting the boundaries of the project with the client and stakeholders.

A scope statement includes project justification, project description, major deliverables, time and cost estimates, success criteria, assumptions, and constraints. The scope management plan documents how you will manage changes to the scope. The work breakdown structure (WBS) is created by taking the major deliverables from the scope statement and decomposing them into smaller, more manageable components. The breakdown continues through multiple levels until the components can be estimated and resourced. Each lower level of deliverables includes the components that produce the next highest level in the tree. The lowest level of decomposition is the work package. The WBS includes all of the work required to complete the project. Any deliverable not listed on the WBS is assumed to be excluded from the project. The WBS is one of the most critical outputs of planning. A WBS is the basis for time estimates, cost estimates, and resource assignments.

Certain elements in IT shops need to be taken into account when dealing with IT projects. The size of the IT shop very definitely affects the project's time estimates, as do deliverables that may be challenging to define. Business clients may have some hidden processes —"sidebars" that they've not revealed when you're busy trying to discover the processes. Success criteria can be especially tough to define in IT projects. A key project team member leaving can have a remarkable affect on the status of the project's scope.

Exam Essentials

Understand the purpose of the scope statement. The scope statement is the basis of the agreement between the project and the client. It defines the project objectives and the deliverables that will meet those objectives.

Be able to list the components of a scope statement.   A scope statement includes a project justification, product description, major deliverables, success criteria, time and cost estimates, a list of assumptions, and constraints.

Describe the purpose of a scope management plan.   A scope management plan documents the procedures that will be used to manage proposed changes to the project scope throughout the life of the project.

Know how to define and create a work breakdown structure (WBS).   The WBS is a graphical depiction of the work required to complete the project. The WBS is a multilevel tree diagram. You decompose the major deliverables into smaller activities and continue to create lower levels for each deliverable until you reach a point where a time and cost estimate can be provided and resources assigned.

Understand the level structure of a WBS.   The highest level of the WBS is the project name. The major deliverables are the next level. The number of levels in a WBS will vary by project; however, the lowest level is called a work package.

Be able to name the constraints common to all projects.   The constraints common to all projects are time, cost, scope, and quality. The constraints commonly referred to as the triple constraints are time, cost, and quality.

Understand the scope-impacting limitations that a small IT shop might encounter.   Because IT shops aren't heavily staffed, nor are they often staffed specifically with projects in mind, it's important to understand how the scope of a project can be impacted.

Key Terms

Before you take the exam, be certain you are familiar with the following terms:

assumption	scope management plan
constraint	scope planning
decomposition	scope statement
integration testing	sequencing
major deliverables	sidebar systems
network operating system (NOS)	success criteria
order of magnitude	triple constraint
product description	unit testing
project justification	User Acceptance Testing (UAT)
scope	work breakdown structure (WBS)
scope creep	work package

Review Questions

1. Which of the following is NOT a key component of scope planning?
   A. Work breakdown structure (WBS)
   B. Scope statement
   C. Project charter
   D. Scope management plan

2. The scope statement provides which of the following?
   A. A basis for confirming a common understanding of the project and making future decisions regarding the project
   B. A detailed list of all resources required for project completion
   C. A schedule of all the key project activities
   D. A process for managing change control

3. Which of the following is a characteristic of a WBS?
   A. A cost center structure of the project
   B. An organization chart of the project team members
   C. Used primarily on large complex projects involving multiple departments
   D. A task oriented structure that defines and organizes the project

4. Which of the following are components of a scope statement?
   A. Assumptions
   B. Product description
   C. Constraints
   D. All of the above

5. A WBS is created using a technique called decomposition. What is decomposition?
   A. Matching resources with deliverables
   B. Breaking down the project deliverables into smaller, more manageable components
   C. Estimating the cost of each individual deliverable
   D. Creating a detailed To Do list for each work package

6. What is the lowest level of the WBS?
   A. Work package
   B. Level 10
   C. Milestone
   D. Product features

7. Which of the following is *not* a guideline for developing a WBS?
   A. Define the highest level of deliverables before you move down to lower levels.
   B. Make sure that each item in a lower level is a component of the level above.
   C. Sequence all your tasks.
   D. Involve project team members in the process.

8. Which of the following is a benefit of a WBS:
   A. A WBS is an excellent tool for team building.
   B. A WBS helps prevents critical work from being overlooked.
   C. The WBS can become a template for future projects.
   D. All of the above.

9. All projects work under constraints. Which of the following is *not* a constraint that is common to all projects?
   A. Time
   B. Scope
   C. Quality
   D. Equipment

10. Your team is working on creating a WBS for the ABC Software Release. Which of the following is an example of what might appear in level 2 of your WBS?
    A. User guide, training materials, training schedule
    B. Report layout, screen design, and screen mock-up
    C. Product requirements, detail design, development
    D. Project meetings, coding guidelines, test scenarios

11. Which testing element is typically performed by a single individual?
    A. Integration
    B. Delivery
    C. Unit
    D. UAT

12. You're the project manager for a medical research corporation. You've been given a new project whose outcome will result in the formulation of a new cancer treatment involving precisely controlled mini-blasts of radiation using robots and computers. Which of these will most likely impact the scope of the project?
    A. Assembly of key team members
    B. Laws and government regulations
    C. News of a competitor working on the same thing
    D. Formulation of the requirements for the project

13. There are three project elements that remain in tension with one another. Your project client will stipulate which of the three is the most important to them. What are these three elements?
    A. Budget and costs
    B. Team members
    C. Quality of deliverables
    D. Anticipated time to produce deliverables
    E. Sponsors and stakeholders

14. Of the following list of constraints, which one is *the* most important to make sure you've completely and accurately identified when preparing your scope statement documentation?
    A. A clearly defined project end date
    B. A clearly defined set of monetary resources or allocation
    C. A clearly defined set of product requirements
    D. Clearly defined testing methodologiess
    E. Clearly defined priorities

15. When communicating with the project sponsor about your project, which elements below will you have to take into account when considering the project? (Select all that apply.)
    A. The priority of your project as it relates to others
    B. The human resources available for the project
    C. The technology that will be used to create the deliverables
    D. The budget dollars that are available
    E. The equipment that will be required

16. Insert these project elements into the appropriate category to identify whether they are valid success criteria.

Possible Success Criteria	Actual Success Criteria
Save $1.25M in processing costs.	
All data entered into computer 100 percent of the time.	
Sales figures increase.	
Data entry efficiency increased.	
100 percent of drawings visible online.	

100 Chapter 3 · Scope Planning

17. Whose job is it to author the project charter?

   A. Customer

   B. Project manager

   C. Stakeholder representatives

   D. Project sponsor

   E. Options A, B, and C

18. You're developing a scope document for a customer request. A couple of the elements that the client wants might be tricky to accomplish, but after consulting with the project team, you think they can be done. These elements are not a part of the most important things the customer wants out of the product. What should you do?

   A. Include these elements in the scope document, trusting your project team to deliver.

   B. Include these elements in the scope document, denoting the problem elements as such in the document.

   C. Discuss the problem elements with the project sponsor. Obtain customer sign-off.

   D. Discuss the problem elements with the project sponsor and the customer. Obtain sponsor sign-off.

   E. Discuss the problem elements with the customer and the project sponsor. Obtain customer sign-off.

19. What are the functions of the Project Sponsor when it comes to the formulation of the Scope Document?

   A. Signs off on the project scope document.

   B. Has input into the project scope document.

   C. Does not interact with the project scope document.

   D. Authors the project scope document.

20. You're developing the scope document and project plan for a new project. What process group are you in?

   A. Initiation

   B. Planning

   C. Executing

   D. Controlling

   E. Closing

Answers to Review Questions

1. C. The key components of scope planning are the scope statement, the scope management plan, and the work breakdown structure. The project charter is created during project initiation.

2. A. The scope statement is a document that is referenced throughout the project to confirm whether the project is on the right track. It is also used to communicate with the client and stakeholders. A scope statement does not provide a detailed list of all resources required for project completion, a schedule for all the key project activities, or a process for managing change control.

3. D. A WBS is a grouping of project tasks around deliverables that defines the complete scope of the project. A WBS is not a cost structure, or an organizational chart of the project team. It can be used on projects of any size.

4. D. The sections of a project scope statement are project justification, product description, major deliverables, success criteria, time and cost estimates, assumptions, and constraints.

5. B. Decomposition breaks the major deliverables down into smaller pieces that can be used to do cost and time estimates and resource planning. Decomposition does not include matching resources with deliverables, estimating the cost of each individual deliverable, or creating a detailed To Do list for each work package.

6. A. The lowest level of a WBS is the work package. The number of levels will vary by project and complexity.

7. C. The purpose of a WBS is to identify all of the work required to complete a project. It is not important at this point to define the order of the tasks. That will come later when the schedule is developed. The project team members or subject matter experts are involved in creating the WBS.

8. D. There are numerous benefits associated with a WBS. It identifies all of the work associated with the project. It can be used for project team communication and team building. A good WBS can be reused in the future as a template for a similar project.

9. D. The four constraints that are common across all projects are scope, time, cost, and quality.

10. C. Level 2 of the WBS is the first level under the project level and represents major project deliverables, project life cycle phases, or departments involved in the project.

11. C. Unit testing involves testing that single element or thing that will contribute with others to make the whole.

12. B. When your project may attract visibility because it's entrenched in a regulated technology, you'll very definitely have to take into consideration the rules and regulations associated with what you're trying to do.

13. A, C, D. The time/budget/quality equilibrium says that if one element falls short, the other two have to stretch to make up the difference. Short on budget? Then in order to successfully conclude your project with a high-quality product, you'll need to extend the time the project takes.

14. C. It is important to understand all of these constraints. However, the other constraints can change if you have not thoroughly decomposed the new system's software and hardware components in order to arrive at well-understood requirements. If you do not accurately flesh out the requirements, everything else is subject to change.

15. A, B, D. The project sponsor will be concerned with the priority of the project as it relates to others that may be in the loop, and the resources, both budgetary and human, that will be available. It's you and your team's job to determine the equipment and technology that's required and put that in the project plan.

16.

Actual Success Criteria
Save $1.25M in processing costs.
All data entered into computer 100 percent of the time.

Success criteria means that you have some metric—some numeric way of identifying that your project was successfully deployed.

17. B. It is the job of the project manager to synthesize the project charter. However, he does that based upon the collected input of the customers and the project sponsor.

18. E. When you're defining the scope, it's important that you and the customer understand the key areas that really make up project success. In this case, the sketchy elements may not matter to the customer and should be scrapped from the scope of the project. Or, it may be that the risks of not being able to get them accomplished are acceptable to the customer. However it goes, the main point here is that you interface with the customer when working out scope definition elements and make sure you understand the key areas.

19. A, B. The project manager is the one who authors the project scope document. But, keep in mind that it is the sponsor who has the ability to authorize the use of resources for the project, thus she must see the scope document, have input into the scope document, and most importantly, *sign off* on the scope document.

20. B. The planning process group is where you begin to define highly important documents such as the scope and project plan. The scope document arises out of the first important document that you develop, the project concept document, which is developed in the initiating process group.

Chapter 4

Schedule Planning

THE COMPTIA IT PROJECT+ EXAM TOPICS COVERED IN THIS CHAPTER INCLUDE:

- ✓ 2.12 Given a project scenario with many phases and activities, set milestones and measurable targets for completion.
- ✓ 2.13 Given a set of specific milestones and their descriptions, specify entry and exit criteria for each.
- ✓ 2.15 Demonstrate the ability to create an activity time estimate (in units of time).
- ✓ 2.17 Identify and list the components needed to generate a workable project schedule.
- ✓ 2.18 Given a scenario with necessary project documents, and given enterprise holiday and individual calendars, demonstrate the ability to develop a project schedule by doing various project-related tasks.

Once you have an approved scope statement, wouldn't it be great if you could just tell the client and the rest of the stakeholders that your team will complete the project as quickly as possible, but you don't know how long that will be? Everyone dreams of having a job with no deadlines, but without them, we have no measurements for when products and services will be released to the public. Revenue projections are based on when a product or service can be purchased, department heads need to staff for new systems, and functional managers need to know how long you need their staff as resources for your project. These are just a few of the reasons a project manager needs to develop a schedule before the actual project work starts.

Most of you are probably familiar with project schedules; you may have provided input to the development of a schedule or seen copies of schedules produced from a project management software package. At first glance, it would seem that a putting together a schedule is a pretty basic activity. The schedule documents the planned start and finish of all of the tasks included in the project. All you need to do is enter the work packages from the WBS into Microsoft Project, and you have the schedule. It can't be that big a deal; how much planning can this take? As you have probably guessed, the answer is that a good project schedule takes a lot of planning. Just think about everything you need to know to produce a schedule. All of the tasks must be identified; the tasks must be sequenced in the order they can be completed; each task must be assigned an estimated length of time to complete; and finally all of this data must be organized to come up with the overall project schedule.

The project schedule will be part of the project manager's daily routine until the project is completed. Progress is reported against the schedule and status updates are provided to the stakeholders on a regular basis. If the project manager doesn't take the time up front to do schedule planning, he or she will be spending a lot of time during project execution making changes to the schedule and explaining why deliverables are not being completed as anticipated.

Now that you understand how important the schedule is, let's take a closer look at each of the components of schedule planning.

Activity Definition

The foundation to developing a project schedule is a list of the activities required to complete the project. If you have not identified the work that needs to be done, there is no point in trying to put together a schedule. Activity definition is the process of breaking down the deliverables and subdeliverables in the work breakdown structure (WBS) that we discussed in Chapter 3. Although the industry standards set by *A Guide to the PMBOK* defines breaking down work packages into activities as a separate process, in reality activity definition is typically not a stand-alone process. It is part of the iterative process of decomposing the WBS down to a manageable level. Depending on how detailed your WBS is, this step may already be completed.

Many guidelines are available on how far down you should break an activity, and none of them are right for every situation. We're sure you have all seen a project manager with a schedule of detailed tasks so large it looks like you'd have to wheel it around on a cart. Breaking down the work required to complete a project to the level of 15-minute tasks does not guarantee project success. In fact, the outcome is usually quite the opposite. Either the project manager spends all day just trying to keep the schedule current, rather than look at the big picture, or the schedule tracking effort is abandoned and the schedule binder starts collecting dust on a shelf.

The key to activity definition is to identify all of the tasks required to produce the deliverable and to confirm that these tasks are small enough to do time and cost estimates. This needs to be balanced with keeping activities at a high enough level that they can be managed effectively. You do not want to end up trying to keep track of each team member's "To Do" list.

If you only get a status update from project team members on a weekly basis, it does not make sense to track tasks that are only a couple of hours or days. Unless your overall project is on a very short timeline, you should define activities that will take one to three weeks to complete. If you have a very critical short task, you may want to make an exception, but you need to do a special follow-up on the status.

Once you have all of your activities defined, you are now ready to start putting them into the sequence in which they will be completed.

Activity Sequence

Life would be so much easier for a project manager if all the project activities could be worked in parallel. Each person working on the project could be given a list of the activities he or she is responsible for, and once everything on the list is done, that person could return to his or her functional organization. Each team member could estimate how long it takes to complete the assigned tasks, and the project completion date would be based on the team member with the longest estimate. Unfortunately, completing project work is not that simple; many of the project activities cannot start independently. The project team has to identify activity *dependencies*, which describe the relationship between two activities.

Activity sequencing is the process of identifying *dependency relationships* between project activities. First, you need to identify the type of dependency; next comes the specific relationship between the activities. Using this data you can create a pictorial representation of the tasks that shows all of the dependencies.

Let's first take a look at the types of dependencies, and then talk about the different dependency relationships.

Types of Dependencies

You need to identify three categories of dependencies when you are doing activity sequencing. A *mandatory dependency* is created by the type of work the project requires. A utility crew in a new subdivision cannot lay the cable until a trench has been dug. A *discretionary dependency* is something that you choose to impose on the project schedule. An example is a decision to complete tasks in a specific sequence to conform to an established corporate practice, even if there is an alternative means to sequencing the tasks. An *external dependency* is a relationship between a project task and some factor outside of the project that drives the scheduling of that task. Installation of a new server is driven by when the vendor can deliver the equipment.

It is important to know the type of dependency because you have more flexibility with a discretionary dependency than a mandatory dependency. This distinction becomes important later on when you look at ways to complete a project in less time.

Once you've identified a linkage between two tasks, you and the project team need to identify exactly how this relationship works.

Task Dependency Relationships

It isn't enough just to know there is a dependency between two tasks. You need to answer several other questions: How does the dependency impact the start and finish of each of the tasks? Does one task have to start first? Can you start the second task before the first task is done? All of these variables impact what your overall project schedule looks like.

Once you identify a dependency between two tasks, you need to determine what that dependency relationship is so that you can sequence the tasks properly. Before we look at those relationships, let's cover a few key terms that are critical to understanding task dependencies.

A *predecessor* is a task that exists on a path with another task and occurs before the task in question. A *successor* is a task that exists on a common path with another task and occurs after the task in question. Figure 4.1 shows a simple predecessor/successor relationship between Task A and Task B.

Four possible dependency relationships exist between the predecessor task and the successor task. Identifying the correct relationship between dependent tasks is critical to developing an accurate schedule. Depending on the type of dependency relationship, you may be able to schedule the tasks in parallel or the successor task may have to wait until the predecessor is completed. Getting this relationship wrong can have a drastic effect on the accuracy of your schedule. Let's look at the four alternatives you need to evaluate for your dependent tasks.

FIGURE 4.1 Predecessor/Successor Relationship

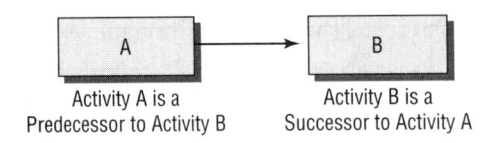

A → B

Activity A is a Predecessor to Activity B
Activity B is a Successor to Activity A

Finish to Start In a *finish to start* relationship, the successor task cannot begin until the predecessor task has completed. This is the most common task relationship. It is the default setting on most project tracking software packages. For example, the user interface must be coded before the printing module can be developed.

Start to Start Use a *start to start* relationship when the start of the successor task depends on the start of the predecessor. These are tasks that can be worked in parallel, but if the first task is delayed, the successor task cannot start. For example, user guide documentation can start when requirements definition starts, but if requirements definition is delayed, the user guide documentation will also be delayed.

Finish to Finish A *finish to finish* relationship has the finish of the successor task dependent on the finish of the predecessor. For example, a new product is finished when the customer manual is complete. If the customer manual is delayed, the release of the product to market is also delayed.

Start to Finish In a *start to finish* relationship, the finish of the successor task is dependent on the start of its predecessor. This relationship is seldom used. Perhaps an example would be that a technical support task cannot be completed until the formation of the technical support team has started.

Once the task dependency relationships have been identified, the project team has the data to create a picture of when the various project tasks can begin and end. This picture is a network diagram.

Creating a Network Diagram

One technique used by project managers for activity sequencing is called a network diagram. Understanding activity relationships is fundamental to using this technique. A *network diagram* depicts the project activities and the interrelationships among these activities. Because you can actually see how the work flows, a network diagram is a great tool to develop with the project team. Using a white board and sticky notes provides an easy way to move activities around and make changes.

The most commonly used network diagraming method is the *precedence diagramming method (PDM)*. PDM uses boxes to represent the project activities and arrows to connect the boxes to depict the dependencies. Figure 4.2 shows a simple PDM network diagram of tasks with finish to start dependencies on this diagram.

Now that the activities are sequenced based on the task dependencies, we are ready to estimate how long it will take to complete each activity.

FIGURE 4.2 Precedence Diagramming Method

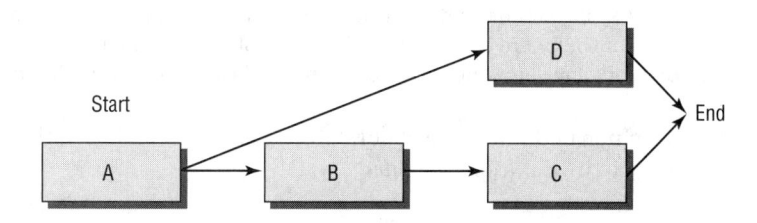

Activity Duration Estimates

We have defined our activities, identified all the dependencies between tasks, and developed a network diagram to depict the flow of the project work. We must be ready to complete the project schedule, right? Not quite yet—we still need a very critical component: how long each task will take to complete. *Activity duration* is the process of estimating the time to complete each item on the activity list. The most common measurements used to define duration are days or weeks, but this can vary based on the size of the project.

Before we explain the techniques you can use to complete your duration estimates, let's make sure we have a common understanding as to what is meant by activity duration.

Defining Duration

When you are estimating duration, you need to make sure that you are looking at the total elapsed time to complete the activity. If you have a task that is estimated to take 5 days, based on an 8-hour day fully dedicated to that task, the actual duration estimate would be 10 days if the resource assigned to the task is only spending 4 hours a day on the task.

You also need to be aware of the difference between work days and calendar days. If your work week is Monday through Friday, and you have a 4-day task starting on Thursday, the duration for that task will be 6 calendar days, because no work will be done on Saturday and Sunday. Figure 4.3 illustrates this situation. The same concept applies to holidays or vacation time.

FIGURE 4.3 A 4-Day Task Separated by the Weekend

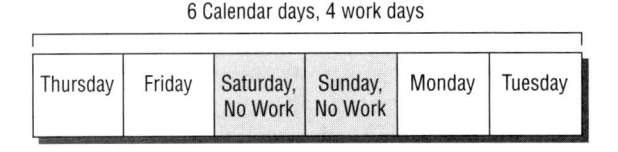

Thursday	Friday	Saturday, No Work	Sunday, No Work	Monday	Tuesday

6 Calendar days, 4 work days

> **NOTE**
> If you have estimated project activity durations in the past, you may not even think about talking about duration with your project team. This could lead to big problems down the road, so make sure that everyone doing estimating is in agreement up front as to whether the estimates will be provided in work days or calendar days. I recommend using work day duration estimates, as the project management software packages allow you to establish a calendar that accounts for non-work days and does not include these days when computing duration.

Now that we have a common understanding of duration, we are ready to discuss the different techniques used to create activity duration estimates.

Estimating Techniques

Where do those task duration estimates come from anyway? Although some cynics may tell you to use a dartboard to estimate duration, there are better ways. Some techniques are designed to provide a ballpark estimate with a wide margin of error when there is not a lot of hard data on the project available. The use of some estimating techniques is driven by the nature of the work involved in completing the task. There is no one right way to do task duration estimates. Just keep in mind that what is being done here is an estimate, and it is not a 100 percent guarantee of the length of time each task will actually take to complete.

Several techniques are used for activity duration estimates. We will take a look at three of the most commonly used and talk about some of the variables that can impact the accuracy of estimates made using each of these techniques.

Analogous estimating, or top down estimating. *Analogous estimating (top down estimating)* is the use of actual durations from similar activities on a previous project. This is most frequently used at the early stages of project planning when you have limited information regarding the project. Although analogous estimating can provide an approximation of a task duration based on the length of similar activities, it is typically the least accurate means of obtaining an estimate. No two projects are exactly the same, and there is the risk that the project used to obtain the analogous estimates is not as similar as it appears.

Results from analogous estimating will be most accurate if the person doing the estimating is familiar with both projects and may be able to better understand differences that could impact the activity durations.

Expert judgment. *Expert judgment* uses the people most familiar with the work to create the estimate. Ideally, the project team member who will be doing the task should complete the estimate. If all team members have not yet been identified, recruit people with expertise for the tasks you need estimated. How do you find people with the required expertise? If you do not have immediate knowledge of who the internal experts are, research the documentation on team members from similar projects or solicit input from your stakeholders. Ask for people who have completed a similar task on a previous project to assist with the estimates for your project.

The most accurate estimates based on expert judgment are those made by the person who will be completing the task, assuming that person can draw on past experience. One of the variables with project duration is the skill set and experience level of the team member performing the work. A duration estimate made by a senior tester will likely be shorter than that of a junior tester. If the person who is responsible for completing the task does not make the estimate, the project manager needs to make sure he or she validates the estimate with the person assigned to the task.

Quantitatively based durations. *Quantitatively based durations* are used when a certain quantity of work is produced, and there is a formula to gauge duration. To apply quantitatively based durations, you must know the productivity rate of the resource performing the task or have a company or industry standard that can be applied to the task in question. The duration is obtained by multiplying the unit of work produced by the productivity rate. If a typical cable crew can bury 5 miles of cable in a day, it should take 10 days to bury 50 miles of cable.

FIGURE 4.4 Network Diagram with Task Duration

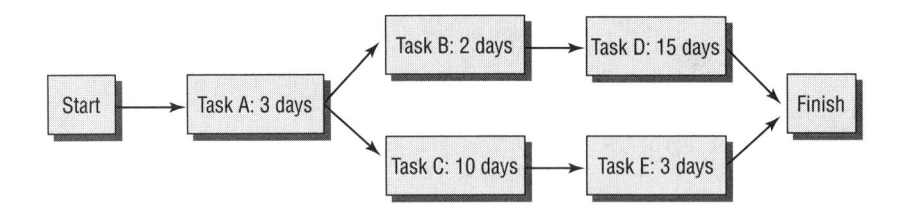

Start → Task A: 3 days → Task B: 2 days → Task D: 15 days → Finish
Task A: 3 days → Task C: 10 days → Task E: 3 days → Finish

This type of estimate can be very accurate for tasks that are repetitive and have a lot of productivity data to assure that the standard productivity rate accounts for variations in skill sets and conditions under which the work is performed. To determine if using quantitatively based durations is applicable to a given project, the project manager needs to understand the criteria for the company or industry standard.

Most projects use some combination of the estimating techniques. If some of the project tasks fit into an established productivity rate formula, they are ideal candidates for quantitatively based estimates; other tasks require the input of an expert familiar with the work.

Once you have determined which estimating technique(s) works best for your project, guide the team members as they work through all of the tasks on the network diagram and assign a duration estimate to each task as illustrated in Figure 4.4.

This will prepare you for the next process, schedule development.

Schedule Development

Schedule development is the establishment of a start date and a finish date for each of the project activities. Schedule development is where we put together all of the other work from schedule planning. An accurate schedule needs all of the activities, the sequence of those activities, and the length of each activity. With all the work we have done so far, you may think this part should be a piece of cake. In reality, putting together all of the data from the other schedule planning processes and creating a project schedule is one of the more complex processes. Luckily, you can use a number of different techniques to develop a project schedule. We will talk in detail about three of the most commonly used techniques: critical path method (CPM), duration compression, and the use of project management software.

Project schedule development also includes the use of milestone dates, which mark a significant project event or the end of a project phase.

Let's get started with the techniques available to develop a schedule.

Schedule Development Techniques

Even though you have a huge pot of data with all of this information about all of the project activities, you still don't have a schedule. Although it may seem at first that the putting all of the activities together is an unwieldy process, you can use a number of techniques to create a meaningful schedule.

A Guide to the PMBOK lists a number of techniques for schedule development. We will focus on three of the most commonly used schedule development techniques:

- Mathematical analysis (specifically the critical path method)
- Duration compression
- Project management software

Critical Path Method (CPM)

A Guide to the PMBOK defines *mathematical analysis* as "calculating theoretical early and late start and finish dates for all project activities without regard for any resource pool limitation." In other words, you are not looking at when any of your resources may be available, but only at when each task can start and end based on dependency relationships with other tasks. A summary of the individual activity time periods provides the project time period.

One of the most widely used mathematical analysis techniques is *critical path method (CPM)*. The critical path in a project schedule is the longest activity sequence path in the project; therefore, it controls the finish date of the project. The purpose of CPM is to identify this path. The activities on the critical path have no *float time*. Float is the time a task may be started late or the additional time that can be used to complete the task without impacting project completion. Critical path tasks have zero float, which is why these tasks get so much attention. If a critical path task does not complete as scheduled and no other changes are made, the project end date will be affected.

> **NOTE** Chapter 9, "Project Control" will cover what you can do if you have critical path tasks that are taking longer than planned.

In addition to calculating the overall time to complete the project and identifying tasks on the critical path, CPM provides other useful data. You will be able to determine which tasks can start late or can take longer than planned without impacting the project end date. This information can be used during project execution to help the project manager focus attention on the tasks that have the most impact on the overall project completion date.

We are going to walk through a simple CPM calculation. CPM is rarely done manually, since a variety of software tools will do these calculations for you. But unless you understand the fundamentals behind what the software is doing, you cannot take advantage of what it is telling you.

The network diagram from activity sequencing and the task duration estimates are the key components of the CPM calculation. Refer to the precedence diagram shown in Figure 4.4 as we walk through this example.

Forward Pass   The first step in determining your critical path is to complete a *forward pass* through the network diagram. This means that you are working from the left to the right of your network diagram. This will give you two calculations for each activity.

Early start is the earliest date an activity may begin as logically constrained by the network. The first activity on the diagram has an early start of 0. Add the duration of that activity to obtain the early finish for that activity. *Early finish* is the earliest date an activity may finish as logically constrained by the network.

In Figure 4.4, the early start for Task A is 0 since it is the first activity on the network. The duration for A is 3 days, so your early finish will be 3. The early finish for A becomes the early start for its successor, Task B. Continue to calculate the early start and finish dates for each activity on the network moving across the diagram until you reach the box marked "Finish."

Table 4.1 shows the completed early start and early finish calculations for each of the tasks in our network diagram. Based on the calculations from this completed forward pass, the project can complete on day 20.

TABLE 4.1 Forward Pass

Task	Early Start	Early Finish
A	0	3
B	3	5
C	3	13
D	5	20
E	13	16

Backward Pass The next step to complete critical path is to complete a *backward pass*. This means you start at the finish of your network diagram and work back though each path until you reach start. This gives you two calculations.

Late finish is the latest date an activity can complete without impacting the project end date. *Late start* is the latest date you can start an activity without impacting the project end date.

In Figure 4.4, the final activity to complete is Task D. The latest it can finish is day 20. To calculate the late start for this activity, subtract the duration of 15 days from the late finish. Your late start is day 5. The late start for Task D becomes the late finish for its predecessor; Task B. Continue back through the network, calculating the late start and late finish for each task on the network diagram.

Then go back and compute the second path starting with Task E. Since the project finish date is day 20, the late finish for Task E is also day 20. By subtracting the duration of 3 days, you obtain the late start of day 17. Continue to calculate the late start and finish dates for each activity on the network.

Table 4.2 shows the completed late start and late finish calculations for our network diagram.

TABLE 4.2 Backward Pass

Task	Late Start	Late Finish
A	0	3
B	3	5
C	7	17
D	5	20
E	17	20

Float The final step in determining critical path is to calculate float for each activity on the network diagram. Float is obtained by subtracting the early start from the late start or the early finish from the late finish for each activity. Use the calculations from Tables 4.1 and 4.2 and start with Task A. The early finish is 3 and the late finish is 3, making the float 0. Continue through the network diagram until you have computed the float time for each activity.

Table 4.3 shows the float for each of our tasks.

TABLE 4.3 Float

Task	Float
A	0
B	0
C	4
D	0
E	4

   You are now ready to determine the critical path. Remember we said earlier that the critical path is the path with no float. In our example in Figure 4.4, both Tasks C and E have float, which means they are not on the critical path. A-B-D is the critical path, as each of these tasks has 0 float. If any of the tasks on the critical path do not start on time or take longer than planned, the end date of the project will be impacted; it will not complete within the 20-day estimate. Remember that you must pay particular attention to the status of your critical path tasks over the course of project execution to keep your schedule on track.

Unfortunately, there are times when you complete the network diagram and calculate the critical path and you determine the length of your project is unacceptable to the project stakeholders or does not complete within a mandated legal requirement. If you find yourself in that situation, you need to utilize duration compression techniques.

Duration Compression

You have just learned how to develop a network diagram of your project tasks and lay out your project schedule using CPM. But what happens if your calculation of the total project duration is longer than your target project completion date?

This is where *duration compression* scheduling techniques come into play. These techniques can be used up front to shorten the planned duration of the project or during project execution to resolve schedule slippage. The two duration compression techniques are crashing and fast track.

Crashing

Crashing is a technique that adds more resources to a task to complete the task more quickly.

> **NOTE** Crashing may have an impact on your budget, so you will need to look at the impacts to both your schedule and your budget.

> **WARNING** One common misconception regarding adding resources is that if you double the resources, you will cut the duration in half. If two programmers can write the code in 4 weeks, then four programmers can do it in 2 weeks. What happens in the real world may be quite the opposite. Typically, the original resources are initially less productive when you add new resources. The work must be reallocated, which takes time away from the work itself. There may be downtime while the experienced team members train the new members.

There is also the issue of diminishing returns. The more resources that are added, the less impact each resource will make on duration reduction.

Crashing can produce the desired results if used wisely, but it is not the solution for a timeline that is unrealistic based on the scope of the project.

Fast Track

When you *fast track* a project, you work tasks in parallel that would normally be done in sequence.

For example, suppose that you have a project in which you have to build four servers that are going to interact with one another. You might have initially created four "build server" tasks that were supposed to happen one right after the other. However, when you decide to fast track the project, you'd probably ask the server administrator building the servers if he or she could build all four in approximately the same time. In a fast-track situation, the admin might assemble the server hardware for server one, then start the OS installing. Once that was going he or she might move to assembling Server 2's hardware and so on. In this way you could shave precious time off of the project.

There is a great deal of risk in fast tracking. If you decide to compress your project schedule using this method, be sure and get input from the team members as to what could go wrong. Document all the risks and present them to your sponsor, your client, and other key stakeholders. Many project managers make the mistake of just trying to do the project faster without any communication as to the impacts on other areas such as quality. You need to make sure that everyone understands the potential consequences. For instance, in the example of the servers above, you can see that the main risk involved is that the admin may get confused as to which step he or she is at in the server-building process and make a critical mistake in bringing up one of the servers.

Project Management Software

Project management software is a wonderful tool that can save you a lot of time. It provides you with the ability to display a number of different views of the project, which can be a great communication tool.

The processes that we have covered in this chapter—activity definition, activity sequence, and schedule development—can all be completed using a project management software package. In fact, you may be wondering why we even bothered to walk through manual examples of these processes, when you can just enter your data in a software package and let it do all the work. In order to effectively use project management software, you must understand the fundamental concepts behind what the software is doing. Otherwise, you will not obtain the full benefit of what the software can provide. Worse yet, you may become frustrated because the way you have entered your tasks causes the software to do things you do not want it to do. Going through each of these processes manually will equip you with the knowledge and understanding to effectively use a software tool.

Keep in mind that even if you will be using software to track the progress of your project, the up-front work that you do as a team to create a WBS and define estimates can still be created manually using a white board and sticky notes. This data can be entered into a software package later for tracking purposes.

If your company provides you with a project management software tool and you have never used one before, ask to attend a class. If that is not possible, try to find someone in your organization who is experienced with the software to give you some on-the-job training.

A good understanding of project management software becomes more important when you start tracking project process, which we will discuss in Chapter 8, "Project Execution."

Use of one or more of these scheduling techniques will assist the project manager in producing a schedule with a start and end date that accounts for all of the project activities and their dependencies. To make your schedule complete, all that remains is the addition of any required milestone dates.

Milestones

Depending on the specific methodology used and the policies within your organization, you may also need to include milestone dates in your project schedule. A *milestone* marks a key event in the project life cycle. Typically milestones are included in the project to identify the completion of a major deliverable. If you will be using milestones in your schedule, be sure that all of the activities required to meet the milestone are scheduled to complete before the milestone date.

Some project life cycle methodologies also use milestones to mark the end of one project phase and the beginning of the next phase. Milestones between phases typically have exit or entrance criteria. For example, a system development project milestone for moving from a test phase to a deployment phase could have a list of specific test scenarios that must be successfully completed before the testing phase is complete. This is the exit criterion that must be met before the test phase is considered complete.

Project managers need to pay close attention to milestone dates, as they are also a communication trigger. Stakeholders need to be informed when major deliverables are completed or when a project has successfully moved to a new phase. If these dates are not met, the project manager needs to communicate the current status, plans to bring the project back on track, and the new milestone date. The details of communications planning will be covered in Chapter 6, "Additional Planning Processes."

Schedule Baseline

The project manager and the project team should review the completed project schedule to address any questions or resolve any outstanding issues. The project team needs to own the schedule and be committed to meeting the planned dates. To facilitate a clear understanding of the schedule, provide each team member with a copy of the schedule to review prior to the meeting. If the project schedule has been developed using a project management software package, you may be able to provide access via a shared folder.

Once the team reviews the project schedule and adds any milestone dates, it is time to establish the *schedule baseline*, which is a copy of the schedule prior to the start of project work. A baseline is a tool used by the project manager during project execution to monitor and communicate project progress.

The project manager communicates the baseline schedule to the stakeholders. The level of detail provided to the stakeholders will vary depending on the detail each stakeholder requires, but at a minimum cover the key milestone dates.

Juggling Project Time in the Real World

In the scope of our experience, the various IT teams we've worked on have been small-ish and incredibly overburdened with projects. On top of that, very little time could actually be devoted during the day to working on projects due to user problems and what we've begun to call "drive-bys" (more on that in a minute). If, in fact, a person did find time to work on a project, it was usually after working hours when there was time to fully concentrate on the tasks.

As for project planning and good quality systems analysis and design? Fuhgeddaboudit!

Generally speaking, based on the size of the organization, IT shops are either:

- Heavily segmented into IT job categories such as application development, open systems (UNIX, Linux, and Windows) server support, mainframe and mid-sized computer support, help-desk and PC-technicians, database administrators and so forth, or...

- An all-one-shop that has one or two people working each type of the above job duties.

We have never run into a company that has a dedicated project team staffed with individuals from various IT persuasions, ready and anxious to work on projects, but we don't suppose that's an altogether bad idea. In any event, most companies staff IT with an eye toward maintaining the day-to-day IT activities and then only secondarily with IT projects in mind.

Drive-Bys—the Non-Project Project

In the IT world, people are often involved with very small teams of people that have an expertise in a given subject here or there and that contribute to the overall health of the network, application development unit, or customer care center simply by bringing forward those bodies of expertise. You may, for example, be on a team of server administrators that has an email admin who basically does nothing but handle the email server farm on a daily basis. Additionally, you've probably got a backup person, someone who manages the file-servers, probably a database server administrator, and a security/perimeter person (running the antivirus, firewalls, DMZ, etc.). Additionally, you probably have some enterprise-class apps running such as an ERP system—requiring some specialty administrators.

The point is, *none* of these individuals have time for projects! And yet, if you work in shops like I've worked in, you *must* make time for projects that come your way. So you somehow apportion your day in order to get your routine server work done, plus your project work. But then, your boss comes by and wants you to drop everything so that you can go work with the guy in the attorney's office who's having a problem connecting to the email server.

Ever had that happen to you? Things are going along fine, and then, wham-o, you have to spend the next (important) two hours working with someone who doesn't understand how to drive Windows XP and Outlook 2000. Now you're way behind in both your project *and* your routine work.

Someone I work with gave these little boss re-directions a great term: "drive-bys." The boss swings by on his way to another meeting and says "By the way, can you run by so-and-so's office and check what's going on with his computer? He keeps calling me!" You're not on the PC technician team, but today you're a PC technician and everything else suffers for it!

Here's the important element: How do you project plan for the inevitable drive-bys? In the scheme of things, when thinking like a project manager who has at your disposal a small team of admins, how do drive-bys fit into the whole resource-planning scheme?

This is tricky and, I think, somewhat isolated to IT shops. There's just only so much expertise to go around.

One way to deal with drive-bys in your resource planning efforts is to create a "project" called "non-project work." Your human resources will keep track of the time that they spend on drive-bys by keying in tasks that they perform on a day-to-day basis that have nothing to do with the actual project itself. Included in these tasks will, of course, be the hours spent on the task. Thus, as the end of a pre-designated period, you can easily show how the drive-bys erode the total time allotted for a project, the result of which is a project that ends after its designated due date.

Since that's the situation, and you're concerned with juggling a busy IT shop's time so that you can get projects done, you need to understand time appropriation in the average IT shop's day.

Server Administrators Most server administrators begin their day by checking each of the servers' log files to make sure there are no glaring errors. If there are errors, then, of course, they have to spend time figuring out what happened and how to rectify the situation. After that, server admins usually have several trouble calls they have to work on. (For example, so-and-so can't log on because his password has expired or the account is locked out due to too many login retries.)

After all that, if there's time left in the day, a server admin is available to work on new projects.

Database Administrators Database administrators (DBAs) also begin their day by checking each of the database log files to make sure nothing's wrong. If there are errors, they also have to spend time figuring out what happened and how to rectify the situation. After that, DBAs work on performance tuning, writing stored procedures, maintaining indexes and triggers, and working on new requests for column additions or deletions.

DBAs begin any new project work by developing a *database schema*, the initial layout and design of a new database. The whole database design component can be quite lengthy because it entails taking what the customer is requesting and converting that into a sensible database layout. Part of this effort includes the task of *normalizing* the database—reducing each table in the database to the elements that most logically belong to it. Also, the notion of relating the tables by one or more keys also takes a great deal of time, especially when dealing with substantial databases.

Application Developers Usually you don't have the luxury of scheduling your applications programmers because they're sitting around waiting for something to do. Most programmers are busy working on other projects so it can be quite challenging to round up the help you need to get some development work done.

On top of that, your programmers may have different languages they're familiar with as well as different levels of experience. For example, your project might require a Java programmer with a good body of background experience—one who's able to quickly get several modules written and functional while operating under a relatively short deadline. Clearly, a C# programmer couldn't fill the bill, nor could one with very little Java experience. You don't have the luxury of waiting while a more junior coder figures out how to write a certain piece of code.

Additionally, development shops typically aren't staffed to maximum capacity and, as if that's not bad enough, the senior, highly experienced folks are usually heavily engaged. They barely have enough time to answer a question from the junior folks, let alone take on another project module. The whole of this leaves you as a project manager scheduling key project tasks very far out there unless, of course, your project takes priority over everything else and managers tell the development department to drop all other work until your project is complete (not likely).

Telecommunications and Internetworking Specialists Very frequently telecommunications and internetworking folks are not even considered to be a part of the IT shop—they're a separate arm, reporting to a different manager. But just as frequently they're needed for your IT projects. And just as frequently they're extremely busy with other priorities and projects.

> **Data Normalization and Conversion Takes Serious Time!**
>
> Some engineers in your company have created an Access database system that has become quite useful to their department. As a consequence, two things have transpired: The system has been significantly tweaked and refined so that it's extremely complementary of the tasks the engineers are trying to accomplish and, as a result, there are between 30–50 people at any one time trying to access the system.
>
> The problem is, Microsoft Access just doesn't scale well to such large concurrent user numbers. Access wasn't designed for that kind of use.
>
> So now you're faced with an engineering department business request to take this system and convert it to a Microsoft SQL Server–based environment. SQL Server has a cool utility in it called Data Transformation Services (DTS), made just for the purpose of migrating data such as Access databases into SQL Server.
>
> During your business requirements analysis, you ask a DBA to take a look at the database itself. She brings back some startling news: the engineers have done a great job of assembling a system, but they clearly have no idea about data normalization. The screens and reports are nice but the database itself is a mess and is going to take significant time to convert to a well-crafted SQL Server layout. She'll have to examine the Access database in order to figure out the best schema for the SQL Server database, then perform complicated data conversion routines to get the data into the proper tables and columns. Her estimate is 3 weeks just for this part of the project! Then there's the whole issue of recoding the reports (because they point to a new data source with columns that are in different tables) and screen redesigns.
>
> There are also difficulties in making sure that the current SQL servers can handle the additional load and setting up new ODBC connections.
>
> Microsoft Access (and to some extent programs such as dBASE, FoxPro, and FileMaker Pro) has made it very easy for neophyte users to create quick and dirty systems that meet a business need. But very often the number of users outgrows the capability of the system to meet everyone's needs. It is then that the IT shop has to get involved and spin up a project to convert the system to something with a little more horsepower. Users are almost always surprised at the amount of time that the project's going to take. It was simple to build—why isn't it that simple to convert?

All of this may sound very doom and gloomish. How can you ever expect to get a project fully staffed and going if you have to wade through a labyrinth of scheduling difficulties? Part of the answer has to do with corporate priorities. If your project is an important one and you have a clear mandate to bring in the deliverables on a certain date, then you've got leverage power to get the people you need to help. However, this leverage depends on whom the mandate is from. If, for example, the project emanates from the marketing department, you might be given a huge sense of urgency by the department's manager, but others in the organization don't share that same rush-rush feeling about it. If, on the other hand, the project you're on is something that the CEO wants to see happen right away, then you're going to have fewer problems lassoing the folks you need.

Managing projects in IT environments can be quite challenging simply because you don't have dedicated staff and the people you do have available may be unavailable for certain lengths of time. It's important that you clearly examine project schedules based on current workloads and communicate real expected finish dates as opposed to those that are overly aggressive.

> **Case Study: Chaptal Wineries—a Closer Look at the WBS**
>
> After looking over your manually created WBS (Chapter 3) and thinking about the dependencies and dates, you've realized there are areas you need to expand, timewise. For example, if you're going to be the one doing the server installation and user training, you're going to have to fly to each location, do your business, then fly to the next. Considering a flight from France to Australia, you've got a minimum of 2 days on the airplane, plus the configuration time to get the server up and running. Then, you have to turn around and do the same thing again for user training, again planning on flight time as a huge part of the task time estimates.
>
> The server installation itself should go fairly smoothly. Using Microsoft Windows Server 2003 and Exchange Server 2003, you'll set all locations up as distinct sites in the same organization. Provided WAN connectivity is set up and working, you should have few issues with the actual software installation. You'll also be setting up Internet Information Server (IIS) 6.0 as the intranet base web server while you're at each foreign location. You believe you can accomplish all installation work in 2 days' time per location and you've given yourself an additional day for any issues that might arise.
>
> You're trusting the local internetworking vendor to handle the internetworking gear installation, as part of the contractual provision. Who better to install a Cisco router and get it working in France than a French Cisco system engineer (SE), for example?
>
> Provisioning the WAN connectivity through the various local telcos seems to you to be the sketchiest part of the whole project. You have to work hand-in-hand with the local winery representative, mostly to provide you with telecommunications company contact info, to relay you important documentation, to give you anticipated installation lead times, and to make sure that the contracts are signed and installation dates set. Still, T1/E1 circuits are the bread and butter of most telcos—you don't anticipate major delivery problems in the 30-day time constraint you've placed. Budget is not a huge priority relative to the WAN circuits. Kim knows you need them, and you're not asking for anything huge in terms of bandwidth (a T1 circuit runs at 1.544 megabits/second).
>
> After installing a copy of Microsoft Project 2002, you whip up your project schedule, keying in the changes and setting up what you believe are accurate task durations and predecessors. The graphics below show the output: the WBS and Gantt chart, respectively. A Gantt chart is a bar chart that shows the relationship between the project tasks and time. Project managers like to use Gantt charts because they quickly give people a visual representation of the tasks and how they play out over time. Project management software can automatically generate Gantt charts, along with the coupling lines that show interesting project features, such as milestones. The main program window in a Microsoft Project screen shows the tasks in the left-hand pane and the Gannt chart in the right-hand pane. In the graphics below we show the two panes one beneath the other.

Juggling Project Time in the Real World

You've included the Early Start, Late Start, Early Finish, and Late Finish columns so you can understand how Project calculates them (based on the predecessors) and what your floats are.

	Task Name	Predecessors	Duration	Early Start	Early Finish	Late Start	Late Finish	Free Slack
1	CHAPTAL INT'L EXPANSION		1 day	Mon 10/27/03	Mon 10/27/03	Tue 3/2/04	Tue 3/2/04	91 days
2	☐ 1.0 Hardware Procurement		30 days	Mon 11/3/03	Fri 12/12/03	Mon 11/3/03	Wed 2/25/04	0 days
3	1.10 Purchase servers		30 days	Mon 11/3/03	Fri 12/12/03	Mon 11/3/03	Fri 12/12/03	0 days
4	1.20 Purchase network gear		30 days	Mon 11/3/03	Fri 12/12/03	Mon 12/15/03	Fri 1/23/04	0 days
5	☐ 2.0 WAN connection provision		30 days	Mon 11/3/03	Fri 12/12/03	Thu 1/15/04	Fri 2/27/04	53 days
6	2.10 E1 circuit/French telco		30 days	Mon 11/3/03	Fri 12/12/03	Mon 12/15/03	Fri 1/23/04	0 days
7	2.20 T1 circuit/Australia telco		30 days	Mon 11/3/03	Fri 12/12/03	Mon 12/15/03	Fri 1/23/04	0 days
8	2.30 T1 circuit/Chile telco		30 days	Mon 11/3/03	Fri 12/12/03	Mon 12/15/03	Fri 1/23/04	0 days
9	2.40 T1 circuit/California telco		30 days	Mon 11/3/03	Fri 12/12/03	Wed 12/17/03	Tue 1/27/04	0 days
10	☐ 3.0 Networking gear installation		4 days	Mon 12/15/03	Thu 12/18/03	Thu 2/26/04	Tue 3/2/04	53 days
11	3.10 French installation	4,6	4 days	Mon 12/15/03	Thu 12/18/03	Thu 2/26/04	Tue 3/2/04	53 days
12	3.20 So. Australia installation	4,7	4 days	Mon 12/15/03	Thu 12/18/03	Thu 2/26/04	Tue 3/2/04	53 days
13	3.30 Chile installation	4,8	4 days	Mon 12/15/03	Thu 12/18/03	Thu 2/26/04	Tue 3/2/04	53 days
14	3.40 California installation	4,9	2 days	Mon 12/15/03	Tue 12/16/03	Mon 3/1/04	Tue 3/2/04	55 days
15	☐ 4.0 Server Installation		17 days	Mon 12/15/03	Tue 1/6/04	Mon 12/15/03	Tue 1/6/04	0 days
16	4.10 Install France server	3	5 days	Mon 12/15/03	Fri 12/19/03	Mon 12/15/03	Fri 12/19/03	0 days
17	4.20 Install Australia server	16	5 days	Mon 12/22/03	Fri 12/26/03	Mon 12/22/03	Fri 12/26/03	0 days
18	4.30 Install Chile server	17	5 days	Mon 12/29/03	Fri 1/2/04	Mon 12/29/03	Fri 1/2/04	0 days
19	4.40 Install California server	18	2 days	Mon 1/5/04	Tue 1/6/04	Mon 1/5/04	Tue 1/6/04	0 days
20	☐ 5.0 Intranet development		14 days	Wed 1/7/04	Mon 1/26/04	Wed 1/7/04	Mon 1/26/04	0 days
21	6.10 Develop intranet pages	19	14 days	Wed 1/7/04	Mon 1/26/04	Wed 1/7/04	Mon 1/26/04	0 days
22	☐ 6.0 Testing		9 days	Tue 1/27/04	Fri 2/6/04	Tue 1/27/04	Fri 2/6/04	0 days
23	6.10 Unit testing (CA)	21	2 days	Tue 1/27/04	Wed 1/28/04	Tue 1/27/04	Wed 1/28/04	0 days
24	6.20 Integ. testing (int'l)	23	5 days	Thu 1/29/04	Wed 2/4/04	Thu 1/29/04	Wed 2/4/04	0 days
25	6.30 User acceptance testing	24	2 days	Thu 2/5/04	Fri 2/6/04	Thu 2/5/04	Fri 2/6/04	0 days
26	☐ 7.0 Training		17 days	Mon 2/9/04	Tue 3/2/04	Mon 2/9/04	Tue 3/2/04	0 days
27	7.10 Train French (email)	25	2 days	Mon 2/9/04	Tue 2/10/04	Mon 2/9/04	Tue 2/10/04	0 days
28	7.20 Train French (intranet)	27	3 days	Wed 2/11/04	Fri 2/13/04	Wed 2/11/04	Fri 2/13/04	0 days
29	7.30 Train Australian (email)	28	2 days	Mon 2/16/04	Tue 2/17/04	Mon 2/16/04	Tue 2/17/04	0 days
30	7.40 Train Australian (intranet)	29	3 days	Wed 2/18/04	Fri 2/20/04	Wed 2/18/04	Fri 2/20/04	0 days
31	7.50 Train Chilean (email)	30	2 days	Mon 2/23/04	Tue 2/24/04	Mon 2/23/04	Tue 2/24/04	0 days
32	7.60 Train Chilean (intranet)	31	3 days	Wed 2/25/04	Fri 2/27/04	Wed 2/25/04	Fri 2/27/04	0 days
33	7.70 Train California (email)	32	1 day	Mon 3/1/04	Mon 3/1/04	Mon 3/1/04	Mon 3/1/04	0 days
34	7.80 Train California (intranet)	33	1 day	Tue 3/2/04	Tue 3/2/04	Tue 3/2/04	Tue 3/2/04	0 days

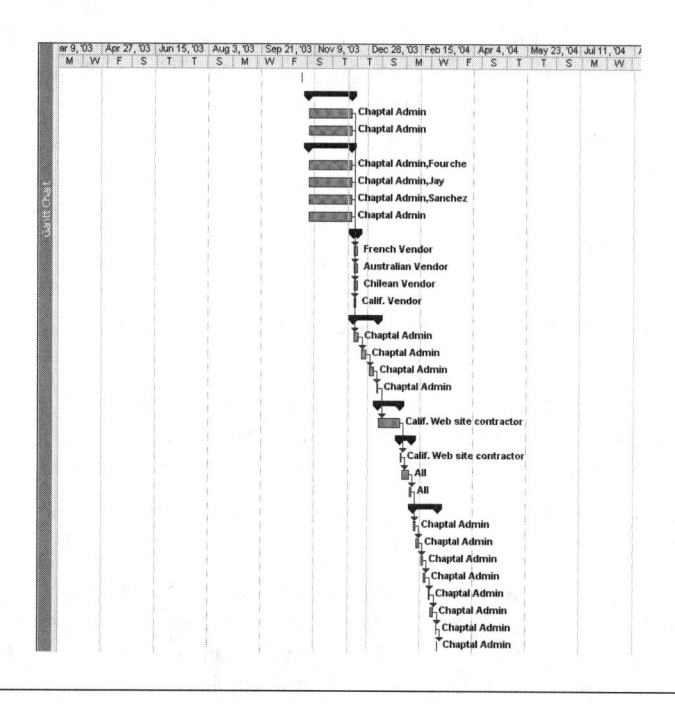

Summary

Many critical processes are included in schedule planning. Activity definition takes the work packages from your WBS and breaks them down into assignable tasks. Activity sequencing looks at dependencies between tasks. These dependencies can be mandatory, discretionary, or external. Dependent tasks are either a successor or a predecessor of a linked task.

There are four types of task dependency relationships: finish to start, start to start, start to finish, and finish to finish. A network diagram is a pictorial representation of the task dependency relationships. Activity duration estimating is obtained using analogous (also called top down) estimating, quantitatively based durations, or expert judgment.

The most complex schedule planning process is schedule development. There are three commonly used schedule development techniques. The mathematical analysis technique critical path method (CPM) creates a schedule through the completion of a forward and backward pass through the network diagram and calculating float.

Duration compression is the technique used to shorten a project schedule to meet a mandated completion date. Duration compression can be obtained by applying either crashing or fast track. Crashing shortens task duration by adding more resources to the project. Fast track works tasks that were originally scheduled in sequence in parallel.

Numerous project management software tools can be used as schedule development tools. A project schedule may also include milestones, which mark major project events such as the completion of major deliverable. A completed project schedule becomes the baseline used to track and report progress of the project.

Finally, various IT professionals find that the nature of their work results in different ways of managing time. As an IT project manager, it's your job to understand the day-to-day responsibilities of those IT professionals in order to determine when they will be available to take on new projects. Often, obtaining the resources and time needed to complete a project depends on who (which department) in the organization requires the help of IT.

Exam Essentials

Describe the activity sequencing process. Activity sequencing is the process of identifying relationships between the project activities.

Name the two major relationships between dependent tasks. A predecessor is a task that exists on a path with another task and occurs before the task in question. A successor is a task that exists on a common path with another task and occurs after the task in question.

Name the four types of task relationships. The four types of task relationships are finish to start, start to start, start to finish, and finish to finish.

Know and understand the three most commonly used techniques to estimate activity duration. Expert judgment relies of the knowledge of someone familiar with the tasks. Analogous or top down estimating bases the estimate on similar activities from a previous project. Quantitatively based durations are used if you can apply a unit-based formula to the activity.

Define the purpose of CPM. CPM identifies the longest activity sequence path in the project. This path controls the finish date of the project.

Explain a network diagram. A network diagram is used in activity sequencing to depict project activities and interrelationships among these activities.

Key Terms

Before you take the exam, be certain you are familiar with the following terms:

activity duration	float time
activity sequencing	forward pass
analogous estimating	late finish
backward pass	late start
crashing	mandatory dependency
critical path method (CPM)	mathematical analysis
database schema	milestone
dependencies	network diagram
dependency relationships	normalizing
discretionary dependency	precedence diagramming method (PDM)
duration compression	predecessor
early finish	quantitatively based duration
early start	schedule baseline
expert judgment	schedule development
external dependency	start to finish
fast track	start to start
finish to finish	successor
finish to start	top down estimating

Review Questions

1. Which is true for the critical path?
   A. Has zero float
   B. Is the shortest activity sequence in the network
   C. Both A and D
   D. Controls the project finish date

2. You are a project manager for a major movie studio. You need to schedule a shoot in Denver during ski season. This is an example of which of the following?
   A. External dependency
   B. Finish to finish relationship
   C. Mandatory dependency
   D. None of the above

3. What is analogous estimating also referred to as?
   A. Fast tracking
   B. Expert judgement
   C. Crashing
   D. Top down estimating

4. You are working on your network diagram. Task A is a predecessor to Task B. Task B cannot begin until Task A is completed. What is this telling you?
   A. There is a mandatory dependency between Task A and Task B.
   B. There is a finish to start dependency relationship between Task A and Task B.
   C. Task A and Task B are both on the critical path.
   D. Task B is a successor to multiple tasks.

5. What is the most commonly used form of network diagramming?
   A. Activity on arrow
   B. Precedence diagramming
   C. CPM
   D. PERT

6. What are crashing and fast track techniques used for?
   A. Duration compression
   B. Activity sequencing
   C. Precedence diagramming
   D. Activity definition

7. Which is true for float or slack time?
   A. Calculated by adding the durations of all activities and dividing by the number of activities
   B. Time that you add to the project schedule to provide a cushion
   C. The amount of time an activity can be delayed without delaying the project completion
   D. Is only calculated on the longest path of the network diagram

8. Which of the following is *not* a tool used to determine a project critical path?
   A. Forward pass
   B. Duration compression
   C. Float calculation
   D. Backward pass

9. Activity B on your network diagram has a duration of 8 days. How do you calculate the early finish date for this task?
   A. Subtract 8 days from the late finish of the next activity on the path.
   B. Add 8 days to the late start date of Activity B.
   C. Take the early start date of Activity B and add 8 days.
   D. None of the above.

10. Which of the following is true for all activities on the critical path?
    A. The early start is always less than the late start.
    B. These activities are on the shortest path on the network diagram.
    C. The float is not important.
    D. The late finish is always the same as the early finish.

11. You're working on a project in which the time to complete the project has been heavily restricted and funds are short. Part of the project consists of your server administrator preparing a half-dozen servers for use in a balanced web array. The servers will all look basically alike. What technique can you use to slim down some of the time required to perform this task in the project?

    A. Fast track
    B. Crashing
    C. Reducing the number of servers
    D. Purchasing a server that runs a number of virtual machines simultaneously

12. Why is it important to understand the critical path of a project?

    A. The tasks on the critical path are the most important.
    B. There is no float in the critical path tasks.
    C. The tasks on the critical path must be done first.
    D. The length of the critical path can change subject to new tasks being added to it.

13. Suppose that you're working on a project in which you've established this milestone: "Database Servers Built and Functional." The following tasks are needed to get to this milestone:

    A. Build 3 database servers—see published burn doc
    B. Install Oracle 9i on each server
    C. Validate that Oracle is running correctly and can be connected to
    D. Install database schemas from development environment — see schema build documentation
    E. Test 100% succesful

    Which of the tasks above would represent entry criteria for the milestone?

    A. Task a
    B. Task b
    C. Task c
    D. Task d
    E. Task e

14. You're working on a project that you and your team have estimated is going to take 15 business days. Given the work calendar shown below with a start date of Monday, November 24, 2003, how many calendar days are actually required?

November 2003

| Sunday 23 | Monday 24 | Tuesday 25 | Wednesday 26 | Thursday 27 Holiday | Friday 28 Holiday | Saturday 29 |

December 2003

Sunday 30	Monday 1	Tuesday 2	Wednesday 3	Thursday 4	Friday 5	Saturday 6
Sunday 7	Monday 8	Tuesday 9	Wednesday 10	Thursday 11	Friday 12	Saturday 13
Sunday 14	Monday 15	Tuesday 16	Wednesday 17	Thursday 18	Friday 19	Saturday 20
Sunday 21	Monday 22	Tuesday 23	Wednesday 24	Thursday 25 Holiday	Friday 26 Holiday	Saturday 27

A. 15
B. 22
C. 23
D. 24
E. 25
F. 30

15. A milestone differs from a task in that it (Select all that apply):

A. Represents the end of a critical project phase
B. Represents the culmination of a given set of tasks
C. Represents the change of ownership in the project (from one sponsor to another, for example)
D. Doesn't necessarily have to be removed from a task—the completion of a given task can *be* the milestone
E. Represents the movement from one process group to another

16. You're in the process of developing a project schedule for a new project in which you've just completed the requirement-gathering and scope document elements. What would be the smart next step in figuring out what tasks go into the project schedule?

    A. Develop a network diagram.

    B. Sit down at your project management software and start hammering out the tasks.

    C. Ascertain who's going to be on the project team.

    D. Hold a white board and sticky note session that creates a network diagram.

    E. Figure out the critical path of the project.

17. You've defined a task in a project schedule in which your team members will develop an XML application that uses a MySQL back end. While the DBA has plenty of experience with Oracle and MS SQL Server, he's pretty new to MySQL. What is the most likely element affected in the tasks of your project schedule?

    A. Resource allocation

    B. Task duration

    C. Task estimation

    D. Critical path

18. You're the project manager for a project in which you're following a specific software development methodology. Some of the developers have observed that a new coding technique could improve the speed with which the code will be developed and ready. How will this affect the current activity duration for the project?

    A. There is a potential for a (large) decrease in the task duration.

    B. The will definitely be a decrease in task duration.

    C. The new methodology probably won't have an effect on task duration.

    D. There will probably be an actual increase in task duration should the new methodology be adopted.

19. The exhibit shows the steps in a network diagram. Task B must occur before Task C. Tasks B, C, and D must all occur after Task A and must all occur before Task E can be accomplished. How long is the critical path, in days?

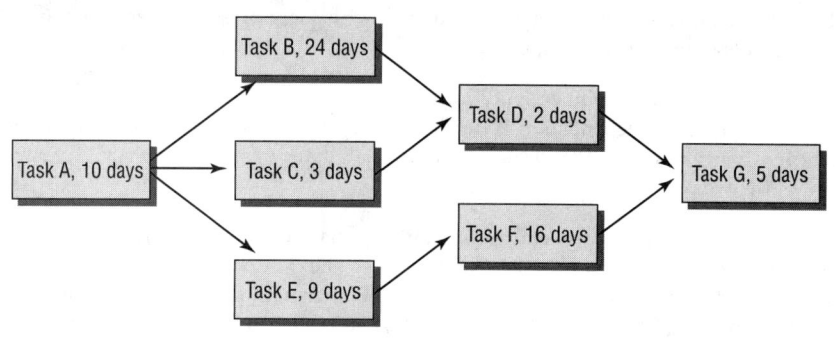

[Network diagram: Task A, 10 days → Task B, 24 days; Task A → Task C, 3 days; Task A → Task E, 9 days. Task B → Task D, 2 days. Task C → Task D. Task E → Task F, 16 days. Task D → Task G, 5 days. Task F → Task G.]

- **A.** 13 days
- **B.** 20 days
- **C.** 27 days
- **D.** 30 days
- **E.** 40 days

20. The exhibit shows a series of steps in a network diagram. Tasks B through F must all wait for Task A to be completed and must all be complete before Task G can begin. Tasks B and C must occur before Task D, and Task E must occur before Task F. How long is the critical path, in days?

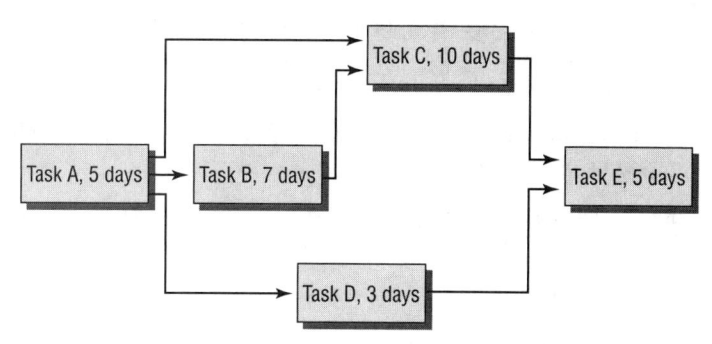

[Network diagram: Task A, 5 days → Task B, 7 days; Task B → Task C, 10 days; Task B → Task D, 3 days; Task C → Task E, 5 days; Task D → Task E.]

- **A.** 20 days
- **B.** 40 days
- **C.** 41 days
- **D.** 55 days
- **E.** 69 days

Answers to Review Questions

1. **C.** The critical path is the longest activity sequence in the network. It has zero float or slack time, and it controls the project end date.

2. **A.** A dependency such as weather conditions or a specific season that is outside the list of project activities is an external dependency. A finish to finish relationship means that the successor task cannot finish until the predecessor task completes. A mandatory dependency is created by the nature of the work.

3. **D.** Analogous estimating is also called top down estimating. It is used early in the project when there is not enough detail to do a detailed estimate. The estimate is done based on a similar project. Expert judgement relies on people most familiar with the tasks to complete the estimates. Fast tracking and crashing are forms of duration compression.

4. **B.** There is a finish to start dependency relationship between Task A and Task B. You do not have enough information to determine if the dependency between the two tasks is mandatory, discretionary, or external.

5. **B.** Precedence diagramming is the most used diagramming method. Activity on arrow is a less-used diagramming method that uses arrows to represent the tasks. CPM is a schedule-development technique. Although network diagrams are sometimes called PERT charts, PERT is actually a seldom-used, specialized schedule-development technique that uses weighted averages.

6. **A.** Duration compression involves either crashing the schedule by adding more resources or creating a fast track by working activities in parallel that would normally be done in sequence. Activity sequencing is the process of determining the order in which tasks must be worked. Precedence diagramming method, the most common form of the network diagram, is a depiction of the project activities and the interrelationships among these activities. Activity definition is the process of defining all the tasks required to complete the project deliverables.

7. **C.** Float or slack time is the time a task may be started late or the additional duration a task may use without impacting project completion.

8. **B.** The tools use to calculate critical path are forward pass, backward pass, and float calculation. Duration compression is a technique used in schedule development.

9. **C.** Early finish is calculated by adding Activity B's task duration to its early start date.

10. **D.** The late finish is always the same as the early finish. Float is always zero on the critical path activities. The critical path is always the longest path on the network diagram.

11. **A.** You only have one admin, so crashing the project (bringing in multiple folks to parallel tasks) probably isn't the solution. You can't reduce the number of servers—ostensibly because by the time you've gotten to this step in the project, requirement-gathering has illustrated that you will need this many. Purchasing a VM server probably won't help because it's as complex to bring up as the six individual servers, what with the underlying VM software and the individual partitions.

12. **B.** Tasks on the critical path aren't necessarily the most important, they're just the ones that have zero float time—meaning you have no wiggle room from start to finish. Because of that, the tasks on the critical path should, if represented well, represent the actual complete duration of the project. Tasks on the critical path don't necessarily have to be done first—but they must be done in the order that you've defined with their predecessors and successors. Once you've defined the tasks and figured out what the critical path is (and obtained sign-off) you don't want to add tasks to it because this represents scope slippage.

13. **E.** Building the servers, installing Oracle on them, and bringing up the schemas represents work *toward* the milestone, but does not adequately represent that you've *reached* the milestone. Only task e, which says that you've successfully tested the servers as database servers, indicates that you've reached your goal.

14. **C.** As you can see from the answer graphic, you have to count the Saturdays and Sundays *plus* the holidays that are included in the project's calendar days. Even though the project only takes 15 days, you'll require 23 to account for days off.

November 2003

| Sunday 23 | Monday 24 | Tuesday 25 | Wednesday 26 | Thursday 27 Holiday | Friday 28 Holiday | Saturday 29 |

December 2003

Sunday 30	Monday 1	Tuesday 2	Wednesday 3	Thursday 4	Friday 5	Saturday 6
Sunday 7	Monday 8	Tuesday 9	Wednesday 10	Thursday 11	Friday 12	Saturday 13
Sunday 14	Monday 15	Tuesday 16	Wednesday 17	Thursday 18	Friday 19	Saturday 20
Sunday 21	Monday 22	Tuesday 23	Wednesday 24	Thursday 25 Holiday	Friday 26 Holiday	Saturday 27

15. **A, B, E.** The 2000 *Guide to the PMBOK* (glossary—page 203) says that a milestone is a representation of a significant event in the project—often the production of a major project deliverable. Therefore, when you shift from one project phase to another in your WBS, representing the completion of a group of tasks that resulted in that phase completion, or you've completed all the deliverables and you've now shifted from the Executing/Controlling to the Closing process group, you have achieved a milestone. There is a lot of room for gray area discussion about what actually makes up a milestone in any given project—it's fundamental that you would arrive at those milestone designations by communicating with your team to determine what the milestones are and then communicate outward to your stakeholders. All interested parties should know when you've hit a key milestone.

16. D. As a result of finishing the scope document and requirements documents, you probably already know who's going to be on the project team. What you *don't* have a good feel for, at least yet, is the tasks that have to be done. A white board and sticky note session with your project team would be a good starting point in directing you to a network diagram that (hopefully) everyone can live with.

17. B. As an experienced DBA, he probably has the ability to give you a fairly good estimate of what it's going to take to build the database in MySQL. Much of the design work in databases is done before the DBA hits the UI (user interface) to actually create the tables so you can be reasonably sure of the estimate of work. However, that being said, you cannot stipulate *for positive* the duration of the task.

18. A. Here's the wrinkle with such a proposal: The developers are smart enough to understand that the amount of time required to write the new programs will be diminished by adopting this new software development methodology; *however, how long will it take them to fully envelop the new principles of this methodology?* In other words, if you're used to doing a thing a certain way—in fact you've been doing it that way for a long time—and then you learn a new, faster way, how long does it take you to integrate the new method into your skill set? As a project manager, you have to somehow figure out the delta in the two (the difference between the improvement in coding speed versus the time required to adopt the new methodology). If there's a significant difference, then it's probably worth your while to adopt the new technique.

19. C. The critical path is the series of consecutive activities that represent the longest necessary path through the network diagram. You use up 5 days with Task A, then 7 days with B, 10 days with C, and a final 5 days with Task E, for a total of 27 days. Even though Task D cannot fire off before Task A is completed, A-D-E only uses 13 days.

20. C. Tasks A, B, D, and G represent the longest dependent path through the network diagram, so the critical path requires 41 days.

Chapter 5

Cost Planning

THE COMPTIA IT PROJECT+ EXAM TOPICS COVERED IN THIS CHAPTER INCLUDE:

- ✓ 1.6 Given a project initiation document (a project charter or contract), including a confirmed high-level scope definition and project justification, demonstrate the ability to identify and define key elements.
- ✓ 2.3 Demonstrate understanding of estimating concepts, techniques, and issues.
- ✓ 2.14 Demonstrate the ability to create an activity cost estimate.
- ✓ 2.15 Demonstrate the ability to create an activity time estimate (in units of time).
- ✓ 2.16 Recognize and explain the difference between a project cost estimate, effort estimate, and time estimate.
- ✓ 2.20 Demonstrate the ability to assign resources to the schedule.
- ✓ 2.21 Given a project scope, timeline, cost, project team, and dependencies, demonstrate the ability to manage key elements of the project budget.

By this time, you may be wondering why you have to have a plan for everything. If you know the scope of your project and you've identified the tasks to complete the project, why can't you just get started? As the project manager, you aren't going to be managing just the scope and the duration of the project; you are also managing the costs. To understand what your project will cost and to create and manage your budget, you need to identify all of the expenses associated with your project. Developing a plan to identify and manage your costs will help you complete your project within the approved budget.

In a fantasy world, corporate funds would be unlimited and projects would be approved based on the result they produce and provided with the funding required to do what it takes to complete the project. In the real world, projects have budgets, and cost overruns are not a good thing. Money is always a hot topic. There is never enough to go around, and you are always asked to do more with less. Going back and asking for more money after the project is underway is not a pleasant undertaking, so you want to do the best job possible of planning for the funds you will need. Estimating project costs can be a tricky undertaking, but luckily project management provides some useful tools and techniques to help you through this effort.

Resource planning looks at identifying the types of resources you need to complete your project and assigning resources by job description or job title to each project task. Cost estimating is the process of determining what you will spend for the resources you need to complete the work on your project. There are three types of cost estimating: analogous estimates, parametric modeling, and definitive estimates. Cost budgeting allocates the approved costs of all the project resources over your project timeline to create a project budget. A copy of the project budget before any work has started is the cost baseline. We'll discuss these topics and more in this chapter. Let's get started.

Resource Planning

You may think you know who and what you need to complete the project work, but if you try to just start grabbing resources where you can and assigning tasks, you may quickly find your project at a standstill. Remember all those task dependencies we identified in Chapter 3? Tasks that must happen in sequence drive the need for the resources to complete those tasks in the same sequence. If you take the time to identify all of the resources you need for the project, you will get the people and the equipment that you need at the time you actually need them.

The first step in cost planning is *resource planning*, which means determining the following:

- The resources the project needs, in the form of both human, equipment, and material resources. The quantity of each resource required to complete the work for your project (e.g., two servers, four person-hours, etc.).

After all, you cannot do an accurate estimate of your project costs if you have not identified the resources to complete the project.

Luckily, your previous planning processes provide the inputs you need to identify your resources. For example, an input you might've received at requirement-gathering time was "the system will be browser-based and made available over the intranet." Intuitively then, you know that you'll need human resources to provide web programming and also human and material resources to hook what was developed into the corporate intranet.

Before you start the resource planning process, review your scope statement and WBS and investigate whether you can obtain historical resource information from similar projects. Understanding the resources from a similar project may help you get started in the right direction. It is also a good idea to review any specific corporate policies regarding allocation of resources to projects. For example, corporate policy may require you to obtain formal department-head approval before utilizing any more than 40 hours of an employee's time who is not in your department.

> One of the good things about a project management office (PMO) is that corporate heads have realized the common sense in formalizing the project management process and will probably have already approved formal standards and policies for how projects are started and run.

Although the project team members may get the most attention during resource planning, there is more to resource planning than just the staffing requirements. We will take you through the three types of project resources you need to identify before you start estimating your costs. After providing an understanding of what is meant by project resources, we will move on to identifying the specific types of resources you need for each of the project tasks.

Types of Resources

When you mention project resources, the first thought that comes to mind is the people required to complete the project activities. Although people are certainly an important component and perhaps the one you'll pay the most attention to, resource planning involves far more than just the project team. Focusing on just the people can cause major disruptions down the road when you find you do not have the workstations you need or there is no power supply in your training room. It turns out that it's the little things that bite you. You must plan for three different and equally important types of resources: human resources, equipment, and material.

Human Resources

Human resources are the people with the background and skills to complete the tasks on your project schedule. You are not going to forget that you need people to complete the work associated with the project, but defining the *right* people can be a little more complicated.

It is important that people knowledgeable in the work required to perform a given task are involved in identifying the skilled labor component for each project task. You need to involve project team members or the functional managers providing the resources. For example, who better to tell you who is the best choice for a web programming project than the manager of the applications development department?

Your request for project staffing may need to span numerous internal organizations, depending on the nature of your project. Do not assume, just because this is an IT project, that all of the resources will come from the IT organization. As an example, an IT technical writer may not be the best choice to develop a user training package if he or she cannot explain the concept in a language the user can understand. A business methods writer from the client organization may be a better choice. By identifying the skill set required for each activity, you will have the data to determine which group can provide the appropriate people.

Equipment

Equipment includes anything from specialized test tools to new servers or additional PCs for the programming team. Equipment is very often a critical component of IT projects. Some types of equipment have long lead times from when the order is placed, so your upfront planning needs to be very thorough.

If you are developing a new piece of software and think your application can run on an existing server, check to make sure that is a correct assumption. Even if the server currently has free space, it may be reserved for another application. If you will be doing extensive testing, determine whether you will have access to existing test equipment or whether special equipment will be needed for your project.

For any task that involves development, testing, or delivery of your product, determine any special equipment needs associated with the completion of that task. Be particularly aware of any needs outside of IT. If the project schedule includes user acceptance testing, how will this be accomplished? Has a location been identified and does that location contain the necessary equipment for the users to complete the test scenarios? If a hardware component isn't identified until after project execution is in progress, an added cost for expedited delivery or a schedule delay may result.

Materials

Materials is kind of a catchall category that includes utility requirements such as software, electricity, or water, any supplies you will need for the project, or other consumable goods.

Failure to think through and plan for materials can lead to major issues. If your project requires a special training room, you will probably identify the need for PCs when you plan your equipment needs. What you may not think about are the connections for power for each of the PCs or a need to have them connect to a corporate local area network (LAN). If you are equipping a training room, make sure you understand what it comes with and what you will need to provide in order to conduct the training associated with your project. This same scenario could apply to any specialized workspace required to complete the project work.

Materials can trip you up if you do not have a good understanding of what is considered a supply that is just part conducting normal business versus what is considered unique to the project. You may not have to identify paper, pens, and file folders, but if you want each team member to have a copy of Microsoft Project, it probably needs to be included as part of the project resource requirements. If there is any question, check out your departmental policy—do not assume it is covered under the functional budget.

> **NOTE** One interesting thing that you'll run into when you begin to test a web application is the idea of mimicking the load that a website can handle, that is, how many thousands of hits can it take at once and still stay functional? One of your material resource planning items might be load software that is able to introduce a load onto the developed website in order to test its ability to withstand numerous hits. You may not have considered this element as you're going through your resource planning efforts, which is why it's good to bounce identified resources off of the tech folks that will be working on the project's deliverables.

Now that you understand the types of resources you need to be concerned with, you can start assigning resources to your project tasks.

Defining Resource Requirements

Armed with an understanding of the three types of project resources, your scope statement, and your WBS, you are ready to start defining the resources needed to complete your project. This process will give you the output of resource planning, the *resource requirements*. The resource requirements document contains a description of the resources needed from all three resource types for each of your work package items from the WBS. Figure 5.1 illustrates resource requirements in a scope statement form.

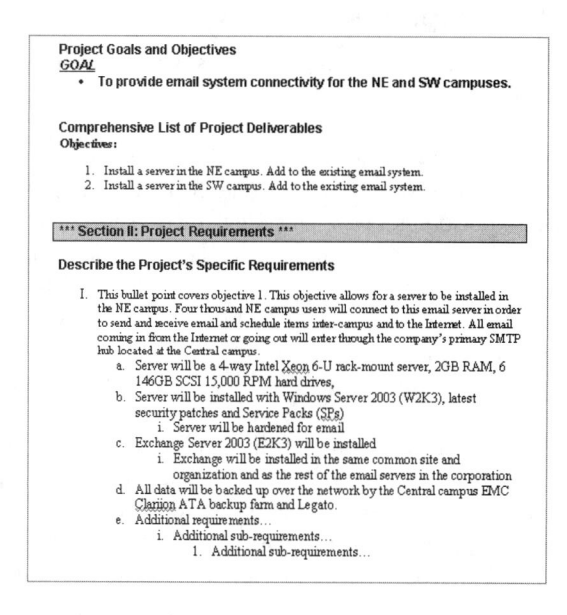

FIGURE 5.1   Resource Requirements

```
Project Goals and Objectives
  GOAL
    • To provide email system connectivity for the NE and SW campuses.

Comprehensive List of Project Deliverables
Objectives:
  1. Install a server in the NE campus. Add to the existing email system.
  2. Install a server in the SW campus. Add to the existing email system.

*** Section II: Project Requirements ***

Describe the Project's Specific Requirements
  I. This bullet point covers objective 1. This objective allows for a server to be installed in
     the NE campus. Four thousand NE campus users will connect to this email server in order
     to send and receive email and schedule items inter-campus and to the Internet. All email
     coming in from the Internet or going out will enter through the company's primary SMTP
     hub located at the Central campus.
       a. Server will be a 4-way Intel Xeon 6-U rack-mount server, 2GB RAM, 6
          146GB SCSI 15,000 RPM hard drives.
       b. Server will be installed with Windows Server 2003 (W2K3), latest
          security patches and Service Packs (SPs)
            i. Server will be hardened for email
       c. Exchange Server 2003 (E2K3) will be installed
            i. Exchange will be installed in the same common site and
               organization and as the rest of the email servers in the corporation
       d. All data will be backed up over the network by the Central campus EMC
          Clariion ATA backup farm and Legato.
       e. Additional requirements…
            i. Additional sub-requirements…
                 1. Additional sub-requirements…
```

During the resource planning process, you do not need to be concerned with identifying the names of people who will complete the work. What you need to identify in resource requirements is a *generic* human resource based on job title or job description, that is, "web programmer" or "server administrator." We will discuss in more detail how you actually go about *acquiring* human resources when we discuss organizational planning in Chapter 6, "Additional Planning Processes."

Job Descriptions and Titles

A tool that can be very useful for developing the human resource requirements is a *resource pool description*. This is a list of all the job titles within your company. If you work in a very large corporation, you may want only those job titles associated with a specific department(s). This list provides a brief description of the job and may identify the number of people currently employed in each job title. Check with your departmental human resources representative to see if this type of information is tracked in your organization, and if it can be made available to you for resource planning purposes. If this type of data is not available or if it is confidential, you could look at resource information from similar projects as a guide to the various job functions you made need to identify. Corporate organizational charts are also a source of information on job titles, although they do not usually include job descriptions.

For some tasks you may not have an exact job title for each of your human resources, but you do know that you need someone from a particular department. For other tasks, you may need to enter into a contract with an outside company, in which case, you may need a resource from the legal department to work on the contract negotiation.

Equipment and Material Descriptions

A description of available equipment or material resources is not as typical as a list of job titles and descriptions, so you may need to do some homework to identify those resources. One of the big questions you need to answer is what materials or equipment the project is expected to provide for the team members. When people are assigned to projects in your organization, do they come with the equipment they will need to do the job? My experience has been that most project team resources supplied by a functional manager have an assigned workspace that includes a PC, phone line, and other basic work tools such as pens, notebooks, etc. In some instances, project workers are collocated, which requires at least part of the team to move to new office space. You need to determine whether the policy of your organization is to move equipment with the person or is the project manager accountable for providing everything. If the team is going to be collocated, is existing workspace available or will the project budget need to fund the build out of cubicles?

New applications projects need a server or mainframe on which to reside. If there are standards as to what hardware platforms can be used, your project application needs to run on approved equipment. An existing piece of hardware may have available space for your application or you may need to purchase hardware. If your project involves a hardware purchase, you need to identify any materials required to house the new equipment, such as power supply or ventilation.

> **Developmental Environments**
>
> In most application development arenas, applications development managers like to maintain three separate environments: development (Dev), test (Test) and production (Prod). Applications programmers (coders) and database administrators (DBAs) work on the software modules in the Dev environment. When a module is ready for testing, it's moved to the Test area where it's tested. When everything works, the code is moved to Prod. In bigger, more stringent shops, the person doing the moving from Dev to Test isn't the same as the one moving from Test to Prod. If you don't maintain a Dev/Test/Prod environment while you develop your project's software, chances are you'll encounter a lot more problems with the code than if you obey the Dev/Test/Prod environment protocol.

Responsibility Assignment Matrix (RAM)

You need some tools or templates to keep track of all the resource requirements. A good tool to use for defining and documenting your resource requirements is a *Responsibility Assignment Matrix (RAM)*. A RAM is a chart that matches your WBS tasks with the required resources. Table 5.1 depicts the start of a RAM for an IT development project.

TABLE 5.1 Sample Project Responsibility Assignment Matrix (RAM)

Task	Programmer	tester	Marketing	Tech Writer	Server
A				1	
B	2				
C		3			1
D	4				
E			1		

> **Note:** Be sure to include any resources with one-time or fixed costs that will be purchased from your project budget.

In the above example, for each task we have identified the resource(s) required to complete the work and inserted the quantity of each resource for each task. This gives us not only the resources needed for each task, but the quantity of each resource as well.

Real World Scenario

The Equipment Was There, but Not the Electricity!

Susan is a project manager for a large corporation based in the Pacific Northwest. The corporate managers decided to build a new building to house all of the departments in one place. The company planned to save money by reducing lease contracts and increasing the level of efficiency because coworkers would be in closer proximity to one another. Susan was put in charge of a project to move all the people into the new building. The project would take about 6 months and she would be required to move 1,000 people in "move waves" with a total of six waves.

Shortly after she received the project, Susan met with the building's contractor to discuss the location of the different departments and the datacenters, for the servers as well as the power, and determine lighting diagrams for the cubicles throughout the building and the datacenter. The contractor noted to Susan that in the interest of saving money, the corporate engineers had opted to reduce the amount of electrical cables—called "whips"—in the datacenter, though he assured her he thought he had planned for enough connections.

Susan discovered, on interviewing the contact in each department, that even though the company had a central IT shop, seven separate mini-IT shops needed to place server equipment in the datacenter, along with the central IT department itself. Going on the word of the contractor, she felt that there would be plenty of electricity to meet the needs of the various IT stakeholders.

During the first wave move some, but not all, of the servers that were going into the datacenter were delivered, and the various administrators showed up to hook them up, Susan was shocked (no pun intended) to find out that all of the electrical connections were used up! Even though there were still more servers to come, she had nowhere for them to hook up to power. The assurance that the contractor gave her was suddenly out the window.

Furthermore, as Susan went back through and inventoried the electrical requirements for the remaining servers, she was startled to find that some had regular 15 amp requirements, others needed 20 amp circuits, and still others required a specialized 277/480 circuit. On revisiting the contractor she found that he had only installed 15 amp circuits—he wasn't aware that server gear may have other power requirements than an ordinary house lamp!

Susan had to assess in a RAM how many circuits she needed for each kind of remaining power requirements. The total was seventeen 15 amp, ten 20 amp, and two 277/480 circuits. She also planned in a little bit extra for growth. Next she went back to the contractor to get an estimate of the cost for the 31 new circuits—a whopping $17,500!

Finally, with much trepidation (she was, after all, a skilled project manager) she went to the project's sponsor, explaining that she had overlooked the power requirements and that significant additional monies were required to complete the project.

Susan now works as a cab driver in a central California city.

Three job titles are listed in the example matrix: programmer, tester, and technical writer. We also know we need someone from the marketing department to handle external customer communication, but we do not have a specific job title. The RAM can also be used to depict materials and equipment. Task C in this example requires a new server.

You can use other tools besides the RAM to identify resource requirements. We have seen project teams use the WBS (created in scope planning) and write in the resources required next to each task. Resource requirements can also be documented using project management software package. You may also use tools or templates from previous projects.

> **TIP** The specifics of how you identify resources are not as important as making sure that you capture everything.

The team continues to work through the task list until resources have been assigned to all of the project tasks. Once you have identified the resources you need, you are ready to start the process of estimating the cost of each of the resources.

Cost Estimating

Now that you have documented your project resource requirements, you are ready to begin *cost estimating*, the process of approximating what you will spend on all of your project resources. A cost estimate is the input for developing the project budget. The key thing to remember about cost estimating is "approximate." Cost estimating is a guess. You have no way of knowing exactly what the cost of your project will be, and some estimating methods are more accurate than others. To increase the precision of your guess, it is important to use all of the data and tools available to you.

> **WARNING** Cost estimates are communicated to the project stakeholders. Any predictions related to the cost of a project tends to be cast in stone, so a project manager needs to be very clear about the potential accuracy of an estimate, especially those estimates made early in the planning process.

If multiple estimates are made during the course of project planning, always communicate the new estimates to the stakeholder group if there is a significant change, and provide background information on the new estimate to explain how it differs from the previous estimate both in terms of content and accuracy. We will discuss the final planning cost estimate a little later in this chapter when we discuss the cost baseline. Communications about revised estimates should highlight the information you now have that was not available when the first estimate was made.

A number of different techniques are used for cost estimating. We will look at three types of cost estimates: analogous estimates, parametric models, and definitive estimates. We will also provide some tips to help you work through the estimating process.

Cost Estimating Techniques

There are three major categories of cost estimating techniques: analogous estimating, definitive estimates, and parametric modeling. You may use each one of these methods at various stages of project planning, or you may use one type of estimating for part of the activities and another method for the rest.

The methods have varying degrees of accuracy and each method can produce different results, so it is very important to communicate which method you are using when you provide cost estimates. Let's take a look at each of these estimating methods in more detail and how they work.

Analogous Estimates

You may remember this term from schedule planning. For cost estimating, an *analogous estimate* approximates the cost of the project at a high level by using a similar past project. (You may also hear this referred to as *top down estimating* or an *order of magnitude* estimate.) This type of estimate is typically done as part of a business case in the initiation process or during the early planning process of scope planning, when there is not a lot of detail on the project. Analogous estimating uses this historical data along with expert judgment of the person responsible for the estimate to create a big picture estimate. An analogous estimate may be done for project as a whole, or for selected phases or deliverables. It is not typically used to estimate individual work packages.

For example, if you know that a sales consultant desktop tool project 2 years ago cost $5 million, an analogous estimate for a customer care desktop tool might be $5.2 million, accounting for increased costs of resources or inflation.

It is impossible to find a previous project exactly like your new project (after all if your exact project had been done before, what you are doing now would not be unique, and therefore, would not be a project). If you are lucky, you may find a project that is similar in size and scope, which at least gives you a starting point.

> **NOTE** Analogous estimates have a very low level of accuracy, and can range between −25% and +75% of the actual cost of the project.

Analogous estimating may be the best you can do at an early stage of the project when you have very little detail to go on. The key here is to make sure that everyone involved understands how imprecise this estimate is. "Because of the newness of this project I am using analogous estimating for these cost figures and they do not have a very high accuracy level," you might say.

Parametric Modeling

Parametric modeling uses a mathematical model to compute costs. The type of project you are working on drives whether parametric modeling is an appropriate estimating technique. The most common parametric models are used in the construction industry. Homebuilders typically estimate new home construction based on a parametric model that provides a cost estimate per square foot.

Probably the most widely known parametric model in the IT world is the COnstructive COst MOdel (COCOMO and COCOMO II) for software development, which uses parameters that address the complexity of the software, the capabilities of the team, the processes used to develop the product, and the tools used for development.

Many organizations have developed a parametric model internally; there are also commercial parametric modeling packages available.

Parametric modeling is dependent on the accuracy of the data used to create the model. The most frequent drawback mentioned in relation to parametric models is that a model may not be scalable.

If your organization uses parametric modeling, you need to learn more about the specific models that are used and if this technique is appropriate for your specific project.

If you want to learn more about COCOMO or parametric modeling, there are numerous websites with more information, including the NASA Parametric Cost Estimating Handbook at www.jsc.nasa.gov/bu2/PCEHHTML/pceh.htm or the USC Center for Software Engineering at http://sunset.usc.edu/research/cocomosuite/suite_main.html.

Definitive Estimates

The most precise cost estimating technique is the *definitive estimate*, which assigns a cost estimate to each work package. The definitive cost estimate typically falls between –5% and +10% of the actual budget. The definitive estimate is also referred to as *bottom up estimating*. The WBS and the project resource requirements are critical inputs for a definitive estimate. You start at the lowest level of activity (the bottom of your WBS) and calculate the cost of each low level task. The sum of all these low level estimates provides the estimate of total project cost.

When we discussed schedule planning in Chapter 4, we talked about duration estimates for each task to determine the length of your project. When you are doing cost estimates, you need to base the estimate on *work effort*, which is the total time it would take for a person to complete the task if they did nothing else from the time they started until the task was complete. A work effort estimate is also referred to as a person-hour estimate. As an example, for schedule planning, a task to write the technical requirements document has an activity duration estimate of 4 days. When you do cost planning, if the technical writer is allocating 5 hours a day to the project, the estimate of the total elapsed time the technical writer spends to complete the task gives you a work effort estimate of 20 hours.

The difference between task duration and task work effort may seem confusing, so you need to remember that you are looking at two entirely different outputs. The duration estimates that you complete in schedule planning help you define how long the project will take to complete. The work effort estimates that you obtain in cost planning are used to define how much the project will cost. For purposes of creating a schedule, you need to know that a task will take 2 weeks. For purposes of a cost estimate, you need to know it will take 30 hours.

Let's take a look at how at how this works by adding a work effort estimate to the tasks from our Resource Assignment Matrix. Table 5.2 shows the work effort estimated for each of these activities.

The final piece of data you need for a definitive cost estimate is the rate for each resource. Rates for labor and leased equipment are typically calculated on an hourly or daily rate. Access to a central or shared system may include a per use fee, while the purchase of materials or equipment will have a fixed price.

TABLE 5.2 Sample Project Work Effort Matrix

Task	Resource	Work Effort
A	Tech Writer	20 hours
B	Programmers (2)	100 hours
C	Server	N/A
C	Testers (3)	60 hours
D	Programmers (4)	200 hours
E	Marketing	30 hours

Deciding the correct rate to use for cost estimating can be tricky. For materials or equipment, the current cost of a similar item is probably as accurate as you will get. The largest overall cost for many projects is the human resource or labor cost, and this cost is often the most difficult to estimate. The actual rate that someone will be paid to perform work, even within the same job title, can fluctuate based on education and experience level. Rates vary if you are contracting temporary resources to complete part of the work or using a consultant. Typically, you can get information on either average rates for a given job title or a range of rates. The people doing the individual estimates need to determine which of these ranges is the most accurate based on the complexity of the task. A task requiring an experienced tester may carry a higher rate than another task that requires a tester with less experience.

Table 5.3 shows the rate assigned for each of the resources we will be using in our sample project. For this example, we have used the current market price for the server and a range of employee rates for the tech writer and the testers. We are estimating the programmers at the standard organizational contract rate. A marketing consultant will perform Task E, with the rate estimate provided by marketing.

TABLE 5.3 Sample Project Resource Rates

Task	Resource	Work Effort	Rate
A	Tech Writer	20 hours	$30/hr
B	Programmers (2)	100 hours	$50/hr
C	Server	Fixed rate	$100,000
C	Testers (3)	60 hours	$30/hr

TABLE 5.3 Sample Project Resource Rates *(continued)*

Task	Resource	Work Effort	Rate
D	Programmers (4)	200 hours	$50/hr
E	Marketing	30 hours	$60/hr

Now that you have the resource requirements and associated work effort and rate for each task, you can complete the cost estimate by adding a total column to your table. The cost of each task is calculated by multiplying the work effort for each resource by the rate for that resource. This will give you the total project cost estimate. Table 5.4 shows a completed cost estimate for the tasks in our sample project.

TABLE 5.4 Sample Project Cost Estimate

Task	Resource	Work Effort	Rate	Total Cost
A	Tech Writer	20 hours	$30/hr	$600
B	Programmers	100 hours	$50/hr	$5,000
C	Server	Fixed rate	$100,000	$100,000
C	Testers	60 hours	$30/hr	$1,800
D	Programmer	200 hours	$50/hr	$10,000
E	Marketing	30 hours	$60/hr	$1,800
TOTAL				$119,200

Estimating Tips

Cost estimating can be very complex, and cost estimates often become broadcast as the official cost of the project before you have the proper level of detail. You will probably never have all of the information that you would like when you do cost estimates, but that is the nature of project management. Here are some thoughts to keep in mind as you work through the estimating process.

Brainstorm with your project team. Although looking to the cost of each activity is a great way to get a detailed cost estimate, you may miss items, because they are not linked to a specific task or they span multiple tasks.

Will any of the project team members require special training? If the project involves deployment of software, will there be travel involved or can the installation be done remotely?

Getting the team together to talk about other possible costs is a good way to catch these items.

Communicate the type of estimate you are providing. Project cost estimates get cast in concrete quickly. Although you may not be able to stop this from happening, you can be crystal clear about the type of estimate you are providing.

If you are preparing an analogous estimate based on a similar project, be very clear on how far off it might be from the actual cost of the project. You should point out any significant cost impacting differences between your project and the project used to create the estimate. Any risk or uncertainly caused by using a previous project for estimating also need to be spelled out.

> **TIP**
>
> In addition to emphasizing the potential inaccuracies of an analogous estimate, provide stakeholders with a timeline for a definitive estimate. A project sponsor is more willing to accept that your current estimate may be 75 percent lower than the actual cost of the project if he or she understands both why the current estimate is vague and what work is being done to provide a more accurate estimate.

Make use of any available templates. Many companies have cost-estimating templates or worksheets. Make sure to use these even if they are not required. Looking at all the possible categories of capital and expense is a good checklist to make sure you have included everything in your cost estimates.

Templates may also be a good source of rate estimates. The salary of the people on your project will vary based on both their job title and specific experience. Standard rates may have been developed for cost-estimating purposes. Standard estimating rates are usually based on either the average salary for a particular job title or what is referred to as a *loaded rate*, which includes a percentage of the salary to cover employee benefits such as medical, disability, or pension plans. Individual corporate policies will determine if loaded rates are used for project cost estimates.

> **NOTE**
>
> Some project managers have a term for the exercise of populating a project template with human and material resources (as well as human resource salaries). We call this *resource loading*.

Get estimates from the people doing the work. The reason that a bottom up estimate is the most accurate is that work effort estimates are provided for each work package. This accuracy will not hold up if someone unfamiliar with the task completes the estimate. If your project includes tasks brand new to your company or uses an untested methodology, you may need to

> ### Real World Scenario
>
> **Resource Loading: Where to Start?**
>
> The reason resource loading is so tricky has to do with the fact that people vary so widely in their operational characteristics. Suppose, for example, that you have a team of four programmers. Imagine that your most senior person isn't exactly a self-starter. While he's very competent and knows what to do and when to do it, you have to really work hard to light a fire under him. Conversely, you might have a junior person who's a firecracker. She's constantly at your door looking for the next project. When she's not tied up with project work, she's researching new resource materials or online Webinars to learn more about her craft. Sure she's slow, but she's steady, persistent, and will stick with the task until it's complete. Further, everyone knows that when she finishes a task, she finishes it correctly and it runs well.
>
> Your senior guy makes $85/hour (including benefits), your junior person only $65. Your senior guy (provided you can get him motivated and working straight ahead on his task) can bring in a project anywhere between a day to a week sooner than his junior counterpart, depending on the complexity of the task.
>
> So, if you decide to resource load your projects, what figure should you pick to represent both sides of the equation? Should you key in $85/hour for all programming tasks, $65/hour, or perhaps strike a middle ground at $75/hour and hope it all comes out in the wash?
>
> Note too that some material resources change very little, are used quite often in projects, and thus qualify for resource loading. Consider a T1 data telecommunications circuit. It's a very common thing to link two buildings in a campus together with T1 lines. Generally speaking, the installation cost and monthly charges are well known for a given telco, as well as the time to deliver. By resource loading well-known resources, you can save time in approximating the budget. However, you always need to keep in mind the "sketchiness" factor that the resources bring with them: that is, they're subject to change, people work differently, rates and prices increase, etc.

look outside for assistance with work effort estimates. This could come from published industry standards or by hiring a consultant to assist with the estimating process.

Include money for team recognition.   Every project manager wants to recognize team members who make an outstanding contribution to the project; however, it is difficult to accomplish this without funding. We will talk about the various types of rewards and recognition later in this book, but whether you are looking at team celebration at the end of the project, prizes for outstanding achievement, or cash bonuses, the money needs to come from somewhere. Not all organizations approve an allocation for rewards and recognition, and you may need help from your sponsor to get this approved.

Document any assumptions you have made. If you have identified hourly rates based on internal resources, note that information on the estimate. IT projects often end up using contract labor, which will have a different hourly rate. If there is a decision at a later point in time to use contract resources, you can immediately advise the stakeholders that there will need to be revisions to the budget to account for this new rate.

Now that you have completed all of these cost estimates, they will be used to create the project budget.

Cost Budgeting

All of this resource planning and cost estimating has not resulted in any real money being earmarked for the project. This is because most companies have a formal process within the finance department for allocating funds to projects.

The project manager gathers and summarizes the cost estimates for the project and provides as input into the budgeting process. An approval process turns a project cost estimate from a request for funds to an approved budget. *Cost budgeting* is the process of allocating your approved project funding across the activities, using your cost estimates, your WBS, and the schedule. The total cost of all of the project resources is allocated in the budget across the project timeline, and as your team starts project execution, the actual costs incurred will be tracked against the budgeted estimates.

A project budget is used to communicate what amounts will be spent on categories of resources within a given time period. Most budgets are broken down by month.

Knowing all of the items being charged to your budget is not an easy task, especially if charge codes are assigned to the resources you use. Before you get started with the project work, determine what your departmental procedure is. You need to ask several questions when ascertaining your budgeting structure:

- Are all project expenses submitted to the project manager for approval?
- Does the project manager approve timesheets for project team members?
- Does the project manager receive weekly reports on the labor hours charged to your project?
- Are there categories of cost or amounts that require approval from the sponsor or client?

Getting the answers to these questions before the money is spent will eliminate problems and confusion later in the project.

The tracking of project expenses as they are incurred is not always the responsibility of the project manager. Once the cost estimates have been provided and the project budget established, the actual tracking may end up in a central organization. The finance department may be responsible for tracking all budgets, including the project budgets. Some organizations have a *program management office (PMO)* to oversee all projects and to define project management standards, tools, and templates. The PMO may track all of the project budgets.

Or, as is the case with some organizations, each department has its own finance and budget person who tracks the departmental budget. If you "borrow" a resource from this department for some of the work, likely as not you'll have to work with the budget person for that department to report the time utilized. Generally you'll be given some sort of a resource code against which you'll record this time expenditure. From there the resource code ("cost-center" or other nomenclature) directly translates into dollars again against the departmental budget sheet—something you'll probably never see.

As a project manager it is your responsibility to know where the budget is tracked and what types of reports show the amounts charged to your project. Even if you or a team member does not actually track the budget, you are accountable for how the money is spent and completing the project within budget. Immediate access to any reports on the budget spent to date is a critical tool for the project manager to identify any significant overruns and take corrective action.

> **NOTE** It would not be out of reason to consider a routine (weekly, biweekly) meeting with each budget analyst for the various departments from which you're deriving project funding so that you both are aware of the funds already spent and the amount left. We have found that budget analysts are much more amenable to being told you're short on funding up front rather than being caught near the end with a terrific shortfall.

As you can see, the budgeting process can get very complex. Let's walk through creating a project budget (including some special funding categories), establishing a budget baseline, and setting budget targets for future tracking.

Creating Your Budget

Using your approved cost estimate and your project schedule, you are now ready to create the project budget. But before we get into details about setting up the project budget, let's take a look at two discretionary funds you may see included in a project budget.

Contingency funds and managerial reserves are two types of special funding that some organizations use. These funds are not allocated to all projects. If your company uses either of these budget categories, you will need to learn the policies that dictate both the allocation of these funds and the authority to spend these funds.

Contingency Fund A *contingency fund* is an amount of money set aside and dedicated to the project to be used to cover unforeseen costs within the original scope of the project that were not identified as part of the planning process. There is no set rule for defining the amount of a contingency fund, but organizations that use this allocation often set the contingency find amount at a percentage of the total project cost.

A contingency fund is designed to help reduce risk. Risk planning is covered in Chapter 6, but for now be aware that a project manager should not request a contingency fund just to have extra money. Contingency funds are frequently used in projects that are considered "leading edge." The cost estimates of projects that are breaking new ground are much more likely to be incorrect, because there is no historical data and people may have little experience with activities required.

The project manager typically controls the use of the money allocated to the contingency fund.

Managerial Reserve A *managerial reserve* is an amount set aside by upper management to cover future situations that cannot be predicted. As with the contingency fund, the amount of a managerial reserve is typically based on a percentage of the total project cost.

What makes the managerial reserve different from the contingency fund is who controls the spending of this fund. Upper management usually controls the managerial reserve, and the project manager cannot spend this money without prior approval from upper management.

One other use you may see for managerial reserve is the funding for rewards and recognition.

> The terms *contingency fund* and *managerial reserve* may be considered interchangeable in some organizations.

Project budgets are usually broken down by specific cost categories defined by finance. A few examples of common cost categories include salary, hardware, software, travel, training, and materials.

In some organizations a finance representative or someone from the PMO may develop the project budget or assist you in developing the budget. In other organizations, and particularly in smaller companies, you may be required to set up the budget as one of your responsibilities as project manager. Either way, you need to obtain a copy of your organization's cost categories with a list of the specific cost items included in each category so that you understand how each of your resources is classified.

A budget is typically created in spreadsheet format broken into monthly or quarterly increments.

Let's take our cost estimate figures from Table 5.4 and spread them across a target 3-month schedule. The salary and contract labor dollars are spread across all 3 months based on when the work is scheduled. The bill for the new server will be paid in February. Table 5.5 is a simple budget spreadsheet for our sample project.

TABLE 5.5 Sample Project Budget

	Jan	Feb	Mar	Total
Salary	$600	$900	$2,700	$4,200
Contract Labor	$5,000	$5,000	$5,000	$15,000
Hardware Server		$100,000		$100,000
TOTAL				**$119,200**

It can be difficult to develop an accurate project baseline, as numerous variables can impact when costs are actually recorded. For that reason, some project managers choose to split costs, especially the salary dollars, equally across all of the months. This certainly makes the budgeting process easier, but this approach can cause problems during project execution when the actual expenses are tracked.

The project budget is used to create the cost baseline, which is a tool used during project execution.

Cost Baseline

The completed project budget should be reviewed with the project team. Depending on who actually created the budget, it may be appropriate to have the review conducted by a representative from the finance department(s) or the PMO. The project team needs to understand the critical link between the schedule and the budget. Any questions about either budget categories or how the dollars are spread across the project timeline should be addressed at this time.

Once the budget review with the project team is complete, it is time to create a *cost baseline*, which is a copy of the budget prior to the start of project work. This is very similar to the schedule baseline created in Chapter 3. The cost baseline is used during project execution to track the actual cost of the project against the planning numbers. It is also used to project future costs based on what has been spent to date and the projected cost of the remaining work. The cost baseline includes all of the estimated project costs, excluding any monies that were approved for either a contingency fund or managerial reserve.

The project manager communicates information about the cost baseline to the project stakeholders. Some stakeholders may want a copy of the total project budget baseline, while others may only be interested in what will be spent during each phase. The spending by phase is obtained by setting budget targets.

Budget Targets

Project budgets are normally set up to meet the guidelines of the finance department. Although the budget categories and monthly reporting provide good detail on how and when project dollars are spent, it is not necessarily the only tool or the best tool to manage the project budget.

As project manager, you may need to report on the amount of money spent on a particular phase of the project, so it is a good idea to set targets based on the activities included in each phase. When you get into project execution and actually start tracking both the schedule and the budget, you will need to know that both of these are on track. If you set target amounts of the budget for each phase, you will have a warning sign that your actual spending may not be as on track as it appears on the monthly report. As an example, let's take a standard IT development project using life cycle phases for requirements, design, build, test, and release. You have estimated that $50,000 of your budget will be spent in the requirements phase, and according to the project schedule baseline, that phase will take 4

152 Chapter 5 • Cost Planning

weeks and should complete March 31. When you get the March monthly budget report, it shows that $49,000 was spent, which might make everyone think you are in great shape; you even have a little money to spare. But if your schedule tracking shows that the requirements phase did not complete on March 31 and will probably take another 3 weeks, your project could be in trouble. You have spent the money allocated to complete the requirements phase, but over half the work is not yet done. This is why it is important to set targets or milestones in your budget.

Don't be concerned right now as to what action you should take if you find yourself in this situation. Sometimes after you've created what you think is a solid budget, you find that there are differences in the costs than what you initially planned. These are called "cost variances" and we will discuss them in depth in Chapter 9.

Case Study: Chaptal Wineries—The Budget

To "load" the salaries, and for ease of understanding in this case study, assume that the salary of each individual who works for the winery and is associated with this project is $50/hour. For the purpose of including the benefits percentage, you'll add 40 percent to come up with a total salary figure of $70/hour.

Next you go into Microsoft Project and click View ➤ Resource Sheet to find the place where you can load your salary values (see graphic below). Note that you've already pre-loaded the various resources for this project. "Chaptal Admin" is you. Also included are St. Croix, Fourche, Jay, and Sanchez, whom you'll be relying on to help with this project. Additionally, you are going to need some contractors in each location to help you set up the WAN gear (routers and switches). Ideally, these contractors will be associated with the telecommunications company through which you provision the E1 or T1 circuits, but you may wind up having to use a third party to do the work. In either case, you're budgeting an estimated fee of $225/hour for each contractor, so you've keyed this into the resource sheet as well.

	Resource Name	Type	Initials	Max. Units	Std. Rate	Ovt. Rate	Cost/Use	Accrue At	Base Calendar
1	Chaptal Admin	Work	C	100%	$70.00/hr	$0.00/hr	$0.00	Prorated	Standard
2	St. Croix	Work	S	100%	$70.00/hr	$0.00/hr	$0.00	Prorated	Standard
3	Fourche	Work	F	100%	$70.00/hr	$0.00/hr	$0.00	Prorated	Standard
4	Jay	Work	J	100%	$70.00/hr	$0.00/hr	$0.00	Prorated	Standard
5	Sanchez	Work	S	100%	$70.00/hr	$0.00/hr	$0.00	Prorated	Standard
6	French Contractor	Work	F	100%	$225.00/hr	$0.00/hr	$0.00	Prorated	Standard
7	Australian Contractor	Work	A	100%	$225.00/hr	$0.00/hr	$0.00	Prorated	Standard
8	Chilean Contractor	Work	C	100%	$225.00/hr	$0.00/hr	$0.00	Prorated	Standard
9	Calif. Contractor	Work	C	100%	$225.00/hr	$0.00/hr	$0.00	Prorated	Standard
10	Calif. Web site contra	Work	C	100%	$225.00/hr	$0.00/hr	$0.00	Prorated	Standard
11	All	Work	A	100%	$575.00/hr	$0.00/hr	$0.00	Prorated	Standard
12	French Vendor	Work	F	100%	$125.00/hr	$0.00/hr	$0.00	Prorated	Standard
13	Australian Vendor	Work	A	100%	$200.00/hr	$0.00/hr	$0.00	Prorated	Standard
14	Chilean Vendor	Work	C	100%	$100.00/hr	$0.00/hr	$0.00	Prorated	Standard
15	Calif. Vendor	Work	C	100%	$225.00/hr	$0.00/hr	$0.00	Prorated	Standard

Cost Budgeting

Note that you're using a resource called "All", which means the intranet programmer and each of the Chaptal winery employees (St. Croix, Fourche, et al). at the various sites to do some testing. Because of this, you can just lump together the hourly figures to come up with a $575/hour cost to perform certain testing elements alongside the contractor.

#	Task Name	Resource Names	Duration	Fixed Cost	Total Cost	Baseline	Variance	Actual	Remaining
1	CHAPTAL INT'L EXPANSION		1 day	$0.00	$0.00	$0.00	$0.00	$0.00	$0.00
2	☐ 1.0 Hardware Procurement		0.5 days	$0.00	$100,602.00	$0.00	$100,602.00	$0.00	$100,602.00
3	1.10 Purchase servers	ptal Admin	4 hrs	$78,879.00	$79,124.00	$90,000.00	($10,876.00)	$0.00	$79,124.00
4	1.20 Purchase network gear	ptal Admin	4 hrs	$21,233.00	$21,478.00	$20,000.00	$1,478.00	$0.00	$21,478.00
5	☐ 2.0 WAN connection provision		1 day	$0.00	$10,180.00	$0.00	$10,180.00	$0.00	$10,180.00
6	2.10 E1 circuit/French telco	in,Fourche	8 hrs	$2,000.00	$2,980.00	$2,000.00	$980.00	$0.00	$2,980.00
7	2.20 T1 circuit/Australia telco	Admin,Jay	8 hrs	$1,500.00	$2,480.00	$2,000.00	$480.00	$0.00	$2,480.00
8	2.30 T1 circuit/Chile telco	n,Sanchez	8 hrs	$1,750.00	$2,730.00	$2,000.00	$730.00	$0.00	$2,730.00
9	2.40 T1 circuit/California telco	ptal Admin	8 hrs	$1,500.00	$1,990.00	$2,000.00	($10.00)	$0.00	$1,990.00
10	☐ 3.0 Networking gear installation		4 days	$0.00	$17,200.00	$0.00	$17,200.00	$0.00	$17,200.00
11	3.10 French installation	ch Vendor	32 hrs	$0.00	$4,000.00	$0.00	$4,000.00	$0.00	$4,000.00
12	3.20 So. Australia installation	an Vendor	32 hrs	$0.00	$6,400.00	$0.00	$6,400.00	$0.00	$6,400.00
13	3.30 Chile installation	an Vendor	32 hrs	$0.00	$3,200.00	$0.00	$3,200.00	$0.00	$3,200.00
14	3.40 California installation	lif. Vendor	16 hrs	$0.00	$3,600.00	$0.00	$3,600.00	$0.00	$3,600.00
15	☐ 4.0 Server Installation		8 days	$0.00	$8,720.00	$0.00	$8,720.00	$0.00	$8,720.00
16	4.10 Install France server	ptal Admin	16 hrs	$1,500.00	$2,480.00	$0.00	$2,480.00	$0.00	$2,480.00
17	4.20 Install Australia server	ptal Admin	16 hrs	$2,000.00	$2,980.00	$0.00	$2,980.00	$0.00	$2,980.00
18	4.30 Install Chile server	ptal Admin	16 hrs	$1,300.00	$2,280.00	$0.00	$2,280.00	$0.00	$2,280.00
19	4.40 Install California server	ptal Admin	16 hrs	$0.00	$980.00	$0.00	$980.00	$0.00	$980.00
20	☐ 5.0 Intranet development		14 days	$0.00	$25,200.00	$0.00	$25,200.00	$0.00	$25,200.00
21	6.10 Develop intranet pages	contractor	112 hrs	$0.00	$25,200.00	$0.00	$25,200.00	$0.00	$25,200.00
22	☐ 6.0 Testing		9 days	$0.00	$33,350.00	$0.00	$33,350.00	$0.00	$33,350.00
23	6.10 Unit testing (CA)	contractor	16 hrs	$0.00	$3,600.00	$0.00	$3,600.00	$0.00	$3,600.00
24	6.20 Integration testing (internation	All	40 hrs	$0.00	$21,250.00	$0.00	$21,250.00	$0.00	$21,250.00
25	6.30 User acceptance testing (UA	All	16 hrs	$0.00	$8,500.00	$0.00	$8,500.00	$0.00	$8,500.00
26	☐ 7.0 Training		17 days	$0.00	$8,330.00	$0.00	$8,330.00	$0.00	$8,330.00
27	7.10 Train French (email)	ptal Admin	16 hrs	$0.00	$980.00	$0.00	$980.00	$0.00	$980.00
28	7.20 Train French (intranet)	ptal Admin	24 hrs	$0.00	$1,470.00	$0.00	$1,470.00	$0.00	$1,470.00
29	7.30 Train Australian (email)	ptal Admin	16 hrs	$0.00	$980.00	$0.00	$980.00	$0.00	$980.00
30	7.40 Train Australian (intranet)	ptal Admin	24 hrs	$0.00	$1,470.00	$0.00	$1,470.00	$0.00	$1,470.00
31	7.50 Train Chilean (email)	ptal Admin	16 hrs	$0.00	$980.00	$0.00	$980.00	$0.00	$980.00
32	7.60 Train Chilean (intranet)	ptal Admin	24 hrs	$0.00	$1,470.00	$0.00	$1,470.00	$0.00	$1,470.00
33	7.70 Train California (email)	ptal Admin	8 hrs	$0.00	$490.00	$0.00	$490.00	$0.00	$490.00
34	7.80 Train California (intranet)	ptal Admin	8 hrs	$0.00	$490.00	$0.00	$490.00	$0.00	$490.00

Finally, you budget money to pay the telecommunications vendors working on the actual T1 connectivity (i.e., the demarcation point, testing, validating the circuit, etc.). So key in figures that represent what you think the costs will be for each these individual's hourly rates. You could obtain this information from the actual telecommunications company or use analogous figures obtained from previous projects or colleagues of yours who've recently provisioned telecommunications circuits.

Note that all employees are *exempt* status, meaning they're not eligible for overtime. If you had a person who could obtain overtime (*non-exempt*), you'd have to figure out and key in that value as well. Common situations where this occurs might be with testers, PC technicians, etc.

Next navigate back to the normal project sheet by clicking View ➤ Gantt Chart. In this view, the columns Fixed Cost, Total Cost, Baseline, Variance, Actual, and Remaining are added. Also in this view you'll see the Resource Names and the Duration that each of the tasks is estimated to take.

> Note that Microsoft Project generally uses a bottom up budget, which means that you don't necessarily know the pot of money you have, you're instead relying on the combination of costs the project will incur plus the estimated hours for each of the tasks in order to arrive at a project budget. Top down budgeting will be a little harder to manage because you're given a pot of money and told to make the project's deliverables come about within those confines. Unless the pot is huge, you have to be very careful to delineate tasks and durations precisely and to clearly understand all facets of the project's requirements so you don't make a false step that costs you (potentially the project). Sometimes companies will use top down budgeting when they're inventing a new service or product and they have a certain profit margin that they need to meet—they cannot exceed that potential for profit with a costly project!
>
> Note that, looking at the graphic above, by keying in the salary figures, Project looks at the hours entered for a given task and calculates the cost of that task. This *does not* account for other costs that might need to be entered in (such as the cost of hardware, per diem and travel expenses, etc.) Also note that you have baseline column in which you can type in your initial expectations (derived from quality estimating techniques) and Project will show you how far away from baseline each of the tasks were. It also tallies the major task subtotals and the total of the project for you.
>
> If you had a contingency pot, you might opt to manage it as a resource within Project or choose to simply keep track of the contingency fund as a separate pot of money that you can draw on in an emergency. Realize that just because there's a contingency fund out there doesn't mean you can loosely manage your project because you have a safety net hanging out there. The fund is there for unforeseen circumstances. Your manager will still be watching you closely to see how well you estimate and how effectively you can bring in a project on time and under budget. Too many times drawing from a contingency fund will get you a reputation for not managing projects very well!

Using Project Management Software

Just as was the case with developing a project schedule, the cost estimates and project budget can also be developed using a project management software package.

Microsoft Project, as an example, has a resource sheet. This view allows the user to enter all of the people, equipment, and materials associated with a project. For each resource there is a column to enter data such as the number of resources, the rate for the resource, overtime rates, a cost per use for the resource, or a fixed rate. Resources can be assigned to each project task, and the software will calculate the total costs based on the data from the resource sheet. Resources can be assigned to multiple tasks, but the cost-related data is only entered once. Microsoft Project can also be linked to data in Excel spreadsheets to avoid duplicate entries.

Using project management software, you can establish both a schedule and a budget baseline to use for tracking purposes during project execution. Most software packages have multiple reports in which you can display the cost data, including a standard budget view, costs per task, and cost per resource. We will talk more about how you use this data when we get into project execution and project control.

> **NOTE:** While covered in Chapter 4, we cannot emphasize enough the importance of understanding both the concepts behind project management software and the details of how your specific package works. Formal training on the package is the best solution, but if that is not possible, find someone with experience who can act as a mentor and assist you in understanding the fundamentals. A project management software package is only effective if the person using this tool understands how to both properly input data and interpret results.

Summary

Dealing with costs, while not the most exciting portion of project management, is certainly one of the most interesting to the sponsor and doubtless to a great majority of your stakeholders. Although you may find cost planning tedious, having an accurate cost estimate will make life a whole lot easier when you start project execution.

Cost planning includes all of the processes to identify what you need to complete the project and what the costs will be. Resource planning is the process of determining what resources you need on your project and the quantity of each resource. Resources include people, equipment, and materials. Cost estimating is the process of determining what you will spend on the work required to complete your project. The accuracy of a cost estimate can vary depending on the type of estimate you are using.

Numerous techniques are used to create project estimates. Analogous or top down estimates use expert judgment and historical data to provide a high level estimate for the entire project or a phase or deliverable. Parametric modeling uses a mathematical model to create the estimates. The definitive method creates the project estimate by adding up individual estimates from each work package.

Cost budgeting takes the cost estimates and allocates them across the project schedule. A cost baseline is produced to use for forecasting and tracking.

Exam Essentials

Know the three types of resources used on a project.   A project needs human resources, equipment, and materials.

Understand how to create a Responsibility Assignment Matrix.   Match each project activity with the appropriate resource from the resource pool. Determine if more than one of these resources is required. Continue the process until resources have been assigned to all of the tasks.

Understand the different types of resource rates and how they are used.   A time-based rate such as an hourly or daily rate is used for labor resources or leased equipment. A per use rate applies to any resource the project incurs a charge from based on usage such as access to a centralized database. A fixed rate applies to the purchase of materials or equipment such as a new server.

Know the difference between analogous, parametric modeling, and definitive estimating techniques. Analogous or top down estimates use expert judgment and historical data to provide a high level estimate for the entire project. Parametric modeling uses a mathematical model to create the estimates. The bottom up method starts at the lowest level of activity on the WBS and calculates the cost of each item to obtain the total cost.

Know the discretionary funding allocations a project may receive. The two types of discretionary funding are a contingency fund and a managerial reserve.

Explain the purpose of a cost baseline. A cost baseline is created to allow for tracking and comparison of actual costs to the original estimates and to project future costs. It includes all of the estimated project costs except for any contingency fund or managerial reserve.

Understand how, why, and when you'd use resource loading in a project plan. Not all resources can be pre-loaded into the project plan. There's also the difficulty associated with salaries and benefits coupled with worker styles.

Understand your company's financing model. Companies have drastically different methods of tracking funds for projects. Some companies allow the PMO to manage its funding; others require that the departmental finance officer handle it; still others require that a centralized finance office manage everything. Then there's the whole thing of understanding corporate cost-centers (i.e., accounting codes for different sections where money is allocated and spent).

Key Terms

Before you take the exam, be certain you are familiar with the following terms:

analogous estimate	managerial reserve
bottom up estimating	materials
contingency fund	parametric modeling
cost baseline	resource planning
cost budgeting	resource pool description
cost estimating	resource requirements
definitive estimate	Responsibility Assignment Matrix (RAM)
equipment	work effort
human resources	
loaded rate	

Review Questions

1. Which of the following are types of resources you must consider when planning your project? Select the best answer.
   A. Technical staff, non-technical staff, and contractors
   B. Human resources, servers, and workstations
   C. Human resources, equipment, and materials
   D. None of the above

2. Name the table that matches the project work packages with the required resources.
   A. Responsibility Assignment Matrix
   B. Resource requirements document
   C. Cost estimate
   D. Budget baseline

3. You are asked to prepare an estimate for a project business case to install a new server group. There is very little detail about this project. What will you use to compute your estimate?
   A. The price the client is willing to pay
   B. A sophisticated modeling technique
   C. The estimate provided by the project sponsor
   D. The actual cost of a similar project

4. Which of the following is *not* one of the cost planning processes?
   A. Cost estimating
   B. Cost control
   C. Resource planning
   D. Cost budgeting

5. A work effort estimate is used to develop
   A. Responsibility Assignment Matrix
   B. Cost estimates
   C. Schedule estimates
   D. All of the above

6. A discretionary fund used by the project manager to cover unforeseen costs within the original project scope is a
   A. Managerial reserve
   B. Parametric model
   C. Contingency fund
   D. Cost baseline

7. You are developing a definitive budget estimate. Which of the following would be the MOST important input to complete this task?

   A. Historic data from a similar project
   B. A list of the budget category items used by finance
   C. The project WBS
   D. The project scope statement

8. Which of the following is a tool for developing the project resource requirements during the resource planning process?

   A. Organization chart
   B. Resource Assignment Matrix
   C. WBS
   D. None of the above

9. What is the most accurate estimate?

   A. Analogous estimate
   B. Definitive estimate
   C. Top down estimate
   D. A and C

10. You are asked to present and explain your project cost baseline. All of the following are true except:

    A. The baseline will be used to track against actual spending.
    B. The baseline can be used to project future project costs.
    C. The baseline includes a contingency fund and a managerial reserve.
    D. The baseline is the estimate prior to the start of project execution of what the project will spend.

11. You're the project manager for a large IT project. At the time you performed your cost estimates, the license structure for some of the software you're going to use was based on a license fee plus a maintenance fee for a specified number of years (e.g., a license fee of $500 plus a 3-year maintenance fee of $2,750). The company has now changed their licensing paradigm to a "software assurance" (SA) model in which you purchase a license at a particular (much higher) fee and are guaranteed upgrades for a specified period of time. If you opt to purchase a non-SA license, you must purchase another license as soon as an upgrade comes out—provided, that is, that you desire to upgrade the software as new editions come out. If you choose not to pay the upgrade license fee, and continue on with the existing software version it will fall behind year after year to the point where it will not be possible to upgrade the software. You may actually have to launch another project at that time to meet the expectations of new version releases. What should you do?

    A. Do nothing. You've got the license purchases accounted for; upgrades are someone else's problem. Update the sponsor.

    B. Determine the cost variance between the current structure versus the new SA structure. Update the sponsor.

    C. Switch to the SA structure. Update the sponsor.

    D. Let the sponsor decide what to do.

12. Suppose that you're the leader of a project management office. You want to baseline any new projects with the salaries that different staff members make. What is this called?

    A. Resource loading

    B. Baseline loading

    C. Resource scheduling

    D. Resource sheet

13. You're using the estimating technique in which you look at previous projects similar to the one you're currently working on in order to figure out what some of the tasks will cost. What is this estimating technique called?

    A. Baseline estimating

    B. Legacy estimating

    C. Analogous estimating

    D. Proficiency estimating

14. You are considering the total time it would take for a person to complete the task if they did nothing else from the time they started until the task was complete. What is this called?

    A. Work hours

    B. Work effort

    C. Work planning

    D. Work substance

15. When you're engaged in the process of allocating the money you've been given for a project to specific categories, you are said to be in the process of doing what?

    A. Cost budgeting

    B. Resource allocation

    C. Cost estimating

    D. Finance management

16. Your programming team is embarking on their first ever intranet development project. The developers have identified Microsoft Visual Studio as the development environment they want to use for this project. Which type of resource is this considered to be?

    A. Human

    B. Material

    C. Equipment

    D. It's not a project resource.

17. Who is responsible for approving the project budget?

    A. Project manager

    B. Project team

    C. Project sponsor

    D. Member of executive staff

18. Who is responsible for estimating the amount of money that a given task will cost, in terms of human, material, and equipment resources?

    A. Project manager

    B. Project team

    C. Project sponsor

    D. Member of the executive staff

19. The *work effort* times the ____ will bring about the *total cost* of each task.

    A. Duration

    B. +/–75% leeway

    C. Rate

    D. Number of people

20. In order to accurately define the resources required for your project, you need three things. What are they?
    A. Understanding of the three types of project resources
    B. Scope statement
    C. Project sponsor buy-in
    D. Stakeholder OK
    E. Work breakdown structure (WBS)
    F. Contingency fund

Answers to Review Questions

1. **C.** The three types of resources used in project planning are human resources, equipment, and materials. Technical staff, non-technical staff, and contractors are categories of human resources. Servers and workstations are both categories of equipment.

2. **A.** A Responsibility Assignment Matrix combines the tasks from the WBS with the project resources. The output of completing a RAM is the resource requirements. A cost estimate is obtained by calculating the work effort associated with each resource on the Responsibility Assignment Matrix. A budget baseline is the allocation of the total cost of the project prior to the start of project execution.

3. **D.** In this situation you would do an analogous estimate, which is based on historical data from a similar project and expert judgment. You would look up cost data on the most recent server installation project.

4. **B.** The cost planning processes are resource planning, cost estimating, and cost budgeting. Cost control is one of the controlling processes that will be discussed in Chapter 9.

5. **B.** A work effort estimate or person-hour estimate is used to develop the cost estimates. A Resource Assignment Matrix is completed prior to the cost estimating process by matching the project tasks with the resources required to complete the work. Schedule estimates calculate the total amount of elapsed time it will take to reach project completion. Project schedules are based on duration estimates, such as the number of work days or weeks required to complete a task.

6. **C.** A contingency fund is an amount allocated under the control of the project manager to cover unforeseen costs. A managerial reserve is under the control of upper management. A parametric model is a mathematical model used to estimate costs. The cost baseline is the amount of the budget before the actual work on the project starts. This is used to track what is actually spent against the original estimate.

7. **C.** The project WBS provides a list of the project activities requiring work effort estimates to produce the overall project definitive estimate. Historical data from a similar project is used primarily for analogous estimates. The budget category list is a useful tool in resource planning to use as a checklist that all resources have been identified. The project scope statement does not contain the activity level detail found in the WBS.

8. **B.** A Resource Assignment Matrix is one of the tools used to create the resource requirements. It displays the type and quantity of resources needed to complete each task.

9. **B.** A definitive estimate is the most accurate, typically falling within −5% and +10% of the actual project cost. This estimate is based on estimating the cost of the resources for each of the project tasks. An analogous estimate (also referred to as a top down estimate) is the least accurate. It is based on historical cost data from a similar project.

10. C. If the project includes a contingency fund or a managerial reserve, these amounts are not included in a project cost baseline. The baseline only includes the estimated cost of the actual project work. The project baseline is used to compare the actual project costs against the projected costs. A baseline can be used as a tool to project future costs by adding the estimate of remaining project work to the total dollars spent to date.

11. B. You need to determine the difference in cost, whether up or down, that you're looking at with the change. If additional money is involved, you'll need to communicate it to the sponsor so that approvals and additional monies can be allocated. If the licensing variance saves money, the sponsor needs to know about it as well.

12. A. Resource loading is the process of entering in resource costs for bottom up budgeting purposes.

13. C. When you examine previous projects in order to derive cost estimates for a current one, you're utilizing analogous cost estimating.

14. B. Work effort is the total amount of time it will take an individual to complete a task.

15. A. Cost budgeting is the process of putting allocated funds into the various categories you have pinpointed to bring about the deliverables of the project.

16. B. Visual Studio, in this case, is a material resource because it wasn't in use prior to this project and we don't know if it will be from here on out. The salient point here is that the software is needed for this project to create the project deliverables.

17. C. Recall that the sponsor is the one who's empowered to expend the resources required to create the deliverables of the project. Hence, he or she is the one who'll approve the budget.

18. A. Ultimately, it is up to the project manager to make the final decision about the cost estimates for the various tasks. However, he or she may well delegate this responsibility to knowledgeable team members who are best equipped to provide estimates for given tasks, or, lacking project team members, he or she might solicit assistance from experts in the various task areas.

19. C. The rate that is established for a given resource times the work effort (usually expressed in hours) will yield the total cost of the task.

20. A, B, E. You need to know what three types of project resources you might be dealing with (so you understand what categories each task may require). You also need the scope statement so you understand the underlying framework of the project as well as the WBS, which details the tasks involved.

Chapter 6

Other Planning Processes

THE COMPTIA IT PROJECT+ EXAM TOPICS COVERED IN THIS CHAPTER INCLUDE:

- ✓ 1.9 Given a proposed scope definition and based on the scope components, assess the feasibility of the project and the viability of a given project component against a predetermined list of constraints.
- ✓ 2.4 Given a team-building scenario, including a scope definition and work breakdown structure (WBS), identify selection criteria for particular team members. Demonstrate the ability to ask interview questions that will assist the team selection process.
- ✓ 2.19 Demonstrate the ability to identify project team organization roles and responsibilities required for the execution of the project.
- ✓ 2.22 Demonstrate an understanding of the components of a project quality management plan (e.g., measured quality checkpoints, assignments for architectural control, systems test, and unit tests, user sign-off, etc.).
- ✓ 2.23 Demonstrate the skills to develop a quality plan.
- ✓ 2.24 Demonstrate the ability to perform risk assessment and mitigation (given a scenario including the appropriate project documentation).
- ✓ 2.25 Demonstrate the ability to create a project communications plan that clearly indicates what needs to be communicated during a project, to whom, when, and how (using formal and informal approaches).
- ✓ 2.31 Be able to secure staffing commitments and resolve staffing issues.
- ✓ 3.21 Recognize the relevance of the organization's quality policy to project quality.

It might appear that we should be done with planning and ready to move into project execution. We have planned our scope, cost, and schedule. What more could there be?

Although scope, schedule, and cost are the foundation of project planning, several other components of project management need to be addressed in the planning process. For instance, human resources planning means deciding how to staff your project—acquiring the people you need to complete the project. Quality planning involves setting the project quality standards. It includes determining what quality variables you will measure and how you will measure them. Risk planning identifies possible risks to your project, quantifies the magnitude and probability of these risks, and defines how to respond if the risk occurs. Communications planning is necessary to identify what people or groups will need information about your project and how you will provide information. Finally, procurement planning becomes necessary if you will be purchasing goods or services for your project from outside vendors. It covers defining a statement of work and vendor selection criteria, as well as the various types of contracts. We'll discuss all of these planning methods in this chapter.

Human Resources Planning

In Chapter 5 we covered resource planning as a process to identify the costs of your project. At that point, we identified human resources primarily by job title; we did not have actual people matched to each deliverable. Before work can actually begin on the project, you need to replace the generic job title requirements you identified with the names of real people. You also need to address how you will organize and manage your team through the completion of the project.

Human resources planning includes defining team member roles and responsibilities, establishing an appropriate structure for team reporting, securing the right team members, and bringing them on the project as needed for the appropriate length of time. Human resources planning results are achieved through the development of an organization plan coupled with the acquisition of the staff necessary to complete the project.

Organizational Planning

Managing a group of people to complete a unique product within a limited time frame can be very challenging. Each team member needs to have a clear picture of their role on the team and what they are accountable for.

Real World Scenario

Building a Rocket Using a Geographically Dispersed Team

Recently one of us took a college class in organizing technical projects. The instructor for that class had as his day job a position as a senior systems analyst for a large aerospace contracting firm. Let's call this instructor "Jim," so we have a common reference name.

Jim's entire premise for the class was that it's very difficult to put together a group of people—especially highly specialized aerospace engineers—some of whom live in California, others overseas, still others in Colorado, and so forth to design, build, assemble, and deploy a rocket. Basically, his points were limited but salient:

- You have to *really* understand the project thoroughly. All team members have to be clear about what it is you're building. There can be no question about vision.

- With big projects you use the "eat an elephant one bite at a time" principle, breaking the project into manageable chunks and grouping the team members together that pertain to the chunk you're interested in talking about today.

- There is a center point to all projects. You can't, for example, design the fuselage first, *then* design an engine to fit around it. All components of a rocket project center on the engine itself. Thus, the engine is a well-known, well-understood quantity—the rest of the parts are designed around it. We believe this is probably true for the vast majority of IT projects.

- In the case of geographically dispersed teams, you simply don't have the funding to fly everyone around the country so they can get together to work on the project (though this happened for Jim's teams at very critical junctures in a project's stage). Jim and his teams rely heavily on online collaboration, using software, audio equipment, and cameras to bring people together over the Internet in order to discuss drawings, design characteristics, and other components of the project. So important to Jim was this topic that the majority of our class time, he talked about the miracle that is online collaboration.

- You don't necessarily need to be afraid of geographic boundaries when assembling people whose skills you need. A little thinking outside the box might lead to a well-formed albeit nonlocal team. That being said, you, the project manager, are the final arbiter of what will and what will not work for a given project.

Moreover, the primary takeaway from the class was that projects—IT or otherwise—of massive proportions are being worked on every day. The power of the Internet has greatly impacted the speed with which team members can communicate and bring their projects to fruition.

Additionally, team members and the other project stakeholders need to understand how the team will be organized. If you have a small 8-person colocated IT team, the team reporting structure will look very different than if you have a team of 150 that is spread across six different organizations in four cities.

Other potential constraints may impact your project staffing. These include labor union agreements, organizational policies, team preferences, and team member knowledge.

Organizational planning is the process of addressing interfaces that may impact how you manage your project team, defining roles and responsibilities for project team members, identifying how your project team will be organized, and documenting your staffing management plan.

Project Interfaces

You need to consider various interfaces as part of your organizational planning, as they may impact both the selection of project team members and how the team is managed.

Organizational interfaces   Organizational interfaces are the relationships that must be managed when a project spans multiple departments. The way you structure your team meetings, how you provide feedback to team members, and how you communicate status are a few of the areas that may be managed differently if you are managing a cross-functional project.

Technical interfaces   Technical interfaces drive how the technical work of the project gets done. The people developing a new software application that interfaces with existing systems must understand application interfaces as well as the operating platform on which the new application will reside.

Interpersonal interfaces   Interpersonal interfaces are the reporting relationships between the people working on the project. In an ideal world, everyone gets along with no conflicts or disputes; in the real world, a project manager needs to be prepared to deal with differences between team members. Knowledge of previous conflicts may even impact the team member selection process.

A key input to organizational planning is the documentation produced from defining your resource requirements during the resource planning process you went through as part of cost estimating that was discussed in Chapter 5. The Resource Assignment Matrix (RAM) or other documentation from resource planning can be used to start your documentation of roles and responsibilities.

> ### Integrated Systems: The "We Can't Figure Out Why It Didn't Work" Project
>
> The above reference regarding technical interfaces is associated with implicit and subtle nuances. It's easy for company executives to say something like this: "You know, we currently have this XYZ system and, while we think it's wonderful—it does all of our company's billing—it really needs to be augmented with a newer, friendlier look for the intranet as well as the Internet. Surely the technology you bring to this project can hook to the current system to do this!?!"
>
> Well, the answer is yes, sort-of, probably, maybe, and no. When we begin to talk about applying new technology to an existing system, *or* bringing two or more totally different systems together, we're talking about integrated systems.

Our experience has been that it's remarkably easy for companies such as Microsoft to advertise a snappy new way to interface with an existing system in order to extract information from it for a totally new form of processing. However, the proof's in the pudding, as they say, and putting an integrated system together is much more difficult in practice than in theory.

Consider a mainframe system running Adabas and Natural (a well-known mainframe database and programming interface, respectively). The system has run successfully for 25+ years and though it's efficient, it has run its technological course. Users are tired of the "green screen" look of the mainframe, and mainframe programmers have run out of ways to make it do what needs to be done for today's billing environment (specifically Internet queries). You're now charged with a project to bring about an application server interface that allows you to extract the data from this system, render it in XML pages, and thrust it out to the intranet for your customer service folks, your Interactive Voice Response (IVR) system for customers who call in, and the Internet for your more progressive customers seeking assistance via the Web.

Where to start? All of your techies say the words "application server" simultaneously as though it's clear this is the magic box that's required. But is anyone aware of the complexity involved here? Is anyone in the company prepared for such an undertaking? Microsoft BizTalk, BEA WebLogic, JBoss, and other such application server software (not to mention Internet interfaces for the mainframe such as IBM WebSphere) could potentially bring about the magic required—but does anyone possess the wand? These application packages are something that a project manager shouldn't just willy-nilly bring into play without first understanding what's required to maintain such a deployment and assessing how much of a corporately internal intellectual grasp there is of such software. After all, you don't want to deploy a project for your company that's going to have to be staffed full-time by expensive contractors. And though it may be acceptable to ask for full-time employees (FTE) trained to handle the care and feeding of such an animal, chances are the first time you say FTE in front of the sponsor you might find your project killed. (It's almost like an allergic reaction with some executives.)

Our point here isn't that you should *never* venture into integrated systems land, but that you should go there with your eyes open. Do not imagine (or let vendors tell you) that it will be easy to connect two disparate applications. It won't be. You'll run into issues that you hadn't counted on—running the gamut from simple things like workstation connectivity to ghostly apparitions taking on the form of mysterious disconnections between the two systems. Not to mention the whole issue of representing the system out on the Demilitarized Zone (DMZ–that area between the Internet and the private internal network where IT shops often put their Web and other servers) to Internet users and all of the assorted security concerns that go along with that idea.

As a wise project manager you'll doubtless interview those who've gone before you in an attempt to figure out what the pitfalls are for the proposed deployment.

Roles and Responsibilities

A roles and responsibilities document lists each group or individual team member on the project and their responsibilities. You have a portion of what you need to document roles and responsibilities if you assigned resources to each task in the schedule or created a RAM to match the activities to the resource doing the work.

But roles and responsibilities of project team members are more than just the assigned tasks. There are standards and methodologies to be adhered to, documentation to be completed, and time reporting responsibilities, to name a few. So in addition to assigning people to tasks, it is a good idea to develop a template to document roles and responsibilities beyond just the task assignment. The more clarity around who is responsible for what, the better.

Roles and Responsibilities Example

Every team member should have clearly documented roles and responsibilities. That includes the project manager; so let's take a look at how you might define the roles and responsibilities for the project manager on the voice-activated dialing project.

Title: Project Manager

Role: Lead the project management activities associated with the launch of voice-activated dialing.

Primary Responsibilities: The project manager may perform some or all of the following:

- Identify any departmental project management standards.
- Lead team in all aspects of project planning.
- Manage the project team in the execution of the project work.
- Develop schedule and maintain updates on a weekly basis.
- Run weekly project team status meeting.
- Track, assign, and report progress on any project issues.
- Track implementation of contingency or mitigation plans.
- Provide a weekly status of critical issues to project sponsor and key stakeholders.
- Prepare and present a formal monthly project status for the stakeholders.

Similar documentation should be developed for each project team member. This document not only clarifies for each team member what he or she will be held accountable for, but can also be used to communicate team member accountabilities with the sponsor, functional managers, or other stakeholders.

Many teams often include the project sponsor in the roles and responsibilities documentation. This can be a good way of confirming joint understanding between the sponsor and the project manager as to when and how the sponsor will be involved in the project work.

Roles and responsibilities can be documented in a variety of ways—bulleted lists, tables, or paragraph format, to name a few. Check for any templates available in your organization or use the format that seems most appropriate for your team.

> **TIP** Whatever format you choose, the intent is to be as clear and precise as possible in defining the key areas of accountability for each team member.

> **TIP** Roles and responsibilities may change over the course of the project, so be sure to update this document as needed.

The development of project roles and responsibilities is a good time to clarify the project manager's authority with the project sponsor, especially if the project charter was vague or did not include this information. The project manager's authority can be formally documented in the roles and responsibilities, or it may be an informal agreement where the sponsor delegates some of his or her authority to the project manager. Any authority surrounding hiring and firing decisions or the spending of the project budget should be documented.

Project Organization Chart

It is always a good idea to develop a project organization chart; not only does it provide a snapshot of who is working on the project, it also shows the reporting structure. Depending on the complexity of your project and the number of people involved, there may be multiple reporting levels.

In a small centrally located project team, all team members may report directly to the project manager. However, for an 85-person team working on a large application development project spanning multiple organizations, the structure will typically have many team members report to someone other than the project manager. Large, complex projects often establish project team lead positions. The project team lead is accountable for either the people assigned to a particular phase such as development or testing or for the team members from a specific department such as sales, training, IT, or network. A sample project organization chart using the team lead concept is shown in Figure 6.1.

Staffing Management Plan

The staffing management plan is a document where you pull all of your staffing data together. The *staffing management plan* documents when and how human resources will be added to and released from the project team and what they will be working on while they are part of the team. Adding and releasing resources may be an informal or a formal process, depending on your organization. Make sure you are familiar with any corporate human resources policies that may impact how you release team members from the project. This is particularly important if any of your team members are covered by a collective bargaining agreement (union). Very specific rules regarding both advance notification and the specific process may be used to move these people on and off a project.

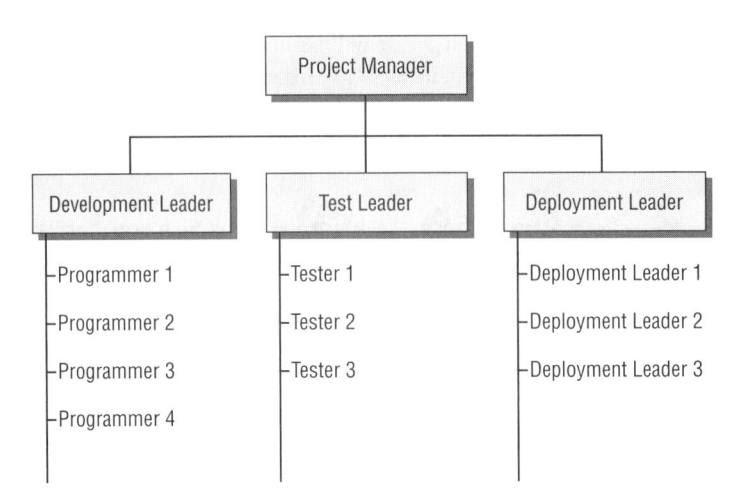

FIGURE 6.1 Project Organization Chart

```
                        Project Manager
                              |
        ┌─────────────────────┼─────────────────────┐
  Development Leader     Test Leader         Deployment Leader
   ─Programmer 1         ─Tester 1           ─Deployment Leader 1
   ─Programmer 2         ─Tester 2           ─Deployment Leader 2
   ─Programmer 3         ─Tester 3           ─Deployment Leader 3
   ─Programmer 4
```

If your project involves complex interfaces, be they organizational, technical, or interpersonal, document how you plan to manage these interfaces. If all software development testing must be assigned to a specific work group, this requirement should be identified. If your team spans multiple cities or crosses multiple departments, you need to document plans to manage these circumstances.

The team member roles and responsibilities and the project organization chart also become a part of the staffing management plan to make this a cohesive, comprehensive document covering all aspects of managing your team.

Staffing management plans can be high level or very detailed, so it is a good idea to see if your organization has any project staffing management standards or templates.

> **TIP** You need to be comfortable that your staffing management plan provides you the blueprint you need to manage the human resources assigned to your project.

Now that you have a plan for managing the staff, it is time to staff your project.

Staff Acquisition

In the *staff acquisition process* you finally get people assigned to the project. During this process you will put to use some of the general management skills we discussed in Chapter 1.

How the project manager actually goes about obtaining project team members and the amount of project manager involvement in the decision making process for staff assignments varies across organizations. In the best case scenario, the project manager interviews candidates for project team positions and has full authority to select the team members; however, in many organizations, project managers must negotiate with the functional managers providing the resources.

Interviewing Potential Team Members

The control a project manager has over the selection of project team members varies with the type of organization structure and the policies associated with project staffing. If you are in a strong matrix or projectized organization there is more opportunity to impact the decision of who will be included on the team. If you will be interviewing candidates for any of the positions on your team, you need to be prepared with the questions you will ask and the factors that you will use to make your decision. When preparing for an interview, you should make sure to cover several areas.

Skill level:

- Does the person have the training and experience to complete the tasks?
- Does the experience level of the candidate match what is required to complete the tasks?

Project experience:

- Does the person have previous experience working on a project team?
- What types of projects has the candidate worked on?
- What were the candidate's previous project responsibilities?

Interpersonal skills:

- Does the person demonstrate the ability to be a team player?
- Does the candidate have strong written and oral communication skills?
- What are the candidate's strengths and weaknesses?

This is a starting point. Based on the specifics of your project, you can add other areas to this list.

> **NOTE** You may find yourself on a project where at least part of the staff is preassigned, if the staff has been defined in the project charter.

> **TIP** The purpose of an interview is to determine the best person for the job. Preparation is the key to conducting a successful interview. Have a list of written questions that you want to ask each candidate and take notes as you conduct each interview. There are laws governing the personal information that can be requested from job applicants. If you do not have experience interviewing job candidates, you should find a mentor to assist you or obtain a template or checklist from your human resources department.

Negotiating with Functional Managers

In a more traditional organization structure, you will need to negotiate with functional managers to obtain your project staff. You may or may not have an opportunity to interview potential candidates, depending on how staffing is handled within your organization. But even if you interview candidates, you will need to work through the functional manager to finalize project staffing decisions.

> **Not a Big Field to Choose From**
>
> Suppose that you're a project manager in the middle of staffing a new software development project. You don't have a large field of developers from which to choose. The senior-level developers are engaged and are using the juniors from time to time for coding assistance. You're going to have to pick from a field of one or two junior-level developers who you've been told are available for your project.
>
> Picking a junior-level developer isn't necessarily a bad thing, it's just that you will need to augment the development time required to compensate for the "junior-ness" of your programmer. He or she can probably do the job, just not as quickly as the senior who has "been there, done that." Skill level and experience will drive task durations out and hence affect the bottom line of the project's due date.
>
> If the project has a hard due date—that is, the sponsor says it *must* be done by such and such a date—then you're faced with working your junior overtime, or telling the sponsor that you need to free up senior-level resources to meet the deadline or you employ the techniques of crashing and fast-tracking.

The functional manager will determine whether resources are available on a full-time or a part-time basis. If you are acquiring people who are assigned to additional projects or other staff work, you must establish a clear understanding as to the numbers of hours each person is dedicated to your project.

In a matrix organization, where the project team members will have multiple bosses (the functional manager and at least one project manager), it is essential to clarify and obtain agreement on the team member accountability. A team member should only be accountable to one person for a given result.

Performance assessment is another topic to be discussed at the time resources are obtained. Your organization may have a formal policy that includes input from the project manager as part of the process, or you may need to reach an agreement with each functional manager as to how you will provide feedback into the performance appraisal process.

As the project manager, you should initiate a meeting with each impacted functional manager to discuss your staffing needs and come to agreement on who will be assigned to your project. Functional managers often have very large teams and are constantly fielding requests to provide staffing resources to project teams. You need to come into the meeting prepared to identify your needs and have a game plan to negotiate with the functional manager. Here are some suggestions to help make this process smoother:

Schedule a separate meeting with each functional manager. Unless your organization has a formal staff allocation process involving all project managers and all impacted functional managers, meet individually with each functional manager so that you can focus on the project needs from that specific area and make the best use of the functional manager's time. When scheduling a meeting, be clear on the purpose, allow adequate time to work through any issues, and hold the meeting in a workroom or private office. Do not try to complete the staff negotiation process in the hall or on the elevator.

Identify who would be part of your "dream team." Do your homework and become familiar with the people who report to each functional manager. Use your staffing management plan, your roles and responsibilities matrix, any documented information regarding the experience and qualification of available resources, and previous work experience with potential team members to pencil out a list of who you would bring to the team if the decision were in your hands.

Plan who you will request from each functional manager. If you want specific people on your team or you require people with a specific experience level, explain to the functional manager who you want and the reason behind your request. Let's face it; every project manager wants the best people, so you will need to make your case. Be prepared to provide a brief overview of your project, its strategic importance, and the importance of the resource(s) coming from this functional area.

Have a backup plan if you cannot obtain the resources you want, and be prepared to negotiate.

Request your most critical resources first. It is very unlikely that you will get everyone you ask for. Certain people may already be committed to other projects or the timing of your request may conflict with critical functional activities. You need to prioritize your staffing needs. Understand which activities are the most complex, are on the critical path, and have the highest risk potential. These activities are the areas where you want to make sure you have the best people. Work through getting these areas assigned first. You have more flexibility to agree to a different resource or accept the person assigned by the functional manager for activities that are less complex or have float time.

Following these steps may not always get you the team members you want, but it will help establish your credibility with the functional managers if you handle your requests in a professional manner. Whatever the outcome of a particular meeting, maintain a good business relationship with the functional managers; you will be back to see them again for future projects.

Other Staffing Scenarios

In some situations you may not be able to negotiate for staff. Only one person may be available with the skill set required. The project sponsor may assign some of the project team members, or the client or other executive stakeholder may request certain team members. Assignments made without your input may be good choices or bad choices. If you choose to challenge one of these assignments, make sure you are doing so based on hard facts such as the lack of the required technical skills. Unless the person simply is not qualified to do the work, you will probably have to live with this decision and make the best of it.

One last staffing scenario involves procuring resources from an outside supplier. Contract workers may be brought in if no internal resources are available for a time-critical project or if internal resources do not have the required skill set. Procurement planning is discussed later in this chapter.

Quality Planning

When we do a project assessment, one of the items we ask to see is the quality plan. In our experience, the quality plan is one of the most frequently ignored areas in the overall project plan. People sometimes just assume that since the team wants to produce a high-quality product, it will happen. But if you just assume that the quality is there, you may be in for some unpleasant surprises. Not everyone defines quality in the same fashion. If you have not defined your approach to quality up front, how can you determine the level of quality in your finished product? *Quality planning* is the process of identifying quality standards that are applicable to your project and deciding how your project will meet these standards.

Numerous articles and books have been written on the subject of quality. You may be familiar with the work of one of the quality movement gurus: Crosby, Juran, or Deming. Although each of these men defined a specific approach to quality, one common thread in their philosophies is that quality must be planned.

> **NOTE** Quality management reaches very esoteric heights. Quality management programs such as total quality management (TQM) and Six Sigma strive for consistent quality modifications that result in nearly 100 percent throughput, in terms of high quality. Do an Internet search for "TQM," "Six Sigma," and "ISO 9000" and you'll get plenty of hits for more thorough reading on this subject.

A key component of quality planning is the corporate quality policy. You need to determine if such a document exists in your organization, and if so, review the quality standards or direction on how to approach your project. If you are referencing a corporate quality policy, review that policy with your project team and the stakeholders to make sure everyone is familiar with the standards. You should also reference the quality policy in your quality management plan.

It would be impractical to quality check every single task on the project plan. Several tools and techniques are available to assist you in determining what to measure and how to measure. These decisions regarding quality measurement are documented in the quality plan.

Quality Planning Tools and Techniques

At this point you may be asking yourself "How do I go about determining what quality activities I should include in my project?" What you need is a way to determine those areas of your project most likely to have quality issues that impact the success of the project.

Your corporate quality plan may include useful tools and techniques to determine where to focus your quality efforts. It may include standard tools that each project is expected to use.

Another area the project manager needs to consider is industry standards or government regulations. In particular, if you are producing a product that is regulated, you must be certain that it meets the criteria defined in the regulations. Failure to meet the provisions of a regulation could result in fines or jail terms. Regulations may also be in place for safety reason to protect workers and/or consumers.

Even if you do not have a corporate quality process and are working on a project with no predefined standards or regulations, you can use several techniques to determine what quality aspects of your project to measure. We will look at four of the most commonly used: cost-benefit analysis, benchmarking, flowcharting, and cost of quality.

Cost-Benefit Analysis

Cost-benefit analysis was discussed earlier in this book in Chapter 2, when we covered project selection. This technique is also useful in planning quality management. You need to identify those quality activities that will provide the most benefit at the least cost.

The benefits of quality are things like client satisfaction, less rework, and lower overall costs. IT projects often have test plans. Cost-benefit analysis can be used to help identify each point in the development phase where test scenarios should be run, as well as the type and number of test scenarios.

Benchmarking

Benchmarking is a technique that uses similar activities as a means of comparison. It is a very useful technique if you are changing or upgrading the way you currently do business. If you are changing the work environment, you want results equal to if not better than the current environment.

For IT projects benchmarking could include such items as a comparison of a new system response time with a similar application or the speed of report generation with the speed of the current system. Benchmarking is only applicable if there is valid data on the capabilities of the original system, and there are enough similarities that the comparison is meaningful.

Flowcharting and Process Diagrams

The notions between a flowchart and DFD are similar—you're trying to map a process flow—but with a DFD you are breaking things down into discreet chunks from which you can begin to develop your code.

Flowcharting uses diagrams that depict the relationship of various elements in the project. Developing a flowchart or a series of Data Flow Diagrams (DFDs) can help you anticipate where and when a problem may occur. You can build in checkpoints to assess the quality of a particular activity before the next step is started. To use a simple example from a home improvement project, you could build in a quality checkpoint to make sure the paint on the walls has dried before you hang your family photo collection.

Figure 6.2 shows a flowchart and a DFD for the process of a customer interacting with a company through a customer service website.

At first glance the flowchart looks considerably more difficult to interpret than the series of DFDs. However, you should note that the flowchart describes the flow from start to finish. DFDs start with what's called a "context zero" diagram (note the 0 in the upper center of the starting box) and drill down into diagram levels 1, 2, and so on. The idea is that as you drill down, you get more and more information about a specific context. At some point, you've finally fleshed out the context so much that you have a solid place from which to begin coding. Some Computer Aided Software Engineering (CASE) tools have the capability of letting you create the DFDs within the CASE tool, then, with the push of a button, create the majority of the code associated with a given context.

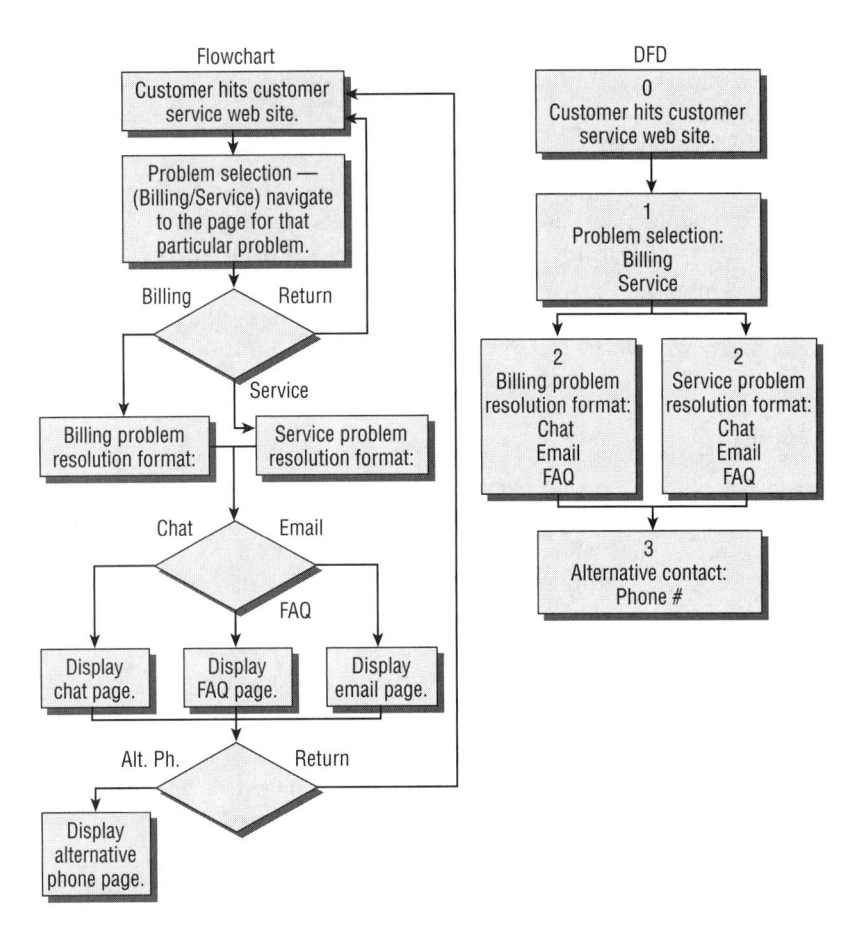

FIGURE 6.2 A Comparison between a Flowchart and a DFD

Cost of Quality

Quality involves added work to the project, and it comes at a cost. *Cost of quality* is the cost of all of the work required to assure the project meets the quality standards. You can have costs associated with both the work you do to assure quality and with the ramifications of a poor-quality product. The three types of costs associated with quality are prevention, appraisal, and failure.

Prevention *Prevention costs* cover the activities performed to avoid quality problems. These costs include quality planning, training, and any product or process testing.

Prevention costs are incurred by planning in activities like testing code at various phases: individual unit tests, integration testing that combines several modules, and in some cases a systems test that tests end to end. The purpose of these tests is to catch any potential problems early on as the work is being done.

Appraisal *Appraisal costs* cover the activities that keep the product defects from reaching the client. Appraisal costs include inspection, testing, and formal quality audits.

User acceptance testing is an appraisal cost. A small, controlled group of users runs scenarios to test the functionality of a new system before it is deployed.

Failure *Failure costs* cover the activities generated if the product fails. Failure costs include downtime, more user support, rework to correct critical problems, and possible scrapping of the project. Failure costs on a new customer support application could include additional user training or the need for extended on-site support.

Further failure costs are incurred if the product has left the organization and reached an external customer. These costs include recalls, warranty work, customer site visits, and the damage to the company's reputation.

As we mentioned in Chapter 2, quality is one of the constraints that all project managers must deal with. It really is a balancing act among the budget you have for the project, the time you're given to accomplish the project's goals, and the overall quality of the product. Quality is not free and it takes time; as project manager you need to plan for the appropriate quality steps and be prepared to explain the consequences of shortchanging quality in terms of failure costs.

The specific quality activities that you identify are documented in the quality management plan.

Quality Management Plan

The *quality management plan* documents the output from the quality planning tools and techniques by listing the quality activities that will be performed, the procedures used to complete the quality activities, and the resources required. This plan will be the basis for doing quality control when you are in project execution.

The procedures section of the plan includes more detailed information regarding the expected results from quality activities and the steps used to determine whether the quality standards are being met. The quality standards and the method used to measure these standards need to be clearly defined. Methods used to measure whether quality standards have been met include metrics, checklists, and exit criteria.

Metrics A *metric* is a standard of measurement that specifically defines how something will be measured. You can define metrics for any area of the project. Let's use a web sales application as an example. If you are going to measure quality of the checkout process, your metric might state that when the customer implements the checkout process, the system will multiply the price of each item by the quantity of items ordered and compute the applicable sales tax and shipping charges 100 percent of the time. This metric would be part of the test scenarios run against both code in the calculation unit and as part of the user acceptance test.

Checklists A checklist is a tool to list a series of steps that must be taken to complete an activity. As each step is completed it is marked off the list. This provides documentation that the steps were done and can also be used to track when the step was taken and who performed the work.

A quality checklist for user acceptance testing might contain the following items:

- Schedule 10 users to complete test scenarios.
- Develop 20 test scenarios.
- Review scenarios and obtain client approval.
- Make copies of scenarios for each user.
- Train the 10 users on how to run the scenarios and document their results.
- Review user results.
- Document defects.

> **NOTE** You can hire contractors who specialize in testing processes. Also note that companies specialize in validation of a specific development process. These specialists are called *Independent Validation and Verification (IV&V)* companies and can be an invaluable aid in large software development and deployment projects. They perform the function of keeping everyone on their toes with eyes fixed straight ahead on the project. (See NASA's IV&V site http://www.ivv.nasa.gov/business/ivv/index.shtml for more in-depth information on this intriguing and substantial subject.)

Exit Criteria We discussed exit criteria briefly in Chapter 4 when we talked about milestones. To refresh your memory, a milestone marks a key event in the project life cycle. If your project life cycle methodology uses milestones to mark the end of one project phase and the beginning of the next phase, the milestones between phases may include quality exit criteria. In this case your quality plan should document the criteria that must be met at each phase to consider that phase complete. Software development projects frequently use a series of tests to confirm the quality of the major deliverables for each phase. These tests can be established as exit or entrance criteria. For example, a unit test can be used as a criterion to signify the completion of code development.

The quality management plan should also address how the results of the quality activities will be reviewed with the project sponsor and other stakeholders. Identification of any activities requiring formal sign-off is also documented. A user acceptance test may not be considered complete until the client or a designated representative approves the results.

Risk Planning

Risk is something that we deal with in our everyday lives. Some people seek out jobs or leisure activities that are considered high risk. They may get a thrill or a feeling of great accomplishment derived from taking on the challenge of skydiving or mountain climbing or working as a lineman on high-voltage electrical lines.

However, if you mention the word risk in association with a project, the majority of people will immediately think of something negative. Risks are not always negative. A project *risk* is simply an element of uncertainty that can have either negative or positive consequences. Remember when we discussed fast tracking as a means to reduce the schedule duration by doing tasks in parallel that would normally be done in sequence? There are definitely risks involved in overlapping tasks, but in this case it is a self-imposed risk that may have a positive outcome of completing the project sooner and meeting the client's needs.

That said, a lot of project risks probably have negative consequences. The best way to handle risk is to acknowledge it and deal with it. In order to more clearly illustrate this, think back a moment about the definition of a project. One of the key factors in defining a project is that it produces a unique result. If you remember that you are not dealing with an operations procedure that has been in place for months or years with fairly predictable results, you'll immediately see the implications of risk. Even if your project is similar to previous projects, it will still produce its own unique result; you do not have a crystal ball to tell you exactly what will happen during the course of the project. You need to plan up front for events that may take your project off course. *Risk planning* deals with how you manage the areas of uncertainty in your project.

Risk planning has three major components: identifying the potential risks to your project, analyzing the potential impact of each risk, and developing an appropriate response for each risk.

Risk Identification

All projects have risks. Project team members can identify a component of their current project that they are not comfortable with. It could be an aggressive schedule with complex task dependencies, team member experience, or lack of confidence in a vendor. Unfortunately, many project managers do not take the time to work with the project team and other stakeholders to formally document where the project is at risk. *Risk identification* is the process of determining and documenting the areas in your project with the potential to take the project off track.

Risks can be viewed from both the global level, looking at the project as a whole, and by analyzing the tasks in the project schedule. Global risks can include such items as the level of funding committed to the project, the overall experience level of the core project team, the use of project management practices, or the strategic significance of the project. Typically, the project manager, the project sponsor, and the client deal with identifying the global risks.

Risks are also identified by the project team from the perspective of the schedule and the tasks required to achieve the project objectives within the committed time and budget. There may be risks associated with particular phases of the project or with certain key tasks. The assessment of risks in the project schedule includes participation from all core project team members and any appropriate subject matter experts.

A series of questions can be developed to pose to the project team for each phase or task. Examples of risk identification questions include:

- Is the task on the critical path?
- Is this a complex task?
- Does the task involve a new or unfamiliar technology?
- Does the task have multiple dependencies?
- Have we had problems with similar tasks in previous projects?
- Is this task controlled by outside influences (permits, county hearings, etc.)?
- Are there inexperienced resources assigned to this task?
- Are there adequate resources assigned to the task?
- Does this task involve an integrated system?
- Are we unfamiliar with the hardware or software we're going to use for the tasks?

For those tasks with yes answers to any of the above questions, move on to questions regarding the potential problems that may be associated with this phase:

- What issues or problems might occur?
- What problems occurred with similar tasks in the past?
- What could cause this problem?

Once you have walked through the process of identifying all the possible risks to your project, you need to use risk analysis to take a closer look at each identified risk to see what the impact really is.

> **What Could Possibly Go Wrong?**
>
> It's also good to have a pre-project brainstorming session with the finalized project team in which you simply use sticky notes and answer this question: What could go wrong?
>
> By letting people free think and blurt out all the possibilities that occur to them, you might get some input that proves to be really valuable in the risk identification step.

Risk Analysis

Risk analysis is the process used to identify and focus on those risks that are the most critical to the success of your project

There is a lot of information out there about risk analysis and the various techniques that can be used. Risk analysis can be approached from a qualitative or quantitative perspective. *Qualitative risk analysis* looks at the likelihood that a risk will actually occur and the impact to the project if it does occur. *Quantitative risk analysis* uses a more complex mathematical approach to numerically analyze the probability that a risk will occur, the effect on the project goals, and the consequences to the overall project. A detailed discussion of quantitative risk analysis methodologies is beyond the scope of this book, but you should be aware of some of the terms you may see. The more advanced techniques for computing quantitative risk analysis include sensitivity analysis, decision tree analysis, simulation using the Monte Carlo technique, and interviewing. Organizations that use these techniques as part of risk management typically have in house experts to complete the assessment or assist project teams. More information on quantitative risk analysis can be found in the *Guide to the PMBOK*.

What we are going to focus on in this section is a simplified approach to qualitative risk analysis that a project manager can lead without the need for special tools or training. If your organization relies on these more sophisticated tools, that is great, but do not think you cannot do risk analysis without them. By using a template and a simple set of criteria, the project can focus the team on the risks that really need attention.

When you are finished with risk identification, you may find that you have several pages of documentation. Numerous tasks on the project schedule are likely to have some degree of risk associated with them, and the thought of all this risk may seem overwhelming. You need to keep in mind that all risks are not equal. Risk identification is a brainstorming session to make sure as many potential risks as possible have been captured. But not all risks will become a reality. Therefore, it is important to quantify the potential risks, so that attention can be focused on those risks whose impacts on the project success are the greatest.

Risk Severity   For each of the items that have been listed on the template, the team identifies the impact to the project if the potential problem does occur. A simple rating can be used:

- High impact
- Medium impact
- Low impact

Some problems have impacts that are very narrow in scope and do not impact the overall success of the project, while others could delay the project completion or cause a significant budget overrun. By relying on the expert knowledge and judgment of the team members and any historical data, your team can rate the severity of the each risk.

Risk Probability   The other key element of risk quantification is the probability of the potential problem actually occurring. Some risks are almost a certainty, while others are an extremely remote possibility. The knowledge of the project team and any historical data is used to rate the probability of risk occurrence. The same high, medium, or low scale can be used.

The risk analysis process can be completed using a simple template as shown in Table 6.1.

The tasks with potential risks can then be prioritized, with those having both a critical severity rating and a high probability of occurrence listed first. For those tasks that have the greatest potential impact on the project, a plan should be developed for an appropriate course of action.

TABLE 6.1   Table 6.1 Risk Analysis Template

Risk	Severity	Probability
Risk A	H	H
Risk B	M	M
Risk C	L	H
Risk D	H	L

Risk Response

Risk analysis provides you with a prioritization for all the risks the team has identified. *Risk response planning* is the process of reviewing each item on the prioritized list of potential project risks to determine what, if any, action should be taken.

The *Guide to the PMBOK* lists four techniques for risk response planning:

- Avoidance—changing the project plan to eliminate the activity that created the risk.
- Transference—moving the liability for the risk to a third party.
- Mitigation—reducing the impact and/or the probability of the risk.
- Acceptance—choosing to accept the consequences of the risk or being unable to identify another response strategy.

Transference is a specific technique involving tools such as insurance premiums, performance bonds, or fixed price contracts to limit financial risk. The other techniques can be grouped together as two types of action can be taken when responding to risk: preventative action and contingency action.

Preventative Action

Preventative action involves the review of potential risks to determine if any steps can be taken to prevent the problem from occurring or reduce the probability that the problem will occur. Preventative action combines the techniques of avoidance and mitigation. The costs of these actions are weighed against the impact of the risk. You determine whether resources are available with the skill set to implement the preventative action. Tasks are added to the project schedule to track preventative actions. Questions to ask the project team as you work to identify preventative actions include:

- What can be done to prevent the problem from occurring (address the causes)?
- What can be done to decrease the likelihood of the problem occurring?
- Are these actions cost-effective?
- Are there resources available to implement these actions?

Contingency Action

Acceptance includes not only those risks you choose to accept, but also those risks you cannot prevent. If the problem is something totally outside the control of the project team (such as pending legislation or a possible work stoppage), a *contingency plan* is developed to identify the most likely impacts to the project and a strategy to deal with the impacts. You want to be able to answer the following:

- If the problem cannot be prevented, what are the most likely impacts to the project?
- What can be done to minimize these impacts?

Your risk management plan can be documented using a simple template as shown in Figure 6.3.

FIGURE 6.3 Risk Management Template

Risk Management Template

Project:_____   Date:_____

DESCRIPTION OF RISK	RISK PROBABILITY (H/M/L)	IMPACT TO PROJECT IF RISK OCCURS	RISK SEVERITY (H/M/L)	PREVENTATIVE OR CONTINGENCY ACTION PLAN

This plan is used to communicate project risks and action plans to other stakeholders. It can be converted into a risk tracking log, which we will discuss further during project control in Chapter 9.

Communications Planning

Good communication is one of the keys to project success. If you ask project managers to tell you how they spend their time, most will state that they spend anywhere from 50 to 80 percent of their time on project communication. You may have noticed in this book, we continually end a planning section with the need to communicate this information to team members or other stakeholders. A need for good communication starts from the day the project charter is issued and you are formally named project manager (perhaps even earlier if you have been filling the project manager role informally). The project charter is the first of many project documents that needs to be reviewed with your stakeholders. Unfortunately, even though project managers usually recognize how much time they spend communicating, this does not always translate into taking the time to develop a good communications plan.

> **Overcommunicating Is Not Necessarily *Good* Communicating!**
>
> Once, one of us was a team lead on a project where the project manager created distribution lists for both email and paper documents and sent everything she received that even remotely involved the project to everyone on the lists. She thought she was doing an excellent job of communicating with the team, but the team was going crazy. We were buried with data, and much of it was not relevant to our role on the project. It got to the point where most of the team members were so overwhelmed we stopped reading everything. That, of course, led us to missing information we did need. The project manager did not understand why there was so much confusion on the team. She had not put any planning into her communications process.

Good communication involves far more than just setting up distribution lists. You need a plan to determine what gets communicated to whom. *Communications planning* is the process of identifying what people or groups need to receive information regarding your project, what information each group needs, and how the information will be distributed. The communication system should monitor the project status and satisfy the diverse communication needs of the project's stakeholders.

We are going to review general principles of project communications strategy and then focus on some specific areas of concern for communicating with project team members and communicating with other stakeholder groups.

Communications Strategy

Communication is a part of our daily lives, both business and personal. Because people communicate all the time, they give little thought to organizing or planning communication.

Regardless whether you are communicating with your sponsor, team members, or your client, some simple steps will make your communication more effective.

- Decide WHAT you wish to communicate.
- Decide TO WHOM you wish to communicate.
- Think about the BIASES of the receivers/listeners.
- Decide HOW you should communicate.
- COMPOSE and TRANSMIT the message.

It is not necessary to document these steps every time you communicate, but taking even 5 minutes to think through them will have the outcome of improving the focus and clarity of project communications. The importance of planning your communications before you speak or write is even more critical if your message is sensitive or controversial. Life is much easier if you send the right message to begin with, rather than apologizing or retracting at a later time.

Communications Planning

Documenting an overall communications plan can be accomplished by:

- Defining who needs information on your project.
- Listing communication objectives for this person or group.
- Identifying the communications vehicle(s).
- Assigning accountability to deliver the communication.
- Determining when the communications will happen.

Figure 6.4 shows an example of a communications plan using this approach.

Although the template from this example can be used to create an overall communications plan for all stakeholder groups, there are some additional considerations when it comes to communicating with your project team.

FIGURE 6.4 Communications Plan Example

Communication Plan Example

Project:_____   Date:_____

STAKEHOLDER AUDIENCE (Who needs this information?)	OBJECTIVE (What do we want to communicate?)	MEDIUM (What is the communications vehicle?)	RESPONSIBILITY (Who is responsible for development and delivery?)	DATE OR FREQUENCY (When will this be completed?)
Project Team	Functional area dependencies Status of key project deliverables Issues impacting project milestones Risks	Project Schedule Issues Log Team meeting Launch Checklist	Project Manager	Weekly
Project Sponsor	Summary of progress Slipping critical tasks Issues Risks	Project Report Card Schedule Summary Issues Log Escalation List Launch Checklist	Project Manager	Weekly
	Financials	Project Review Budget Summary	Functional Team Leads Finance Lead	Monthly
Functional Directors	Summary of progress Functional Issues Functional Risks Functional Financials	Functional Status Project Report Card Stakeholder Review	Functional Team Leads Project Manager Project Sponsor	Weekly Weekly Monthly
Executive Team	Milestone progress Cross-functional Risks Financials	Executive Review	Project Sponsor	Monthly/Quarterly
	Launch status	Voicemail Updates	Project Manager	Weekly/As Needed

Communicating with Project Team Members

One of your most important jobs as project manager will be communicating with your project team members. It is your responsibility to make sure all the team members understand the project goals and objectives and how their contribution fits into the big picture. Unfortunately, this is an area that is frequently overlooked in communications planning.

Your interactions with your project team will involve both formal and informal communications. *Formal communications* include project kickoff meetings, team status meetings, written status reports, team building sessions, or other planned sessions that you hold with the team. *Informal communications* include phone calls and emails to and from your team members, conversations in the hallway, and impromptu meetings.

The challenge that project managers face is to match their communication style with that of each team member. Getting input from your team members will help you better communicate with them. If you are scheduling a kickoff meeting or other team building session, ask for suggestions on agenda items or areas for team discussion. Team members may have suggestions for the structure and frequency of the team meetings or format for status reporting, based on their previous project experience. The project manager may not be able to accommodate all suggestions, but taking the time to consider input and reviewing the final format will go a long way toward building a cohesive team.

Everyone has a communications method they are most comfortable with; some of your team members may prefer to primarily use email, while other rely on phone calls or voicemail. For these informal one-on-one communications, where possible, work to accommodate what is most comfortable for each team member.

You may note that some of the other stakeholders may not understand how they are involved with the project. Extra steps are required to properly engage these people.

Engaging Stakeholders

Before you can develop a communications plan for the other stakeholders on your project, you need to identify who they are. In Chapter 2 we identified some of the typical project stakeholders: project sponsor, functional managers, customers, and end users. Remember that a stakeholder is anyone who will be positively or negatively affected by the outcome of a project.

On large projects that cross multiple functional areas, you may identify stakeholders who are not participating in the project or do not fully understand their role. This commonly occurs with large systems applications or new products that are deployed across geographic regions such as multistate customer operations areas or multicampus sites. If the customer operations director does not understand how his team is involved or what will be the total impact on his group, you need to get him connected to what's going on. But he may be busy and not paying attention to your project. So, if you can only get 5 minutes of time with an uninvolved stakeholder, it's vital that you spend your time wisely.

To accomplish your mission, it can be useful to develop an engagement plan that describes the key points you need to get across:

- Identify which aspects of the project plan to communicate.
- List any known or probable benefits or concerns from the stakeholder.
- Determine key message(s) to convey to each stakeholder.

An example of a stakeholder engagement plan using the customer operations scenario for a new product deployment is shown in Figure 6.5.

This particular example uses three scenarios based on the amount of time you are spending with the stakeholder. This approach has two key benefits:

- You have carefully thought out what you need to say if your time is limited.
- You are ready for the next meeting or to extend your current meeting if the stakeholder wants more detail immediately.

Your communications plan is a document you need to review with your sponsor. If your project requires communication to executive team members, the sponsor can help develop the communications plan by identifying what information the group needs, and how and when communication will take place. In addition to the communications distribution structure, your communications plan may include information on how you will gather and store information, how to obtain information between communications, and how to update the communications plan.

FIGURE 6.5 Stakeholder Engagement Plan

Communications Plan Stakeholder Engagement Example

Project:_____Stakeholder Group: <u>Customer Operations</u>

	HIGH LEVEL OVERVIEW (5 minutes)	KEY POINTS (30 minutes)	SUPPORTING DETAIL (1-2 hours)
WHY (are we doing this project?)	Expand product offering	Increase customer base and projected revenue	Market research
WHAT (does this mean to the stakeholder?)	All sales channels will require training	Product functionality highlights Training expectations	Product functionality detail Product demos
HOW (will the project goal be achieved?)	Launch product in selected channels on March 7	Channel sales goals Channel training dates	Sales channel product proficiency
WHEN (will the stakeholder be involved?)	Supply Core Team lead starting November 9	Development of training Delivery of training	Interface with Human Factors team Interface with Customer Care

Procurement Planning

Many projects are completed using external resources for part of the project deliverables. For a variety of reasons, another company may complete pieces of the project work or on occasion even the entire project. You may have been part of a project team that included contractors to complete certain tasks. IT projects often use outside resources on large projects rather than hire more employees who may not have any work when the project is done. If your project includes outside resources, you need to be familiar with the procurement process. *Procurement planning* is the process of identifying the goods and services required for your project that will be purchased from an outside organization. If your project is completely internal, you do not need a procurement plan, unless internal departments bid on the work and sign a contract.

As a project manager, you are the buyer of goods and services for your project, so because of that we will cover the procurement process from the buyer's perspective.

The organization selling the goods or services is referred to as a vendor, a supplier, a consultant, or a contractor.

The procurement process is very complex and often involves the legal department or in the case of larger companies a separate procurement department that manages the process across the organization. This book will not make you an expert in procurement, but we will cover many of the basic concepts.

Procurement planning starts with the decision to procure goods or services outside the organization. Once that decision has been made, you need to determine what type of contract would be best. A statement of work (SOW) is developed to define exactly what work the vendor is being asked to deliver. The SOW is incorporated in a document distributed to the vendors who will be bidding on the work. Vendor evaluation criteria are developed to use in evaluating the bids or proposals that are received.

Let's start by looking at some of the circumstances that might cause you to procure outside resources.

Make or Buy Analysis

Before you can define a procurement plan, you need to determine whether you need to procure anything. The general management technique known as *make or buy analysis* is often used to make that determination. What it involves is looking at the trade-offs between doing something in-house versus procuring it outside the organization. Here are some of the more common areas to consider:

Equipment

For some of your project resources, this may be fairly simple. If you are developing a new application that requires new hardware, you will need to obtain the hardware from outside your company. But you still have a decision point of purchasing the hardware outright or leasing it. You need to look at the life expectancy of the application as well as such things as whether other applications could run on the hardware and share some of the cost.

Staff Augmentation

The use of outside human resources can range from paying a vendor to run the entire project to contracting for specific resources to perform certain tasks.

Using a vendor can be driven by a lack of organizational expertise. If none of your programmers are skilled in the programming language required for your new application, you could hire people who have this expertise, but there may not be a need for all of those people once the development work is complete. Contracting for programmers with the required skill set to complete the project work may be a better plan. If the new system will be maintained internally after the project is completed, you need to determine how you will train existing employees or add to the current maintenance staff.

Time-critical projects may also require more resources than are currently available. Contract resources can fill this gap.

Other Goods or Services

Projects may have specific deliverables that are appropriate to have completed by a vendor. If you are installing a new commercial software application, you can schedule resources to develop training or you can purchase the training. If you do not have a dedicated in-house training development and delivery team, it may be more effective to contract these services. There may even be existing training developed that you can purchase either with or without resources to do the training.

IV&V and testing services are an ideal candidate for this kind of outsourcing as well. Unless you've got a formal testing department with an established set of procedures, you'll get much better results from outsourcing the testing to a group of professionals.

Once you determine which aspects of the project to procure from outside the organization, you need to have a basic understanding of the types of contracts you can use to authorize this work.

Types of Contracts

A *contract* is a legal document that covers the work that will be done, how the work will be compensated, and any penalties for noncompliance. Entire law school courses are devoted to contract management, so this book is not going to make you a contract expert, but you should be able to understand differences between the types of contracts. Most contracts fall into one of the following categories: fixed price contracts, cost reimbursable contracts, and time and materials contracts. Let's take a more detailed look at each of these.

Fixed price contracts *Fixed price contracts* have a fixed fee for the work that the vendor will provide. This type of contract works best when the product is very well defined and there is good historical information. Using a fixed price contract on a product or service that is not well defined or has never been done before is risky for both the buyer and the seller.

Cost reimbursable contract A *cost reimbursable contract* provides a seller with payment of all costs he or she incurs to deliver the product and includes a fee to cover the seller's profit. This type of contract has the most risk for the buyer, as you do not know what the total cost will be. Although this may not be the most desirable contract from a buyer perspective, it may be your only option if you do not have a well-defined product or if you are asking the vendor to provide something that has never been done before.

Time and materials contract   A *time and materials contract* is a cross between a fixed price and cost reimbursable contract. The buyer and the seller agree on a unit rate, such as the hourly rate for a programmer, but the total cost is unknown and will depend on the amount of time spent to produce the product. This type of contract is often used for staff augmentation, where contract workers are brought on to perform specific tasks on the project.

Keep in mind the types of contracts as you define the work you want completed in the statement of work (SOW).

Statement of Work

If you are going to have outside vendors involved in the project, it is critical that they know exactly what you are asking them to do. The *statement of work (SOW)* details the goods or services you wish to procure. In many respects it is similar to the project scope statement; it contains the project description, major deliverables, success criteria, and any assumptions or constraints. It will also generally include information about any warranties the vendor is supplying and will detail payment expectations. The portion of your project scope statement pertaining to the work you are putting out for bid is a good starting point for the SOW.

Even if the SOW is actually created by another department, the project manager should be involved in the process to ensure accuracy of the project requirements. Vendors use the SOW to determine if they are both capable and interested in bidding on your project work. It must be very clear and precise. Anything in the SOW that is ambiguous could lead to a less than satisfactory deliverable.

Many companies have templates for creating a SOW; this ensures that all required items are covered and provides consistent information to vendors.

Completion of the SOW means you are ready to start vendor solicitation.

Vendor Solicitation

Once you have decided that some of the project work will be completed outside the organization and have developed a SOW defining what you want done, you need to notify vendors. *Solicitation* is the process of obtaining responses from vendors to complete your project work as documented in the SOW.

Typically a procurement document is prepared to notify prospective sellers of work. There are several terms associated with these documents. Three of the more common terms are:

- Request For Proposal (RFP)
- Request For Quotation (RFQ)
- Invitation For Bid (IFB)

These terms are often used interchangeably and may have different meanings in different organizations. Regardless of what these documents are called, they should include your SOW, information regarding how responses are to be formatted and delivered, and a date by which responses must be received. Potential vendors may be required to make a formal presentation or they may just be asked to submit a bid. Depending on the industry you are in, these procurement documents may be extremely detailed.

Before providing a copy of your procurement document to any potential seller, always determine if your company has an approved vendor list. Many companies have a formal process that vendors must comply with before they can do business with the company. If your company has such a policy, you should only be soliciting bids from those approved vendors. If no such list exists, the project team or the procurement department will need to research potential vendors through trade association, Internet, or other available sources of information.

At the time the procurement documents are distributed (or earlier), you need to develop the criteria to be used to evaluate the bids, quotes, or proposals you receive.

Vendor Selection Criteria

The amount of time that the project manager spends on vendor selection is driven by whether the company has a separate procurement department. If your company has a specialized group that handles vendor contracts, they will advise you what information you need to provide and a member of their team will work on your project to manage the vendor selection process and the contract.

If you are responsible for vendor selection, then you will need to develop criteria to use when evaluating vendor bids or proposals. It helps to decide up front with the sponsor and other key stakeholders who will be involved in the review and selection of vendor proposals. This group should develop the selection criteria as a team and reach agreement ahead of time as to any weighting of the criteria.

Sole-Source Documentation

For those of you who work in government, your procurement job is even harder! Governments typically not only create an approved vendor list—you *must* buy from the vendors on the list unless you can prove that they can't supply it, *never mind* whether another manufacturer makes a superior product or not!

The only way you can get around this problem is to provide what is called *sole-source* documentation stating that the vendor you're buying from is the only one that carries the thing that you need along with the reasons why you need that specific thing. If you don't carefully document the exact reasons why you need the thing you need and you don't make a convincing case of it, you're likely to be forced to go with someone else's product and make it work.

The vendor evaluation criteria you develop will be used to rank the various proposals. The criteria may be both objective and subjective. An example of criteria you might use includes:

- Overall cost of the vendor proposal.
- Vendor understanding of the business need.
- Qualifications of the vendor staff—both managerial and technical.
- Vendor experience with similar products.
- Cultural fit with your organization.
- Vendor financial status.

> **Case Study: Chaptal Wineries Email and Intranet Systems—Formulating the Final Plans in the Project Planning Process**
>
> You're very close to finally being able to begin the Chaptal project plan. However, you need to focus on some final planning elements that will help bring about a solidly deployed project. You'll develop a roles and responsibilities worksheet, communications plan, quality plan, and you'll perform risk assessment and team member designations and procurement planning in this section.
>
> **Roles and Responsibilities and Team Member Designations**
>
> **Title:** Yourself—project manager and IT Director for Chaptal
>
> **Role:** Project planner, initiator, and coordinator
>
> **Primary responsibilities:** Acquisition of project hardware and software, also WAN telecommunications connections
> Vendor contracts and maintenance agreements
> Managing contractors and other winery employees in bringing about the deliverables
> Work with day-to-day IT duties as required
>
> **Title:** Guillaume Fourche, Metor Sanchez, Jason Jay—project team members
>
> **Role:** Assist with WAN connectivity issues, testing, and server deployment at the various winery sites
>
> **Title:** Intranet contractor
>
> **Role:** Develop all intranet pages for use by the Chaptal winery group
>
> **Title:** Telecommunications contractors
>
> **Role:** Provide T1/E1 connectivity from the winery site to the telecommunications cloud.

Procurement Planning

Communications Plan Kim Cox—your boss, also the project sponsor. You've decided she'll need daily updates on your progress. Since you don't have email yet, you'll either give her a quick heads-up in person, or over the phone. She says she doesn't expect a blow-by-blow synopsis, just any standout issues or problems that you've run into. She'd also like a quick update on any significant project progress.

Guillaume Fourche, Metor Sanchez, and Jason Jay need to hear from you at a minimum of once a week, even if you have nothing to share. Since they will be working with you to get things done for their particular areas of the world, you'll also need to get any news, updates, or issues while you're talking with them.

All of the telecommunications companies will require direct dialog as needed.

When your intranet contractor begins work, he or she will dialog with you on a daily basis, giving you status updates, showing you the work to date, and working with you on testing procedures.

Winery Expansion Communication Plan

Project: Chaptal Wineries   Date: _____

STAKEHOLDER AUDIENCE Who needs this information	OBJECTIVE What do we want to communicate	MEDIUM What is the communications vehicle What will be communicated	RESPONSIBILITY Who is responsible for development and delivery	DATE OR FREQUENCY When will this be completed
Project Team 1. Chaptal IT Manager (Project Manager) 2. Jason Jay 3. Guillaume Fourche 4. Metor Sanchez	Functional area dependencies Status of key project deliverables Issues impacting project milestones Risks	In-person (Kim) or con-call (Internationals) Project Schedule Issues Log Team meeting (con-call) Launch Checklist	Project Manager	Weekly
Project Sponsor Kim Cox	Summary of progress Slipping critical tasks Issues Risks Financials	In-person Project Report Card Schedule Summary Issues Log Escalation List Launch Checklist Project Review Budget Summary	Project Manager Project Manager (for Finance Department)	Weekly Monthly
Vendors 1. Telecommunications providers 2. Internetworking contractors 3. Intranet contractor	Milestone progress Cross-functional Risks SOW and contract status Payment information	Voicemail or Email Executive Review	Project Manager Project Manager	Weekly Weekly

Quality Plan Your quality plan consists of three elements:

- Server hardware and software testing and validation—You will be responsible for verifying that all server software has been correctly installed, that all service packs and necessary security patches have been applied and that all hardware is functional and operating correctly with the software.

- The telecommunications contractors will be responsible for testing and validating that the telecommunications circuits (T1 and E1) are operational, fully functional, and error-free. Telecommunications companies will provide a warranty of error-free operation and an Operational Level Agreement (OLA) that specifies how they will perform if any problems occur.

- There will be significant unit, system, and UAT testing on the intranet pages. There will be UAT with regard to the email system.

Risk Assessment After performing a risk assessment analysis with Kim Cox and others from the Chaptal management team, the following subjects were determined to have some element of risk associated with them:

T1/E1 WAN Circuits—There is a marginal (20 percent) probability that the minimal speed of the circuit (1.44 Mb/s) could introduce bottlenecking at peak information load times. Risk mitigation involves either waiting out the peak, or purchasing a higher-load circuit (such as a double T1). Chaptal management thinks that the best approach is to monitor the circuits for load at deployment time and to probably live with any minor bottlenecks that might occur. Load testing will be able to show if there are more significant load factors than anticipated as of this writing.

Hardware failure—There is a 2 percent probability that the hardware will fail upon initial power-up and short-term operation, or that it will be delivered in a nonfunctional state. The vendor contract calls for a next-day air shipment on all defective parts that cannot be replaced by in-the-field warranty personnel. Otherwise, there is a 3-hour turnaround time on warranty work for hardware. Thus, mitigation will be to utilize vendor warranty services.

Software failure—It is anticipated that there is less than a 1 percent chance of the software incorrectly working, *provided* it is configured correctly. Risk protection involves developing a configuration "burn document" ahead of time and validating it through the software company to make sure that all correct steps are followed and all service packs and security patches are applied in the correct order. Mitigation means that a re-burn would have to happen after it was determined what went wrong in the first place.

Internetworking gear failure—Mean time between failure (MTBF) history shows a less than 0.2 percent chance of a failure on all new router and switchgear that's deployed in the field—regardless of international location. Mitigation involves warranty replacement (3-hour window) by contract field personnel.

Programming errors—The vendor has provided documentation on several other intranet sites he has created and he stipulates that there is less than a 1 percent chance of anything going wrong because he's going to follow the same development characteristics on the same platforms as he's worked with before. However, he has put a warranty stipulation in his SOW that details he will thoroughly test and validate that all systems are working as advertised before he receives his last 50 percent payout.

> **Procurement Plan** Server Gear: Bids and SOWs received will determine the winning server hardware vendor. Terms: Net 30. Order will include Windows Server 2003 and 25-client license pack as well as comprehensive customer service plan. Vendor has complied with the hardware you specified with no substitutions. Servers shipped to respective locales to avoid additional delivery charges.
> Telecommunications Gear: Provided by respective telecommunications providers upon signing of provision agreement contract (Kim Cox).
> Internetworking Gear: Bids and SOWs received will determine the winning internetworking hardware vendor. Terms: Net 30. Order will include routers, switches, software, network cabling and electrical cabling appropriate for the country the gear will reside in. Internetworking gear shipped to respective locales to avoid additional delivery charges. Internetworking contractors for each country obtained through a reference obtained from the winning internetworking company.
> Intranet contractor: Ads in San Francisco Chronicle and Napa News soliciting bids for contracting work. Sealed bids will be received after a "show-n-tell" session held at Chaptal headquarters describing the nature of the work.

Summary

Human resource planning identifies the specific resources that will be assigned to your project as well as how and when they will join the project team and be returned to their functional department. Quality planning determines the quality standards that the project will be measured on and defines how that will be accomplished. Risk planning covers the identification of risks to your project, the quantification of those risks, and a response plan. Communications planning names the people or groups requiring information on the project, the specific information required by each group, and how that information will be provided. Procurement planning is completed if any goods or services for the project will be provided outside the organization. Procurement planning involves a make or buy analysis, a SOW, vendor bid solicitation, and vendor selection criteria.

If you think about the above paragraph, the sum total describes how you're going to work with the *people* who will bring about the project. You identify the team members who will participate. You determine how people will ascertain the quality levels and how they will keep those levels to customer expectations. Risk identification and mitigation strategies show that people have put some effort into thinking about the problems a project could encounter and have come up with ways to avoid those problems. Your communications plan illustrates how you're going to make sure everyone is in the know regarding the project. And your Procurement plan describes how you're going to interface with people to obtain the goods and services you need to start the project and keep it going. So, if you take the tack that your planning process focuses on people, and you think about the needs those people will have relative to your project, you'll be successful.

Exam Essentials

Be able to name the two major components of human resources planning. The human resources planning processes are organizational planning and staff acquisition.

Know the four techniques used to determine what quality aspects to measure. The four most commonly used techniques are cost-benefit analysis, benchmarking, flowcharting, and cost of quality.

Be able to name the types of cost of quality. The types of costs are prevention costs, appraisal costs, and failure costs.

Explain the three processes used to develop a risk management plan. Risk identification is the process of identifying and documenting the potential danger areas in your project. Risk analysis evaluates the severity of the impact to the project and the probability that the risk will actually occur. Risk response planning is the process of reviewing each item on the prioritized list of potential risks impacting the project to determine what, if any, action should be taken.

Know and understand the information to include in a communications management plan. A communications plan identifies the audience, objective, medium, responsibility, and frequency.

Be able to name the types of contracts. Contracts can be fixed price, cost reimbursable, or time and materials.

Key Terms

Before you take the exam, be certain you are familiar with the following terms:

- appraisal costs
- benchmarking
- communications planning
- contract
- cost of quality
- cost reimbursable contract
- failure costs
- fixed price contracts
- formal communications
- human resources planning
- informal communications
- make or buy analysis
- metric
- organizational planning
- planning
- preventative action
- prevention costs
- procurement planning
- quality management plan
- quality planning
- risk
- risk analysis
- risk identification
- risk planning
- risk response planning
- sole source
- solicitation
- staff acquisition process
- staffing management plan
- statement of work (SOW)
- time and materials contract

Review Questions

1. What are the processes that you use for human resources planning?
   A. Staff acquisition
   B. Contract administration
   C. Organizational planning
   D. Performance reporting

2. You have been assigned as project manager for a major software development project. Andy is the functional manager who will be providing the resources for your development team. Andy is being asked to supply resources to several projects concurrently. You have a list of the people you want assigned to your team, but you fear other project managers may want these same people. How should you approach Andy regarding the assignment of his people to the project? Choose the best answer.
   A. Schedule a meeting with Andy to discuss resources. Explain your project deliverables and the skill sets you need. Negotiate for your most critical resources first. Negotiate with Andy.
   B. Send Andy a memo listing the resources you need and the start date for each resource.
   C. Catch up with Andy just before a meeting both of you need to attend so that he will not have time to think up reasons to turn down part of your request.
   D. Meet with Andy's boss to let her know that your project is critical and provide her with the list of resources you need from Andy.

3. A quality technique that analyzes similar activities as a means of comparison is:
   A. Cost-benefit analysis
   B. Corporate quality policy
   C. Flowcharting
   D. Benchmarking

4. The total cost of all the work required to assure the project conforms to quality standards is referred to as the cost of quality. Which of the following are types of costs associated with quality?
   A. Failure costs
   B. Prevention costs
   C. Appraisal costs
   D. All of the above

5. Risk identification is the process of:
   A. Quantifying the impact to the project of a potential problem
   B. Determining and documenting potential danger areas in your project
   C. Assigning a probability that a particular problem will occur
   D. Defining the action to take in response to a potential risk

6. What types of activities are documented in a risk response plan?
   A. Risk probabilities
   B. Preventative actions
   C. Contingency actions
   D. B and C

7. Communications planning is the process of:
   A. Scheduling a regular meeting for the project team.
   B. Developing a distribution list for the stakeholders
   C. Identifying the people or groups who need information on your project
   D. Creating a template to report project status

8. You are the project manager for a new software application that will provide online help to sales consultants regarding the features of the products they sell. One of your stakeholders is the VP of sales, who has committed to a 5 percent increase in product revenue based on this tool to assist his sales team. You have an opportunity to present an overview of this project to the VP. Based on the why, what, how, and when categories in the stakeholder engagement template, which of the following would be appropriate messages in the presentation?
   A. A summary of the detailed technical design.
   B. A demonstration of how the help function is accessed and the type of product information that is displayed.
   C. An overview of the programming language used to develop the code.
   D. A review of the plans to involve a small group of sales consultants in a pilot of the application to identify any concerns before the system is deployed to 4,000 users.

9. The technique of looking at the trade-offs between doing something internally and procuring it from outside the organization is referred to as:
   A. Cost estimating
   B. Vendor selection criteria
   C. Staff augmentation
   D. Make or buy analysis

10. You are a project manager for a telecommunications company assigned to a project to deploy a new wireless network using a technology that does not have a proven track record. You have requested vendor bids for portions of the development that will include researching various scenarios. What type of contract is the most likely in this situation? Choose the best answer.
   A. Fixed price contract
   B. Time and materials contract
   C. Cost reimbursable contract
   D. None of the above

11. You're stuck with a hard project end date and your budget is fixed. If you don't manage the project extremely well, which component is most likely to suffer?
    A. Project plan
    B. Quality
    C. Documentation
    D. Project book

12. Who is responsible for identifying and mitigating risk in the project?
    A. Sponsors
    B. Stakeholders
    C. Project manager
    D. Corporate management

13. You're well under way with a major project when one of your development engineers alerts you to an unforeseen problem—a delay in the procurement of a specific piece of hardware—that is going to require a significant addition of time to the deadline of the project. What should you do? Please select the best answer(s).
    A. Adjust the timeline of the project and notify the stakeholders.
    B. Consult your risk assessment and mitigation strategies for this risk.
    C. Adjust the timeline of the project and notify the sponsors.
    D. Adjust the timeline of the project and obtain sign-off from the sponsors.
    E. Tell the engineer that he must complete the project on time.
    F. Add developers to the project.

14. Who is responsible for accepting or not accepting the risks associated with a project?
    A. Project sponsors
    B. Project stakeholders
    C. Project client
    D. Project manager

15. You are the project manager for a large, complex project that is in the middle of an 18-month estimated timeline. Some important vendors are now entering into the delivery of key project parts (servers, cabling, etc.). What crucial part of project planning will now play out as you take delivery of the components? Select all that apply.
    A. Procurement planning
    B. Human resources planning
    C. Communications planning
    D. Risk planning

16. Why do you spend time developing a solid communications plan? Select all that apply.

   A. To set and meet stakeholder expectations.

   B. To set aside time for your own needs.

   C. To make sure vendors are in the loop.

   D. To understand where the blame lies when something goes wrong.

   E. To keep company executives updated on your progress.

17. When developing projects, your company has determined that quality is the most important of the three elements that affect any project (time, money, quality). What corporate strategy would assist with such a mandate?

   A. Project management plan

   B. Corporate quality officer

   C. Corporate quality policy

   D. Project manager bonuses

18. Your project involves a complicated system that enables communication among several disparate systems. What component of the project planning may require additional (perhaps substantial) communications work on your part with team members and stakeholders in order to clearly elucidate the complexity of the project?

   A. Deliverables

   B. Project end date

   C. Budget and additional resources

   D. Risk assessment

19. You're the project manager for a project in which you're following a specific software development methodology. Some of the developers went to a presentation by a well-known company that manufactures software development software. They saw a new coding technique that could improve the speed with which the code will be developed and ready. They come back energized and ready to shift everything over to the new coding paradigm. How should you handle this recommendation?

   A. Since there's a cost/time-savings benefit, go with the recommendation.

   B. Obtain project sponsor approval to implement the new methodology.

   C. Run the recommendation through the change-management process.

   D. Development methodologies aren't something that the project manager needs to be concerned with.

   E. Assess the risks of adopting the new development methodology. If acceptable, go forward.

   F. Nix the idea and save for the next project.

20. In your risk assessment activities, why would it be more important for you to evaluate potential risks for steps in the critical path than for those steps that are not? (Choose the best answer.)

    A. Steps in the critical path directly affect the project's duration.
    B. Steps in the critical path are the most critical to the project's successful outcome.
    C. Steps in the critical path are those that are the most time-intensive.
    D. Steps in the critical path are those that are the most complicated.

Answers to Review Questions

1. **A, C.** Organizational planning is the process used to define roles and responsibilities for project team members and a plan to manage the project team. Staff acquisition is the actual assignment of people to the project team.

2. **A.** Obtaining the right resources for your project requires good planning and skillful negotiation. An individual meeting with each functional manager who will be providing resources is the best approach. Although you identify all the ideal resources you need, do not expect that you will get everyone you want. Negotiate for your most critical resources first and be willing to compromise. An assumption that the functional manager just needs your list or an attempt to obtain resources by circumventing the functional manager provides a perception that you do not value the functional manager and can create a poor working relationship.

3. **D.** Benchmarking is a technique that uses similar activities as a means of comparison. It is a good quality tool for projects designed to improve the current business operation. Cost-benefit analysis is another quality tool that looks at proposed quality activities to determine which one will provide the most benefit to the project at the least cost. Flowcharting uses diagrams that depict the way work flows. The corporate quality policy is an existing document that can provide information on existing corporate quality standards.

4. **D.** All of these are components of the cost of quality. Prevention costs cover activities that keep quality problems from occurring. Appraisal costs keep any product defects from reaching the customer. Failure costs include any work associated with the failure of the product.

5. **B.** Risk identification is the process of determining and documenting the potential danger areas in your project. Quantifying the impact to the project of a potential problem is risk severity. Risk probability deals with the likelihood that a particular problem will occur. Risk response defines the action to take in response to a potential risk.

6. **D.** A risk response plan contains preventative actions and contingency actions. A preventative action is an activity designed to prevent a risk from occurring. A contingency action is an activity designed to deal with the impacts of a risk that is out of your control. Risk probability is part of risk analysis. You must determine how likely it is that the potential problem will occur in order to prioritize your risks. Risk analysis is done prior to the risk response plan.

7. **C.** Communications planning is the process of identifying who needs to receive information on the project, what information they need, and how they will get that information. Scheduling project team meeting, developing distribution lists, and creating a project status template are all activities that might be a result of the communications plan.

8. **B, D.** The VP of sales is accountable for the increased revenue resulting from this application. He is concerned that the functionality the application will provide is easy to use and contains the data users need to close sales. He would also be interested in any processes that will ensure the system is ready for mass deployment. A review of the technical design and programmer language is more appropriate for functional manager stakeholders in the IT organization who are providing the people who will be doing the design and code work.

9. D. Make or buy analysis is the technique of determining the benefits of procuring goods or services outside the organization. Staff augmentation is the term used for contract labor that is added either for a fixed amount of time or to complete specific tasks. Vendor selection criteria are the items you use to evaluate and select a vendor.

10. C. A cost reimbursable contract is often the only option if you do not have a well-defined product or if the vendor is being asked to provide something that has not been done before. A fixed price contract would not be feasible for the vendor or the buyer, as there is not any historical information to use as a basis for the fee. A time and materials contract would also be problematic, as the vendor may not have enough data to know what type of resources will be applied to the contract.

11. B. If your budget and project end date are fixed, then the thing that's going to represent the point of variance will be the quality. Managing quality in such an environment can be very difficult.

12. C. It is the responsibility of the project manager to identify those risks associated with the project.

13. B, C. You've encountered a risk to the project that you (hopefully) identified in your risk assessment process. The mitigation strategy shows that when the scope of the project has changed, which it has in this case due to the pushing out of the targeted completion date, you must obtain sign-off from the project sponsor. Adding developers won't help in this situation because the problem's been determined and a solution proposed but there is a time requirement.

14. B. The stakeholders of the project (which includes the sponsor and the clients) are the ones who'll have to live with any associated risks and need to be the ones who decide whether the risks are acceptable. On the other hand, it is up to the project manager to make sure he or she has assessed the risk situation and has come up with ways to avoid any pitfalls, as well as mitigation strategies to deal with risks that arise. Stakeholders should be made aware of the risks that were discovered at risk assessment time.

15. A, C, D. When you develop a procurement plan, you put out a request for bids and perform an analysis of the subsequent bids for the work. You should pay attention to the way that the vendor describes how the gear will be shipped, how it will be warranted, and how its safe arrival will be guaranteed. Thus procurement planning is critical to making sure that the long-term delivery initiatives pointed out above (18 months) will be met. Additionally, risk planning will help define those areas where problems may arise. While not necessary, you could certainly add communications planning details on how you'll interact with vendors.

16. A, C, E. While a nice advantage to a good communications plan is that you are able to carve out some time for yourself, it is *not* the reason you develop such a plan. Similarly, with a good communications plan, you'll be updating the sponsor who, *in turn*, will update the executives, but your communications plan may not directly update them.

17. C. A corporate quality officer is probably a good idea, but how will she enforce quality if there's not a quality policy in place to start with? A project management plan should be in place for *adhering* to a corporate quality policy and the project manager might be lucky enough to work for a company that gives bonuses for superior project management quality.

18. D. When faced with an integrated system deployment, it's wise to understand that the complexities can frequently be more plentiful than your team may at first be willing to admit. In an integrated systems project, it would be prudent to spend extra time on risk assessment as well as allocating extra testing time when connecting systems.

19. F. A methodology change involves in a change in the project's scope, which, in turn, involves sponsor sign-off and a brand new risk assessment. While it may be attractive to go forward with something that has the promise of saving you time, you've already settled on a given methodology that has sign-off and you should not experiment at this point in time with new techniques as you're not sure whether you'd have a positive outcome.

20. A. The critical path is the series of consecutive activities that represent the longest dependent path through the project. Since a risk to a step in the critical path could potentially increase the time it takes to get the step done, it can directly affect the project's completion date. While it's important that you strive to uncover as many risks as possible prior to the project getting under way, it's very important that you pay special attention in terms of risk assessment to tasks on the critical path.

Chapter 7

Comprehensive Project Plan

THE COMPTIA IT PROJECT+ EXAM TOPICS COVERED IN THIS CHAPTER INCLUDE:

- ✓ 2.2 Given an approved project charter, high-level scope documents, and schedule/budget objectives demonstrate the ability to create a project management plan that illustrates key knowledge and understanding.

- ✓ 2.26 Identify the components/documents of an adequate project plan and explain the function of each.

- ✓ 2.27 Identify the steps involved in organizing a comprehensive project plan and using it to close out the planning phase of a project.

- ✓ 2.28 Demonstrate knowledge of how to set performance baselines.

- ✓ 2.29 Demonstrate knowledge of the need to create change management procedures for the project plan.

- ✓ 2.30 Be able to identify project performance indicators that will be used to monitor and control performance during execution.

- ✓ 2.32 Recognize the need to conduct a review meeting as the project transitions from the planning phase to the execution/control/coordination phase. The review would include an assessment of all planning documents.

Finally, we have reached the last chapter dealing with project planning. Critical data is generated from all of the planning processes we discussed in the first six chapters, and you must be wondering what do you do with this information and how to track it. This is where an overall planning document comes into play.

At this point in the project, you are almost ready to start the project execution phase, and all of the planning output needs to be organized in a way that creates a handbook you can use to lead the completion of the project work.

The planning data is integrated into one comprehensive planning document that contains output from all of the applicable planning processes we have covered so far: Initiation, Scope, Time, Cost, Human Resources, Quality, Communications, Risk, and Procurement.

A typical project plan contains several categories of components such as administrative, planning, templates and checklists, references, and an appendix, all of which we'll discuss in more detail in this chapter.

The development of a project plan is more than just taking all of your planning documents and putting them in a binder. The development of a meaningful project plan requires time and input from your sponsor, project team members, and other stakeholders. A detailed outline or table of contents (TOC) and organization of your planning documents around this outline or TOC are key elements to writing a plan.

Finally, the review, formal approval, and distribution of the project plan signifies the transition of the project from the planning phase into the execution phase.

What Is a Project Plan?

As you have learned from previous chapters, the project planning process commences with initiation and includes processes from the entire *Guide to the PMBOK* knowledge areas. A *comprehensive project plan* is a document that integrates all planning data into one document that the project manager can be use as a guidebook for moving the project into the execution phase and overseeing the project. The project plan uses the output from the planning processes to create a consistent end-to-end document covering all project phases. The project plan is maintained and updated throughout the life of the project.

Creating a comprehensive project plan is a very important component of project planning that is often overlooked. It may not seem important that all of your planning data is organized into one central document, but without it you will find yourself constantly fielding questions regarding the project requiring you to search for the file on the project charter, the scope statement, the WBS, or some other planning document.

Further, a lot of important data is created during the planning process. If this data is not clearly organized and distributed to the right people, it will be of little value.

The purpose of a project plan extends beyond just a collection of project data, and there are also benefits from a high-quality plan you will realize during project execution and control.

Purpose   The final step in the project planning phase produces a formal, approved document that is used to guide project execution and control. It provides the basis for performing and managing all project-related activities.

The project plan is the document you will use during project execution and control as the foundation to track the performance of your project and take any needed corrective action. It is used to communicate key information to the project stakeholders.

Benefits   The project plan is a single source of information regarding all key elements of the project—available to everyone associated with the project.

The plan is a reference source that can clarify questions such as what is or is not included in the scope of the project, who the key stakeholders are, and what the major deliverables are, along with many others.

The project plan is a guidebook that can be used during project execution to focus team members, thus keeping the project on course.

To better understand what the comprehensive project plan is all about, let's take a look at the components you will find in a typical project plan.

Project Plan Components

The comprehensive project plan should bring together information obtained from all the various planning processes you've undertaken in an organized, cohesive fashion. You can organize data in a number of ways to produce an integrated project plan. Many organizations use a standard template for project plans. Although the format and structure may vary, the key components of a project plan, as we mentioned in the chapter introduction, usually include (but are not limited to) the following:

- Administrative information regarding the organization and revision of the document
- Outputs of your planning processes
- Any applicable templates or checklists that will be used to manage the project
- Any reference material
- An appendix

No standard sequence drives the order of the project plan components. Both the components themselves and the component sequence vary between organizations, and an abbreviated version may be used for small projects.

If your organization has a program management office (PMO), there is probably a standard project plan template. If you do not have a template, you can use examples of project plans from previous projects to develop your particular plan. (You could try visiting well-known websites such as www.gantthead.com or www.techrepublic.com for project planning examples or simply do a Google search for "project plan template"). Communicating your project plan is much easier if you are using a format people are familiar with.

It is a good idea to review carefully the contents of any planning template you are expected to complete to determine whether your planning activities to date have produced all of the data required in the document. You may find your team has additional work to do to provide all of the information required in the template.

Let's take a closer look at the components of a typical project plan.

Administrative Components

A comprehensive project plan can be a very lengthy document. To facilitate ease of use and ensure that updates are properly tracked, a project plan may include the following administrative components:

Document Information   This section contains information regarding the update and maintenance of the plan. A document history lists the version numbers and revision dates, and contact information to obtain copies of the document.

Table of Contents   The table of contents displays how the information is organized, so that the reader can access a particular component. If you do not have a project plan template to follow, find examples from other projects in your organization. It is helpful to the people who will be referencing the plan to have the data in a recognizable sequence.

Planning Components

The planning components are the main body of the document, and they appear as sequenced in the table of contents. The components listed below are typical of how a project plan is organized, although it is always best to determine if you are expected to follow specific standards.

Executive Summary   An executive summary is included to communicate with executives who are responsible for corporate business strategy or funding decisions, and any managers whose personnel the project will impact. It should contain high-level information written in nontechnical terms.

The executive summary typically starts with a brief project description that explains the business need or problem that generated the project request. It should include the overall goal of the project as it relates to corporate goals or strategies, the targeted completion date, and overall budget. The goal of the Executive Summary is to give busy executives a quick high-level overview of the project so they can be knowledgeable about what's going on. It does not go deep into the nuts and bolts of the project.

Requirements   The requirements section lists the functional, technical, and business requirements for the project, as defined during project initiation.

Scope   The project scope defines the boundaries of the project based on the deliverables agreed to by the client.

> **Note:** Remember, this section describes both what is included and excluded in the product being produced by the project.

Stakeholders The stakeholder component identifies the people responsible for the success of the project. This includes the sponsor, client(s), project manager, and project team members, as well as other work groups whose assistance is required to complete the project (such as vendors).

> **Note:** There is debate among project managers as to the amount of detail to include in this section. For large projects that will last over six months, it may not be practical to list all of the project team members, as the baseline resource list you create during planning may change significantly multiple times over the course of the project. (For example, Kimmie may be the programmer initially, but she resigns to pursue writing a novel so you replace her with Susan.) Rather than constantly updating the project plan, you may choose to list only the project manager, sponsor, and client(s), with a reference to how readers can obtain the current project team organization chart or directory. You may opt, for example, to publish this information on an intranet site.

Expected Resources The expected resources section lists non–human resources such as servers, software, etc., that you anticipate using. You may also list vendors in this section.

Assumption and/or Constraints The assumptions that were agreed on during the planning process and any known constraints that will impact the outcome of the project are documented in this section. These are outputs from your planning process. A typical assumption statement might read: "The vendor will deliver on time."

Major Deliverables/Scheduled Tasks The major deliverables section lists the *summary level* achievements that make up the delivery of the product. You should include the major deliverables from each project phase. This information typically is obtained by using the highest level of the WBS or the summary tasks from the project schedule.

You may also be required to provide information on how to view the current version of the project schedule (e.g., intranet page or other electronic location).

A copy of the project schedule baseline may be included as an appendix.

Budget The project budget is discussed here. This section may be very high level with only a summary figure for the entire project budget or it may break the budget down into various spending categories. Some plans also detail the method used to purchase capital equipment and track project capital and expenses.

A copy of the budget baseline may be included as an appendix.

> **Racing to the Finish**
>
> One project we were familiar with (but did not work on) used a cute way to illustrate the project baseline. The project managers got foam board from the stationery store. They printed out clip art of different racehorses and cut them out. Then they glued the horses to more foam board and cut them out. Next, they attached Velcro dots to the horses and also to percentages to complete milestones along the baseline. When the final "baseline board" was done you had a "lane" for each racehorse—each lane representing a phase or deliverable. As each phase or deliverable was worked on and progress was made, its horse was advanced one more step. The end result was that you had a very clear illustration of where we were at in the project, similar to the graphic shown below.
>
> Unfortunately, the project was a flop—but hey, the baseline board has stuck in our minds all these years.

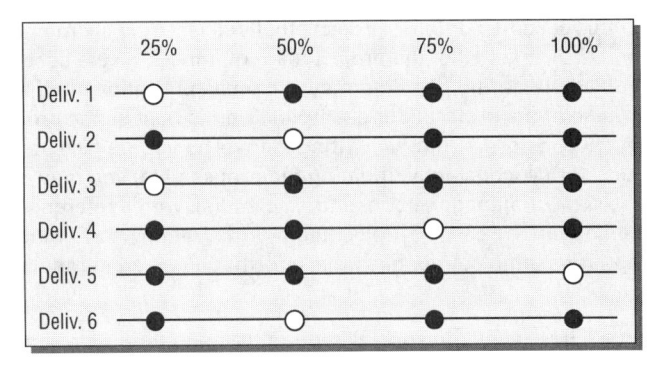

Risks The identified risks that could affect the success of the project and plans to avoid or mitigate the risks are listed in this section.

Issues The method used to identify project issues, assign responsibility for resolution, define escalation procedures, and track and report progress is described in this section. This section can also include a discussion of the overall environmental issues the project could run into, including the overall computing environment as well as the political, geographical, and integrated systems environments.

Communications The communications component describes the method and frequency of communication with sponsor, clients, project team, and other stakeholders. For example, you might say something like this: "Sponsor communications—one-on-one meeting every Monday at 10:00 A.M. for the duration of the project," and "Team communications—biweekly team meeting every Thursday at 2:00 P.M.; email or one-on-one conferences as required for the duration of the project."

Implementation Plan   The implementation plan is an overview of the methodology used to implement the project schedule. The plans you've created for development, hardware, installation, securing, configuration, testing as well as other plans for correct implementation of the project schedule are included.

Support Plan   The support plan documents how the new system will be supported once the project is complete. Support may be limited to the update and maintenance of a new system or piece of hardware, or it may include a technical group that will support the users of a new application.

Training Plan   The training plan documents how training on the new system will be accomplished. This includes training for end users, help-desk staff, operations staff, or other groups, as applicable.

Templates and Checklists

If you are using any existing checklists or have developed checklists during the planning processes, you can include copies in this section. Examples of checklists in this section are:

- Installation checklist
- Testing checklist
- Other quality checklists

References

The reference section lists any sources used for project methodology, corporate standards, or best practices. A reference list may include:

- *A Guide to the PMBOK*
- Your Corporation's quality standards
- Your corporation's system development methodology
- Your corporation's project management methodology
- ISO 9000 standards
- Any applicable regulations or standards

Appendix

An appendix can be used to provide a copy of detailed documents not normally included in the body of the project plan:

- Project schedule baseline
- Project budget baseline

With all of these components to consider, writing a comprehensive project plan can overwhelm a new project manager. Don't worry, we can share a lot of tips on how to make this come together smoothly with all of the data you need to oversee the project.

Putting It All Together

The project plan can be created either by putting all of your critical data in a formal document or by organizing a series of existing documents, depending on what is expected in your organization. If your initial planning processes are thorough and involve the right participants, the revisions should be kept to those aspects of the project that are formally changed during the course of the project. If the up-front planning activities are shortchanged, the project plan will probably be inaccurate or important data will be missing.

In order to finish out project planning there are some final required steps:

- Organize and write the plan.
- Define a plan update process.
- Review the plan with stakeholders.
- Close out the planning phase.

Organizing and Writing the Plan

Although you may be tempted to just jump in and start writing, it is much better to take time to review your documentation and organize it to match the outline or template you will be using. Otherwise you may find that you are moving data around, entering data multiple times, or omitting key points.

> ### Real World Scenario
>
> #### After-the-Fact Plan
>
> We can remember being on a project with a very large project plan binder that was updated on a weekly basis during project execution because most of the sections were created as the project work was being done.
>
> This method of developing the comprehensive project plan created a scenario where the project manager, the project team members, and other stakeholders did not have a plan to guide execution of the project. What we received instead was a history of what was decided after the fact.
>
> As you can imagine, confusion was rampant, and to no one's surprise, the project was quickly off track.
>
> This is definitely not the way you want to transition into project execution. A project plan binder isn't a reflection of what has been done, but what has been *planned to be* done.

You also need to define a *document control process* if there is not a standard in your organization. How revisions are made, the version numbering system, and the placement of the version number and revision date are items that should be defined before even a draft project plan is distributed. Without a document control system in place, you cannot properly account for all updates to the plan.

With today's file-sharing technology, more project managers are taking advantage of distributing project data electronically. This eliminates a lot of the manual work involved in printing and distributing the original project plan and then distributing any changed pages as the plan is updated.

You should decide prior to starting the document whether you are going to distribute the plan via paper or electronically. A project plan accessed via a shared file has its own unique challenges. You need to determine the level of security required to access your documents, and make sure all stakeholders have access to the server where your project file is stored. All of the documents on the server should be "read only" to prevent any accidental changes. You do not want to start putting documentation out on a server until you have established the access and security procedures.

Once you have completed these up-front steps and have all of your planning output organized around your outline, you are ready to write the plan. Your plan will be read in part or in total by many people at many different levels in your organization, so make sure that you have checked grammar and spelling and that each section of the plan is complete and all of the data is correct. A plan that is thrown together without the proper review and editing will provide the impression that the project itself was not thoroughly thought out or properly planned.

Even as you are writing the initial version of the plan, you need to be developing change management processes for updating the plan.

Updating the Plan

Even after you complete the initial project plan document, reviewed the document with all the stakeholders, and obtained formal sponsor approval, your project plan may still change as you move into the project execution phase.

Updating the project plan is an *iterative process*; meaning that as key components documented in the plan change throughout the course of the project, various sections of the project plan will require updates. The scope may change, a new stakeholder may become involved, or an additional major deliverable may be added, to name just a few examples. The challenge of maintaining a project plan has always been the logistics of keeping the plan current and communicating updates to the project team, the sponsor, and other key stakeholders. Plans that are updated haphazardly will quickly become inaccurate and lose their usefulness as a road map for project execution.

To help alleviate these difficulties, you need a documented change process. Additionally, unless your PMO provides the updates, you will need to designate a person to actually make the changes and distribute the revised pages. The process for updating the plan needs to be communicated to all stakeholders.

Any change to project plan data that is controlled by a change process should only be made as a result of output from the corresponding process. A change to the scope should only include official scope changes that have been approved via the process established in the scope management plan. Budget or schedule changes should also be linked to the formal approval process for such changes.

Throughout the process of putting together your planning data, you will need to schedule ongoing reviews with the sponsor and other stakeholders.

Reviewing the Plan

A good project plan is a document that the project manager uses to drive the successful development of the project's product. The people involved with the project should have an opportunity to participate in the creation of the plan. The project plan is usually developed in multiple steps and evolves throughout the planning process. Ongoing review of the plan with both the sponsor and the other stakeholders is critical to the success of the project.

Sponsor Review

The sponsor review starts when you are developing your outline or table of contents. Review of a plan outline will provide the sponsor with an opportunity to comment on the content of the document. Even if you are following an approved template, it is your responsibility as project manager to confirm that the sponsor is familiar with the contents of the template.

Schedule periodic reviews with the sponsor as you add data to the various sections. The sponsor must sign off on the project plan to make it official. The end result should not be a surprise, merely the finished product the sponsor has seen through various stages of development.

Other Stakeholder Review

The creation of the comprehensive project plan is actually a great opportunity for the project manager to solidify involvement and commitment of the stakeholders. Your client, your project team, and other key stakeholders are key participants in the creation of the project plan. At a minimum, these people should receive a copy of the outline or TOC so that they are aware of what information is included in the plan. Even though the information being compiled in the project plan should not be news to the stakeholders, they may have different expectations for the project plan. Thus, up-front resolution of any issues or concerns will facilitate the writing of the plan.

Interim reviews with the stakeholder team may be appropriate for a complex and detailed project plan. In other situations it may be appropriate to meet with individual stakeholders only if they have questions.

The final review of the project plan is a formal process that signifies the end of the planning.

Closing Out the Planning Phase

The completion of the comprehensive project plan signals the transition from the planning phase to the execution and control phases. When the initial project plan document is complete, the comprehensive project plan is circulated to all the stakeholders. The planning phase can be closed out with a formal stakeholder review meeting to transition to the execution and control phases.

Throughout the project, you will constantly be assessing whether the project should move forward. The meeting to close out the planning process is an excellent opportunity to obtain stakeholder concurrence regarding the viability of the project business case. If there have been any substantial changes in the business need that initially drove the approval of the project, now is the time, before the project work begins, to evaluate whether the project should move forward.

This review session should bring closure to any outstanding issues from the planning process. Hopefully, any issues that were raised earlier have been addressed and resolved throughout the planning phase. But don't assume that issues do not exist just because you are not made aware of them. Be sure to ask the stakeholders directly if anything regarding the planning phase is unresolved in their minds. It is much easier to resolve any planning disputes before the project work begins.

> **NOTE** It might be helpful to remember that as project manager, in some people's eyes you are in a position of power. They may be reluctant to reveal a problem to you because they don't want to appear as non–team players or as troublemakers. It's important to try to foster open, honest, straightforward communication that supports a sense of security for people to be able to speak their minds about issues they see forthcoming. Yes, there are people who will freely speak their minds no matter what. But you know who those people are. It's up to you to try to get the information out of those who know, but won't tell.

Another key focus of the planning review is to assure that stakeholder expectations of the project are aligned with what is detailed in the plan. If any component of the plan was a surprise, find out what the real expectation was. It is the project manager's responsibility to make sure that everyone involved in the project understands and supports not only the end result of the project, but the road map to reach that end result.

After making any changes as a result of the review meeting, the plan is formally approved by the sponsor and, in some cases, by the client. The approved document is then distributed to all stakeholders.

As a transition into the execution and controlling phases, the planning close out meeting may also be used to discuss indicators used to monitor and control project performance as the project work begins. *Project performance indicators* are measures the project manager uses to determine whether the project is on track, such as any deviation from the baseline schedule or the baseline budget. For example, you should know that your development phase is scheduled to complete in 8 weeks and be tracking progress to meet that target. The use of performance indicators will be discussed in more detail in Chapters 8 and 9.

A successful transition from planning into execution should leave everyone clear about his or her individual role on the project and excited about moving forward to actually get the work done.

> **Case Study: Chaptal Wineries—Finalized Project Plan**
>
> You're now ready to go forward and prepare your finalized project plan for presentation to Kim Cox, the owner of Chaptal. Following are the elements that you prepare:
>
> **Table of Contents**
>
> 1. Executive Summary
> 2. Requirements
> 3. Scope
> 4. Stakeholders
> 5. Expected Resources
> 6. Assumptions and Constraints
> 7. Major Deliverables
> 8. Budget
> 9. Risks
> 10. Issues
> 11. Communication
> 12. Implementation Plan
> 13. Support Plan
> 14. Training Plan
>
> **1. Executive Summary** Chaptal Wineries recently purchased wineries in France, Southeastern Australia, and Chile. It is now necessary to electronically connect the wineries so that workers in each location can send and receive email, as well as look at one another's calendars. Additionally, it is necessary to set up a Chaptal intranet site so that critical information such as the numbers of cases of wine produced, vine health, winemaker notes, and other similar pieces of information critical to the business can be posted for corporatewide consumption. The IT manager at Chaptal's Sonoma, California location will be responsible for procuring the necessary hardware and software, telecommunications connections, and installation expertise.
>
> **2. Requirements**
>
> > A. Install T1 or E1 telecommunications circuits at each of the newly purchased sites, thus preparing the sites for WAN communications. Telecommunications companies and their third-party vendor representatives will be used for this work.

B. Set up an email system between the four sites. This will allow for all sites to email one another using an internal email system, thus preventing the possibility that someone outside the organization can get inside information via email regarding new vintages, wines, wine-making methods, case lots, or other business-critical information. There will be an email server at each of the four geographically disbursed sites. The Chaptal IT manager will be responsible for procuring the servers and installing and configuring them.

C. Set up an intranet. The intranet server will be hosted at the Sonoma location. This server will host web pages that perform such business-critical functions as corporate timekeeping, winemaker's notes, barrel-tasting notes, vintages, diseases encountered, vinekeeper notes, and other data relevant to the performance of our vineyards and the wine. The Chaptal IT manager will procure the server and install it. A contractor will be used for the programming work.

D. Test all connections and train users.

3. Scope This project includes the elements necessary to connect the four sites together by wide area networking. Additionally, the project accounts for setting up an email system that includes an email server at each site. As well, an intranet server and the programming of relevant intranet pages are included. Procurement of all necessary hardware and software, as well as installation configuration, testing, deployment, maintenance, and training are included. *Not* included in this project is a system for managing corporate finances, HR, or assembly-line/manufacturing work (such as the actual bottling and labeling of the wine bottles). Our enterprise resource planning (ERP) software handles this function. A later project will bring all three new sites into utilization of the ERP.

4. Stakeholders Stakeholders include:

Kim Cox Project Sponsor and owner of Chaptal Wineries.

Guillaume Fourche A Bordeaux *negociant* specializing in fine red wines. Fourche's cabernet sauvignon wine will be re-branded as Les Chaptalè Bordeaux Villages.

Metor Sanchez Owner of a Chilean winery in the Aconcagua valley. Sanchez's Syrah, cabernet sauvignon, and Malbec wines will be re-branded as Casa Sanchez Chaptal.

Jason Jay Proprietor of Roo wines. His Shiraz wines will be re-branded as Chaptal Roo.

Others Chaptal wineries employees to assist with UAT.

5. Expected Resources

Five Intel-based midrange class servers.

Carrier Sensing Units/Data Sensing Units (CSU/DSU) for demarcation connectivity.

One router and switch per location.

Telecommunications vendors and consultants (including demarcation installers and router and switch internetworking specialists).

Contractor to develop and test intranet pages.

Email software.

Web software.

Virus-scanning software.

6. Assumptions and Constraints

Assumptions

1. No variance in the behavior of like hardware.
2. Telecommunications companies in each nation will have reasonable wide area network setup request procedures and installation timelines.
3. Average T1/E1 cost is assumed to be $350/month U.S. dollars.
4. Intranet development time is assumed to be 60 person days (30 working days, 2 persons).
5. All sites will provide reasonable access for installers and a secure, climate-controlled, power-conditioned room for the electronic gear.
6. Routers will use Open Shortest Path First (OSPF) routing protocol.
7. Contractual help will be used for configuration of the routers.
8. The network operating system (NOS) will be Windows Server 2003 (W2K3) and the email server software will be Exchange 2003 (E2K3).

Constraints

1. Language barriers
2. Availability of people at any given site to be able to help with setup due to problems with the winemaking efforts
3. Harvest and crush seasons

7. Major Deliverables

1. Procure server and internetworking hardware
2. Procure wide area networking connections
3. Internetworking gear installation
4. Server installation

> 5. Email software installation
>
> 6. Intranet development
>
> 7. Training of users
>
> 8. Unit, Integration, and User Acceptance Testing
>
> **8. Budget** It is projected that the total project, not including the Chaptal IT Manager's regular salary, will be $205,000. Kim Cox has agreed to subsidize the project with a $25,000 contingency fund.
>
> **9. Risks**
>
> T1/E1 circuit bandwidth not sufficient
>
> Hardware failure
>
> Software failure
>
> Internetworking gear failure
>
> Programming errors
>
> **10. Issues** It is vital that the project be completed before the September "crush" of the grapes and preparation for new vintage wine making. Kim Cox has made it clear that no Chaptal employees are to be doing anything else but concentrating on the wine in September and October.
>
> **11. Communication** Because the email and intranet servers are not up yet, all communications will be by phone or by free temporary Internet mail such as Hotmail. Kim Cox will be updated daily. Jason Jay, Metor Sanchez, and Guillaume Fourche will be updated weekly.
>
> **12. Implementation Plan** Due to the requirements of the email software, procurement and installation of the WAN circuits must happen first, followed by installation of the internetworking gear. After that, server builds can take place following by intranet programming and testing.
>
> **13. Support Plan** The Chaptal IT manager will be the primary support entity, assisted by a designated individual at each of the remote sites.
>
> **14. Training Plan** The Chaptal IT manager will handle all of the training efforts at all sites.

Summary

The comprehensive project plan is your guidebook that will be used throughout the life of the project.

The project plan contains outputs from the various planning processes put together in one all-inclusive document. It should include the critical planning outputs for initiation, scope, time, cost, human resources, quality, communications, risk, and procurement.

Although a project plan has historically been a paper document, today there are more examples of project managers who distribute plans electronically in a shared folder environment.

The comprehensive project plan is created with ongoing input and review from the sponsor, the client, the project team, and other stakeholders.

A formal review, with official sign off and approval of the plan, marks the transition from project planning to project execution.

Exam Essentials

Explain the purpose of a comprehensive project plan. A comprehensive project plan is the document you will use during execution and control to track the performance of the project and take any needed corrective action. It is used to communicate key information to the project stakeholders.

Be familiar with the components of a comprehensive project plan. A comprehensive project plan contains components such as documentation revision control, a table of contents, executive summary, a list of stakeholders, project requirements, major deliverables, expected resources, environmental issues, and plans for implementation, support, and training.

Understand what is meant when project plan development is described as an iterative process. The planning process is repeated in cycles as more information is obtained or changes are made to the project.

Explain the importance of performance baselines. Baselines are a picture of what is expected to happen before the project work begins. They are used to measure the progress being made. Common baselines include the scope statement, the schedule, and the budget.

Demonstrate knowledge of the importance of a formal review of the project plan. A formal review is scheduled to assure a common understanding of the project plan by all stakeholders. Stakeholders have an opportunity to ask questions and provide feedback before the plan is finalized.

Identify the steps involved in creating a project plan. The project manager should create an outline or table of contents for review with the sponsor and other stakeholders. The writing of the plan involves bringing together and integrating all of the output from the planning processes. A review of the draft plan is held with all stakeholders. The project sponsor provides formal approval or sign off of the plan.

Key Terms

Before you take the exam, be certain you are familiar with the following terms:

comprehensive project plan

iterative process

document control process

project performance indicators

Review Questions

1. What document integrates the information from all of the planning processes into one cohesive road map for managing the project?
   A. Project charter
   B. Scope management plan
   C. Comprehensive project plan
   D. Schedule baseline

2. Which of the following best describes the iterative nature of the development of the project plan?
   A. The project plan is never "final." The process is repeated as new information is obtained or if there is a major change to the project.
   B. The project plan is circulated to each of the stakeholders and comments are incorporated as they are received.
   C. The project plan is updated weekly to make sure everyone understands the importance of the project.
   D. Multiple versions of the project plan are created to cause confusion and lessen the likelihood that you will be blamed if the project fails.

3. Which of the following is the best method to organize of the project plan?
   A. Because compiling the project plan is really an administrative task, you should solicit clerical support to sort through all of the planning data and put together a table of contents.
   B. You need to develop an outline of what will be included in the plan, but don't spend a lot of time incorporating your planning outputs into the outline. You will save time if you just wait until the project is underway to see what really happens and complete the outline after the fact.
   C. You should gather your output data from the planning processes and organize the data in a logical fashion. You are now ready to send the document to your sponsor with a signature sheet. You can distribute the approved plan to the stakeholders so they know what you and the sponsor have agreed to.
   D. You start by gathering all of your output data from the planning processes. Next, you develop an outline or table of contents to review with the project sponsor and other stakeholders. After you have updated the outline based on feedback from the sponsor or the other stakeholders, write the plan by integrating the data from your planning output documents into your outline. The completed document should be distributed to all stakeholders in preparation for a formal review session. After incorporating any changes from the review session, obtain formal approval from the sponsor, and distribute the approved document.

4. Which of the following best reflects the purpose of a formal review of the comprehensive project plan?

   A. A formal review of the project plan provides an opportunity for stakeholders to ask questions and provide feedback on the contents of the plan.

   B. A formal review is held to fill in any gaps in the project plan.

   C. A formal review is a means of shifting accountability to the stakeholders if they agree with the plan.

   D. A formal review is a great way to impress the stakeholder team by using elaborate slides with a lot of artwork.

5. Not all project plans will contain the same components. Which of the following components would you expect to see in all plans?

   A. Training plan

   B. Overview or executive summary

   C. Procurement plan

   D. None of the above

6. What is the best way to handle a potential change to the project plan?

   A. You should have a documented procedure to handle changes to the project plan. This plan needs to be communicated to all stakeholders.

   B. You must update the plan and distribute the new version as quickly as you hear of any changes.

   C. You need to set a schedule for project plan updates and only reissue the plan according to that schedule.

   D. A meeting of all project stakeholders should be scheduled to discuss and vote on any proposed change to the project plan.

7. You are being pressured to get your team started on project execution, but you have not completed the comprehensive project plan. In the interest of time, you decide not to include any stakeholders in this process. Which of the following is a likely result of your decision?

   A. The project will start on time and be a success due to your creative thinking.

   B. The project plan will be clear and concise, as you will not have to make any of those additions or changes that the stakeholders might want.

   C. There will not be a common understanding of how the project execution and control will proceed. Key stakeholders may feel that their input is not valued, and support for the project may diminish.

   D. There may be a few complaints, but you can easily handle any issues that might arise once you get the team members working on the project tasks.

8. A project plan often includes a baseline for the project scope, schedule, and budget. What is the importance of these documents?

    A. Baselines are used to show how poorly the project was planned.

    B. A baseline is a picture of what is planned prior to the start of project execution and can be used to monitor project progress.

    C. Baselines have no relevance to project execution.

    D. Baselines are used to show stakeholders what they want to hear.

9. Which of the following is the best example of a project performance indicator?

    A. There have been 10 scope change requests.

    B. The length of the weekly project status meeting has increased.

    C. Your team member Jane reports that her task will not complete on time.

    D. There was $250,000 spent on the development phase, as compared to a budgeted amount of $200,000.

10. You need an assessment of the ongoing viability of the project business case, the completeness of planning documents, and the resolution of all planning issues. What is the best method to accomplish this?

    A. Distribute a memo requesting submission of planning input and any issues related to planning.

    B. Distribute all planning documentation to the stakeholder team.

    C. Schedule a meeting with all stakeholders to transition the project from planning to execution.

    D. Discuss these items with the project sponsor.

11. Of the following elements, which one is not a requirement for the project plan?

    A. Detailed WBS

    B. Training plan

    C. Risks

    D. Executive summary

12. Whose responsibility is it to prepare the project plan?

    A. Sponsor

    B. Project manager

    C. Project team

    D. PMO administrative assistant

13. Which is true for a comprehensive project plan? (Select all that apply.)
    A. Is optional
    B. Can be assembled and delivered at any time during the project
    C. Signals the end of the planning process
    D. Must be signed by all stakeholders
    E. Must at least be signed by the sponsor

14. In order to make sure that changes are adequately tracked, what sort of process must be in place for comprehensive electronic project plans?
    A. Change management process
    B. Document management process
    C. Quality management process
    D. Electronic signature process

15. Ongoing comprehensive plan reviews with the sponsor and stakeholders should be held:
    A. Only once, at the time that you write and release the project plan.
    B. On a regularly scheduled, routine basis.
    C. As needed.
    D. Stakeholders need not be included.

16. What is the reason for using a project performance indicator?
    A. To track the output of your project team members
    B. To make sure the project has not exceeded budget or timeline constraints
    C. To assure that you've not added additional deliverables to the project
    D. To be able to add a visual element to the project plan for those who are kinesthetically oriented learners

17. From the list below, select some examples of things you might consider including in the appendix section of your comprehensive project plan. (Select all that apply.)
    A. *A Guide to the PMBOK*
    B. Your corporation's quality standards
    C. Thanks and signatory pages for all those who participated
    D. Photos of the project team and team members' contact information
    E. Your corporation's system development methodology
    F. Your corporation's project management methodology
    G. ISO 9000 standards

18. Which is true for the Executive Summary? (Select all that apply.)
    A. Is a technical section
    B. Is a nontechnical section
    C. Is a complete synopsis
    D. Is a brief summary

19. What is the purpose of the comprehensive project plan? (Select all that apply.)
    A. A guidebook for focusing team members
    B. A reference source for clarifying questions
    C. A budget book for the finance office
    D. A single source of information regarding all key elements of the project
    E. An input into the corporate strategic plan

20. Name the three plans that you would include in your comprehensive project plan document.
    A. Implementation plan
    B. Budgeting plan
    C. Training plan
    D. Team member performance review plan
    E. Support plan

Answers to Review Questions

1. **C.** The comprehensive project plan is the document that pulls together all of the output from the previous planning processes. A typical project plan contains elements from the project charter, the scope management plan, and the schedule baseline.

2. **A.** The project plan is a living document. Multiple iterations of a project plan are a reflection of new information regarding project stakeholders or a major approved change to the scope, schedule, or budget.

3. **D.** A good project plan is instrumental in the smooth execution of the project work. Putting thought into the plan, taking time to review the plan with your sponsor and other stakeholders, and obtaining formal approval will increase commitment to the project and reduce later misunderstandings that could impact the outcome of the project.

4. **A.** A formal review of the project plan is your last opportunity prior to project execution to obtain feedback or input on the project work. It can be used as a checkpoint to make sure all of the stakeholders are on the same page.

5. **B.** All plans should contain an overview or executive summary that contains a brief description of the project and how the project links to the organizational strategy. Executives do not have the time to read through the entire comprehensive project plan for each project in their organization; they need a clear, concise summary that provides them the basic information in nontechnical terms. Training plans and procurement plans do not pertain to all projects.

6. **A.** There should be documented change control procedures for handling any change to the project plan. These should be closely linked to procedures for changing the scope, budget, or schedule. Updates should only be made as required by this process.

7. **C.** It is always tempting to take shortcuts in the planning process, but doing so usually just creates bigger issues. Involving the stakeholders in the development of the project plan will help focus everyone on the project goals, clarify any misunderstandings, and solidify support for the project.

8. **B.** A baseline represents some of the key outputs of the planning process. A schedule baseline, as an example, depicts what tasks should be completed at a given point in time. By comparing actual results to the baseline document, a project manager can assess the progress being made.

9. **D.** A comparison of actual spending against the baseline budget is a good indicator of project performance. The number of scope change requests and the length of a project status meeting do not by themselves provide a measurable indication of how the project is going. There is not enough information on Jane's task to determine whether this delay could have an overall impact on the status of the project schedule.

10. **C.** The transition from the planning phase to the execution phase is an important step that needs to be officially acknowledged with a meeting to ensure all stakeholders' expectations for the planning process have been met and that there are no outstanding issues as project execution begins.

11. A. A *detailed* WBS isn't required for the project plan. The high-level summary tasks associated with the WBS should be included, however.

12. B. The project manager will be responsible for preparing the project plan, but it should be noted that he or she does not work in a vacuum. Up to now, input from the project team and the stakeholders has been required to assimilate all of the correct information about the project and when writing the project plan; you may need to consult them again and they will provide updates to the plan as you move forward.

13. C, E. The comprehensive project plan is a formal project document that signals the end of the planning process (and the beginning of executing and controlling). Further, it is an *approved* document, meaning that it is signed by at least the sponsor. You should consider having all stakeholders review it prior to sending it up for approval by the sponsor.

14. B. To make sure that changes and updates to the comprehensive project plan are accounted for, you should consider a document management process in which the documents live under some sort of version control methodology. In other words, when someone "checks out" a document for review and updating, the document version number is updated if updates are indeed made. Good workflow software such as Microsoft SharePoint Portal Server or others easily handles this requirement.

15. C. If changes are made that affect the comprehensive project plan, you must meet to review the prospective changes and gain buy in and acceptance. If there's nothing new in the project plan, then you're wasting everyone's time by having a meeting to review an unchanged document.

16. B. Performance indicators are a method you can use (talked about more in Chapters 8 and 9) for monitoring that you've not gone off budget or over the allotted time.

17. A, B, E, F, G. Not all of these elements are required, but they may be things you'd consider for your project plan. For instance, if your development team uses the so-called agile form of software development, you might include a section in the appendix that talks about what agile software development is and how it differs from ordinary application work.

18. B, D. The Executive Summary is a high-level overview of the project, its deliverables, and other nontechnical elements that you think a busy executive would be interested in relative to your project. You should take as much space as required to accurately and adequately summarize your project, but it needs to be a brief summary—something that can be reviewed by executives in a couple-minute read.

19. A, B, D. The comprehensive project plan is a document that describes all of the key elements of your project to those with an interest in it and who are authorized to view it. As such, it can act as a clarification reference for people who have questions about the direction the project is going in. While a large IT project might certainly wind up on a corporate strategic plan, it's doubtful that the full project plan would be included. Additionally, while the project plan contains high-level budget information, it is not a resource for the finance office. Your full project budget would be useful for that.

20. A, C, E. In your comprehensive project plan, you'll include that plans you have made for how you're going to deploy the system, how you'll support it once it's deployed, and how you'll train people to use it. The budget and performance review plans don't need to be a part of the project plan, although you'll include high-level budget information in your plan.

Chapter 8

Project Execution

THE COMPTIA IT PROJECT+ EXAM TOPICS COVERED IN THIS CHAPTER INCLUDE:

- ✓ 2.5: Identify methods for resolving disagreements among team members when evaluating the suitability of deliverables at each point in their evolution.
- ✓ 3.1: Identify the tasks that should be accomplished on a weekly basis in the course of tracking an "up and running" project.
- ✓ 3.6: Given a scenario in which a vendor requests a 2-week delay in delivering its product, explain the appropriate action.
- ✓ 3.7: Given a scenario in which there is a disagreement between a vendor and your project team, identify methods for resolving the problem.
- ✓ 3.8: Identify issues to consider when trying to rebuild active project support from a wavering executive (e.g., the need to identify the source of doubts, interpersonal communications skills that might be employed, the need to act without creating negative impact, the need to identify and utilize various allies and influences, etc.). Given a scenario involving a wavering executive, choose an appropriate course of action.
- ✓ 3.11: Demonstrate the ability to track the financial performance of a project, given the financial management baseline and data on the actual performance of the project.
- ✓ 3.22: Identify effective strategies for providing timely performance feedback to team members.
- ✓ 3.23: Demonstrate an understanding of how to effectively manage disgruntled team members so that team performance is not adversely affected.
- ✓ 3.24: Demonstrate an understanding of how to recognize individual team member performance issues and to identify effective strategies for corrective action.

- ✓ 3.25: Given an initial high-level scope, budget, and resource allocation, demonstrate understanding of the need to investigate the aspects of the project that could be modified to improve outcomes (i.e., find out what is negotiable, prepare to negotiate).
- ✓ 3.26: Given a project scenario, demonstrate the ability to resolve a resource availability (staffing) issue requiring escalation to the project sponsor and senior-level stakeholders.
- ✓ 3.27: Given a project scenario during the implementation phases, demonstrate the understanding of the need to organize and effectively run meetings.
- ✓ 3.28: Given a project team meeting scenario in which a decision must be made with imperfect information, demonstrate the knowledge of problem-solving techniques to help the team through a decision making process.
- ✓ 3.29: Given a project team meeting scenario, demonstrate the awareness of the need to provide direction and clarify work instructions to team members.
- ✓ 3.30: Given a project team meeting scenario under a situation whereby the project is behind plan, demonstrate the awareness of the need to identify, clarify, develop, and implement key strategies.
- ✓ 3.31: Given a project scenario in which intra-team communication is inadequate, demonstrate the ability to improve communication to an appropriate level.
- ✓ 3.39: Recognize potential organizational and political barriers inhibiting an effective working relationship between the IT organization and the client/business organization.
- ✓ 3.40: Demonstrate an understanding of methods to develop and maintain an effective working relationship during projects between the IT organization and the client/business organization.

Now is where the real work begins—project execution. You are in charge of managing the project to a successful completion. Successful project execution involves development of your project team, performing according to the project plan, information distribution, and contract administration.

You will have relationships with a number of individuals and groups during the life of the project. All of your people-management skills will come into play as you negotiate with the sponsor, team members, vendors, functional managers, clients, users, and other internal organizations such as finance or legal.

If you talk to veteran project managers about what makes them successful, many will list the project team. Understanding how to build this temporary group into a team, making sure appropriate training is provided, and implementing a meaningful rewards and recognition plan are all challenges you face in developing a cohesive team.

Other stakeholder relationships are also critical to the success of a project. Building a good working relationship between IT and the client organization can be a challenge. You also need to continually monitor your relationship with the project sponsor. To verify that the project work is performed according to plan, you are collecting data, reviewing performance against the baselines that were set in planning, and documenting and reporting progress.

Contract administration is an important component of managing vendors. The project manager reviews vendor progress, resolves disputes between the project team and vendors, works with the vendor on the impact of delayed deliverables, and approves invoices for payment.

We will start by looking at the various aspects of developing and managing a project team.

Team Development

Managing a project team differs from managing a functional work group. Project teams are temporary, and getting everyone to work together on a common goal can be a challenge, especially if your team members are specialists in a given discipline without a lot of broad business background. As project manager, you must mold this group into an efficient team that can work together to deliver the project as defined on time, within budget, and with quality. Not an easy undertaking, especially if you factor in a combination of full- and part-time team members, technical and nontechnical people, and in some cases a team dispersed over a large geographic area.

As project manager you need to be concerned with building and managing a cohesive team, providing appropriate training to team members, and using an effective rewards and recognition system.

Building and Managing a Cohesive Team

Before we begin discussing techniques to manage a temporary team, it is helpful to look at the progressive stages that a team goes through. You may be familiar with this concept from a general management perspective, but it applies to project teams as well.

Forming The forming stage is where the team members go through the process of getting oriented to the project's objectives, the project manager, and each other.

Storming Storming is the struggle for control, power, and influence as the team members work to establish themselves in the project structure.

Norming As the project evolves and the team settles in to a routine, the norming stage brings cooperation and establishment of beneficial work practices.

Performing The last team stage is the performing stage that brings interdependence, cohesiveness, and high productivity.

It takes both time and good management to bring a team through these stages. A good starting point is a project kickoff.

Project Kickoff

If you think about past experiences you have had being involved in a new project, you can probably break down most of your concerns into these questions:

- Why am I here?
- Who are you and what do you expect of me?
- What are we doing?
- How will we do our work?

As project manager, you need to take the steps necessary to ensure that team members have answers to those questions. A good project kickoff meeting will do a lot to answer those questions and establish a foundation for your team members.

A project kickoff meeting is the best way to formally introduce team members and other stakeholders and convey the same message to everyone at the same time. Typically, you may not know all of your team members, and you may not even have had the opportunity to interview them for the positions they will fill. Not the best way to start a relationship, but in some organizations team members are provided by the functional manager with little input from the project manager.

The tone that you set at the project kickoff meeting can make or break your relationship with the team. An ideal project kickoff session is a combination of serious business and fun. Your goal is to get the team aligned around the project goals and to get the team members comfortable with each other. This is a great opportunity to begin the forming stage.

You may know project managers who dislike the idea of a project kickoff and consider it a waste of time and money, but experience proves that the results of a good kickoff meeting make it well worth the effort. There are a lot of different ways to structure a kickoff meeting. Here are some of the key components you may choose to include.

Welcome

It is a good idea to start the meeting by welcoming the team members and letting them know that you are looking forward to working with them. The welcome also gives you an opportunity to set the stage for the rest of the day. Take a few minutes to run through what participants can expect out of the meeting and what activities they will be involved in.

Introductions

A typical introduction format may include the person's functional area, brief background, and role in the project. The project manager should start the process to set an example of the appropriate length and detail. Put some thought into the information you want team members to share so that the time invested is worthwhile.

Guest Speakers

Invite the sponsor, the client, and any other executive stakeholders; it is important that the team members know them and hear first-hand their goals for the project. These people may not be able to stay for the whole session, but do your best to get them to at least make an appearance and say a few words to the team.

You may need to do some coaching here, so spend time prior to the session to communicate with the executive stakeholders regarding the message they will deliver. The client is often the best candidate to provide the business justification for the project and the link to the corporate strategy. If your client or sponsor is a dynamic speaker, you might want to schedule them for a little more time to get the troops excited about the project they are working on.

Project Overview

Covering the project scope statement is key to starting the team on the right track. A summary of the key deliverables from each of the project phases, as well as the high-level schedule and budget will help team members get the big picture and understand how they fit. The kickoff meeting is an excellent opportunity to get everyone on the same page, especially as project team members typically do not come on board at the same time. At the time you start project execution, you will probably have a combination of people who have been involved with the project since initiation and those who are relatively new to the project.

Project Manager Expectations

This is your chance to communicate how you will be managing the project and your expectations for how the team will function. Many of the team members may not know you or be familiar your management style.

This is not the place for a detailed review of a progress report template or a team meeting agenda, but is it important for the team to know whether you plan weekly team meetings, what you expect in terms of progress reports, and how they will be asked to provide input into project progress reports.

Question and Answer

One of the most important items of the kickoff session is the time you allocate for team members to ask questions. Ideally, this is a panel session so that questions can be directed to the project manager, the sponsor, the client, or other executive stakeholders, but it is just as important even if the questions are only directed to the project manager.

> ### 🌐 Real World Scenario
>
> **Kickoff for Remote Team Members**
>
> For a project kickoff to work, it needs to include all the team members. But what do you do if part of your team is located in a different city or state?
>
> Remote team members often feel left out, especially if the majority of the team, including the project manager, sponsor, and client is located at corporate headquarters where all of the action is.
>
> Getting approval to bring in remote team members is a battle worth fighting, because it is so important to making everyone feel like a part of the team. If you exclude your remote team members, you are sending them a message that they are less important before the project work is even underway.
>
> With more companies looking closely at travel related expenses, bringing in remote team members may require prior approval of the sponsor, even if the budget will cover the expense. When making your case with the project sponsor, make sure you explain the importance of this meeting and the benefits to the project. Your sponsor will be much more receptive to the idea if he or she knows what will be covered and can see that this is far more than people getting together for a free lunch.
>
> But what if you cannot get this to happen? It doesn't mean that there is not still a way to include them.
>
> I was on a project where we had a large group of team members in a remote state. The company was really cutting back on travel, and even though the sponsor wanted to bring everyone to the same city, he could not get approval from the CEO. But we were able to get approval for the next best thing: the sponsor, the client, and the project manager traveled to the remote city and held a separate kick-off for those people. It took extra time to do this, but this project was critical to the corporate strategy. We were able to use that day to build a sold foundation for dealing with the challenges of remote management.

Not only is this an opportunity to clarify any misunderstanding regarding the project, it is also a chance to do rumor control. Having everyone hear the same message from the same person at the same time can remove a lot of confusion.

Social Interaction

Another goal of a project kickoff meeting is to get the team members to start feeling comfortable with each other, so it is a good idea to plan activities that require interaction. A proven method to move a team forward is the ability to get team members to self disclose. When they get to this point they will tell you what is going right and wrong on your project. Social interaction will help get them to self disclosure.

This can be a tricky area to maneuver, as people have different interests and different tolerances for games and icebreakers. You can plan a scavenger hunt, a trivia game, or even a crossword puzzle based on key elements in the project plan. The point is to break the team into smaller groups and get people to start interacting with each other. This will also give you some insight into the various personalities and styles that you will be dealing with.

Monitoring Team Performance

As the leader of the project team, your role involves teaching the members of the team to take responsibility for task and relationship processes and outcomes. Through monitoring performance you should assure responsibility and accountability. To build and maintain the trust of your project team members you need to demonstrate competence, respect, honesty, integrity, and openness. You must also demonstrate that you are willing to act if there are performance problems.

Performance Feedback

Managing team member performance can be a complex undertaking. A successful project manager needs to let the people do the work they were assigned without approving every action taken. This may be a new concept for team members who are used to being micromanaged by a functional manager, or even to you as project managers. Team member performance will be enhanced if activities can be modified to fit individual needs. As long as the end result is the same and there is no impact on scope, schedule, budget, or quality, team members should be given freedom and choices in how to complete their tasks.

Although you should not micromanage team members, they do need feedback on how they are doing—good, bad, or otherwise. Most team members perform well in some areas and need improvement in others. Even if your organization structure does not require project managers to conduct formal written appraisals, you need to take care not to get so caught up in managing the project issues that you neglect to provide performance feedback. The following are important areas of focus as you prepare to discuss performance with a team member:

- Specify performance expectations.
- Identify inadequate performance behaviors.
- Reward superior performance.
- Reprimand inadequate performance.
- Provide specific consequences for choices made.

Performance feedback should be given in a timely fashion. It is of little value to attempt corrective action on something that happened several weeks ago. The team member may not even remember the specifics of the performance in question.

Rewards for superior performance can be given publicly, but a discussion of inadequate performance should always be done privately. Berating a team member in front of others is totally inappropriate and will likely make the person angry and defensive.

We are going to take a closer look at team management scenarios that involve conflict. Before we get into a discussion of the more challenging aspects of project team management, let's take a quick look at some styles that people use to deal with conflict:

Accommodating A person using an accommodating style attempts to meet the other person's needs at the expense of their own concerns.

Avoiding   Avoiding finds the person "dropping out" of the conflict situation; they choose to not bring the issue to the other person's attention and to not deal with the problem.

Competing   A person who uses a competing style uses any actions available to satisfy his or her own needs, often at the other person's expense.

Compromising   A compromising style attempts to resolve the conflict by partially satisfying the needs of both parties by having each give up something in order to reach an agreement.

Collaborating   In the collaborating style, a person works with the other party to explore alternate solutions and agree on a solution that will satisfy each of their needs and concerns.

These conflict management styles can help you understand behavior you observe and must deal with when you need to correct team member behavior. Two situations that require special treatment are dealing with team member disputes and handling disgruntled team members, which we'll discuss next.

Team Member Disputes

Given the diverse backgrounds and varying areas of expertise you find in project team members, it should come as no surprise that team members will have disagreements. Sometimes people just need to have a conversation and work though the issues, but other times disputes require the intervention of the project manager.

You may be tempted to make a snap judgment based on what you see at any given point in time, but this may only exacerbate the situation. You need to get the facts and understand what is behind the dispute. If an experienced team member is trying to tell a more junior member how to do his or her work, this advice may have been unsolicited. If the junior member is completing activities according to plan, it does not matter if the approach is different than what the senior member uses. In a case like this, you may need to take the senior member aside and discuss the situation. You want to handle the situation carefully, as you do not want to alienate anyone, but you need to explain that each person is accountable for his or her own work. If the senior member has extra time, perhaps there is another person who wants and needs some guidance.

Team members may also disagree over the suitability of deliverables. Suggestions to make a deliverable better or more effective may be a sign of scope creep that can lead the project off track. You should establish and enforce a policy that any comments regarding the adequacy of a deliverable need to be stated in the context of the project scope and the project requirements. If a deliverable fails to meet the documented requirements, you have a valid issue, but if a person is just looking to add bells and whistles, you need to keep the project on track. These types of disputes can be eliminated if you define acceptance criteria for your deliverables in the planning phase. The project manager needs to act quickly to resolve these disagreements so that project time is not wasted.

Disgruntled Team Member

Few situations can poison team morale more quickly than a disgruntled team member. This can happen at any time during the project, and can involve anyone on the team.

The behavior of a discontented team member can take a variety of forms. A person may become argumentative in meetings or continually make side comments putting down the project. Even worse, this unhappy camper may spend time moving from cubicle to cubicle sharing these negative feelings about the project with other team members. When team members constantly hear statements that the project is stupid, doomed to fail, or on the cutting block, overall team productivity will be impacted.

As the project manager, you need to spend some private time with this employee to determine the cause of the dissatisfaction. It may be that the unhappy team member doesn't fully understand the project scope and how his or her contribution will lead to the project success, or at the other extreme, this could be an assignment the person did not want.

It is best to start by listening: stick to the facts and ask the person to clarify the negative comments. If the team member is repeating incorrect information, set the record straight. If he is frustrated about some aspect of the project and feels no one is listening, find out what the issue is and explain that going around bad-mouthing the project is not the way issues get resolved. If the person truly does not want to be a part of the project team or does not want to do her assigned tasks, work quickly with the functional manager or your sponsor to get this person replaced.

Developing your team and improving overall performance can also be accomplished through training.

Training

Depending on the nature of your project, another element of team development may be scheduling training for some or all of the project team members. In some companies, one of the perks associated with being assigned to do project work is the opportunity to expand a skill set or get information on new products or processes.

If you are developing a system using a new, evolving technology, the project may include sending the technical team to a class on the technology. A project manager for a new product team may provide training for the whole team on the product itself, including hands-on use of a prototype or assigning project team members to be a pilot group of users.

One of the more common types of training provided to project teams is project management training. Project management training can include a session developed by the project manager, formal training provided by an outside company, or training from an internal PMO on the standard methodologies, tools, and templates all project members are expected to use.

Team development and proper performance feedback are important, but another aspect of team development is rewards and recognition.

Rewards and Recognition

Some project managers (or maybe more frequently project sponsors) may tell you that project team members are just doing their job and should not be getting anything extra. But excellent performance is rewarded in most organizations, and project work should not be an exception.

Project teams work hard and often overcome numerous challenges to deliver a project. If your company has a functional organization structure, the project work may not receive the appropriate recognition from the functional managers. It is your job as project manager to recognize the job your team does and implement a reward system.

> ### 🌐 Real World Scenario
>
> **Project Management 101**
>
> One of the more successful experiences we have had with project management training involved a project team in an organization that was just starting to implement the project management discipline. Based on the chaos that had been created on earlier attempts at running projects, it was clear that the team members needed a common understanding on what project management was all about.
>
> We contracted with a professional project management training company to teach a beginner class in project management concepts. All project team members were required to attend this session.
>
> All of the exercises associated with the class were based on the actual project the team members were assigned to. Not only did the team members gain knowledge of the project management discipline, they were able to contribute to the project while in class.
>
> Although this took some time and money, it was well worth the effort. All team members used common definitions of terms, and it was much easier to talk about meeting requirements, the project baseline, scope creep, and other fundamental project management concepts. The success of this project resulted in the organization setting goals around various levels of project management training for the entire group.

A reward system is typically associated with money allocated in the project budget for the project manager to use for on-the-spot awards for outstanding performance or end-of-project merit awards. Depending on your organization's policies, rewards may be limited to merchandise or gift certificates.

If you are lucky enough to have money for a reward system, either as a direct budget line or as part of a managerial reserve, you must decide what constitutes performance worthy of receiving a reward. Anytime that you do provide an award, you should always state clearly what the person did that made you decide to make the award.

An alternate means of implementing a reward system is to reward the team as a whole, rather than individual performance. In this scenario, you are combining a reward system with ongoing team building. You can take the team to a sporting or cultural event after the completion of a particularly difficult phase. Team dinners or other celebrations to mark project completion are another popular choice. Team rewards are appropriate in situations where you have a cohesive, high-performing team with all members making a substantial contribution to the project success.

Not all project mangers have the resources to reward team members either individually or collectively, but that does not mean that superior performance should go unrecognized. One of the easiest things you can do is simply telling people that you are aware of what they have accomplished and that you appreciate their efforts.

A "team member of the month" concept is a frequently used recognition technique. You can create a certificate or have a trophy that is passed on to the employee who has made the most significant contribution to the project for the previous month. With a program like this, you can solicit nominees from the team.

A letter of recognition to an employee's manager, with copies to the appropriate organizational executives and the project sponsor can be a very powerful means of communicating your appreciation for an outstanding performance.

The key to rewards and recognition is to establish a program to acknowledge the efforts of your project team members, whether it involves money, prizes, letters of commendation, or a simple "thank you." Whatever form your rewards and recognition program takes, you must make sure that it is applied consistently to all project team members. Inconsistent application of rewards is often construed as favoritism.

Your team is not the only group you interface with during project execution; you have ongoing relationships with all the stakeholders.

Other Stakeholder Relationships

In addition to developing the project team members, you must maintain an ongoing relationship with the sponsor, client, and other project stakeholders. Although you may not interact with these people as frequently, they are critical to project success. Let's take a closer look at a few scenarios involving other stakeholders: building a productive IT/client relationship, dealing with a disengaged project sponsor, and resolving staffing issues with functional managers.

Relationship Management with the Client

In many organizations, the IT group and its internal business clients are known for having adversarial relationships. This is not healthy for either the people involved or the project itself. If you are the IT project manager, you need to recognize and address any barriers that may be inhibiting an effective working relationship with your client.

A client may not recognize the complex application development required to produce what he or she believes is a simple product feature, but on the other hand, the IT project manager may not fully understand the business impact of this feature.

Clients have a wide range of technical background. The relationship will be much more effective if you establish the client's knowledge of the technology being used. Clients can be frustrated by technical jargon, but they can also be offended if you talk down to them. Asking a few background questions regarding the client's familiarity with the technology in question can guide your discussion to the proper level.

Some basic principles go a long way in maintaining an effective working relationship with a client:

Frequent Communication   Regular updates to the client organization are a must. The "us against them" mentality and the political battles for control will do nothing to improve the relationship. In addition to distributing written status reports to provide the client with a roadmap of project progress, call the client to see if he or she has any questions or would like to meet with you to clarify any aspects of the project. Being proactive sends the message that you will listen to client concerns.

Team Building   Client involvement in a project kickoff meeting or any team event or celebration demonstrates that you view them as a critical part of the team and goes a long way to taking down some of those political fences that may have been built between the organizations.

Gaining Consensus   Just as you worked with the client to gain consensus during requirements definition in the initiation phase, you need to include the client in the problem solving and issues management. You may resolve purely technical issues, but if they impact the scope or the deliverables, client input is important. A client will not feel ownership in a solution if it was developed in an IT vacuum.

Timely Decision Making   A sense of urgency is important. If you need additional information or approval to make a decision, explain the process to the client and provide a commitment as to when your decision will be made.

Managing Expectations   Over the course of the project, clients may forget the specifics of requirements, assumptions, constraints, and other information obtained during the planning process. A continued review of the project progress compared to the project plan will reinforce what the client can expect from the project.

Managing by Facts   Disputes between IT and client organizations can escalate quickly based on mere rumors or speculation. If you hear that a client representative is unhappy with a project deliverable, get the facts and find out what the real issues are. If the deliverable does not meet the documented requirements, admit there is a problem and work to correct the situation. If a client is asking for something that is out of scope, review the scope statement and requirements to reset client expectations and if needed, walk them though the scope change process.

Managing a Wavering Sponsor

All sorts of kinks can occur to make life challenging for a project manager. As if you don't have enough to do assembling a cohesive team and building a good relationship with your client, you may reach a time during the project where you are not getting the support you expect from your sponsor. Wavering support can manifest itself in a number of ways. Maybe your review meetings are being canceled, or the sponsor suddenly does not have time to talk about project issues. The sponsor may even indicate that you should be able to handle situations that are clearly part of the sponsor role.

A sponsor may back away from a project for a variety of reasons:

- A change in top management may be driving a new corporate strategy.
- Rumors circulating that the project is in trouble may be driving the sponsor to take a hands-off approach.
- The sponsor may have an increased workload.
- The sponsor may be working through personal problems that are taking focus off the project.

Regardless of why the sponsor's commitment to the project has changed, you need to confront the problem and seek a resolution.

Identify the source of the doubts. You need to meet with the sponsor and raise the issue. "I noticed that your interest and support of this project is not the same level as it was during project planning." Have all of your concerns organized and list the reasons behind your statement. Ask the sponsor if they have issues with how the project is being managed and what you can do to help correct the situation. The sponsor has a choice of two responses in this situation—they can acknowledge that something has changed or simply deny that there's a problem. Listen not only to what is being said, but what is not said, and watch the sponsor's body language.

Communicate your concerns with care. No matter how you approach the sponsor, this will not be a comfortable situation, but the last thing you want to do is alienate them. Stick to the facts, choose your words carefully, and allow the sponsor time to think through a response. If you come across as criticizing, judging, or accusing, you will more than likely put the sponsor on the defensive.

Utilize allies and influences. If your sponsor denies a wavering support of the project during your meeting, but continues to be unavailable and unsupportive, what can you do next? You may want to involve others by asking executive allies in your department or other stakeholders who may have influence on the sponsor if they know what the issue is. You can be on very slippery ground here, so make sure you choose these people carefully.

If the situation persists with no resolution, you need to determine whether you should seek a new sponsor or recommend canceling the project. If the sponsor has taken on additional job duties, perhaps sponsorship needs to be transitioned. If the waning sponsor support is instead a signal that the project is no longer viable, letting it die slowly is of no benefit to anyone.

Relationships with Functional Managers

You may have thought that dealing with functional managers are limited to the initial request for project resources. This is rarely the case, as resources that were committed during project planning may suddenly be unavailable. Overall team performance can also be impacted if a planned resource is not brought onto the team as promised or if a functional manager attempts to pull a resource off the project before the assigned tasks are complete.

In this situation, you need to work with the functional manager to try to come up with a resolution that is satisfactory to all parties. You need to know the reason a resource is being pulled from your project and how the functional manager proposes to handle the replacement. If there will be a transition period and the substitute resource can perform the tasks with no impact to the project end result, you may just want to accept the change and work at integrating the new person into the team.

Proposed staffing changes sometimes occur at very critical stages in the project. If you get a call from a functional manager in the middle of the development phase telling you the lead programmer has been assigned to a special project, the negative impact to your project could be great. You want to attempt to resolve the issue by explaining how critical the lead programmer's position is and the impact of making a change at this juncture.

If the functional manager is not willing to negotiate and if the ramp-up time for a new person will delay the project, you need to escalate this situation to your project sponsor for resolution. Be prepared to review with the sponsor the consequences to the project if you lose the lead programmer and explain the actions you have taken to attempt a resolution with the functional manager. The project sponsor can work at the executive level to confirm the priority of the project and the need to maintain resource commitments.

Project execution is the phase that delivers the work results, so in addition to developing your project team and managing stakeholder relationships, you are tracking the overall project performance.

Perform According to Plan

Once the project work is underway, the project manager needs to track numerous items to make sure the project is on schedule, on budget, and delivering a quality product that meets the requirement of the scope statement. For a typical up and running project, these tasks should be completed on a weekly basis. To effectively coordinate all of this work, the project manager must collect data about the project work and compare project execution against the baselines that were established during project planning.

Collect Data

You need a lot of information to be able to accurately track project performance. You need an organized, consistent means of collecting data. Tools that can be used to assist in data collection include progress reports, an issues log, and budget reports.

Progress Reports

A lot of the data you need to collect on the project work relates to the progress of tasks on the project schedule. One of the first things that you need to establish is the format and timing of regular *progress reports* from your team members. With everything you need to keep track of, it is important that there is a consistency to these reports, so that you can scan them quickly to get a big picture of how the team is doing. These reports should list the tasks each team member is working on, the current progress of each task, and the work remaining.

TABLE 8.1 A Sample Progress Report

Task	hours worked	hours left	percent complete	notes

On most projects, you need to receive weekly progress reports from your team members to stay on top of project progress. The team should agree on when the reports are due and how they will be provided (email, paper copy, etc.).

You may find some team members who are lax in submitting progress reports. You need to stress with the team how critical it is to the success of the project that these reports be timely and accurate. You need to monitor progress reports and follow up with team members who do not submit reports. If the tardiness becomes habitual, schedule a meeting with the offender to discuss this as a performance concern.

If your project software is set up for updates to be made centrally by one person, the progress report may also be used as input to update schedule progress.

Issues

Every project will have issues that need to be resolved. In order to assure that issues are communicated and resolved, you need to develop and maintain an issues log. Various formats can be used to track project issues, and your PMO or other projects may provide an existing template.

Identify these key elements:

- What the issue is.
- How the issue affects the project.
- Who is accountable for resolving the issue.
- Current status of resolving the issue.

An issues log is often tracked using a spreadsheet, which allows for easy sorting by date or status. Figure 8.1 displays a sample log for tracking project issues.

FIGURE 8.1 Issues Tracking Log

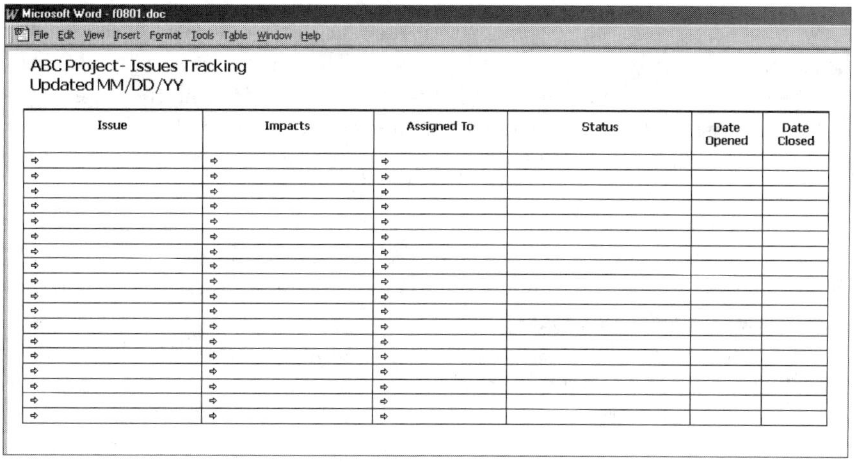

ABC Project- Issues Tracking
Updated MM/DD/YY

Issue	Impacts	Assigned To	Status	Date Opened	Date Closed
⇨	⇨	⇨			
⇨	⇨	⇨			
⇨	⇨	⇨			
⇨	⇨	⇨			
⇨	⇨	⇨			
⇨	⇨	⇨			
⇨	⇨	⇨			
⇨	⇨	⇨			
⇨	⇨	⇨			
⇨	⇨	⇨			
⇨	⇨	⇨			
⇨	⇨	⇨			
⇨	⇨	⇨			
⇨	⇨	⇨			
⇨	⇨	⇨			
⇨	⇨	⇨			
⇨	⇨	⇨			
⇨	⇨	⇨			

An issues log can become very lengthy, especially on large, complex projects. You may opt to display only the open issues or leave issues on the log for a predetermined time period after the issue is closed.

The issues log is typically reviewed and updated during the project team meeting, which we will discuss later in this chapter.

> **NOTE** You can find a version of the Issues Tracking Log on this book's companion CD, for your own use in project management.

Spending

The other important piece of data for the project manager to collect is the amount of money spent on the project. Tracking financial data is greatly simplified if your project has a dedicated financial analyst who can access the necessary reports from the finance systems. If that is not the case, you will need to take the necessary steps to receive the official budget reports for your project.

Depending on how current your financial management systems data are, you may need to do some manual tracking as well. Many project managers review and/or approve both the weekly time reporting of the project team members and any materials or equipment charged to the project. The last thing you want to see is a $100,000 surprise that hits the official budget tracking 2 months after the fact.

The data that you obtain from the progress reports, issues log, and spending reports are all key inputs in your quest to complete the project work according to the baselines created during project planning.

Progress Against Baselines

Now you will start to see the importance of the schedule and budget baselines that you established as part of scope planning and cost planning. These documents are used as a roadmap during project execution to determine whether the project work is being completed as planned. The schedule baseline, cost baseline, and scope statement are continually compared with the actual progress of the project. If you find deviations from any of these baselines, you must determine if any action is required.

The question to continually answer is where are you in your project as of this date? From the schedule perspective, did you plan to be further along, are you ahead of schedule, or are you right on track? Do the project budget reports indicate more or less spending than you had planned based on schedule progress?

In this chapter we will discuss what items you should focus on. Analyzing deviations from any of the project baselines and controlling risk and change will be discussed in detail in Chapter 9, "Project Control."

Schedule Baseline

Project team members may input task progress on a server-based project management software system or a central project administrator may complete the updates working off of the progress reports. Either way, the project manager needs to compare actual progress to the baseline on a regular basis. You may have been alerted to a potential problem by notes in the progress report or discussion from the team meeting, but you cannot assume that all existing or potential deviations from the baseline will be bought to your attention. Individual team members tend to focus on their assigned tasks rather than the impact to downstream tasks. A task that will last two extra days may not seem like a big deal, but if three other people cannot start their work until this task is done, there could be major impacts. A project manager will not have time to analyze every task that has deviated from the baseline, so particular attention must be paid to critical path tasks or tasks with multiple dependent tasks.

Evaluating Costs

Official corporate project budget reports contain budgeted dollars per task or per budget category and the corresponding dollars that were actually spent. Project budget reports compare what was planned with what has really happened from the perspective of dollars and indicate where the project has overspent or under spent. The budget report provides a basis for variance analysis.

Time reporting or invoices submitted for approval may provide an early warning that your budget report will not match plan. You want to pay particular attention to time reports that consistently exceed the number of hours a team member is dedicated to the project. Any given task estimate may not be accurate, but if a team member is working more hours than planned on a weekly basis, your salary budget is going to be overspent.

Scope Statement

Another document that tells you if you are on track is the scope statement. As milestones are reached for the completion of major deliverables, make sure these deliverables match what was documented in the scope statement.

You should be on the lookout for red flags that may indicate potential scope creep. If tasks from various team members on a particular deliverable are consistently taking longer than planned, don't wait for the deliverable to be completed to start asking questions. If scope has changed without an approved change request, you need to resolve this issue quickly.

Deliverable Sign-Off

As your project progresses, more and more tasks on the project schedule should be shown as complete. You need to be alert to any tasks that are reported as "almost complete" for more than one progress reporting period. This may be a sign that the team member is behind or has found the task more complex than planned. In other cases, there may be uncertainty about closing the task. A few key questions can help determine the real issue and push for task completion.

The completion of a series of tasks leads to completion of a deliverable. Pay special attention to the completion of deliverable, as they may be associated with a milestone that requires sponsor or stakeholder review or sign off. If there are any issues with a deliverable, fixes may need to be made before additional work begins, so delaying sign off of deliverables can create a chain of rework.

The acceptance of all of the project work and the associated deliverables by the stakeholders is referred to as *scope verification*. The data you gather is compiled and communicated to the project stakeholders.

Information Distribution

It should be obvious at this point that the project manager reviews a lot of data. Much of this data needs to be summarized and shared with others. *Information distribution* is the process of providing project stakeholders with the information they need when they need it. When you distribute information about the project, you are implementing your communications plan. Information can be distributed using a variety of methods, including project meetings, status reports, and formal project reviews.

Project Team Meetings

The project team meeting is the best tool for ongoing communication between the project team members, yet it is often the source of the greatest frustration and the most complaints. A successful project meeting needs to be well organized and tightly focused. A well-run meeting can be instrumental in moving a project to completion.

Leading a Meeting

Project team meetings can be the best or the worst aspect of being on a project team, depending on how the meetings are structured. You may have heard your fellow employees complain about sitting in endless meetings that accomplish nothing. A productive team meeting is an ongoing opportunity for the project manager to provide direction to the team and clarify any questions regarding completion of the project work. Successful team meetings do not just happen; they require a good deal of effort in both planning and execution. You can take a number of steps to establish a foundation for productive team meetings:

Designate a consistent day and time for the team meeting. You should obtain input from team members and determine the best time to schedule the meeting.

Stress the importance of consistent attendance. Team meetings will not be effective if key members are missing. Establishing a policy where team members will provide information in advance or send a representative if unable to attend adds emphasis to the importance of being at the meeting.

Prepare and distribute a written agenda. Team members need to know what topics to be prepared to discuss, and the time that will be allocated to each topic. Even if the team meeting topics are consistent week to week, an agenda reinforces both the structure and the need to be ready for discussion.

Start and end the meeting on time. If you schedule your team meeting for one hour, that is how long it should last. Team members need to be told, perhaps multiple times, that you will start and end meetings on time. Some people are habitually late, but delaying the start of a meeting only rewards bad behavior and punishes those who are on time. If someone arrives late and starts questioning topics that were already covered, advise them to get with you or another team member after the meeting.

Follow the agenda and keep the meeting on track. It is very frustrating to be a participant in a meeting that seems to wander from topic to topic. You developed the agenda for a reason. You can ask team members for input into the agenda prior to the meeting. If a particular subject is taking more time than planned, decide whether to remove some items from the agenda or schedule a separate meeting to allocate more time to a given issue.

Solicit participation from all team members. Some people just love to talk. You need to be aware if a few team members are monopolizing the meeting. Direct questions to individual team members to level the playing field.

Distribute meeting minutes. People will inevitably remember different outcomes to items discussed during the team meeting unless the outcome of the meeting is captured in writing. Meeting minutes should summarize the key points of the meeting, including the key elements discussed, recommendations, and action items for different team members.

Meeting Outcomes

A project meeting can be much more than just a time to update status of assigned tasks. An effective meeting can result in improved team member interaction, issues resolution, and problem solving.

Team Member Interaction The team meeting is an excellent venue to observe the interaction between team members. If there are too many surprises or people with linked tasks are clueless as to their impact on one another, you may have a group that is operating in silo mode. Team members are not expected to know every detail on every task, but there should be ongoing interaction between team members. If necessary, you may need to schedule time to review key dependencies between major deliverables.

If you perceive that intra-team communication is weak and could impact task dependencies on your critical path, you may need to take extra steps to ensure that people in charge of downstream tasks are getting the information they need regarding the progress and deliverables of any predecessor tasks.

Poor intra-team communication can be a major issue on cross-functional projects. A client representative who is writing customer manuals may need to start documentation while development and testing are still in progress, and it is essential that the writer get ongoing updates on items such as screen shots and feature functionality. If your technical team members are reluctant to interface with the client team members, the project end date could be jeopardized if the documentation is started late or requires multiple revisions due to poor team member communication. As project manager, it is your responsibility to establish the importance of effective communication between all team members.

Issues Log Updates A review of the issues log should be part of every project team meeting. This does not require a huge amount of time, as each issue is assigned to a team member for resolution at the time it is added to the issues log. You should request the responsible party(s) to review the status of a current, open issue where a promised action is in progress or should be completed. The work to resolve the issue takes place outside of the team meeting.

Problem Solving   Project teams are constantly called on to make decisions with imperfect information. This can be a frustrating and scary proposition, and it is your job to lead the team members through the problem-solving process. People tend to rush into a solution, so make sure that the problem is clearly defined and there is consensus. Dedicating a short amount of time to brainstorming may uncover a solution that would not have been thought of without encouraging team input.

An example of a common problem that may be appropriate for project team discussion is delays to the project. A consistent approach to the resolving delays will make the team more effective:

- Determine the root cause of the delay.
- Identify the responsible team member.
- Develop a corrective action plan.
- Implement the corrective action.
- Track results.

Team members are not the only stakeholders who need to be informed of project progress. Status reports are another method to share project information.

Status Reports

The project sponsor, the client, and other stakeholders do not need the same level of detail regarding project progress as project team members, but they do need to be kept apprised of project progress. This is why most project communications plans include the regular distribution of a status report.

The status report can be provided via access to a shared folder, email, or even voicemail. The specific distribution method should be identified in the communications plan. The key to success is a consistent report format that paints a clear picture of the current state of the project. A typical status report will include:

- Summary of project progress compared to schedule and cost baseline.
- Completion of any major deliverables or milestones.
- Status of outstanding issues.

A more formal method for communicating information on the project is a project review.

Project Reviews

A *project review* is a formal presentation by the project manager or project team members to the sponsor, the client, and other executive stakeholders. While some sort of status report is produced on almost all projects, a project review is optional in nature and will vary greatly in structure and content between organizations.

Organizations that regularly conduct formal project reviews may have a set monthly or quarterly schedule. We have seen project reviews done at the executive level that cover numerous projects and span several days, with all involved project managers presenting to an executive team.

The information in a project review will be based on your organizational or sponsor needs. A review presented for just the sponsor is easier to prepare for, as you can set the agenda based on what is important to the sponsor. If the audience includes the client or other executives, you may want to solicit input from the attendees regarding expectations for the review session.

The presentation should include an agenda with time limits for each topic. Your time with these busy executives will be limited, so you will need to stay focused and to the point. Topics to consider for a review agenda include:

- Major achievements for current review period
- Budget summary
- Major issues
- Risks and mitigation or contingency plans
- Planned achievements for next reporting period

Project reviews usually include both handouts and slides, so make sure your presentation room has all of the equipment you will need. An example of a project review handout is shown in Figure 8.2. Either the project manager or project team members may be involved in the presentation. The key to success is to make sure that each presenter is clear on the information they will provide and the time allocated to the session. If project team members will be making portions of the presentation, it may be worthwhile to do a practice session, at least for the first review.

FIGURE 8.2 Project Review Template

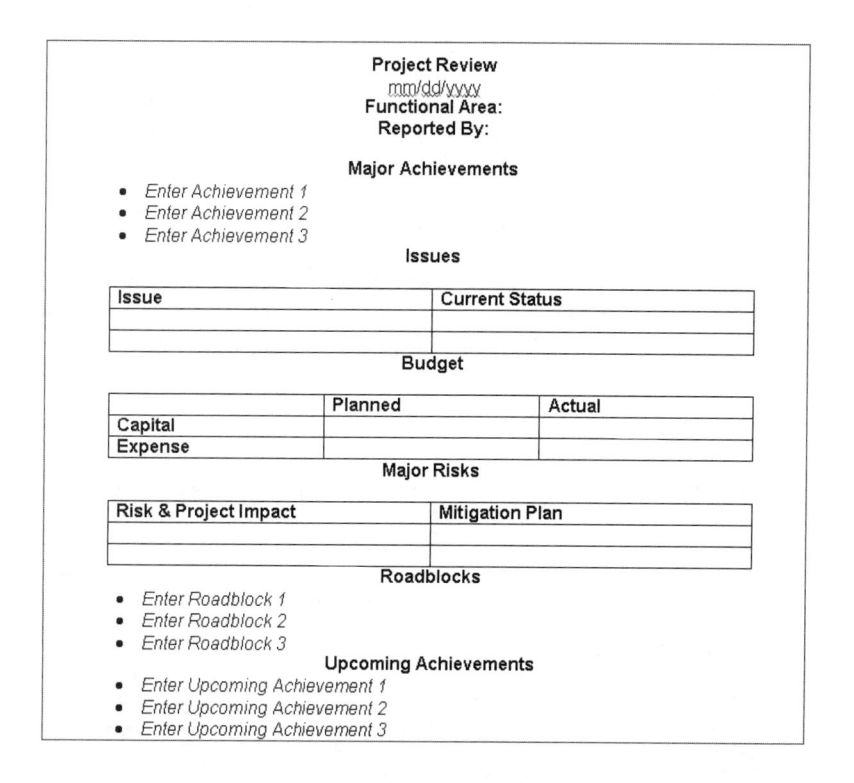

Project Review
mm/dd/yyyy
Functional Area:
Reported By:

Major Achievements

- Enter Achievement 1
- Enter Achievement 2
- Enter Achievement 3

Issues

Issue	Current Status

Budget

	Planned	Actual
Capital		
Expense		

Major Risks

Risk & Project Impact	Mitigation Plan

Roadblocks

- Enter Roadblock 1
- Enter Roadblock 2
- Enter Roadblock 3

Upcoming Achievements

- Enter Upcoming Achievement 1
- Enter Upcoming Achievement 2
- Enter Upcoming Achievement 3

> **Note:** You'll find a sample of the Project Review Template, which you can use for your own project reviews, on the CD-ROM that accompanies this book.

When you report a project's progress to an executive body (a function you'll undoubtedly be actively and routinely involved in during your project career), you'll want to go prepared with a document that presents the important things these folks will want to know in a summary fashion. Generally speaking, unless there's some technical issue that they need to know about in order to help you make an operational decision affecting the project, you'll want to avoid anything remotely technical regarding the project. Instead, you should focus on things that are relevant to decision makers:

- Tasks you're currently working on.
- Issues that you've encountered.
- Estimated percentage complete.
- Estimates of how closely you're following your project budget and timelines.

Some project reports also include a set of characters that help identify whether a manager should be concerned about a project element. For example, you might use an open circle to denote that everything's moving along just fine, a gray triangle to note that there's some concern for a given element and a black diamond to illustrate a major problem. The idea is to give executives something to scan that allows them to easily drill into hot spots and get more information about a key issue as Figure 8.3 illustrates.

When you're reporting to a formal project review body such as a project review board (PRB), you'll take more time to elucidate detailed components of the project—but you'll still want to avoid technical discussions. For the majority of people, you'll lose them more quickly by having a technical discussion than you'll help them. The key here is to find a way to say what you need to say without resorting to technical acronyms or expecting that people will understand what even simple terms like "server" and "router" mean.

> **Note:** You'll find The Executive Project Summary Worksheet template on this book's companion CD-ROM, for use in your own project management.

FIGURE 8.3 The Executive Project Summary Worksheet

Vendor Contract Administration

Many projects cannot go forward without the products or services from third-party sources, or vendors. If you have contracted with vendors for work on your project, you will have a role in *contract administration*. This is the process of tracking and verifying that the vendor meets the terms of the agreement.

Although some of the contract administration may be done through a separate procurement department, your relationship with the vendor is key to a successful project. You will need to receive progress reports from the vendor, resolve disputes between the vendor and your team members, and deal with vendor delays.

Progress Reporting

Progress reports from vendors are just as important as progress reports from your team members. Your vendor deliverables are part of your project schedule and may have dependencies with other tasks assigned to your team members.

The specifics of progress reporting from vendors should be documented in your statement of work (SOW). Communications with vendors tends to be more formal due to the nature of working from a contract, which has legal implications.

Even though the progress reporting requirements are detailed in your SOW, you need to make sure you are getting the data you need in a usable format. A written weekly report should provide a clear status on the vendor deliverables, including percent of work completed, confirmation of target delivery date, and any issues or risks that might impact delivery.

Some project managers also have a monthly meeting with the vendor to review progress and discuss any issues. The need for regular meetings fluctuates based on the complexity of the vendor deliverable and the length of time a vendor is involved on the project.

Managing Vendor Disagreements

Project team members and vendors may not always see eye to eye on how to approach a particular deliverable. This puts you in a difficult situation. The vendor has been hired because of expertise or experience in producing something you need, but the vendor deliverable has to integrate with the rest of your project. So if a team member tells you the vendor is going down the wrong path, what should you do?

You need to sit down with the team member to hear what they are really saying. You also need to hear the vendor side. The source of the friction could be any number of elements, which we will discuss in this section.

Misunderstanding on the Part of Team Members

It could be that the source of the disagreement is merely a misunderstanding. Perhaps your team members have always worked with one product; this new product behaves differently, but they're expecting the same outcome as with the old.

Misunderstanding on the Part of Vendors

Alternatively, perhaps the vendor has misunderstood what your actual intent is for the product it's going to supply. The vendor, after understanding the nature of the misunderstanding, might respond, "Oh, well, Widget A won't do that, but Widget B will." Sure, you should've gone through this discovery process at design time, but this kind of thing has a way of slipping through the cracks.

Paradigm Shift

It could be that the vendor's product is just fine for what you're trying to do, but team members have to go through a paradigm shift in order to effectively use the new product, and they simply have not yet made that leap. Think about the shift that old-school mainframe programmers might have had to make when object-oriented (OO) programming methodologies came about. In this example, you may have had several mainframe programmers who were used to thinking in top-down programming format and might've had a hard time grappling with object-oriented code (where you put an object on a screen, then write the underlying code for that object). A paradigm shift was required. Unfortunately, especially in OO, that shift is a hard one to make, especially if you're coming from the old school of programming.

The Ego Factor

Sadly, IT is an industry that's fraught with large egos. It could very well be that one of your team members has forgotten more about the product than the vendor will ever know, and he's prepared to tell the vendor so. Managing this kind of thing may require that you use "tough love" tactics where you tell the team member to do things the way the vendor says they need to be done. Alternatively (and most often), you may have to replace this talented team member, because he will derail the project, by doing things his own way, more than he will help to get his tasks done. In the final analysis, it is, after all, all about tasks and their timely and successful completion that makes a project successful.

The 800-Pound-Gorilla Vendor

Some vendors have a "my way or the highway" attitude when it comes to their product. Some products, especially enterprise-class software, are so cumbersome that companies are forced to wrap their way of doing business around the product, rather than the product wrapping itself around the way the company does business. Additionally, some of these 800-pound-gorilla companies think nothing of calling you up, telling you that the latest revision is out, that your current version will become unsupported in a few months, and asking how soon you can be converted—all at a substantial cost to you.

If it's apparent that this phenomenon may come into effect, project managers can benefit from heavily weighing this 800-pound-gorilla incident to see if this is somewhere they think the project should go. In other words, if you marry into a software or hardware product that's a phenomenon all unto itself, then you're stuck with that phenomenon. When you're on board the *Queen Elizabeth II*, you go where the captain wants you to go (unless you buy the boat).

This is a place to weigh the disadvantages of integrated systems against the advantages. Suppose that you're using an enterprise-class relational database management system (RDBMS), one that comes with its own software development environment (SDE) or perhaps even with some canned apps that may loosely fit some of the stated deliverables of your project. Should you invest your company's development environment completely in this one large offering, or should you investigate to see whether other SDEs and tool sets may do a better job—if for no other reason than simply to avoid having all of your eggs in a single vendor's basket? Normally, with integrated systems, you're worried about two different platforms (whether hardware or software) talking to one another. But don't forget to ask, "Should I sell my soul to this company?"

A very germane (and often overlooked) element of project planning is to analyze the proposed platform to make sure that you're not steering your passengers onto a ship that they will have to be aboard for many years to come. If you were not far-sighted enough to spot this in the initial planning phases, then the best you can do at execution time is to make sure that the future caretakers of the system are aware that there will be ongoing maintenance issues they'll need to routinely deal with.

> **TIP** Project managers who unknowingly lead companies into an unwanted marriage with an 800-pound gorilla may experience what a project management expert friend of mine lovingly calls a career-limiting move (CLM).

Platform Wars

This phenomenon is especially prevalent in the network operating system (NOS), SDE, and RDBMS camps. One person likes Unix; another won't do anything that's not Microsoft-oriented. One group loves Oracle; another thinks that Sybase is the best. Developers are really funny about stuff like this—one talented developer will insist on using the Java language and a particular Java SDE, while another says that the best code comes from C++ and has the SDE to prove it.

Proactively, as the project manager, it's up to you to create early on a standards-based environment that utilizes the best-of-breed technologies for the given task at hand—often regardless of one individual's personal preferences. This is a really difficult call to make. You can reduce the difficulty by going to websites that specialize in IT research, sites that can give you vendor-independent advice about choosing a product. Gartner Inc. (www.gartner.com) and IDC Corp. (www.idc.com) are two such companies involved in this kind of research. You can do a lot of your research for free without having to purchase a subscription to their extended services, but for heavy detail and Q&A, you'll need a subscription membership.

At project execution time, if you find that platform wars exist you have to manage them by keeping people focused on the goal of the project, and try to steer folks away from the platform religious wars.

> **TIP** Check first. Your company may have a subscription to one of the research groups, and you can set up conference calls with SMEs in the subject you're interested in researching.

Vendors may experience delays in completing deliverables, and you need to be prepared to handle these according to the provisions of the contract.

Vendor Delays

Some project managers mistakenly believe that just because you have hired an outside vendor to complete a portion of the project work, nothing will go wrong, and you can just sit back and wait for the deliverable to appear. This is not how it works in real life.

You may be getting ready to distribute your latest status report, when you get a call from your vendor telling you that their next deliverable will be two weeks late. What should you do now?

Meet with the vendor. You need to sit down with the vendor to get more specific information about the delay. This discussion can help you determine if there are alternative approaches to the issue that can shorten the delay, or if a portion of the deliverable can be completed as planned. You may not be able to resolve the vendor issue, but you need to make sure you have all the facts and understand what action the vendor is taking.

Involve your procurement or legal department. A vendor is doing project work based on a legal contract. If there is going to be a delay in the vendor deliverable, you need to understand the potential contractual impacts. There may be penalties or fines associated with any vendor delay, or you could even have cause to terminate the contract. You should not agree to any change in the vendor deliverable or schedule without the involvement of your procurement or legal representative.

Review impact to the overall project plan. Any time there is a delay in a deliverable, you need to assess the impact this delay will have to the project scope, the schedule baseline, the cost baseline, and resource requirements. A delay in a major vendor deliverable may create new risks that need to be added to the risk management plan.

Notify the sponsor. You need to get with your sponsor as soon as you have all the facts regarding the delay and have assessed the impact to the project plan. If the impact of the vendor delay is severe, the sponsor may choose to escalate the problem with a vendor executive.

Communicate to stakeholders. Information needs to be provided to the project team, the client, and any other impacted stakeholders as quickly as possible. Vendor delays can drive all sorts of rumors about the viability of the project, so you want to make sure that everyone has the facts.

Another difference in dealing with vendors versus employee team members is the oversight of the payments vendors receive.

Vendor Payment Process

The contract with the vendor should spell out how and when the vendor is paid. There may be a regular payment schedule or payment may be tied to completion and acceptance of specific deliverables. Although your accounting department will probably handle the actual payment of vendor invoices, the project manager may be the initial recipient of the invoice.

If you are responsible for approving payment of an invoice, make sure you understand what you are being billed for and do adequate research to confirm the payment is warranted.

If a vendor is being reimbursed based on a phased schedule of deliverables, you need to confirm both receipt and acceptance of the deliverable. Review the process and quality checks that were established to approve vendor deliverables before you approve payment.

Reimbursement of vendor personnel expenses should include receipts and an accounting of the purpose of the expense. If you are not certain of what is required, ask your accounting representative to walk you through the process.

If you are not clear on how the payment process is stated in the contract, request clarification from your procurement team. They are the contract experts, and can help you through the legal terms. If there is a difference of opinion regarding the money owed to a vendor, you will need to involve a procurement expert to work through the resolution of the dispute.

Dealing with Vendors

In this section, we'll discuss some of the methods you can use when working with third-party sources.

Communicate Effectively with Vendors

As the project progresses, you will be maintaining high-quality ongoing communications with the vendors who are engaged in your project. "High-quality" means that you have set up routine meetings in which you and the vendor have an opportunity to bring out issues and discuss solutions within a framework that allows for positive communications and problem-solving. If you have not arrived at consensus on what the work would be when you first started out designing your project and you did not thoroughly review the SOW, project progress meetings will clearly reveal the shortcomings as you may hit problem areas where the vendor won't go any further because they are not within the boundaries of the co-agreed-upon SOW.

In other words, you will find that most vendors are eager to work with you toward solving problems on the project within which they have proper purview. But vendors understandably get a little nervous when you're asking them to help you with something that was not clearly delineated at project creation time. This seems to be the area in which most project manager and vendor relations get into trouble.

Make Sure the Vendor Really Knows Your Needs

Be sure to carefully scrutinize the SOW. It's entirely possible that a vendor will leave out an element you specifically asked for (and that they agreed to) just because they overlooked putting it into the SOW. The SOW is a document that specifies *exactly* what the vendor is going to do, in return for a given amount of money. If you initially thought you had everything you needed stipulated in the SOW, but at project execution you see that there are missing elements, you're going to wind up doing some things you may have wanted the vendor to do. Or you're going to have to pay the vendor extra money to handle the extra work. This is why it's critical to understand exactly what the SOW is saying.

> ### Real World Scenario
>
> **Vendor Pushing Back Due to Incompletely Defined Requirements**
>
> Theresa is a project manager working on a large software-development project. The new software will replace an old legacy mainframe system.
>
> When Theresa began the project she and the business analysts performed interviews with various business subject matter experts (i.e., people who understood the business process flows thoroughly) to determine how the new system should behave. However, due to the large geographic dispersion of the system, it was difficult to pin down certain individuals who were deemed key to the project. They were busy, or it was expensive to fly someone out to do the business interviews—it just seemed to Theresa like it was difficult to get good quality information out of some of the individuals affiliated with the initial requirements-gathering and design efforts of the project. Hence, the information, while certainly not describable as "dicey," wasn't exactly complete either. Even though Theresa submitted this as an issue, project stakeholders felt that there was sufficient information to go ahead and begin the project.
>
> Now well into the project, some of the business subject matter experts have come back to look at what has been done so far and don't like what they see! They have asked for changes—substantial ones—that impact the scope of the project. Because they are deemed critical business experts, the sponsor thinks that their ideas have credibility and that Theresa need to take them into consideration. In fact, she wonders why Theresa didn't initially "hear these people out."
>
> The vendor, a good one of high reputation, is working under a contract and has worked solidly with Theresa throughout the life of the project so far. The vendor has been there for all design and construction meetings and has complied fully with every letter of what Theresa had asked them to do. The vendor is now into other development phases and does not want to go back to re-visit previous work, especially because what they have done meets the criteria Theresa asked for and the system works perfectly. The vendor is now saying that they will have to charge extra money to put in the additions being asked for.
>
> The sponsor is insisting that they did not live up to their end of the bargain. Theresa has documents detailing the deliverables that have been signed off by all parties as well as successful phase completion documentation that was signed off.
>
> Theresa feels as though she is in a no-win situation. She cannot ask the vendor to go back and put in the additions and corrections without being able to pay them for the additional work. The sponsor thinks that Theresa should've gotten the straight story at design time and isn't willing to pay extra for the vendor to make the changes. She says that the vendor should assume responsibility for the changes because "it's the right thing to do."

> Unfortunately, there are no good solutions to this problem. You have a sponsor who is pushing the onus onto you to solve the problem and yet the vendor is pushing back on you to keep moving forward.
>
> The recommended approach in this case would be for Theresa to set up a meeting with herself, the vendor, and the sponsor in which she lays the cards out on the table. If there are areas where she made mistakes, now is the time for her to own those mistakes so she can move forward. The primary point here is to focus on truth-telling and getting the whole story across to all sides so that the vendor can clearly hear the sponsor say that they need to help make things right and the sponsor can hear them say that they're not going to do so. This takes Theresa out of the middle of the equation and gets both sides talking. Theresa is going to be held responsible for whatever outcome is derived from such a meeting. However, it is crucial that all sides meet together to hash out and work on this one specific problem until there is a satisfactory solution for each side.

Additionally, you'll find that a vendor agreement isn't a "set it and forget it" type of arrangement. Even reputable vendors with your best interests in mind lose their way from time to time and forget to include an element you talked about. If a vendor says that they'll have a part to you on Tuesday at 9:00 A.M. by Federal Express, then you'd better have your eyes open looking for that part. If you see the FedEx truck come and go, you should be on the phone asking the vendor where the part is.

Do Your Homework before Vendor Discussions

You should ignore the "our product can do that" statements when you're in your initial discovery meetings with the salesperson and SE. Their system might very well "do that," but you should do some investigative work outside the heat of the sales presentation moment before signing on the dotted line. Suppose, for example, that you want a website software package that will calculate sales tax for anywhere in the state of California. The SE might blurt out "our product can do that," knowing full well that it really can't, but if you're willing to write some code that digs into the vendor's API then it can. Unfortunately, in a sales presentation, the products usually look really, really good, so you may be inclined to accept the "our product can do that" at face value and not investigate further.

Unfortunately, usually it's at execution time that you find out exactly what the software will and will not do. If you've hung everything on the initial sales meeting phrase, "our product can do that," and you find out it really can't, the project execution phase is *not* the time to find out about it! A little pre-project research into the capabilities of the products being considered will go a long way toward eliminating this issue.

Practice Smart Negotiations

Finally, things get tacitly agreed to when it's you and the salesperson and he thinks he's closing the deal. As a general rule of thumb, the larger the sale, the more likely you're going to get a bone or two thrown your way at deal-arranging (but not necessarily closing) time. Be sure to write down those promises for later when you go into the room and close that deal. You'll actually say, "OK, before we go forward, I just want to validate what you communicated to me the other day—that you'd do blah blah, and also blah blah." You'll want these commitments in writing because after the deal's closed and the salesperson's onto other accounts, it may difficult getting him back to the table to talk about those add-ons he committed to.

Tacit agreements especially play themselves out during project execution. Suppose, for example, that you and the vendor were going over a component of the project and he said, "I'll do some checking and get back to you. I think I can get the company to provide you that part at no charge." You leave it at that for the moment. Now well into project execution, you need that part! Because the agreement wasn't committed to paper and agreed to by both parties, you may have a difficult time getting the vendor to do that checking and find that free part.

> **TIP** Be sure to understand a vendor's maintenance and support policies as well. Lots of vendors offer Bronze, Silver, and Gold support plans. What is it you're signing up for and what do you get with that? What will be the annual maintenance costs (if any) that you'll incur as a result of purchasing this vendor's software or hardware? Some vendors make their real money through support and maintenance, not necessarily the software or hardware they're selling. So be sure you understand what their complete offering is going to cost you from this time forward.

Case Study: Chaptal Wineries—Email and Intranet

You're several weeks into the effort to bring your international winery acquisitions into the fold. France's and Australia's server and telco installations are complete. Weekly reports to Kim Cox look similar to the graphic below.

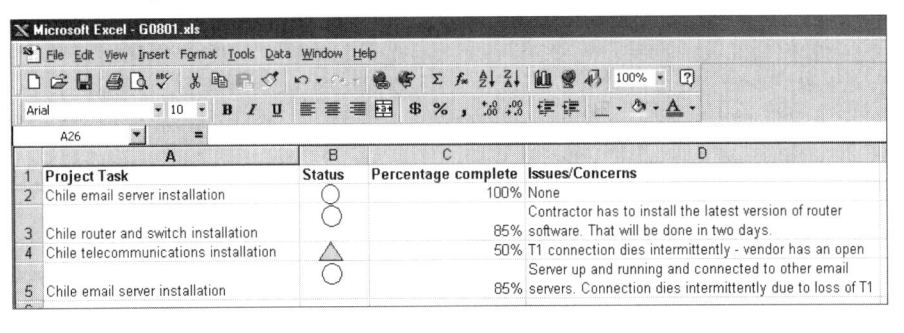

	A	B	C	D
1	Project Task	Status	Percentage complete	Issues/Concerns
2	Chile email server installation	○	100%	None
3	Chile router and switch installation	○	85%	Contractor has to install the latest version of router software. That will be done in two days.
4	Chile telecommunications installation	△	50%	T1 connection dies intermittently - vendor has an open
5	Chile email server installation	○	85%	Server up and running and connected to other email servers. Connection dies intermittently due to loss of T1

> You've approved several invoices for payment—forwarding them back to the Chaptal finance office to cut the checks. You've approved payments for the Australian and French telecommunications installations (after validating that the installations were up and completely operational). The internetworking gear contractors for both of these regions have been paid and you've noted the tasks complete on the project plan.
>
> Now you're concerned about the T1 dropping in Chile. You're beginning to wonder if maybe the internetworking contractor you retained has something misconfigured and doesn't realize it. You make a call to Metor and ask him to call the vendor to have someone else other than the contractor you've been dealing with come out to verify the configuration. Metor's afraid that the contractor may want to charge you more money for validating the configuration, but you fax Metor the SOW and point out to him that the contractor has committed to making sure that connectivity is up 99.8 percent of the time until you've released the vendor and okayed payment. Because the circuit has been up only about 50 percent of the time, you're clearly within your rights to force the vendor to send someone else out to validate the configuration.
>
> Metor agrees to call the vendor and get a different technician out to check the configuration. Sure enough, the Open Shortest Path First (OSPF) settings in the router are not correct for the circuit. When the new technician makes an adjustment, the circuit comes up and stays up full-time thereafter. At next project status meeting, you note that the task is 100 percent complete.

Summary

Project execution is an exciting time as you finally get to see results of the hard work from the Initiating and Planning phases. But just because you are executing against a well-defined plan does not mean that you can sit back and just watch the project phases complete. The project manager is very busy during this phase.

Project execution is where the people assigned to do the project work need to work as a team. Successful team development includes ongoing team building and management, appropriate team member training, and a meaningful rewards and recognition system.

Although you will spend the most time with the project team members, there are other critical relationships you must establish and maintain with the client and your sponsor.

An effective working relationship between the IT department and the business client requires the use of numerous management skills, especially consensus building and frequent communication.

The role of the project sponsor is to act as a mentor for the project manager and remove roadblocks that are beyond the authority of the project manager. If you see signs that the sponsor no longer supports the project, you need to determine the cause of these doubts and work to a satisfactory resolution, even if the ideal solution means canceling the project.

Staffing issues may arise with the functional managers who provide your human resources. You need to attempt to resolve these issues with the functional manager, but if a compromise cannot be reached and the project is in jeopardy, escalation to the sponsor may be required.

As the work on the project progresses, you need to collect data through team member progress reports, timesheets, spending requests, and the documentation of issues. The data you collect can be used as input into analysis of how the project performance compares to the schedule and cost baseline and the scope statement.

There is a great deal of project information, and distributing that information can be accomplished in a variety of means. Project meetings provide a regular point for team members to share progress, solve problems, and update issues. Status reports keep all stakeholders informed on a regular basis, while a formal project review can provide an opportunity to interact face to face with the sponsor, the client, and other executive stakeholders.

Contract administration is an additional process for those project managers dealing with vendors. Although a procurement specialist may handle much of the contract work, the project manager must work with the vendor to obtain progress reports and to resolve disagreements between the vendor and team members. The impact of vendor delays on the project plan must be assessed. The project manager also needs to be involved in the approval of payment for vendor invoices.

Exam Essentials

Identify the ongoing weekly activities a project manager performs as part of executing according to the baseline. A project manager reviews progress reports, spending reports, issues tracking logs, the project scope, the schedule baseline, the budget baseline, and the status and approval of major deliverables.

Understand the impact of a delay of a vendor deliverable to the project plan. Any changes to the project deliverables can impact the scope, the critical path end date, the budget, and the required resources. A vendor deliverable delay may add new risks to the project or create the need to establish new baselines for the schedule or budget.

Name the key components of an effective team meeting. A successful meeting has a stated purpose, a defined time limit, and a documented agenda distributed in advance. The project manager is accountable for setting a consistent day/time for the meeting, keeping the meeting on track, obtaining input from all appropriate team members, and sticking to the agenda.

Understand the various means to recognize or reward team members. Team member contributions can be recognized with monetary rewards or prizes, mention in a formal project review, a letter to executive management, or a team celebration.

Define a strategy for dealing with wavering project support from the sponsor. The strategy for dealing with wavering project support includes identifying the reason for the lack of support, determining the most effective means of communicating with the sponsor, enlisting the support of the allies, and potentially requesting a new sponsor or recommending cancellation of the project.

Recognize the components of an effective working relationship between the IT organization and the client organization. An effective working relationship requires team building, regular written and verbal communications based on the facts, joint issues management, timely decisions, and ongoing management of client expectations.

Understand that vendor relationships are critical to the process of getting your project finished. Be aware that often you come into a relationship with a vendor with one set of expectations, the vendor with quite a different set. Managing those expectations by coming to consensus and making sure that you're on top of what the vendor is going to deliver is critical to project success.

Key Terms

Before you take the exam, be certain you are familiar with the following terms:

- contract administration
- information distribution
- progress reports
- project review
- scope verification

Review Questions

1. There are numerous reasons why a particular project task may not be progressing as planned. Of the following reasons for a task delay, which one is most likely to require a change to the project team composition?

    A. Team member is spending time on another assignment.

    B. Team member is ill or takes a vacation day.

    C. Team member does not have the skill set to complete the work.

    D. Team member does not understand what is expected.

2. Which of the following project manager responsibilities is not part of the project execution phase?

    A. Setting the schedule baseline

    B. Identifying, assigning, and tracking resolution of project issues

    C. Obtaining sign-off as required on major deliverables

    D. Reporting project status

3. Which of the following are components of vendor contract administration? Select the best answer.

    A. Request for proposal, statement of work, and vendor solicitation

    B. Progress reporting, vendor disputes, and vendor delays

    C. Bidders' conferences, vendor selection criteria, and progress reporting

    D. Statement of work, progress reporting, and payment process

4. Which of the following is the most effective method to provide a weekly status report to your client and other executive stakeholders?

    A. The more information that you send to stakeholders, the better. Distribute detailed minutes from your weekly project team meeting to all the stakeholders.

    B. Stakeholders outside of the project team members are not concerned with the project status unless things are going wrong. You can contact them if there is an issue requiring their input.

    C. Stakeholders should be able to analyze the updates from your project management software package. A copy of the current project schedule should be sent to all the stakeholders.

    D. A status report template provides a consistency for stakeholders to quickly identify the information they need. You should include a summary of project progress, the completion of any major deliverables or milestones, and a status of any outstanding issues.

5. During a review of unit test results, two of your programmers disagree on the correctness of the deliverable from one of the units of code. How should you resolve this dispute?

   A. The programmers should take the issue to the test manager.

   B. You should ask clarifying questions to determine the specific issue surrounding the deliverable. Ask the team member disputing the deliverable to reference a specific requirement that is not being met.

   C. A separate meeting should be scheduled to conduct a detailed analysis of the code in question. The programming team and the test team should both be involved in this session.

   D. The project team members should decide who is correct. This item can be added to the agenda for the next regularly scheduled team meeting.

6. When comparing the actual schedule progress to the schedule baseline, which of the following should receive the most attention?

   A. The tasks on the critical path are the most important, as any delay in these tasks can delay the project end date.

   B. The tasks assigned to the technical team members are the most important. The marketing plan and the end-user training do not impact the development and delivery of your system.

   C. The tasks assigned to inexperienced resources are the most likely to get off track and should be closely monitored.

   D. All tasks are equally important, and you should request a detailed explanation and recovery plan for any task that is not 100 percent on track.

7. A functional manager has put you on notice that your lead tester is being pulled from the project to do a special assignment. You have asked around, but no one knows of another qualified person currently available. The timing could not be worse, as your integration testing is scheduled to begin next week. You have requested a meeting with the functional manager to discuss alternatives, but all of your voicemails and emails have been ignored. When you stopped by the functional manager's office, the only response you received was a lecture on the organizational reporting structure. Which of the following would be the best next step?

   A. The functional manager has ultimate say over the resources, so the best you can do is request a replacement resource and move forward. You don't want to raise an alarm prematurely, so don't make an issue out of this unless the integration testing runs into problems.

   B. You should immediately write a letter to the functional manager's department head demanding an explanation for this deliberate attempt to sabotage your project.

   C. Based on the steps you have taken and the responses you have received, resolution of this issue requires escalation. You should meet with your project sponsor to request assistance in resolving this impasse.

   D. You have done everything you can, but you need to make sure all of your attempts are thoroughly documented. When the project falls apart, you can easily put the blame on the functional manager.

8. Just prior to the weekly project team meeting you compare the latest schedule update with the schedule baseline. Based on current progress, the development phase will be completed a month later than planned. What is the best action to take at this point?

   A. You should call an emergency meeting with the sponsor and the client to advise them that the project end date has been delayed by 4 weeks.

   B. The schedule issue should be covered during the team meeting, but this is not the time to solve the problem. You should isolate the critical path tasks that are off track and identify the team member(s) accountable for these tasks. You can work separately with the responsible team member(s) to determine the root cause of the delay and develop a strategy for corrective action.

   C. This issue needs to be resolved immediately by the project team. You should discard the planned team meeting agenda and advise the team how disappointed you are that they have caused a schedule delay. You may need to extend the length of the meeting.

   D. The potential schedule delay should not be communicated to anyone; it will just cause the team to panic. You should email the people responsible for the delayed task(s) and advise them you are confident they will find a way to meet the target end date.

9. Your system engineer has started making negative comments during your weekly team meeting. He has had a heated argument with the marketing manager and you have heard from various team members that he has become difficult to work with. What is the best course of action for you to take?

   A. You should write a memo to the system engineer's functional manager and request a replacement as soon as possible.

   B. The system engineer is critical to the project, so you should give him some slack.

   C. You should confront the system engineer openly at the next team meeting. Let him know that his performance is unacceptable and that he will be replaced if there is not an immediate change.

   D. You should schedule an individual meeting with the system engineer to determine if he has issues with the project that need to be resolved. Get his perspective on how the project is progressing and how he feels about his role.

10. You are preparing for a formal monthly project review session with your sponsor and client. Which of the following is the best approach for making this an effective review?
    A. The project manager creates an agenda giving each team member an equal amount of time to provide task status.
    B. The preparation for a formal review takes valuable time that the project manager could put to better use. Assign one of the team members the task of putting together a summary of the meeting minutes from project team meetings for the last month.
    C. The project manager, with input from the project team, prepares a formal presentation that covers the following: previous months' key achievements, the current month planned deliverables, actual spending compared to budget estimate, overall schedule status, and any issues that could delay the project. The team determines in advance which team member will present each aspect.
    D. The project manager creates a presentation to put the project in the best possible light. Any delays, overruns, or other issues should be downplayed, to avoid making the sponsor look bad in front of the client.

11. Choose the project component that's most important to individual team effectiveness.
    A. Project cost
    B. Project size
    C. Project schedule
    D. Project value
    E. Project budget

12. You're the project manager for a large IT project that's going to take a year and require input from a vast array of IT technicians. Recently you've discovered that some fighting is going on between the person who's developing and implementing your security policies and a senior developer. You've found both to be highly credible, valuable players on your team. What's the best way to handle this situation?
    A. Call both to a meeting. Specify exactly what you're seeing happening between them. Ask for a plan from both to work out the differences. Stress the importance each of them contributes to the project.
    B. Ask the HR office to put together a meeting between you and the two fighting team members. Ask HR to work out the differences between the team members. Stress the importance each of them contributes to the project.
    C. Call both to a meeting with you and the project sponsor. Specify to the sponsor exactly what you're seeing happening between the two. Allow the sponsor to lead the group toward an amicable solution. Stress the importance each of them contributes to the project.
    D. Replace the security specialist with someone else.

13. You're the project manager for a large IT project that's going to take a year and require input from a vast array of IT technicians. Recently you've discovered that some fighting is going on between the person who's developing and implementing your security policies and a senior developer. The senior developer argues that the security specialist has no idea what she's doing and that she's not following good quality security guidelines. He produces some documentation to back up his claims. In researching the work that each is doing, along with his documentation, you find that the claims of the senior developer, while exaggerated, are not without merit. What's the best way to handle this situation?

   A. Call both to a meeting. Specify exactly what you're seeing happening between them. Ask for a plan from both to work out the differences. Stress the importance each of them contributes to the project.

   B. Call the security specialist into a meeting. Tell her that you've been looking at her work and that you'd like some input as to why she made the decisions she made. Without including the fact that the developer brought it up, ask her why the decisions that she made didn't follow the decisions the developer might have made, were he to be in her place. If you find the rationale to be reasonable and proper, tell the senior developer that you're behind the actions of the security specialist. If not, ask her to begin meeting the standard security guidelines and illustrate with your documentation what you're talking about. Ask if there are ways that you can assist her with her work. Stress the importance of her contributions to the project.

   C. Call both to a meeting with you and the project sponsor. Specify to the sponsor exactly what you're seeing happening between the two. Illustrate the developer's point with the documentation he has provided. Put the security specialist on a 30-day action plan to improve her processes. Stress the importance each of them contributes to the project.

   D. Replace the security specialist with someone else.

14. You've recently acquired $20,000 worth of hardware from a server vendor for an activity in your project with a promise from the vendor that he will supply some additional software modules that are required at no cost. Where are these additional software modules noted?

   A. Project charter
   B. Project budget
   C. SOW
   D. WBS

15. You're well into the project execution/controlling phases of your project. After a "here's where we're at" overview of the current work, business experts have come back to you to complain that the product they see being built right now does not address their needs. Yet you have in hand a design document that was signed off by key stakeholders and the sponsor and denotes exactly what the vendor has delivered so far. The vendor says that to go back and make the changes recommended by the business experts will require additional funding, as the vendor sees himself on time, on budget, and within the constraints of the SOW. What do you do?

    A. After performing an investigation, present your findings to the sponsor.

    B. After performing an investigation, authorize the expenditure of the additional funds to meet the business expert's needs.

    C. Do nothing—the business experts agreed to the initial design and the vendor is working according to the agreed-to SOW.

    D. Instruct the vendor that he must implement the changes at no cost.

16. Of these communication situations, which would be best suited to team-building efforts? (Select all that apply.)

    A. Schedule changes

    B. Resource loss

    C. Personality clashes

    D. Budget changes

    E. Low morale

    F. Organizational changes

    G. Project phase completion

17. Of these communication situations, which would you immediately communicate to the project sponsor? (Select all that apply.)

    A. Schedule changes

    B. Resource loss

    C. Personality clashes

    D. Budget changes

    E. Low morale

    F. Organizational changes

    G. Project phase completion

18. You are a project manager for an IT project that's in the executing phases. A vendor has notified you that a server you require for a given task in the project, a task that's on the critical path, will not be able to ship for 2 weeks. What is your course of action?

    A. Set up a meeting with stakeholders. Explain the situation; ask for an extension to the project deadline.

    B. Meet with the vendor; see if you can shorten the delay. Set up a meeting with stakeholders. Explain the situation; ask for an extension to the project deadline.

    C. Meet with the vendor; see if you can shorten the delay. Set up a meeting with stakeholders. Explain the situation; ask for an extension to the project deadline. Get extension approved through project sponsor.

    D. Meet with the vendor; see if you can shorten the delay. Set up a meeting with stakeholders. Explain the situation; ask for an extension to the project deadline. Get extension approved through project sponsor. Revise project plan.

19. Your project has taken a serious turn for the worse. While your project team is working its heart out to meet deadlines, it appears that the executive project sponsor has lost all enthusiasm for the project. You're not sure why. The project is near death, and if you cannot clear up this problem, you're close to the point where you're going to have to kill the project. What steps should you take?

    A. Set up a meeting with the executive project sponsor. See if you can determine why the problem exists.

    B. Set up a meeting with the executive project sponsor. See if you can determine why the problem exists. If you can't get anywhere with the executive project sponsor, try to get an ally or someone with influence on the sponsor to get at the heart of the matter. Meet with the stakeholders to apprise them of the situation—maybe you can get a new sponsor appointed. If you can't get anywhere, you're better off killing the project.

    C. Set up a meeting with the executive project sponsor. See if you can determine why the problem exists. If you can't get anywhere with the executive project sponsor, try to get an ally or someone with influence on the sponsor to get at the heart of the matter.

    D. Set up a meeting with the executive project sponsor. See if you can determine why the problem exists. If you can't get anywhere with the executive project sponsor, try to get an ally or someone with influence on the sponsor to get at the heart of the matter. If you can't get anywhere, you're better off killing the project.

20. One of your senior network engineers, Marty, is absolutely insistent that the vendor who's supplying your routers is "all wet" when it comes to a facet of a router that he's been tasked to install. However, when you consult with the systems engineers who work for the vendor, they tell you that Marty has misunderstood the way the product works and that it works the way they've advertised it. How do you handle this problem?

   A. Call the vendor and Marty to a meeting. Sit back and watch them hash it out.

   B. Call the vendor and Marty to a meeting. Act as arbitrator in an effort to get at the root of what the problem might be.

   C. Arrange to have some of the vendor's engineers meet Marty on site to work through a sample configuration on one of the routers. That way if he's right, they can see what he's talking about; if he's wrong, he'll see why.

   D. Tell Marty to listen to what the vendor has to say—after all, they invented it.

Answers to Review Questions

1. **C.** A team member lacking the required skill set is almost always doomed to fail. Whatever the reason, be it a communication breakdown on the skill set required or a functional manager who simply assigned the next person in line, if you determine that a team member does not know how to complete assigned tasks, you need to consider requesting a replacement. Unless there is a lot of slack time associated with the task, it is not possible to train the person so he or she can do the work. If a team member is spending time on another assignment, you need to confirm with the functional manager the amount of time committed to your project. Confusion over project expectations can normally be clarified with a one-on-one meeting. Illness or unplanned days off are a part of project life.

2. **A.** The schedule baseline is set during project planning before the project work begins. This provides a method to track project progress during execution against what was planned.

3. **B.** During contract administration, the project manager needs to review regular progress reports from the vendor as defined in the statement of work. Disputes between the vendor and team members must be investigated and resolved. Delays to vendor deliverables need to be analyzed for impacts on the project baseline and communicated to the project stakeholders. The other components listed in this question are part of procurement planning.

4. **D.** A weekly status report should be distributed in a consistent format and provide the stakeholders with a snapshot of progress on major deliverables and resolution of issues. Stakeholders do not have time to read through team minutes to obtain information, and many of them may not be familiar with how to interpret a project schedule.

5. **B.** Disputes over project deliverables should always be resolved by referring to the data in the project plan. If a deliverable does not meet the documented project requirements, you have an issue that needs resolution. If you are dealing with a matter of personal preference, the person or group responsible for delivery chooses how to complete the tasks.

6. **A.** The critical path tasks will impact the project end date, and you should focus on these tasks regardless of whether they are technical or business focused. The experience level of a resource does not guarantee that the task will be completed as scheduled. Tasks not on the critical path have built-in slack, but don't forget that if these tasks slip they may become critical path. Your project management software will automatically compute critical path as progress updates are made.

7. **C.** A project manager should always attempt to resolve staffing disputes with the appropriate functional manager providing the resource, but sometimes you reach an impasse. If you are dealing with a resource critical to the success of the project and all your attempts have failed, it is time to escalate the issue to the project sponsor. Writing a letter to the department head will not only alienate the functional manager, it could cause repercussions for your project sponsor. Ignoring the issue will not solve anything.

8. **B.** The people accountable for the work need to identify the problem and work with the project manager on a solution. Involving the entire team in an issue where many members may have no expertise is a waste of valuable time. The worst thing you can do is avoid the issue; chances are it will only get worse. You should meet with the sponsor and the client only after you have more information regarding the cause of the delay and potential solutions.

9. D. In order to address the issue, you need to understand what is behind the system engineer's current behavior. He may have been given additional work that you are not aware of or he may misunderstand the project goals, to name just a couple of possibilities. The situation cannot be ignored, no matter how valuable the person is, and it should be handled in private.

10. C. The purpose of a formal project review is to communicate to key executives current progress, planned progress, and any roadblocks the project may be facing. This is the group of people that can make the hard decisions as to what the priority is between your constraints.

11. D. The project's value—that is, how important it's perceived by management, stakeholders, and perhaps even the corporate body at large—contributes to the team's effectiveness, simply because team members feel like they're working toward something that's held in high esteem. No one wants to work on a project that doesn't mean much to anybody. That being said, picture yourself as a project manager for a project that's going to update the internal piping in a sewage treatment plant. Chances are the overall corporate body isn't going to recognize the importance of your work, but stakeholders certainly are aware of what you're getting done.

12. A. These are always tough situations to arbitrate. Your primary goal is to bring the two together to try to air the differences in a way that's constructive. If possible, don't meet with them in your office; instead, choose a place that's neutral to all of you. Point out that you notice some friction going on and that you're wondering what the elements of that friction might be, because it's having an effect, or will have shortly, on the outcome of the project. Stress how valuable each of them is to the efforts of the project. Ask questions that don't give either other person an opportunity to blame the other. Try to find creative solutions to the problems.

    If this fails, the next step might be to consider asking HR to take a more active role, either through a team-building exercise (which could only occur on larger longer projects where team members work full-time on the project) or in individual counseling.

13. B. The developer should not be a part of the conversation. He has his own work to do and is her peer, not her supervisor. Point out that you've researched some security methodologies and illustrate where you find her work to be different than the standards you've discovered. Ask her why and try to get her rationale behind the decision. If you find the rationale to be wanting, then tell her you need for her to begin to work toward the standards you're talking about. Otherwise, let it go. Speak with the developer to tell him that you've investigated the situation and dealt with it. Ask him to try to work more harmoniously with the security specialist. Be sure you tell both what an important part they play in the project.

14. C. Tacit vendor agreements such as this need to be noted somewhere and agreed to by both parties so that you save yourself embarrassment and expense when you actually call for the promised items. The SOW would be the most logical place to insert the statements that stipulated the promised modules.

15. A. First you must get both sides of the story. You must make sure that the changes being asked for are actually really required and that they were somehow missed at requirements-gathering time. Also you need to determine that the functionality being asked for is a "need to have" versus a "nice to have." You also need to talk to the vendor to get their impression of the situation. Finally, you prepare a report and go to the sponsor for final instructions on how to handle the situation. If the sponsor says that no additional funds are authorized, then the business experts will have to deal with the system as-is (though you may have a "this project stinks" issue on your hands). If the sponsor says that the changes must be made, then she has to authorize the expenses required to make those changes. You cannot simply stipulate that a vendor make changes just because it's the right thing to do, and you cannot operate outside the boundaries of a jointly agreed-to SOW.

16. C, E, F. Personality clashes and low morale can be urgent situations, but not necessarily of the type that require outside intervention. Your team-building skills would be useful in solving problems in these areas. Organizational changes require quick communication from the project manager. As a rule, most people are generally sensitive to change and are asking this question: "What does this mean for me?" This has a tendency to disrupt working patterns, decrease efficiencies, and requires that you act as a change agent—getting people through the change, while continuing the work of your project. Additionally, it's quite possible that an organizational change may directly affect your project in which case you, too, need to ask: "What does this mean for the project?"

17. A, B. Probably, the project sponsor will communicate to you any budget or organizational changes. Project phase completion isn't something you immediately need to communicate. Personality clashes and low morale should first be treated with team-building efforts before escalating any further.

18. D. First, you should meet with the vendor to see whether you can negotiate a shorter delay. Working with tasks on the critical path allows for very little room for finagling other tasks without consulting with the project sponsor and stakeholders. Next, you should meet with the stakeholders to apprise them of the delay. If they're okay with the deadline extension, you should modify the project plan and obtain formal sign-off from the project sponsor.

19. B. You start by going directly to the executive project sponsor to try to get at the heart of what's going on. Careful communication techniques are required so that you don't make the problem worse than it already is. If you can't get anywhere, you should seek out an ally or an influence that might be able to find out what's going on. Barring that, it may be worth your while to take the matter to the stakeholders, though they'll probably have little power to change the sponsor of the project. Finally, if things continue to deteriorate, you'll have to pull the plug on the project.

20. C. Getting vendor SEs in a room with your engineer and letting them work through a sample configuration is the best way to handle the situation. You don't have enough information to know who is right. If the vendor is wrong, you'll be able to address it. Otherwise, you've provided your engineer with a great lesson about configuring this particular router. You should be there with them to make sure that the fisticuffs and name calling are kept to a minimum.

Chapter 9

Project Control

THE COMPTIA IT PROJECT+ EXAM TOPICS COVERED IN THIS CHAPTER INCLUDE:

✓ 3.1: Identify the specific tasks that should be accomplished on a weekly basis in the course of tracking an "up and running" project.

✓ 3.2: Given a scenario with a set of project performance indicators, demonstrate the ability to recognize when performance problems are occurring on the project and determine if/when corrective action/recovery needs to occur.

✓ 3.3: Given a scenario with updates/changes made to the project plan, demonstrate the need to check for various project impacts.

✓ 3.4: Given a scenario involving a project with a schedule delay, choose an appropriate course of action.

✓ 3.5: Given an approved project and a status report scenario containing a significant variance from plan (e.g., excessive overtime, purchased items more expensive than anticipated), identify and determine solutions and accommodations for such a variance.

✓ 3.9: Identify issues to consider when trying to obtain approval of a changed project plan that is still within expected budget, but has a schedule that extends outside of the original baseline end date.

✓ 3.10: Define and explain estimate to complete (ETC), estimate at completion (EAC), and budget at completion (BAC).

✓ 3.11: Demonstrate the ability to track the financial performance of a project, given the financial management baseline and data on the actual performance of the project.

✓ 3.12: Given an approved project plan and a specific scope deviation (e.g., design, schedule, or cost change), demonstrate your ability to identify, prepare, determine, and quantify key elements of change control.

- ✓ **3.13:** Identify and justify the conditions for initiating a change control process.
- ✓ **3.14:** Given scenarios involving requests for changes from sponsors, team members, or third parties, recognize and explain how to prevent scope creep.
- ✓ **3.15:** Recognize and explain the importance of communicating significant proposed changes in project scope, and their impacts, to management, and getting management review and formal approval.
- ✓ **3.16:** Identify and explain strategies and requirements for maintaining qualified deliverables, given a large project with many team members at multiple locations (e.g., communication standards, work standards).
- ✓ **3.17:** Recognize and explain the importance of testing in situations where tasks are being performed by both project team members and third parties.
- ✓ **3.18:** Identify and explain strategies and requirements for assuring quality during the turnover phase (e.g., user docs, user training, help-desk training, or support structure).
- ✓ **3.19:** Identify and explain strategies and requirements for assuring quality of deliverables and meeting sufficiency standards during each phase.
- ✓ **3.20:** Recognize the need and explain the importance of controlling changes on the configuration of the project deliverable.
- ✓ **3.25:** Given an initial high-level scope, budget, and resource allocation, demonstrate understanding of the need to investigate the aspects of the project that could be modified to improve outcomes (i.e., find out what is negotiable, prepare to negotiate).
- ✓ **3.32:** Given a project team meeting scenario, demonstrate the knowledge to review an issue log with team members and secure closure of issues.
- ✓ **3.33:** Demonstrate the ability to prioritize issues by severity and impact on quality.

- ✓ **3.34:** Demonstrate understanding of how to determine if/when planned risks have materialized and how to implement planned risk mitigation and removal strategies.
- ✓ **3.35:** Demonstrate the ability to prioritize risks by severity and impact on quality.
- ✓ **3.36:** Demonstrate the ability to remove/mitigate a project risk.
- ✓ **3.37:** Demonstrate an understanding of how to report to the project sponsor that a project is in jeopardy and how to report corrective action strategies that are under way.
- ✓ **3.38:** Demonstrate understanding of how to determine when a project should be prematurely terminated.
- ✓ **4.3:** Recognize the need for acceptance testing (user acceptance testing, factory acceptance testing, site acceptance testing) of the project deliverable.

In the course of executing your project plan, you continually monitor results. Deviations from the project plan can be warnings that changes may be required to your original project plan. Requests are received during the course of the project to add new requirements or to expand the scope of the project work. You need to implement change control processes to deal with these requests.

Integrated change control looks at the overall impact of change and manages updates across all elements of the project plan. Scope change control includes recognizing that a scope change has occurred, taking appropriate action relative to a scope change, and managing a process to review and approve or reject requests for scope changes. Schedule control entails knowing that a change to the schedule has occurred, taking the appropriate action to deal with the schedule change, and updating the schedule based on changes in other areas of the project plan. Cost control involves being aware that the project costs have changed from the estimate, understanding when cost changes require response, and updating the budget

Quality control monitors the project deliverables against the project requirements to ensure that the project is delivering according to plan.

Performance reporting provides information to the project stakeholders comparing the work results produced by the project with the information contained in the comprehensive project plan. Variance analysis, trend analysis, and earned value are used to assess project performance.

Risk control implements the risk prevention strategies or contingency plans developed in your risk response plan, monitors the results of preventative actions, and assesses new risks to the project.

Changes to the project plan may result in stakeholder action requiring trade-offs between scope, cost, time, and quality. We'll discuss these processes and techniques in this chapter.

Integrated Change Control

At this point you probably are thinking that with all the time and effort that went into planning, you should not have to worry about any changes. Everything is documented in the plan and the stakeholders signed off, so it should just be a matter of execution. That would be nice, but in the real world things change: a new business strategy, a competitive threat, or a new technology that was not available when you did project planning.

All aspects of the project plan are subject to change as the project progresses; the key to avoiding chaos is to manage any change in an organized fashion with an *integrated change control* system that looks at the impact of any change across all aspects of the project plan. A lot of time is spent in the planning phase developing estimates and plans for managing the project. Unfortunately, some project managers tend to forget all of that and just shoot from the hip if things go astray. You need to keep referring back to your planning documents and the management processes you put in place to update the plan.

Depending on how your change control process is set up, there may be a change control committee including the sponsor, the client, and other executives that reviews all changes, or the changes may be worked though the project team. Typically, larger and more complex projects have more formal change control. Regardless of who is involved in reviewing and approving changes to the project plan, changes that go outside established limits need to be presented to the stakeholder team. We will discuss stakeholder action later in this chapter.

Let's take a look at what is involved in controlling changes to scope, schedule, cost, and other elements of the plan.

Scope Change Control

As part of Scope Planning in Chapter 3, we discussed the need to define and document a scope management plan. As your project work progresses, you will implement this plan to control the scope of your project. *Scope change control* is the management and documentation of any changes to the project scope.

The following are some of the events that can trigger the need for the scope change process:

- A review of a major deliverable determines that there have been additions to what was defined in the project plan.
- Project team members indicate that they have made changes to a requirement.
- There is a formal request to add to the project deliverables.
- There is a design change.

In an ideal world, no change would be made to the project scope without going through a formal scope change approval process. In the real world, developers have conversations with end users or someone comes up with a different way of doing things and suddenly your scope has changed. If you discover that you are a victim of scope creep and a change has already occurred, you should still run the change through the scope change process to analyze the impacts to the other parts of the project plan and to secure formal approval for the change.

Let's review the key steps of the scope change process:

- Use a standard scope change request form with a description of the change, the reason for the change, and the originator of the request.
- Analyze the impact of the scope change request on the budget, schedule, and quality of the project.
- Use an approval process to accept or reject requests.
- Communicate results of scope change requests to all stakeholders.
- Incorporate approved changes into the project plan.

Scope changes may require corrective action and/or changes to the baseline.

Corrective Action If your project has become the victim of scope creep, you may or may not want to continue down the path that has created the scope change. You may need to determine what action is required to get the project back on track. It may take time to undo what has been done. In addition, you will want to investigate how the scope creep occurred and take steps to prevent future scope creep, such as educating team members on the scope change process.

Baseline Adjustments Any scope change, either planned or unplanned, will require updates to at least a portion of your baseline planning documents. At a minimum, you will update the scope statement. You may also make changes to the schedule baseline and the cost baseline, depending on the magnitude of the change.

Scope change control results may have a significant impact on schedule control, as you will see in the next section.

Schedule Control

As you review progress reports from project team members and the updates to the project schedule, your goal is to confirm that activities are on track or that any changes have been analyzed for impact to the critical path. Changes to the project scope will also require analysis regarding impact to the schedule. *Schedule control* is the process of managing and documenting any changes to the project schedule.

Project management software is an extremely useful tool for schedule control. Software packages can provide an individual task view of planned start and finish dates compared to actual dates, as well as forecast the impact of any changes from the baseline schedule to linked tasks, the critical path, and the project end date. You can also do what-if scenarios, to show the impact on a particular phase or even the project end date if task duration is changed or new tasks are added due to an approved scope change.

The key to making the best use of team member progress reports and the various reports and views using project management software is to focus on the critical path tasks. Remember that the critical path tasks are on the longest path of your network diagram and drive the end date of the project, so any delay to one of these tasks may lengthen the total project time.

Schedule control results include schedule updates, corrective action, and lessons learned.

Schedule Updates A *schedule update* is any change made to the project schedule as part of the ongoing work involved with managing the project. Schedules are typically updated weekly based on the team member progress reports to provide a current view of schedule progress and a comparison of status of the completed project work to the schedule baseline. Schedules are also updated to reflect new activities.

You may hear two terms in relation to schedule update. A *revision* is an update to the approved start or end date of the schedule baseline. Revisions are typically a result of approved scope changes. If a schedule change is substantial and impacts dates for multiple milestones or major deliverables, *rebaselining* may be required to provide a new means of measuring performance. Rebaselining should not be done lightly, as it distorts the accuracy of your original plan.

Corrective Action A number of factors come into play when considering whether corrective action is required as part of schedule control. Activity duration estimates are not expected to be perfect, so don't think you need to do something every time the actual time required to complete a task does not match the estimates. If an activity has a delayed start or is taking longer than expected, but has float time such that there is no impact to successor tasks, you don't need to take any action at this point. Your emphasis on corrective action should focus on critical path tasks.

Performance indicators can tell you that things are going wrong. Let's take a situation where critical path tasks are taking longer than planned and a major milestone may potentially be missed and/or the project end date is in jeopardy. The performance of critical path tasks impacts your ability to complete the project on time, so you need to look at what can be done to get the project back on schedule. Your first course of action should be to determine why the critical task is behind schedule and work with the person(s) assigned to the task to get it back on track. If you have a part-time resource, you should investigate bringing that person on full-time until the task is complete.

If nothing can be done about the activity creating the potential delay, your analysis will need to encompass the rest of the project work. You may implement fast tracking by having some tasks worked in parallel or crashing by bringing on additional resources to complete the remaining work in less time. If you choose to implement either of these techniques, be sure to document the risks associated with this course of action.

Lessons Learned Major changes to the project schedule should be analyzed to determine what caused the deviation from the plan so that steps can be taken to prevent the situation from happening again. These lessons may apply either to the remaining work on your project or to future projects. If all of the tasks assigned to a particular resource or group require more time than planned, you may want to have the people involved revise estimates for any future tasks or have the remaining estimates reviewed by a third party with experience completing similar tasks.

Changes to your scope or schedule may involve extra costs that need to be managed.

Cost Control

Another key project result is the tracking of project spending. Formal reports from the finance systems, project team member time reporting, and requests for purchase approval all provide a picture of how the project spending is tracking with the budget. The budget impacts from scope changes also need to be analyzed. The *cost control* process includes being aware of the project spending to date, determining that a change to the cost baseline has occurred, and taking appropriate action to deal with the change.

Project management software is also useful in tracking project spending, if cost figures have been loaded. You can run reports that show spending to date and projected spending. You can also look at the impact of adding new tasks using what-if scenarios.

Any major change to the project plan that will impact cost should include securing additional funding as part of the approval process. Adding requirements to the project and starting work on new tasks prior to securing funding is a sure way to overrun your budget.

Cost control results include revised cost estimates, corrective action, and lessons learned.

Revised Cost Estimates As actual costs are incurred and tracked, you are able to project how the actual costs for a particular project phase or even the entire project will differ from the original estimates. As with any deviation from the project plan, you should review the revised cost estimate to determine any impacts to other aspects of the project plan. An increase in overtime hours, for example, may be an early warning that a task is taking longer than planned. Frequently, revised cost estimates are the result of changes originating in other parts of the project plan, such as a scope change or schedule change.

Just as with schedule updates, there can be revisions to the cost baseline, typically in response to a scope change, or there can be rebaselining if the cost variances are so extreme as to make a change necessary in order to track performance

Corrective Action   General cost overruns that are not tied to a change in another part of the project plan such as a scope change or a schedule delay may not require any further action if they are below some predefined level. Many organizations consider projects on track if the actual spending is plus or minus a predefined percentage of the overall project budget. If you have a 10 percent leeway on a project budgeted at $1,000,000, an extra $50,000 spent will be acceptable; an extra $200,000 would require the approval for additional funding.

If the problem rests with the accuracy of the initial cost estimates and there are no additional funds available, you may need to discuss trade-offs with your stakeholders, such as reducing the scope or lowering the quality. We discuss trade-offs in more detail later in this chapter.

Lessons Learned   Major deviations from the cost baseline need to be analyzed to determine what caused the difference so that steps can be taken to prevent the situation from happening again. These lessons may apply to either the remaining work on your project or to future projects. If a number of work effort estimates from the same resource or group are not being met, you may want to have revised work effort estimates for any remaining tasks.

Now let's look at controlling change for some other aspects of the project plan.

Other Plan Changes

Scope, schedule, and budget are the items that are most frequently mentioned targets of change control, but these are not the only components of the project plan that may change. Let's take a brief look at four other elements: resource changes, requirements changes, infrastructure changes, and configuration changes.

Resource Changes   Whenever a project team member is added or leaves, it is important to document the reason for the change, the name of the replacement (if any), the person requesting the change, and any impact the change will have on the project.

Requirements Changes   This can be a tricky area to manage. As detail is added to a requirement or it is updated to clarify expectations, you need be taking a look at these changes to make sure they do not involve a scope change. Any new requirement should always go through the change control process.

Infrastructure Changes   Infrastructure is the elements of a project that will remain permanently after the project is completed. As an example, a team member may have planned for a Sun server running UNIX for your database, but as the project moves forward, the network team requests that you change this operating environment to Windows 2003 Enterprise Server. Infrastructure components that may change include:

- Computing systems
- Software development environments
- Server operating system platforms
- Networking infrastructures
- Delivery methodologies

Infrastructure changes can have a major impact on your overall project plan, particularly if your project includes equipment orders that were based on different infrastructure assumptions.

Configuration Changes Frequently, the design team will make a decision about a software or hardware configuration only to find out as the software is installed that another configuration would work better for the requirements or that the suggested configuration won't work with another system in an integrated system environment. One of the more frequent examples of a configuration change is when the database design team determines that a given set of indexes is required for the database being designed. But then, as the programmers begin to write code that runs against the database, they may decide that another type of index would be useful and effective as well. So a configuration change is required to add the new proposed index.

Configuration changes can be very simple or quite complex—it just depends on the nature of the configuration and what is expected of the software or hardware. However, generally speaking most configuration changes don't require a lot of time and can be accomplished within a couple of hours, so they're really not project showstoppers. Keep in mind that some configuration changes will require a reboot of the equipment and thus may not be able to be put into effect until after hours.

As your project moves forward and major deliverables are produced, you will start implementing your quality management plan.

Quality Control

Although quality is one of the common constraints all projects share, it is an area that does not always receive the same amount of focus as the scope, budget, or schedule. However, lack of quality management can have severe negative impact on the project. *Quality control* is the process of reviewing project results to confirm compliance with defined standards and making appropriate changes to remove causes of unacceptable quality. The quality management plan discussed in Chapter 6 is the foundation for the specific activities carried out during quality control. The quality activities, the procedures used to complete the quality activities, and the resources required are documented in the quality management plan.

Quality control is done throughout the project. As we have mentioned in earlier chapters, milestones are often included in a project schedule to mark the completion of a project phase or major deliverable. Quality tools and techniques are used to determine compliance with a minimum sufficiency standard, and quality activities are often a key part of the formal process of approving the completion of a phase.

We will focus on the use of testing to monitor the project work results, as well as mention some other tools and techniques that are used in quality control. The results of your quality control activities may result in rework, process changes, or acceptance of any defects that are found.

Inspection (Testing)

Inspection is a broad category that includes examining, measuring, or testing work results. The most common use of inspection on IT projects is testing.

Testing is something you should always try to devote extra time to. Testing is a boring job—someone has to run the code over and over again, testing different things in different modules, taking notes about its performance. But it's got to be done. You should have at your disposal testers who are ready and willing to thoroughly run your new code through its paces.

Testing is done throughout the project, and several kinds of testing are common on IT projects:

Module Testing   A programmer completes a module of code and needs to test it. Some modules don't lend themselves to module testing, because they're designed to interface with other modules. Still, the programmer can check that variables load correctly, that the code goes to the places it's supposed to go to depending on the input, and that memory gets cleaned up and the program exits correctly. Often developers can run code through a checker that steps the code line by line to see how it behaves and how it loads memory variables. The process can be at once very interesting and yet extremely frustrating, because the developer has something going wrong but can't figure out where—all of the code appears to be doing what he or she wants it to do.

At this stage of the game, dynamic link libraries (DLLs) and other informational files are also tested for complete and accurate content.

Unit Testing   Once several modules that go together have been satisfactorily tested, the developer can test them all at once in unit testing. They might test an entire printing system or a set of algorithms that calculates something. They're testing the functionality of pieces that have been put together to form a cohesive group.

System Testing   Next, the developers test the entire system as a whole. They make sure the system flows as expected, that the user doesn't encounter unexpected loops or gotchas (such as "deer in the headlights" frozen screens), that the system is fast and functional, and that it delivers what the customer is expecting. System testing should take a long time, because they thoroughly test each component and the whole.

User Acceptance Testing (UAT)   This is the time when they actually bring in a small set of users to begin testing the deliverable. By the time developers get to UAT, they should've worked out all bugs, speed or logic issues, and flow problems. The system should be at its best, most pristine state. This is the system they currently expect the user to utilize in production—until the UAT testers find the problems others missed.

Factory Acceptance Testing (FAT)   Sometimes a system is so large it's better if testing by the users is done on site at the place where the initial development was done. Think of the development of a new radar system for weather forecasting in which there is new gear being developed *plus* new software. All of this is done at the vendor's site in preparation for delivery to the new location once the customer has accepted the new system. FAT is part and parcel of big government contractors such as Raytheon and other companies that specialize in big development work.

Site Acceptance Testing   Site acceptance testing involves customer testing at the customer premises. Consider the radar system example above. A radar specialty contractor has developed the new radar system and all of its elements. The customer has come out to the factory for FAT and finds the system acceptable. Now the company delivers the new system to the customer and they go through another round of testing to make sure that all things are operational and that the system operates as expected.

Testing is always an important step in confirming the quality of an IT project, and in a couple of scenarios you may need to conduct even more testing.

Geographically Dispersed Team Project teams are often dispersed across multiple locations. A major software deliverable may be the result of code compiled from modules written by several programming teams. Even though you have established communications and work standards for the teams, the lack of daily face-to-face contact can increase the risk of misinterpretations, which could lead to differences in the modules that may impact the compiled package. In this situation, you may want to have more detailed testing on the individual modules to catch problems early on.

Vendor Deliverables Another scenario where testing takes on significant importance is when a vendor produces deliverables. The specifics of how and when you can test during the development process should be included in the contract. Integration testing of the vendor deliverable with the rest of the system is commonly a requirement for final acceptance of the vendor work. Acceptance of a vendor deliverable equates to vendor payment, so these tests need to cover all requirements associated with the work the vendor was contracted to produce.

Although testing is the most frequently used for quality control in IT projects, it is not the only method available.

Other Quality Control Tools and Techniques

Anyone who has been on an IT project is probably familiar to some degree with the amount of testing that is conducted over the course of a project. Other tools and techniques can be used in combination with testing to address quality defects.

Pareto Diagram A *Pareto diagram* is used to rank the importance of a problem based on its frequency of occurrence over time. This diagram is based on the Pareto principle, which is more commonly referred to as the 80/20 rule. The Pareto principle is named after Vilfredo Pareto, an Italian sociologist and economist, who observed that 80 percent of the wealth in Italy was held by 20 percent of the population. This principle has been applied to many disciplines since Pareto first discovered it. Applying the principle to quality control, it says that the majority of the project defects are caused by a small set of problems. A Pareto diagram helps to isolate what the major problems are, so that you can take action that will have the greatest impact. A bar graph is used to display problems in decreasing order of occurrence so that priorities for improvement can be established.

The purpose of a Pareto diagram is twofold:

- It displays the relative importance of the defects.
- It directs the improvement efforts to those areas that will have the biggest impact.

FIGURE 9.1 Pareto diagram

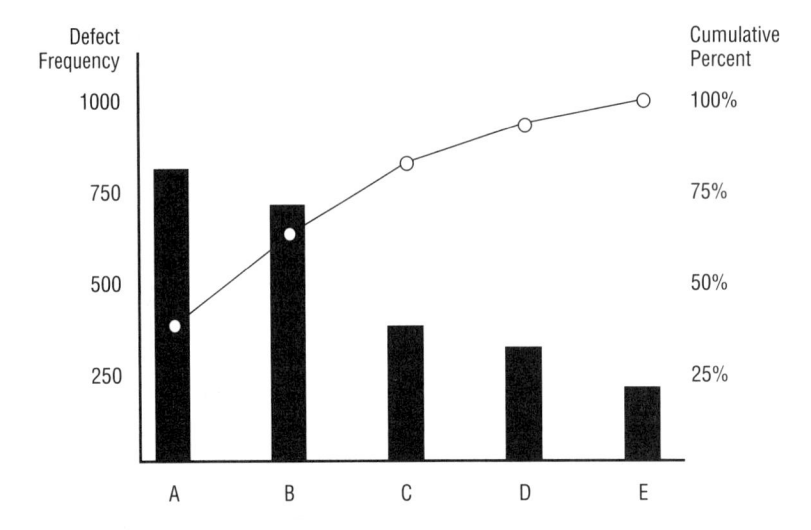

Let's take a look at how this works. A Pareto diagram typically starts with a table that lists information regarding the frequency of the defects or failures uncovered during testing. Table 9.1 shows the following frequency of failure for items A–E: the number of occurrences, the percent of defects that this item represents, and a cumulative percent.

With this data in hand, you can create a Pareto diagram, as shown in Figure 9.1 The bars are ordered from left to right based on the frequency. The bars depict the defect numbers, and the cumulative percentages are plotted using the circles. By looking at the data in Figure 9.1, you can see that the most significant problems you want to focus on are A and B. Fixing these two items will resolve over half of the defects.

TABLE 9.1 Frequency of Failures

Item	Defect Frequency	Percent of Defects	Cumulative Percent
A	800	.33	.33
B	700	.29	.62
C	400	.17	.79
D	300	.13	.92
E	200	.08	1.0

FIGURE 9.2 Control chart

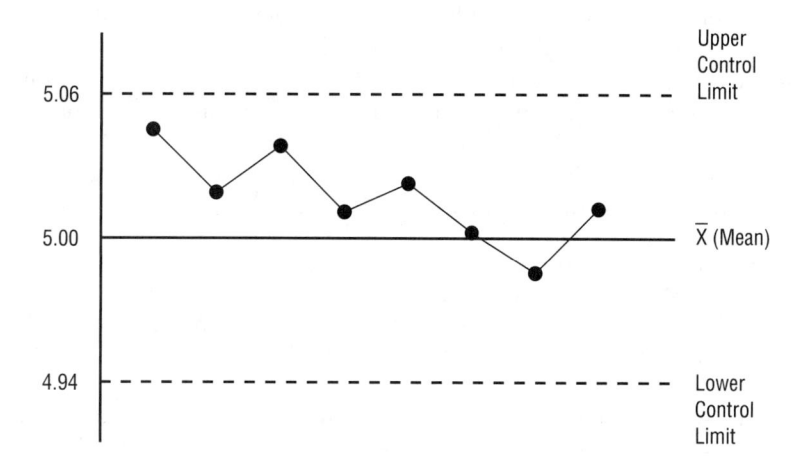

Control Charts   A *control chart* is a picture of the variance of several samples of the same process over time. It is most commonly used in manufacturing. A control chart is based on a mean, an upper control limit, and a lower control limit. The upper control limit is the point beyond which preventing additional defects becomes cost prohibitive. The lower level is the limit at which the client or end user will reject the product because of the defects. The goal is to stay in the middle area (the mean), where the best product for the lowest cost is obtained. An example of a control chart is shown in Figure 9.2.

Statistical Sampling   If you have numerous work results that require inspection or testing, you may decide to use statistical sampling, which gathers a subset of all the applicable work results and randomly selects a small number for testing or examination. Statistical sampling can be very cost effective, especially in projects where multiple versions of the same product are produced.

Flowcharting   Flowcharting was discussed in the quality planning section of Chapter 6 as a means to create the process that produces the product. Flowcharting can also be an effective tool during quality control to help determine the how the problem occurred.

Trend Analysis   *Trend analysis* is a mathematical technique that can be used to predict future defects based on historical results. We will discuss trend analysis in more detail later in this chapter.

The results you obtain from testing or other quality control tools and techniques are used to determine whether any action should be taken to correct poor quality.

Quality Control Actions

As you implement your quality control activities, you need to make decisions on the appropriate course of action based on the results received. Any action taken to resolve quality problems has trade-offs, so you will need to involve other stakeholders in the decision process. The most common actions taken as a result of quality activities are rework, process adjustments, and acceptance.

Rework

Rework is any action that is taken as a result of quality activities to correct a defect. A module test may result in the rewrite of a section of code from the module tested.

Rework sounds like the ideal solution to any quality problem that is found. If you discover a problem, you should fix it—right? In an ideal world with no time and budget constraints that would be true, but rework often impacts both the project schedule and the budget. The time to complete the deliverable will be longer than estimated to account for the time it takes to fix the problem, and the people doing the rework will be billing additional hours to your project.

> There may be exceptions to the increase in billable hours, if you are working with a vendor and have quality standards written into the contract. However, you should always consider the possible financial impacts.

A decision on rework is often tied to the severity of the defect and its impact on the ability of the end user to use the product. Your client, sponsor, and other impacted stakeholders need to be involved in rework decisions.

Process Adjustments

Changing a process can ripple throughout the rest of the project. Unless it is very clear that a process change is contained to a small work group or a few team members with no downstream effects, it is best to use the change control process to analyze the impacts of a process change and obtain formal approval before making any changes.

Acceptance

Acceptance is the decision to accept any defects that are found as a result of the quality testing. Acceptance is a common action based on analysis of the severity and frequency of the defects uncovered during testing. For example, some commercially available software products are released for sale to the public with known defects to be fixed with an upgrade later. Meeting the publicized release date for the product is more important than fixing defects; in other words, the schedule takes priority over quality. The overall impact of accepting a defect should be analyzed and communicated to project stakeholders. You need to get stakeholder sign-off to accept defects.

Another important aspect of quality control is the documentation quality.

Documentation Quality

IT projects often produce documentation, both technical and nontechnical. Your quality control activities include ensuring the quality of all project-related documentation and other material turned over to groups who use or manage your deliverable. This includes user documentation, user training, help-desk training, and documentation for other support groups.

User Documentation

Any documentation—whether online or paper copy—that the user requires in order to use the system should be proofread for spelling, grammar, and content. All instructions regarding the use of the system should be tested to confirm accuracy. Paper copies should be prepared and bound for distribution to the users. Help-screen documentation should be complete and thorough. There is nothing more annoying than hitting F1 for help only to find "No help is available for this topic" or extremely minimal information.

User Training

User training may be instructor led, a self-paced workbook, or online. Regardless of the delivery medium, the curricula should be checked for content and completeness. A pilot class may be held to confirm that the training is thorough and understandable and that any online practice features of a training database work correctly. The trainers who will provide or support the training should be educated on the new system and ready to go, and any training documentation should be printed and bound, ready for class. Training materials such as demonstrations and visuals should be ready. The scheduling of training classes should be part of the project schedule to ensure that users will be ready for the deployment.

Help-Desk Training

IT project managers are often good about considering end-user training and getting classes ready for users, but they may overlook the person in the trenches, the help-desk technician, who will wind up getting calls from users about how the new system works. Take into consideration where the help desk is going to fit in terms of supporting the new system, and prepare help-desk technicians in advance with the training they will need to support users. Help-desk training should include all of the aspects of end-user training as well as the more detailed aspects of resolving problems and troubleshooting. All of the proofreading and testing discussed in reference to user training quality also applies to help-desk training. Especially during the early phases of new system release, users are going to have questions about how the system works and may turn to the help desk for answers. The help desk needs to be ready to go at deployment time.

Other Support Group Documentation

Producing quality deliverables goes well beyond fulfilling the customer's requirements. Others involved with the system need to know how the deliverables will affect their daily business operations. Therefore, it's important to take into consideration, well in advance of the project's closure, the documentation deliverables that apply to other groups in the overall support structure. It may be easy to overlook these people, but the overall success of the project requires accurate and usable documentation for all groups who play a part in the operation and maintenance of your system.

Server administrators must be aware of the impact that the new system will have on servers. It is unreasonable to install new server software on servers and not relay information about it to the server administrators.

PC technicians may also need to be aware of any impact the new system will have on the client computer. For example, if your new app uses Oracle forms or a Visual Basic front-end, or if a thin-client application requires the download of a Java client, problems may be introduced to client computers. It's important that PC technicians know how the new system impacts the client computers so they can, in turn, support the end user.

Database administrators (DBAs) must also be aware of modifications or changes in the enterprise database environment. Especially critical to DBAs is information about indexes, relationships, triggers, stored procedures, table layouts, column names, and other information pertinent to the system databases. It's not wise to put a new system out on the floor without updating DBAs on what the system is about; that amounts to expecting them to go into discovery mode on the fly, finding out how your system works (and fixing it) when you already know this.

New systems that use telephony or internetworking infrastructures (routers, WAN links, etc.) will require assistance from the people who are experts in these areas. During project development time, you may have interfaced with these people, but it's important that they have documentation as to how the new system will work on their equipment.

IT Quality Control

Quality control in the IT world begins by following a twofold path:

- Sticking to well-known, widely established standards for the work that you do
- Setting up your initial environment in such a way that you are guaranteed success

Neither of these items are easy to quickly establish—they take buy in at all levels and a dedication to the process. Let's talk about each one separately so you can get a feel for what's involved.

Standards

When IT shops sit down as a group and hammer out standards, the result is almost always a more consistent way of doing business. Consider, for example, the following applications development standards:

- All new applications will be developed so that they run from a browser utilizing XML.
- All applications will utilize server-side Web services such as J2EE, not localized services.
- All applications will use Simple Object Access Protocol (SOAP) as the transport method from the application to the client.

These standards certainly aren't inclusive and may not be the standards that a given IT shop would set, but you can see that they are fundamental, simple to understand, and use commonly held protocols as the binding glue. By setting these standards, you have a firm way of controlling new applications enterprise-wide. If someone's entertaining the notion of bringing in a COTS software product, you can insist that the vendor(s) being considered are required to adhere to the standards.

In setting up a PMO that's going to handle IT projects, it's wise to get all the IT stakeholders in a room and see if you can generate a list of common standards that all groups will adhere to. These standards can include:

- Server burn documents—that is, how servers will be built
- Workstation installation standards—that is, the OS and office automation suite versions, patches and service packs, browser settings, control panel settings, profiles, etc.
- Application development standards
- Network operation standards, including acceptable network protocols

Standards Organizations

Standards organizations develop standards for almost everything you can imagine (from software protocols to street signs to wine glasses). One organization is called the International Organization for Standardization (ISO—see www.iso.org). Specifically, ISO 9000 can be (and is) utilized by corporations for the management of their quality control. While ISO 9000 is a large thing, perhaps you can glean standards information by visiting the site and determining how ISO derives the standards and what standards are available.

Another is the Distributed Management Task Force (DMTF—see www.dmtf.org). This organization acts to bring about ways to manage systems by a standardized interface. Microsoft introduced this standard into its Windows product through the Web-Based Enterprise Management (WBEM) standard, which utilizes a management interface and database on each Windows 2x computer and higher. WBEM is utilized by Microsoft Systems Management Server (SMS) for the purpose of gathering inventory information from PCs and uploading the data to a central database for the purpose of maintaining a centralized system inventory.

Another is the Institute of Electronic and Electric Engineers (IEEE—see www.ieee.org), an organization instrumental in producing widely adapted networking protocols. The wireless networking protocol suite 802.11 is an IEEE standard that has evolved out of hours of work by committee experts.

Another useful and interesting standards organization centers its philosophy on the best way to manage operations environment (servers, network infrastructure, mainframe, etc.) This organization, the Information Technology Infrastructure Library (ITIL—see www.ogc.gov.uk/index.asp?id=2261) has standards that will assist you in formulating great operational methodologies. ITIL is the entity responsible for saying that one must understand a business process flow before applying technology.

Another standards body is the American National Standards Institute (ANSI— see www.ansi.org). Interestingly, the PMI's *A Guide to the PMBOK* is an ANSI standard.

As you can see from these organizations, thought and effort has been put into developing standards whereby computing systems can "play in the sandbox" with one another. So, at the very least, it's to your benefit to understand those standards and to insist that they're used throughout the organization as best practices.

Setting Up Your Environmental Processes

There are many good ways to get started in organizing a PMO that continuously puts out high-quality projects. Perhaps the first place to start is to assess your organization to see just how healthy it actually is in terms of its ability to actually generate good-quality projects. A *Capability Maturity Model (CMM)* analysis might be in order. CMM was developed by the Software Engineering Institute (SEI) at Carnegie Mellon University (CMU)—see www.sei.cmu.edu/cmmi/adoption/cmmi-start.html for more information on the various CMM implementations to date.

The idea behind any CMM is that five operational levels describe any given organization's project development efforts: Initial, Repeatable, Defined, Managed, and Optimizing.

Initial Processes are ad hoc and occasionally even chaotic. Does this describe your organization? It sure does some of the ones we've worked for! When a project is required, it just sort of gets thrown together. There's not really any commonsense pragmatism put toward the effort. This level is the lowest level of CMM. Organizations at this stage are CMM 1.

Repeatable At this level of CMM, an organization has established basic project management processes that serve to define the costs, schedules, and projected outcomes of any given project. At CMM 2, an organization is not considered to be "project-mature," but has definitely taken strides toward cleaning up its processes.

Defined At CMM 3, processes have been defined, published, standardized, and put into operation by some sort of project overseer entity—typically a PMO. All projects utilize standard documentation, project requests, approvals, and so forth to implement the deliverables. Organizations at CMM 3 are starting to get their stuff together, but they've got a way to go before they're fully functional.

Managed CMM 4 organizations qualitatively control the output of their projects. Any project is subject to strict quantitative scrutiny (in large organizations and projects this happens through Six Sigma techniques) to assess the quality of the outputs. Controls are tight, operations are well understood, and projects are cranked out in a uniform way with consistent quality. Understand that the operative word with CMM 4 is *quantitative*. At this level, we're applying quantitative measures and analysis to assure that our quality output is high.

Optimizing Like Abraham Maslow's top rung (self-actualizing) of his famous hierarchy of needs, an organization at CMM 5 is not only generating projects of consistent high quality and that are expertly monitored and managed, they're also constantly looking for ways to improve processes.

> **NOTE** You may not work for a manufacturing entity or other concern that has a vested interest in quantitatively managing quality, but if you're good with math, especially statistics, you may find a large measure of success in your employment efforts by getting a Six Sigma "belt." Six Sigma (www.isixsigma.com) is a program that teaches people how to monitor quality outputs through statistical analysis. The program uses the various colors of martial arts belts to denote how far you've gone in the program. There are Six Sigma green, brown, and black belts—the top, of course, being a black belt. Companies like General Electric (GE), Boeing, and others use Six Sigma types to assist in the management of their quality output.

The key to any IT undertaking lies in the ability of the IT organization to smartly implement project management methodologies and to undertake projects with consistency of action. By first understanding where your organization is at relative to its ability and aligning your efforts with good-quality, well-known standards, you have a very high chance of success.

> **TIP** Remember that it is key that we always understand a business unit's *process* or *flows* before we apply technology. If you're careful to keep that order straight, all else should fall into place.

Risk Monitoring and Control

Part of project planning was the identification of potential risks to the project and the development of a risk response plan. *Risk monitoring and control* is the process of implementing the risk response plan. This process includes not only tracking the risks identified during planning, but evaluating the effectiveness of the actions you identified. Have the steps you identified to prevent the risk or mitigate the impact been implemented? Is the result what was expected? For those risks you could not control, you must track the status of the risk to determine whether to implement the contingency plan that was developed to deal with the risk.

Risk monitoring and control also includes identifying any new risks throughout the life of the project. Regardless of the level of detail in your original risk identification, as the project progresses conditions change, the business changes, and other components of the project plan change, all of which can produce new risks that must be dealt with.

Closely linked to risk control is the control of project issues. You must monitor and update the progress of current issues, evaluate the progress of resolution, and identify new issues.

Let's start with the risk response plan results.

Monitoring Risk Response Results

During risk planning, you identified risks to the project and prioritized those risks based on the probability of occurrence and the impact to the project if the risk occurred. The risk response plan includes a planned response for each of your high priority risks—action that will either avoid the risk or lessen its impact or a contingency plan to deal with the results of the risk.

Preventative Action Risks that can be avoided or mitigated should have specific actions associated with preventing the risk, often involving the addition of new tasks to the schedule.

In these cases, you should be tracking the implementation of the planned action and evaluating the impact of the action(s) on removing or mitigating the risk. If the action is not mitigating the risk, you will need to review the risk response and either choose to accept the risk or develop a new response.

When you review an action that is not having the desired result, you need to determine if other factors involved have changed the nature of the risk. If what you really have is a different risk, it may require a completely different approach.

> ### Real World Scenario
>
> #### Keeping Your Eye on the Trigger
>
> One of us was on a project a few years ago that involved extensive user training in multiple locations as part of the deployment of a new user interface. The training had to take place before the new application was deployed at each location, which drove the development of a very complex dependency between the training and deployment schedules.
>
> Just when we thought we had this schedule planned out to perfection, we were advised that the end users were represented by a labor union in the midst of negotiating a new contract. Talks were not going well, and a labor strike could start in the middle of our deployment. No one associated with the project could do anything to impact the outcome of the labor negotiations, so we had to develop a contingency plan.
>
> We discussed several options, one being to tighten up the deployment schedule to complete all locations prior to the end of the current contract. That plan would have required additional resources to both train the end users and deploy the system, which we did not have. We opted to keep the existing training plan and develop an alternate plan for those offices that would not be trained before the strike date. The contingency plan called for the training to start 2 weeks after the end of the strike and to keep the same sequence and time between training as existed in the current schedule. All deployments scheduled prior to the strike date would continue as planned. No training or deployments would be canceled until after a strike was declared.
>
> The client approved this plan, a team member was assigned to monitor the progress of negotiations, and we established two triggers. The first was a vote by the union members to authorize a strike. When this occurred, a conference call was established with the managers of all offices impacted by the contingency plan. We reviewed the plan and made sure everyone understood the formula for calculating the new training date. It was agreed that a project team member would contact each office manager to confirm the training dates if we had to implement the contingency plan.
>
> Our second trigger was the official start of the strike, which came at 12:01 A.M. on a Sunday morning. When the strike was declared, a message was sent to all training and deployment managers to cancel travel plans for that coming week.
>
> Although the work stoppage delayed the overall deployment schedule by 6 weeks, the contingency was implemented smoothly and the remaining offices were deployed in an orderly fashion with no disruption to customer service.
>
> The key to a successfully implementing a contingency plan is identifying your triggers and good communication.

Contingency Action The other type of action that you identified in your risk response plan was a contingency action to deal with a risk you could not avoid or mitigate. This requires a different approach to risk monitoring. A contingency plan is implemented only if a risk actually occurs, so you need to be monitoring for a *risk trigger*, which is an event that tells you that the risk is imminent.

As the project moves forward, you need to be alert to any signals that either the risk or the trigger is changing. The key to a successful contingency plan is knowledge that the risk is forthcoming.

Identifying New Risks

The risk response plan evolves throughout the project life cycle. Some risks identified during planning may not materialize, and new risks may arise that were not previously included in the response plan. As the project work completes, you need to be aware of any new unplanned risks.

> **WARNING** Any change to the project scope has a potential to add risk to the project, because it changes or adds to the major deliverables of a project. Because the new activities associated with the scope change frequently lengthen the project schedule, they may be on the critical path as well. A scope change should always include a risk analysis and review of the risk response plan.

New risks may also impact the risk priority listing. A new risk may have a greater probability and a more severe impact than previously identified risks. Changes to the project plan may also change the relative ranking of existing risks. For example, as actual work progress is reported, the schedule critical path may change, impacting the urgency of dealing with risks that were previously a low priority.

As you modify a response to an existing risk or identify a new risk, the action proposed to deal with the risk may itself result in a change to the project plan. The response may involve a change to the project scope, a change to the schedule, or money. In this case, your risk response should go through the appropriate change control procedures, like any other change.

Your issues log is another important document that requires ongoing monitoring and updates.

Monitoring Issue Resolution

Monitoring the progress of issues resolution is very similar to monitoring risk; you need to make sure appropriate action is taken to close the issue. An issues log that is not carefully managed can turn into an unwieldy monster, with new issues added weekly, and nothing getting resolved.

As you review your issues log in a project team meeting, you want to be sure the person who has been assigned to resolve the issue is working toward closure. Sometimes project issues will remain open for weeks or even months, especially if you consider "we are still working on this one" an acceptable progress report. The status you request should always include both a plan for resolution and a target date to resolve the issue. If no progress is made, perhaps the responsible party needs assistance or does not really understand the issue. It may require escalation to the sponsor to overcome roadblocks.

Although the goal is to assign all issues and resolve them as quickly as possible, in some instances you need to prioritize issues and have them worked in sequence. You can use some of the tools from risk planning to complete this prioritization. If multiple issues require the same team member or group, review the impact of each issue on the outcome of the project and establish a priority list.

A Project in Jeopardy

What starts out as a risk or issue to be resolved by project team member action can sometimes escalate into a situation that can jeopardize project completion. If the actions you have taken are not having the desired impact or if you are identifying new risks that you cannot control, it is time to get with the project sponsor to determine the appropriate course of action.

Escalation to the project sponsor is a delicate balancing act. You do not want to get the reputation that you panic every time something goes off course or that you cannot handle tough decisions. On the other hand, if you have done everything you can, do not delay involving the sponsor on the faint hope that things will change. If you do not raise a red flag until the project is in serious trouble, it may be too late for the sponsor to do anything.

When you come to the project sponsor, be prepared to communicate clearly the issue or risk, the actions you have taken so far, and the impact to the project if nothing changes. Your briefing with the sponsor should be at a high level; he or she does not need to know every step taken along the way.

You should request specific action from the sponsor. You will not come off well if you go into your sponsor wringing your hands and saying you don't know what to do. If you are having issues with another department that requires a decision at the executive level, let the sponsor know who is involved and what you need done to get the project on track.

Sometimes nothing can be done to change the situation. Perhaps a new regulation has invalidated key project assumptions or new corporate leadership has implemented a strategy that nullifies the justification for your project. If this is the case, your request to the sponsor may be a recommendation that the project be canceled.

Project control results need to be reported to the stakeholders, and in some cases stakeholder decisions must be made regarding the future of the project.

Performance Reporting

Control activities uncover important information about your project that you need to communicate to stakeholders. *Performance reporting* provides progress and forecast information on the project scope, schedule, cost, and quality. Risks or issues that that are jeopardizing the success of the project also need to be reported to the stakeholders.

Performance results should be distributed based on your communications plan for each stakeholder group. Performance reporting includes information on what has been accomplished to date and is typically stated in terms of what has been completed and what remains to be done.

A number of analytical tools can assist you in obtaining meaningful data to communicate project progress.

In addition to communicating project results and forecasts, performance reports often require action on the part of the stakeholder team.

Performance Reporting Tools and Techniques

A meaningful performance report needs to contain more specific information than simply stating whether the project is on schedule, over budget, or out of scope. Deviations have a wide range of impacts on the overall success of the project. As part of your performance report, you need to include an analysis of the problems to quantify the impact to the project.

Techniques that can be used to clarify the impacts of deviations from the plan include variance analysis, trend analysis, estimate at completion, and earned value.

Variance Analysis

Variance analysis is the comparison of planned project results with actual project results. Variance analysis is most frequently used on the project schedule and project budget.

Most project management software tools include a tracking feature that allows you to display the baseline schedule compared to the actual schedule. You can see which tasks took longer than predicted, as well as any impacts to project milestones. You can create views that show results down to the task level, or you can do a summary view that shows the overall results for a particular phase. This tracking feature also recalculates project end data based on any delays.

Project budget reports can be compared to the cost baseline to show how much has been spent compared to what was budgeted for the same period of time. These reports can also include a comparison of the hours expended on tasks by individual resources to the work effort estimate that was part of the cost baseline.

Percentages can be used to quantify variance. You may have seen performance reports stating that a major deliverable is 75 percent complete or a statement indicating that the project schedule is 50 percent complete and 35 percent of the budget has been spent.

> **WARNING** Exercise caution when using percent complete or percent of total budget. These numbers may be misinterpreted if they are used out of context. The budget needs to be looked at in terms of the work completed and the work remaining. Being on schedule and over budget is not a good thing, but being behind schedule and over budget should send up a big red flag.

Trend Analysis

Past performance may give you a clearer picture of what to expect from future performance. Trend analysis is based on mathematical calculations used to show whether performance is improving or declining over time.

These historical trends are used to forecast future project performance. Various formulas are used to calculate trends and predict future results. It is outside the scope of this book to go into this subject in detail.

Estimate at Completion

As your project progresses and you obtain your official budget reports, you will be asked to predict the total cost of the budget. An *estimate at completion (EAC)* is a forecast of the total cost of the project based on both current project performance and the remaining work. To understand how EAC works, you need to know a couple of other terms:

- *Actual cost (AC)* is the total amount spent on the project to date or through the end of a particular phase.
- *Budget at completion (BAC)* is the total amount of the project budget.
- *Estimate to complete (ETC)* is the cost estimate for the remaining project work.

EAC = AC + ETC

A comparison of your EAC figure to your BAC figure provides you with a current estimate of any deviation from the original budget.

> **NOTE** There are two other methods for calculating EAC. One uses actual spending to date plus remaining budget. The other method uses actual spending to date plus the remaining budget modified by a performance factor. It is beyond the scope of this book to go into detail on these methods. Further information can be found in *A Guide to the PMBOK*.

Earned Value

In your future, more advanced PM studies, you'll encounter some financial management variables that you may want to pay attention to—especially if your project is one that's massive and requires that you pay special attention to all the financial details.

> **NOTE** Although Objective 3.10 only lists the three terms associated with estimate at completion, the intent of this section is to provide a broader explanation of financial management variables.

There are several variables, each of which could be easily calculated through spreadsheet or project management software calculations. We need to take some time to build some of the numbers that you'll use to calculate these variables, so we'll start with some basic definitions, then move into how they combine with each other in real use.

A Guide to the PMBOK has changed some of the earned value management terms. Both sets of terms are still in use, which can cause confusion if you do not realize that two terms are interchangeable. Table 9.2 lists both the current term and the term it replaces.

When you perform analysis on your project using the following formulas and variables, you're performing *earned value analysis*. When you perform assessment on a project's *earned value*, you're measuring how much of the budget you predict that you should have spent so far, given the amount of work already done on the task. You're calculating the *budgeted cost of work performed (BCWP)*. (The terms *earned value* and *BCWP* can be used synonymously.) It's

TABLE 9.2 Earned Value Terms

Current Term	Also Known As
Actual Cost (AC)	Actual Cost of Work Performed (ACWP)
Earned Value (EV)	Budgeted Cost of Work Performed (BCWP)
Planned Value (PV)	Budgeted Cost of Work Scheduled (BCWS)

important to also understand that your pristine project starting point—nobody working on any tasks yet, no money spent—represents the baseline of the project. It's important to fully describe your project's beginning prior to calculating any financial management variables. Project management software allows you to save your work with a baseline before you start entering hours or materials costs.

Earned Value Basics

Start with a *status date*—simply, the date when you're going to take a measurement of how much has been spent on a specific task.

Next, you must understand several different ways of looking at a task's cost. The first way is the *planned value (PV)*, also referred to as *budgeted cost of work scheduled (BCWS)*. Generally, you apportion out a task's total cost evenly over the number of days that the task is scheduled to take. If a task is predicted to take 5 days and cost $100, for example, each day represents $20 of a task. You arrive at the BCWS by comparing the amount that's budgeted to be spent on a task between its start date and the status date (not necessarily the same as the end date). For example, if you have a 5-day task that's going to cost $250, then you can break the per-day cost out to $50 a day. If you set your status date to Thursday, for example, you've used 4 days of the 5 and your BCWS is $200. Figure 9.3 illustrates this concept.

Another component of earned value is the *actual cost of work performed (ACWP)*. This is the actual cost incurred for each day that you worked on a project within a given period. In our example in Figure 9.3, the project has a budgeted cost per day of $50, for a total of $250 for the task. But what if you spent only $45 on Monday, $30 on Tuesday, $45 on Wednesday, and $35 on Thursday? Then your ACWP for the 4 days would be $155, even though your BCWS is still $200. Figure 9.4 shows this relationship.

FIGURE 9.3 Budgeted cost of work scheduled (BCWS) or planned value at status date

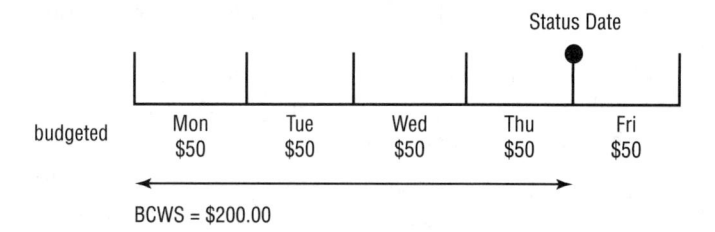

FIGURE 9.4 Actual cost of work performed or actual cost

	Mon	Tue	Wed	Thu	Fri
budgeted	$50	$50	$50	$50	$50
actual	$45	$30	$45	$35	

Status Date (Thu)

BCWS = $200.00
ACWP = $155.00

FIGURE 9.5 Budgeted cost of work performed or earned value

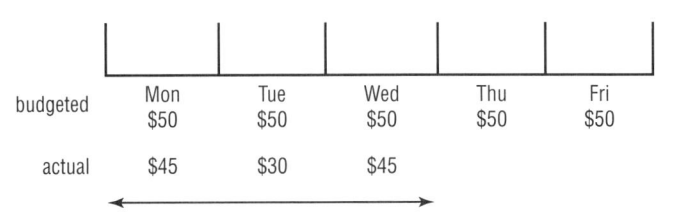

	Mon	Tue	Wed	Thu	Fri
budgeted	$50	$50	$50	$50	$50
actual	$45	$30	$45		

By Wednesday, 75% of work is done.
$250 × 75% = $187.50; therefore, BCWP is $187.50, even though actual expenditures are only $120.

Finally, you have another straightforward calculation you can make: budgeted cost of work performed (BCWP, as mentioned earlier). This figure represents the comparison of the percentage of work performed to the expected, budgeted amount. If by Wednesday you've met 75 percent of the task's budgeted work (even though you've got until Friday), then the work you've done was budgeted to cost $187.50 even though you've only really spent $120. You're comparing the amount you've actually spent to the amount you'd expect to have spent based on the percentage of work completed thus far. Figure 9.5 demonstrates this calculation.

Now that we know the differences in these earned value components, we can go forward and calculate some basic financial management variables. The BCWS, ACWP, and BCWP figures you have go into the remaining calculations.

The BAC and EAC acronyms that were described earlier in this chapter will also play into an index described later.

All these calculations deal with comparing the current status to the budget in some way. One group simply subtracts, producing a variance that is the difference between actual and budgeted; the second group, the *indexes*, divide to show you the ratios relative to those measurements. All these numbers might be useful to calculate, although in smaller IT projects not all of them will be necessary.

Variances

Variances show the difference between that which was budgeted and the actual costs expended. A positive variance shows that you've saved money or time and might be able to reapportion the savings elsewhere in the project. A negative variance states that you're either over budget or behind schedule for a given task—requiring that you take action.

Cost Variance The *cost variance (CV)* simply represents the difference between a task's estimated (budgeted) cost and its actual cost. The formula is CV = BCWP – ACWP.

Schedule Variance The *schedule variance (SV)* simply represents the difference between a task's progress as compared to its estimated progress and is represented in terms of cost. The formula is SV = BCWP – BCWS.

Indexes (Ratios)

Indexes are designed to show a ratio between one project budgetary component and another. The most common of these numbers are extremely useful, because they are simple to gauge: either greater than 1 or less than 1. If a ratio's value is greater than 1, the task is either ahead of schedule or under budget. A ratio less than 1 indicates that your task is behind schedule or over budget.

Note that ratios can also be expressed as percentages, which may be an easier way to think of the numbers. For example, if one of these indexes calculates to 0.971, you can multiply by 100 to state that index as 97.1 percent.

When you commit these formulas to memory and understand what they're representing, you can use earned value analysis to get a much better handle on where you're at with a given project. You can answer questions such as "Is there enough money in the budget so that I can finish the project?" or "Do I have enough time left to finish the project on time?" Again, you would use these calculations with very complex projects and probably wouldn't need them with simpler ones.

COST PERFORMANCE INDEX

The *cost performance index (CPI)* shows the ratio between a task's budgeted and actual costs. The formula is CPI = BCWP/ACWP.

A CPI of less than 1.0 means you're over budget; a value over 1.0 means you're spending less than you expected.

SCHEDULE PERFORMANCE INDEX

The *schedule performance index (SPI)* is a ratio of the work performed on a task versus the work scheduled. The formula is SPI = BCWP/BCWS.

An SPI of less than 1.0 means you're behind schedule; a value over 1.0 means you're taking less time than you expected.

TO-COMPLETE PERFORMANCE INDEX

The *to-complete performance index (TCPI)* is a ratio of remaining work compared to remaining budget and is represented as a percentage. It can be viewed as an efficiency formula where the higher the percentage, the more efficiency you're currently getting out of the task. A TCPI that is more than 20 percent higher or lower than the CPI means that the current EAC is not representative of past performance. Here is the TCPI formula:

TCPI = work remaining / funds remaining

where: work remaining = BAC − BCWP

funds remaining = BAC − ACWP

For example, given the following project numbers, here's how you'd calculate the TCPI:

BAC = 250,000

BCWP = 175,000

ACWP = 180,000

CPI = (175,000 / 180,000)

= 0.972 (or, as a percentage, 97.2%)

TCPI = (250,000 − 175,000) / (250,000 − 180,000)

= 75,000 / 70,000

= 1.071 (or, rendered as a percentage: 107.1%)

To compare TCPI to CPI, divide one into the other. If the result is between 1.2 and 0.8, then you're within the +/− 20% guideline:

TCPI / CPI = efficiency compared to past performance

1.071 / 0.972 = 1.102

In this case, a comparison of 1.1 means we're essentially on track in our project relative to past performance (provided, of course, that *past* performance was in line with our expectations).

The results of all this analysis may require decisions by the stakeholders on how (or if) the project will move forward.

Driving Stakeholder Action

During the project control phase many hard decisions regarding the future of the project are made. The project manager is responsible for communicating not only the nature of deviations from the project plan, but also the impact of these deviations and recommendations for moving forward. Trade-offs may be required in order to complete the project. In some cases, the project may no longer be viable and the stakeholders may be asked to officially cancel the project.

Communicating Performance Deviations

As you analyze progress throughout the life cycle of your project, it is important to keep stakeholders advised of any variance that could impact the outcome of the project. You may choose to supplement your project status report with charts or tables to clarify and summarize the results of your analysis. Several useful charts and reports can be produced using your project management software. For example, a tracking chart can be produced in Microsoft Project that displays the status of major deliverables or milestones compared to the schedule baseline. If you have loaded cost data into the software, other reports compare what was spent to what was budgeted.

> **TIP** The key to success is to keep things as simple as possible. The point of using graphs or charts is to clarify how the project is performing compared to the plan. Avoid using acronyms or other analytical terms the stakeholders may not be familiar with. Translate your results into language everyone can understand.

Managing Trade-Offs

Early on in this book we mentioned that all projects share common constraints: scope, time, cost, and quality. If any one of these changes during the course of a project, it impacts at least one of the other three. Change of some form is inevitable in all projects; so don't think that you can keep all the variables stagnant.

As project manager, you need to communicate the trade-offs to the stakeholders if there is a change to one of the constraints. You should have an idea regarding the importance of the constraints from your planning meetings with the client, so that you can present the trade-offs based on the constraint the client does not want to change. Let's look at how changes in one area of the plan impact the others.

Scope Trade-Offs

A scope change request is often one of the easiest to deal with from a communications perspective, because your change control process includes an analysis of the impact of the proposed scope before the change is approved.

If your client wants a new feature added to the address validation project, you need to communicate the increased cost and/or increased time it will take to add that feature. Additional resources or team members with different skill sets may be required. Clients may often push back and want you to just do it all within the same time period with the money currently budgeted. The client needs to understand that the only way to accomplish that is to give up quality by eliminating or shortening test cycles.

When dealing with scope changes, look for alternate solutions that may be acceptable to the client. If a new feature cannot be added to the existing project without a schedule change, perhaps it can be looked at as a future enhancement. There may be other ways to obtain the result the client needs, so always ask questions to clarify what is behind the scope change request.

Schedule Trade-Offs

The importance of a schedule delay can run from an inconvenience to a disaster, so it is critical that you know and understand the relative importance of this constraint for your project. Let's look at a situation where your 10-month project is staying within budget and has not been subject to scope changes, but you need to obtain approval from your stakeholders to extend the project end date 3 weeks. On the surface this request seems reasonable; we all know that the estimates made during project planning are educated guesses. In many situations, the logical course of action may be to recommend delaying the end date rather than to add risk to the project by implementing crashing or fast tracking. However, if the project was designed to meet a regulatory action with a mandated implementation date, you would certainly lose credibility making a recommendation that would cause your organization to be in noncompliance and subject to fines or other legal action. You should always consider the priority of the target end date and the impacts of missing this date before you recommend a schedule delay.

If your actual results indicate that you are behind schedule in several areas, it is likely that the work effort was underestimated or the requirements did not communicate the true complexity of the project. Regardless of the reason, if you are behind schedule and see no viable means of catching up with the current resources, you need to present your stakeholder with options. Assuming the project delivery date is the highest priority, you need to assess how the date can be met. If your issue is resources, explain to the stakeholders the resources required and the estimated cost. If more resources will not impact the end date or if no funds can be secured, you should be prepared to discuss removing functionality from the project.

A Phased Delay

Telling your stakeholders that there will be a delay in the project delivery is no fun, but sometimes you just can't avoid it. It may even be a big delay. But don't make it worse by downplaying the length of the delay and crossing your fingers.

One of our early project experiences involved a new system application that was being developed for customer care representatives from two recently merged companies. Although the requirements and all of the major deliverables referenced one system, each company had separate backend systems to interface with the new customer care system. So in reality, the development team had twice the application interface work than had been planned.

Everyone on the team knew there was no way that the project would deliver as scheduled, and the development team completed a revised estimate that would delay the project by 6 months. Both the development manager and the project manager were afraid to go to the sponsor and the client with this news, so they communicated a 2-week delay and hoped for a miracle. The 2 weeks didn't change anything, so they communicated another 2-week delay. At this point the sponsor started asking a lot of questions, and the project manager had to admit that the best estimates of the additional work required indicated a 6-month delay. The sponsor was furious that she had not been told the truth from the beginning, and the credibility of the project manager was nonexistent. In fact, a new project manager was named shortly after this incident.

No one likes bad news, but you will be much better off if you take one big hit and present all the facts. Too many project managers try to sugarcoat project problems and convince themselves that the project will turn around—that rarely happens.

Schedule delays may be inevitable. If the original requirements were not clear or a required element was missed, the project may be more complex than anticipated. Work may have progressed beyond the point where functionality can be removed without creating rework. If there is no way to avoid moving out the schedule, and the project is still viable, you need to make sure that the new end date reflects all changes that have occurred since the project was planned.

Cost Trade-Offs

Cost overruns can be the result of inaccurate estimates, schedule delays, scope creep, or omission of critical items from the cost baseline. Because costs may increase from so many areas, it is important to track costs relative to the work that has been completed. What has been spent at a given point in time may be over budget, under budget, or right on track depending on what milestones have been reached. If you budgeted $50,000 for a project phase, have spent $50,000, and the phase is complete, you are right on track. However, if you have spent $50,000 and the phase is only 30 percent complete, you have a problem.

If the project budget is cast in stone and you are experiencing overruns, the only way to make up the difference is to shrink the project. The best way to accomplish this is to meet with the client and the sponsor to decrease the scope of the project that will allow the project to complete with fewer resources and stay within budget. If you find yourself in this situation, make sure you are fully aware of the work that remains. It will accomplish nothing if the client agrees to give up functionality that has already been delivered.

A sponsor or client may push to retain the current scope, and make up for the budget overrun by short cutting testing or other quality activities. If this happens you need to make sure they are willing to accept the consequences of defects that may not be found until the system is in production.

Negotiating project trade-offs may not always be the best solution. If there are no viable alternatives, you need to present a recommendation to cancel the project.

Canceling a Project

In some cases, the best solution for dealing with project variance may be a recommendation to cancel the project. It is better to cancel a project that cannot be adequately funded or staffed to produce the needed deliverables than to let it continue and fail. If a project was approved without adequate planning, you may find yourself in a situation in which there is no viable solution. If requirements are constantly changing, or the client expectation is totally out of synch with the plan, you need to ask the sponsor and the other stakeholders if the project is still viable. If it seems that everything needs to be changed, perhaps there has been a change to the business strategy and this project is no longer needed.

Recommending cancellation of a project does not mean that the project manager has failed, it means he/she is forcing the sponsor and the client to reassess the original objectives and determine if this project still makes good business sense.

> **Case Study: Chaptal Wineries—Intranet and Email**
>
> You've been evaluating the project for quality, budget, and timeliness.
>
> **Budget** While the majority of the budget has gone well—there have not been huge budget shortfalls—you perform a quick estimate from the place where you've gotten hit the hardest—hardware. The result shows that you're almost $3,000 over budget, or about 3 percent of the overall $100,000 cost of the project.
>
> | Category | Actual | Estimated | Difference |
> | --- | --- | --- | --- |
> | Servers | 79,124 | 80,000 | $876.00 |
> | Network | 21,478 | 20,000 | $(1,478.00) |
> | French E1 | 2,980 | 2,000 | $(980.00) |
> | Australia T1 | 2,480 | 2,000 | $(480.00) |
> | Chile T1 | 2,730 | 2,000 | $(730.00) |
> | California T1 | 1,990 | 2,000 | $10.00 |
> | | | Total | $(2,782.00) |
>
> Since you had not ascertained a predetermined variance number for the project, you decide to visit Kim Cox to see what she thinks about the overage. Kim tells you that she had in mind a +/- 5% variance, so she's OK with the fact that you're slightly over. However, just because you're within variance does not mean that you can call yourself overly successful with the project budget.
>
> **Quality** The overall quality of the various elements of the project have, in your opinion, been high. Signal over the T1s is now good throughout—the Chilean telecommunications contractor was able to fix the problem easily (after Metor asked for a replacement from the first person who did the configuration). Customer response on the contractor's part was excellent and took no time at all to get going.
>
> You're also especially pleased with your intranet developer, Susan Wilcox. She has produced high-quality pages at a rapid rate. While she'll use up every bit of the allotted time you've given her, she has committed to not going over and has made all of her deadlines so far. You're quite pleased with the responsiveness and completeness of the pages.
>
> **Timeliness** With the exception of the 2 weeks wasted waiting on the Chilean telecommunications contractor to produce someone else who could figure out what was wrong with the T1 configuration, there have been no timeliness issues.

Summary

As we discussed earlier in the chapter: things change. Project control can be viewed as the glue that holds hold the project together. Continuous monitoring of project results and the implementation of appropriate action to make course corrections are the keys to delivering a successful project.

An integrated change control system is an umbrella that recognizes change or requests for change, determines the global impacts of a change, and updates all impacted portion of the project plan when a change is made.

You'll use scope change control to handle such issues as scope creep, reviewing and analyzing requests for scope changes, and updating all impacted documents if a scope change occurs.

As project manager, your concerns center around many change control issues. For instance, schedule control requires ongoing review of progress reports and schedule updates, with a focus on any delays to critical path tasks. Cost control compares actual spending with the cost baseline as it relates to the completion of specific deliverables or phases. When providing quality control, you'll implement the quality activities defined as part of the quality management plan.

Of course, any project has its risks. A project manager must use risk monitoring and assess the impact of the risk prevention steps identified during planning, identifying and prioritizing new risks, and implementing contingency plans based on a trigger event. Furthermore, the project manager must review and monitor the issues log to confirm that issues are being resolved and closed appropriately.

A project manager is also in charge of determining whether all of the project team players are doing what they set out to do at the cost they had originally estimated. Performance reporting uses a variety of analysis techniques to quantify the project control results for communication with the project stakeholders. Performance in any project element that goes outside predefined limits requires action on the part of the stakeholder team. Trade-offs between quality, scope, schedule, and cost are presented by the project manager. Cancellation of the project is also an action for consideration if the project is no longer viable based on any of the trade-off options.

Exam Essentials

Explain variance analysis.   Variance analysis compares actual project results from the schedule tracking or budget reporting to the planned results as documented in the baseline.

Describe the possible impacts to check for when evaluating a major change to the project scope. A major change to the project scope may impact project objectives, the critical path, the schedule end date, budget, project performance indicators, resources, and risks.

Understand the steps involved in responding to a significant variance from plan, such as increased overtime.   The reason behind the variance needs to be identified to determine whether scope creep is occurring. The impact on the budget and schedule need to be determined, followed by a plan for corrective action.

Explain how to prevent scope creep when handling requests for changes.   The change control process, which includes a thorough analysis of each request and a formal approval process, is used to manage all requests for a change to the project.

Understand the options to present to stakeholders when a project is not progressing as planned. The stakeholders need to be given options that include trade-offs on scope, schedule, budget, or quality. In some cases, project cancellation may also be an option.

Define estimate to complete (ETC), estimate at completion (EAC), and budget at completion (BAC). Estimate to complete (ETC) is a forecast of the cost of all remaining project work. Estimate at completion (EAC) is a projection of final project costs obtained by adding the ETC to the actual project costs to date. Budget at completion (BAC) is the amount of the project budget that remains after subtracting the actual costs spent to date.

Understand who the various standards bodies are that develop some of the essential standards used in IT. It's important to be aware that organizations such as ISO 9000 and ITIL help with quality and operational standards.

Be familiar with the Capability Maturity Model. Understand what CMM represents in helping organizations understand where they are in terms of how they implement projects.

Key Terms

Before you take the exam, be certain you are familiar with the following terms:

acceptance

actual cost (AC)

actual cost of work performed (ACWP)

budget at completion (BAC)

budgeted cost of work performed (BCWP)

budgeted cost of work scheduled (BCWS)

Capability Maturity Model (CMM)

control chart

cost control

cost performance index (CPI)

cost variance (CV)

earned value

earned value analysis

estimate at completion (EAC)

estimate to complete (ETC)

inspection

integrated change control

Pareto diagram

performance reporting

planned value (PV)

quality control

rebaselining

revision

rework

risk monitoring and control

risk trigger

schedule control

schedule performance index (SPI)

schedule update

schedule variance (SV)

scope change control

status date

to-complete performance index (TCPI)

trend analysis

variance analysis

Review Questions

1. You are a project manager for a new software application. You have just learned that one of your programmers is adding several new features to one of the deliverables. What is the best action to take?

    A. Make any needed adjustments to the schedule and cost baseline and tell the programmer that any future changes must be approved by you.

    B. Request the programmer to remove the coding for the new features, as he is outside the boundaries of the original scope statement.

    C. Contact the appropriate functional manager and request a replacement for this programmer.

    D. Determine the source of the request for the new features and run this change through the scope change process to determine the impact of the changes and obtain formal approval to change the scope.

2. You have just received the latest update to the project schedule. Based on the progress to date, system testing is projected to take 3 weeks longer than planned. If this happens, user acceptance testing will have to start 3 weeks late and the project will not complete on the planned finish date. The client scheduled the user acceptance testing participants weeks in advance. What is the best course of action?

    A. Explain to the test team that system test will end on the scheduled date and they are accountable for the accuracy of the testing results.

    B. Meet with the test team to determine the cause of the delay. If you determine that there are not enough testers to complete all of the scenarios in the time allotted, work with the sponsor to secure additional testers to complete system test as planned. If no alternatives can be implemented, work with the client to resolve the impacts to user acceptance testing.

    C. Write a memo to the client stating that you have a new date when the project will be ready for the end user testers.

    D. Escalate the issue of the system test delay to the sponsor and let her decide what action to take.

3. Your $5,000,000 application development project includes the purchase of two new servers, which are currently listed in the cost baseline at $50,000 each for a total of $100,000. Between the time the estimate was made and the equipment was purchased, there was a 10 percent price increase. The bill for the servers will be a total of $110,000. What action should you take? Choose the best answer.

   A. Use the new figure to revise your cost estimate and communicate the change to the project team and other stakeholders as part of your ongoing performance reporting.

   B. Add the additional server costs as an agenda item for the next project team meeting and work with the project team to develop a recommendation to take to the sponsor on scope reduction to cover the increased cost of the server.

   C. Review the scope statement and the schedule baseline for adjustments to make due to the impact of the server cost.

   D. Schedule a performance review meeting with the project team member responsible for the estimate.

4. You are the project manager for a new address verification system. The development phase has experienced some delays, and you are meeting with the development team to look at alternatives to get back on schedule. A suggestion is made by the development manager to skip unit testing and go right to the system test. What is the best response to this suggestion?

   A. The development lead has the most information about the complexity of the individual modules. You decide to accept the suggestion, as you already have 3 weeks scheduled for the system test. That should be more than enough time to find any problems.

   B. You agree to accept the suggestion, but make it clear to the development lead that she is accountable if this decision leads to rework or problems as a result of the system test.

   C. You need to request more information from both the development lead and the test manager regarding the complexity of the unit tests and the potential impacts to the system test if this step is omitted.

   D. You should explain to the development lead that no quality activities can be removed from the schedule, but you can agree to a scaled back version of what is reviewed during testing.

5. The system test results of your address verification system have uncovered a problem with the screen flow that is presented to the end user. Fixing the problem will involve a major rewrite of a portion of the screen flow logic. The end user can still access the "missing" screens, but this involves additional user training on commands to manually request a specific screen. What is the best course of action?

   A. You should send a memo to the client and copy the stakeholder team explaining both the problem and the action required of the end user. Ask the client to determine if there are any schedule changes related to end user training.

   B. You should review the test results with the stakeholder team and provide estimates on the impact to the schedule and the budget if the rework is done. This information should be compared with the cost of additional user training and the impact of the manual override on productivity of the customer experience.

   C. You should escalate the problem to your sponsor for resolution.

   D. You should call an emergency meeting with the team that developed the screen flow logic. Let them know that the problem must be fixed without any impact to the schedule regardless of the hours they must put in. They are salaried employees and are not eligible for overtime, so there will not be any impact to the budget.

6. Which of the following is *not* one of the results of completing quality control activities?

   A. Acceptance of defects

   B. Rework to correct defects

   C. Development of a Pareto diagram

   D. Process changes

7. The project you are currently managing requires a new piece of equipment that has only been available in limited quantity in a beta test mode. The manufacturer has assured you that the device will be in production mode in time to meet the committed delivery in your project schedule. Delivery of this device was identified as a high priority risk during risk planning. Because you have no authority to impact the production of the device, your team designed a contingency plan that uses a different device that will allow the project to move forward with reduced functionality. Which of the following is the best example of a trigger that indicated that you need to implement the contingency plan?

   A. A major trade magazine has just printed a story quoting "informed sources" predicting the resignation of the manufacturer's CIO.

   B. Several of your project team members have come to you to express concern regarding the dependency on this one vendor.

   C. Rumors are circulating that testing of the device is not progressing as planned and major rework will be required.

   D. The vendor is scheduled to ship the first set of devices on March 1. It is February 3 and you have not received the required written confirmation from the vendor regarding the shipping date.

8. Which of the following is the correct term for the forecast of the total project cost based on current performance results?

   A. Actual cost (AC)
   B. Estimate at completion (EAC)
   C. Budget at completion (BAC)
   D. Estimate to complete (ETC)

9. Which of the following statements is most effective to communicate a budget overrun to stakeholders?

   A. We have spent $325,000 on the development phase compared to the cost baseline estimate of $250,000.
   B. We are overrunning our budget by 30 percent.
   C. We ran a little over budget in the development phase, but plan to make it up later on.
   D. Project expenditures to date have been $325,000.

10. You are a project manager for a new product your company will be aggressively promoting. Your client is the VP of Marketing and Sales, and at the time the project charter was approved, she was very clear that the product would be launched on June 15, and information regarding the launch has already been provided to several trade publications. Things have been going great to this point: you are within the budget range and all the major milestones have been met. You have just been advised that one feature of the new product is not functioning properly and will require rework. To launch the product with the new feature, you will need to extend the launch date to July 1. How should you communicate this schedule delay to the VP? Choose the best answer.

    A. Advise your client that the product release will be delayed 2 weeks because the user requirements for the new feature were not clear.
    B. Tell the rework team to do whatever it takes to get the feature in the product, not worry about any testing, and plan on fixing any problems after launch.
    C. Advise the VP that you can meet the committed launch date of June 15, but only by releasing the product without this one feature, and adding the feature in 2 weeks to existing customers via a download from the company website.
    D. Update the project schedule and communicate the change as part of your regular status report. A 2-week delay is not that big a deal.

11. You have just received this Pareto diagram (see exhibit) displaying the results of unit testing. Based on what you see here, what action should you take?

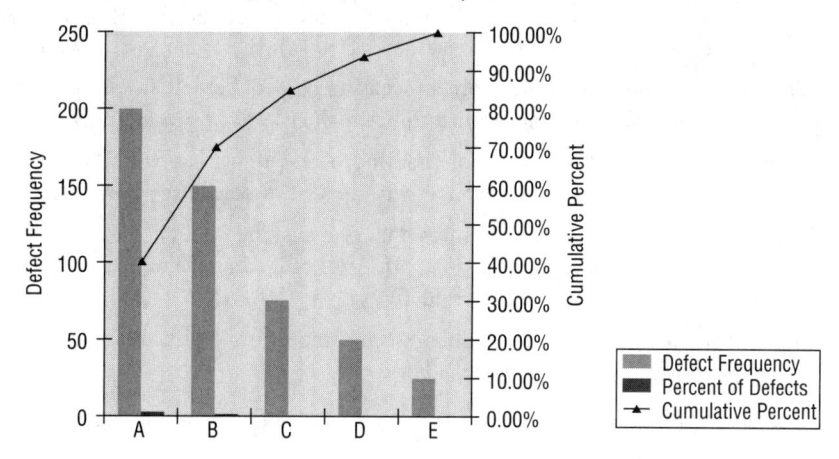

[Pareto diagram showing Defect Frequency and Cumulative Percent for categories A through E. Category A has ~200 defects, B ~150, C ~75, D ~50, E ~25.]

- **A.** Have the programmers start working on the category E errors. Since there are fewer errors here, it should be easier to fix and you can complete one of the five categories and report that you are 20 percent done.
- **B.** Send a memo to the programming lead advising him that all the defects must be fixed in one week.
- **C.** Focus the programming team on the defects in category A.
- **D.** Escalate this to the project sponsor, so she can decide which category is most important.

12. You're a project manager for a complex IT project that's well under way; you're in the middle of the executing/controlling phase. You have a disgruntled team member who is severely distracting the team's focus. The team member came to the team with some sort of chip on his shoulder but managed to keep it low-key until now. The team member has skills that are critical to the project's success. What's the best plan to deal with this issue?

- **A.** Ask him to seek a new team to work with.
- **B.** Ask the team member what the issues seem to be. Tell him that things aren't working out and that you're seeking a new team to work with.
- **C.** Ask the team member what the issues seem to be. Try to get to the heart of what's bothering him. Ask him how you can help correct the issues, if possible. Stress the importance of the project and his role on the team.
- **D.** Tell the team member what you perceive the issues to be. Ask him what's bothering him. Stress the importance of the project and his role on the team.

13. You're a project manager for a complex IT project that's well under way; you're in the middle of the executing/controlling phase. You have a team member who was at one time a star performer but has now begun to slack off. As a result, the tasks she has been working on are behind schedule. You're beginning to become concerned. What's the best plan to deal with this issue?

    A. Ask the team member what the problem seems to be with her late work. Ask her if there are ways that you can help her return to her former level of productivity.

    B. Ask the team member what the problem seems to be with her late work. Tell her that she needs to get back to the level of productivity she was at before she started slacking off.

    C. Tell the team member that other team members are asking about her—wanting to know why her performance level has dropped off. Ask her if there are ways that you can help her return to her former level of productivity.

    D. Ask the team member what the problem seems to be with the late work. Ask her if you can get an assistant to help her finish her work.

14. What are some methods you can use to control the quality of server installations? (Select all that apply.)

    A. Obtain all the gear from the same vendor.

    B. Assure that all servers have a 10Mb or higher connection.

    C. Assure that all gear comes from the same manufacturer.

    D. Create a burn document against which all servers are burned.

    E. Make sure you've got a gold-level maintenance agreement.

15. Stakeholders have come to you to tell you they want to change the scope. Before agreeing to the scope change, what things should you do next? (Select all that apply.)

    A. Determine which project constraint (time, budget, quality) is most important to stakeholders.

    B. Discuss the proposed scope change with the sponsor.

    C. Ask team members what they think about the scope change.

    D. Define alternatives and trade-offs that you can offer back to stakeholders.

16. You are the project manager for a project that's implementing a new manufacturing system that controls the output of widgets. You have just received this Pareto diagram (see exhibit) displaying the results of how the system performed on several different test days, given different system configuration settings. The test basis was 10,000 widgets manufactured per test. Based on what you see here, what action should you take?

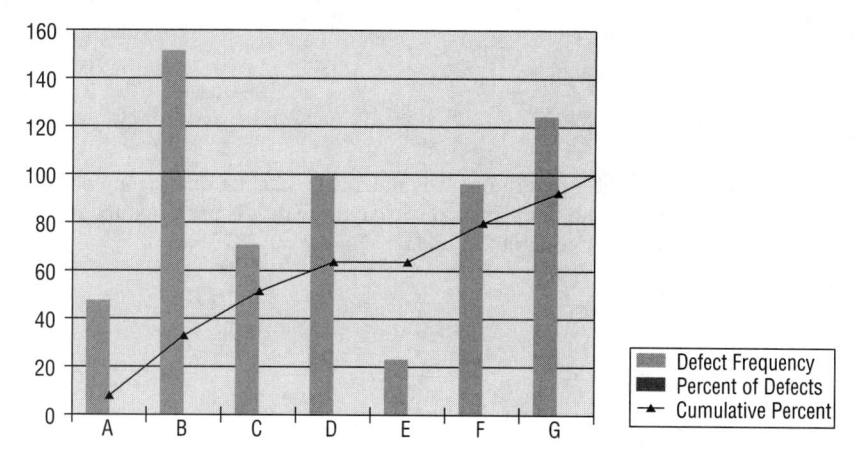

- **A.** Scrap the new system. None of the configurations are worth using.
- **B.** Use configuration E.
- **C.** Use configuration B.
- **D.** Not enough data in this chart to allow for a good choice.

17. Which calculation will show you the ratio of remaining work compared to remaining budget and is represented as a percentage?

- **A.** TCPI
- **B.** BWCP
- **C.** SPI
- **D.** CPI

18. You're preparing some variance figures for your project and you want to show the variance between a task's estimated progress versus its actual progress. What variance formula should you use?

- **A.** SV = BCWS − BCWP
- **B.** CV = BCWS − BCWP
- **C.** SV = BCWP − BCWS
- **D.** CV = BCWP − BCWS

Chapter 9 · Project Control

19. Suppose that you've got a task that's going to take 5 days starting on opening of business on Monday and ending on closing of business on Friday. The task is projected to cost $250. The task concludes successfully at noon on Thursday. What is the BCWS?

   A. $100

   B. $150

   C. $175

   D. $200

   E. $250

20. Suppose that you've got a task that's going to take 5 days starting on opening of business on Monday and ending on closing of business on Friday. The task is projected to cost $250. The task concludes successfully at noon on Thursday. What is the ACWS?

   A. $100

   B. $150

   C. $175

   D. $200

   E. $250

Answers to Review Questions

1. **D.** The client may have requested the new features. If these are required features omitted from the original scope statement, you need to analyze the impact to the project and obtain approval for the change. If you just make adjustments to the budget and schedule without any analysis, you not only risk being late and over budget, there may be impacts to other areas of the plan or risks associated with this change. Removing the new features may add additional cost and time to the schedule as well as create a potentially hostile relationship with the client. Unless this is a situation where the programmer has repeatedly changed scope outside of the approval process, requesting a replacement resource is not an appropriate response.

2. **B.** Any time you have a projected delay in a major deliverable, you want to immediately determine what is causing the delay, as you may determine steps to bring the deliverable back on track. If you determine that there are no options to prevent the delay, you should meet with the client to develop a workable solution to providing testing resources at a later time. Setting an arbitrary finish date for a deliverable that is already behind will almost assure incomplete testing and a potentially poor quality product. Given the magnitude of the impact to the client, this is not a situation that should be communicated in a memo. You need to be part of the solution.

3. **A.** A price increase of that magnitude has a negligible impact on a project with a $5,000,000 budget. The change needs to be documented and communicated, but it does not warrant a scope reduction. The estimate was made with the best information available at the time, so the project team member who provided the estimate did nothing wrong. An equipment cost increase alone will not impact the scope or the schedule baseline.

4. **C.** Even reducing the number of planned quality activities or the scope of an activity can be risky. Leaving out the unit test could result in defects that could have been corrected early on not being found until the system is being tested end to end. You do not have enough information at this point to assess the impact of that suggestion, and you need to involve the test manager. Regardless of what you may say to the development lead, you are accountable for the entire project and would take the blame if this approach backfires.

5. **B.** This is a classic case of the need to evaluate trade-offs with the stakeholder. There is no perfect solution in this case, but situations similar to this occur on a daily basis in the world of project management. Making unreasonable demands on the project team will not resolve the situation; it may even make it worse. This is not an issue that should be decided in a vacuum by the project manager or even the sponsor; it requires input and consensus from the stakeholder team, particularly the client, regarding the best course of action.

6. **C.** A Pareto diagram is one of the quality control tools and techniques. It is used to rank importance of a problem based on its frequency of occurrence over time. The actions that are taken following the completion of a quality activity are accepting the defects that were found, reworking the deliverables involved to correct the defects, or changing processes to prevent defects from happening in the future.

318 Chapter 9 • Project Control

7. D. The vendor has missed a key milestone date—the written confirmation of the device shipping date. The team member concerns may be valid, but the risk associated with a new device produced by only one vendor was accepted when the project was authorized. The speculation regarding the status of device testing may be indications that the device will not be available, but you need to contact the vendor and ask specific questions. The other answers may all warrant further investigation, but you would not want to implement your contingency plan based on unconfirmed rumors.

8. B. Estimate to complete (ETC) is a forecast of the cost of all remaining project work. Estimate at completion (EAC) is a projection of final project costs obtained by adding the ETC to the actual project costs to date (the AC). Budget at completion (BAC) is the amount of the project budget that remains after subtracting the actual costs spent to date.

9. A. The stakeholders need to know the amount of money that has been spent, the amount of money that was budgeted, and what portion of the project is included in that number. Presenting just the amount spent or just the percentage overrun does not provide stakeholders with the context they need. Answer C is an attempt to mask what could be a serious issue.

10. C. Since you are aware that the product release date is the client's top priority, your first option should be one that keeps the launch date and proposes trade-offs in another area. Trying to shift blame to the user requirements will make the situation worse. If the requirements were unclear, you should have resolved this issue during planning. Releasing a product with an untested feature is very risky and a shoddy product could do major damage to the company's reputation. There may be cases where a 2-week delay is not a big issue, but this is definitely not one of them.

11. C. A Pareto diagram ranks problems based on the frequency of occurrence. The purpose of a Pareto diagram is to direct the quality improvement efforts to those areas that will have the biggest impact. The defects in category A account for 40 percent of the problems, so you want to address those first. Fixing category E may be quicker, but it will resolve only 5 percent of your problems. A Pareto chart is unrelated to the amount of time it should take to fix defects.

12. C. People, not equipment or code, are the most important thing your project team has going for it. Clearly, this individual came to the team with some sort of issue. It's important that you work with him, not because he's mission-critical to the project, but because he has issues that you might be able to help him with so he can enjoy his time working on the project just like everyone else. It's important that he knows his importance to the team and the project as well.

13. A. This team member has demonstrated that she's able to handle the level of work you've given her and can produce quality output. Now she's begun to slack off. The problem could be that she's been working too much overtime or that she's lost energy for the project. It's up to you to figure out what's bothering her, then see if you can fix it and get her back on track. You should never bring up that others are asking about her (even if they are). You also shouldn't resort to ordering someone to do something. Telling her to increase her productivity is going to result in exactly the opposite effect. She's able to do the work, an assistant isn't required—getting at the heart of the issue is what's needed.

14. A, C, D. While it's not altogether important that you get all of your gear from one vendor (because most large hardware vendors outsource huge lots of components for their setups anyway), it has support implications for the servers. Settling on a given manufacturer and making sure all the gear is from that manufacturer or that the manufacturer has operational agreements with his outsourced suppliers may go a long way toward making sure the installations are uniform and of good quality. For example, you may have an item in your burn doc that requires that the BIOS for each computer be upgraded to the latest version before the NOS is installed. If you're working with different server manufacturers, then you have to worry about each manufacturer's implementation of BIOS updates. A standardized burn doc is mandatory—one standard burn doc for each type of server you're burning.

15. A, D. Determining the constraint that stakeholders think is driving the project will help you determine the kinds of trade-offs or alternatives you can propose to lessen the effect of the proposed scope change.

16. B. A Pareto diagram ranks problems based on the frequency of occurrence. The purpose of a Pareto diagram is to direct the quality improvement efforts to those areas that will have the biggest impact. The defects in category E reflect a much smaller percentage of the problems, so this would prove to be the most likely configuration to utilize. Using item B would result in disaster as this bar represents the most defects of all of the manufacturing runs.

17. A. The to-complete performance index measures remaining work to remaining budget. TCP can be viewed as an efficiency formula where the higher the percentage you derive, the more efficiency you're currently getting out of a task. A TCPI that is more than 20 percent higher or lower than the cost performance index (the ratio of each of the project's tasks to its costs) means that the current estimate at completion (EAC) is not representative of past performance. Here is the TCPI formula:

TCPI = work remaining / funds remaining

Where: work remaining = BAC − BCWP

Funds remaining = BAC − ACWP

18. C. The schedule variance (SV) is calculated by taking the budgeted cost of work performed (BCWP) and subtracting the budgeted cost of work scheduled (BCWS). Recall that the BCWS and BCWP are derived from the estimated figures for a task as compared to actual performance (see definitions of these items earlier in the chapter).

19. E. The BCWS is calculated by dividing the number of days projected for a task by its budgeted cost. So a task that you think will take 5 days and cost $250 is going to cost $50 a day. Regardless of how quickly you finished the task though, your *budgeted* cost of work scheduled is still $250.

20. C. The ACWS is calculated by dividing the number of days projected for a task by its budgeted cost, then multiplying the result times the number of days it took to complete the task. So a task that you think will take 5 days and cost $250 is going to cost $50 a day. Since you finished the task at noon on Thursday, you multiply by 3.5 to derive an ACWS of $175.

Chapter 10

Project Closure

THE COMPTIA IT PROJECT+ EXAM TOPICS COVERED IN THIS CHAPTER INCLUDE:

- ✓ 4.1: Recognize and explain the value of conducting a comprehensive review process that identifies the lessons learned and evaluates the planning, organizing, directing, controlling, execution, and budget phases of the project, identifying both the positive and negative aspects in a written report.
- ✓ 4.2: Recognize the need to plan to transfer the project deliverable to support and maintenance and to budget for these resources including help desk.
- ✓ 4.4: Recognize the need to obtain formal customer sign-off of the project deliverable and hand off to the customer.
- ✓ 4.5: Recognize the need to complete project documentation, secure approvals, and archive/store appropriately.
- ✓ 4.6: Recognize the need to close out contracts and sign-off for vendors.

Finally, your project is winding down and the end date is in sight. But don't get too excited, your job is not over yet.

A project does not magically end when the last deliverable on the project schedule is complete. Your project plan should also include all the tasks required to transition the project to an ongoing operation. A good project manager follows processes to formally close the project. The good news regarding these additional tasks is that much of the work you do during project closure will help you do a better job managing future projects.

Project closure activities apply regardless of the reason the project is ending or at what point you are at in the project life cycle. Even if your project is canceled, there is still a closeout phase.

Contract closeout is the completion of all items documented in a vendor contract and the formal acceptance of all vendor work.

Administrative closure involves finishing and archiving project documentation, obtaining formal sign-off from the client, conducting a comprehensive review of the project to document lessons learned, turning over the project to operations and maintenance, and releasing project team members to their functional organizations.

Types of Closure

Project closure is the activities required to formally end the project work. This stage often includes formal acceptance of the project; however, a project doesn't always have its success and completion criteria met in order to be concluded. A project might end for other reasons.

Canceled or postponed A project may be canceled or postponed indefinitely, whether or not the products and results have been completed. A project that's going nowhere may be hard to cancel for those involved, but management will eventually make the call. Projects that should rightfully be postponed if the technology just isn't there yet or the funding isn't available also fall into this category.

Plan not approved The project plan is not approved, and instead of sending you back to the project management drawing board, the project is simply canceled. Projects that are *proof of concept* could easily fall into this genre; management simply feels that the project has untenable deliverables. A proof of concept undertakes to prove that a specific activity can be done or an idea can be accomplished. If the concept is not feasible, the project is not approved to move forward.

Resources not available There are not enough resources available to complete the project. You have run out of money, hardware, people, or some other resource, and you have no choice but to conclude the project. This situation may arise due to poor estimating, or you may find that your resources are being diverted to another project with a higher priority. Either way, if you are not getting the resources you need, the project will end.

> **NOTE:** If a project is canceled or the project plan is rejected, you may be within the planning process, well ahead of project implementation. Even then, you would still run through the closing elements of the project, because the metrics you developed might prove useful in another project.

There are two major processes in project closure: contract closeout and administrative closure. Let's start with the process for closing out vendor contracts.

Contract Closeout

When a vendor completes any portion of your project work, project closure needs to deal with the vendor contract. *Contract closeout* is the process of completing the terms of the contract and documenting acceptance. Even if the procurement department is managing the contract, you will need to provide information regarding the acceptance of the vendor deliverables.

As we discussed in Chapter 9, you should perform quality control activities on vendor deliverables as you receive them and provide feedback regarding acceptance throughout the project life cycle. Any rework you require of the vendor should not come as a big surprise at the end of the project.

The procurement department needs to provide the vendor with formal written notice that the deliverables have been accepted and the contract has been completed. This letter will more than likely be sent based on your approval, so make certain that all vendor deliverables have met all required testing and acceptance criteria before you agree to have procurement release the vendor. Once the contract has been completed you may have no recourse if you find missing deliverables or poor quality work.

You should retain a copy of any completed contracts to include in the archives, which we will discuss later in this chapter.

Contract closure only applies to some projects, but all projects should go through the administrative closure process.

Administrative Closure

Once the project work is done, you may be tempted to quickly move on to a new assignment. But you still have important work to finalize your project. *Administrative closure* involves gathering and centralizing project documents, obtaining sign-offs, and communicating the finish of the project.

Some administrative work is tedious, but without it you have no point of reference for any future questions that may arise regarding why this project was authorized and what it accomplished.

Administrative closure also provides a reference source that can be used to improve the success of future projects. There is no reason for another project to make the same mistakes or recreate a useful tool or template that is already available.

We are going to take a closer look at several aspects of administrative closure: project archive, formal acceptance, comprehensive review (often know as lessons learned), turnover, and release of team members.

Project Archive

You have created a lot of documentation over the course of your project, and it was organized to fit your needs for overseeing the project work. One of the benefits of all this project documentation is that it can be used to help you or other project managers on future projects. Your planning documents can be a reference for cost and time estimates or used as templates for planning similar projects. But that can only happen if you create a project archive.

There are a variety of ways to create a project archive. Some organizations have a room dedicated to the storage of project binders for completed projects, and this area may even be set up like a mini-library where project documentation may be checked out. Your PMO may maintain a centralized project archive. If you have a project library or a centrally maintained archive, you should check what the guidelines are for documentation and how to organize it.

Even if your organization has no formal rule regarding project archives, you should create a project binder. Not only will the binder be a good reference tool on future projects, it will facilitate answering any questions you receive about your project's history. Even though you may be tempted to just empty your project files and shove all that paper in a binder, put some thought and effort into organizing the data so that it can be easily retrieved.

Electronic archives are also becoming more popular. Your organization may have a secure file server where it stores project documentation.

One of the documents that will eventually be placed in the project archive is the final acceptance and sign-off for your project.

Formal Acceptance

By this time, you should be very familiar with the importance of doing reviews with stakeholders to get sign-off on major deliverables or milestones to move from one phase to the next. If you have followed this process throughout the project, formal acceptance of the project itself should be easy.

After completion of the final project deliverable, you should bring the stakeholders together for one last formal review of the project. The purpose of this review is to officially declare the project work complete by obtaining stakeholder acceptance and sign-off on the project

Depending on the policies of your organization, there may be a specific format or template for formal project sign-off. Make sure you are aware of all the signatures you need to obtain. On some projects, you may need just the signatures of the sponsor and the client; for other projects you may need a signature from every work group impacted by the project. The formal approval document with all required signatures is your paper trail of project acceptance and should be included in your permanent project archive.

You can clear up any unanswered questions or issues regarding the project. You want everyone to walk away from this review with the agreement that the project is complete and has met the requirements.

Although you should have already communicated to the stakeholders changes to the project plan, some of the players may not remember all of these changes. You should cover any changes to requirements or scope to make sure everyone is on the same page regarding expectations of what the project will do. This is of particular importance if there was a decision to remove features or functionality from the original requirements.

Occasionally, stakeholders may panic as a project draws to a close and ask for all sorts of additions. If project closure were postponed until the project had everything it "needed," most projects would never end. This is why obtaining the necessary approvals for changes, communicating how changes will be implemented, and updating your project plan is so important. The best defense against any last minute concerns is to continually focus on what stakeholders requested and agreed to in the project plan.

The stakeholders should also be made aware of which groups are responsible for the ongoing operation of the system. We will talk more about these people later in this chapter when we get to project turnover.

One of the last major accomplishments for you and your project team will be a comprehensive project review and documentation of lessons learned.

Comprehensive Review (Lessons Learned)

At the end of your project, you should conduct a comprehensive review to assess the good and the not so good aspects of the project. During this process, you evaluate each phase of the project in order to determine which things went right and which things could have been improved. This kind of review provides you an opportunity to improve your overall project management quality on the next project and benefits other projects. The most critical thing to derive from an end of project assessment is the lessons you learned from the project. You want to assess what went wrong and why, not so you can point fingers at the guilty parties, but so that you can do better next time by avoiding the pitfalls you encountered this time. Lessons learned is something project managers like to avoid working on because they're afraid of backwash on the job they did, but the idea is to gain knowledge about how to better manage projects.

If you are managing a cross-functional project, make sure that the review covers both the technical and nontechnical components of the project. Managing a project with deliverables from multiple disciplines has unique complexities. Even though you may be more interested in documenting what happened during development and testing, information on marketing and sales is equally important.

The following subsections describe some of the areas in which you'll concentrate your review process. All of the information generated can be kept in a single document, or you can choose to write a document for each category. Obviously, the larger the project, the more documentation you're going to need to create for any given category. All of this documentation will go into the project archive, whether it is electronic or paper in form. Whatever format you choose for capturing the output from the review process, keep in mind you will need to summarize this data in a written report, which we discuss later in this section.

Planning

When reviewing the planning process, ask yourself how well the project was planned in general. Were the tasks, activities, and phases well thought out and orderly, or did you have to backtrack to fix some things that you originally had set up in the wrong order? When you have to backtrack on things like this, you can get into a situation where you actually can't go back and fix, or at the very minimum precious time is taken up getting back to the place you can continue from.

Also, you should pay attention to the project plan itself, evaluating its complexity, the number of milestones, and whether you filled it out correctly. Project plans can be laborious if they're too detailed and useless if they don't include enough information.

Organizing

How well did the overall project come together? When you examine the organizational characteristics of your now-finished project, you're interested in more than the project plan itself. Did the team members come in for their various tasks at just the right time, or did some of them have to wait for something else to happen before they could go to work? You should examine how well processes went into place and where you can improve next time. Things like equipment burn documents (documentation that stipulates the steps involved in the installation and configuration of computing equipment), network protocol assignments, coordination of physical equipment installations, and other orchestrated functions should be examined closely to see how you could improve them the next time.

It's especially critical to pay attention to the details of any software development involved in your project. Examine the coding, documentation, and testing of the software development. Pay close attention to the development tools used to see whether they were adequate for the process. Did the code repository system you used to store developed modules meet the developer's needs? Further, was the choice of development language appropriate for the project? Often, developers have pet languages that they'll use for all their work, but some projects may be better suited for a different language.

Executing

The executing phase deals with bringing performance in line with your plans. Things such as team development, stakeholder relationships, performing according to schedule and cost baseline, information distribution, and vendor contract administration happened in this phase.

When examining this phase, you should take a look at things such as vendor relationships and how well they worked out, the value of team meetings in maintaining team member linkages and revolving issues, and effectiveness of stakeholder communications.

You may ask yourself a number of other questions about the execution phase. Were the team meetings effective for team communications and issues resolution? Did the weekly progress reports from the team members provide you with accurate and timely data to assess project performance? Did project status reports paint a clear picture of project progress? Was vendor progress adequately monitored?

Your focus here should be on looking at where the project worked flowed smoothly versus where problems or issues you did not expect arose.

Directing

Examine your work. Take a look at how well the project was directed through its steps. Like a movie director helping the actors play out the various shots, you should have been there for your team members at all points of the action. It's important to pay attention to the places where the project got off track and how you got it back on. Perhaps you can make adjustments to your next project to avoid such scenarios.

Look closely at the places where team members fell behind schedule. Determine whether what you had to deal with was personnel management or a technical issue. Defining people issues can help you work more closely with team members in the future.

Controlling

Controlling differs from directing. When you have a finalized project plan and are making sure that the deliverables you're creating meet the metrics you set down during requirements definition, you are controlling the project. For example, a piece of code that does a calculation should meet a success criterion that clearly indicates whether the code works as needed and expected. The controlling aspect of the project looks at metrics. When assessing the project, you might ask, "How well were the metrics formulated, and did they meet expectations?"

Don't forget that during the planning stages you pinpointed the risks to the project. Did any of those risks materialize while in the controlling phase? If so, how did you spot them and then deal with them? Risk monitoring and control is an important facet of any project.

Budget

This is an important end-of-project category. First, take a look at the variances that occurred during the project to see if you can match them to a reason for their occurrence. Spotting the reason could potentially help avoid the same thing next time.

Also, you should evaluate the project budget compared to the way that the corporate budget outlined your budget categories. You do this to make sure that you effectively used the money the way that the company intended you to. Chances are you "robbed Peter to pay Paul" in certain cases, and this is acceptable, but you need to reconcile that with the company's budget.

Prepare reports that represent what was spent, on what, and where your closing budget stands. You should also show the hours spent on the project compared to the salaries of the individuals working on various tasks.

Preparing a Written Project Assessment

A finalized project assessment needs to be prepared and distributed to all of the project stakeholders. The size of the project and the amount of feedback provided by the project team will dictate how large the report should be; a small project might only contain a paragraph or two for each section, while a large project might wind up being a fairly comprehensive document of many pages.

As with any other project documentation, you should check to see whether your organization has standards or a template for documenting lessons learned. If you have no specific guidelines or template, organize your material around topics such as the project phases discussed earlier. For each section, cover the positive aspects, the negative aspects, and plans for improvement.

> ### Real World Scenario
>
> **Involving Project Team Members in Lessons Learned**
>
> Although you can evaluate the various components of the project on your own using the project plan and the project results, to get a more comprehensive lessons learned you should involve the team members.
>
> One way to organize a project review session is to make the session very interactive. Let the team members know in advance which aspects of the project the review will focus on, and ask them to be prepared to contribute input on both what went well and what did not.
>
> You should always set ground rules before you start. You want to stress that the purpose of this session is not to assign blame, but to assess the project so that both this team and other project teams can learn from your experience.
>
> Just sitting around a conference table for several hours can get boring, so we like to keep people moving around. One way to do this is to prepare the meeting room in advance with easel paper listing all the areas of the project you want to cover, and provide each team member with a pad of sticky notes. For each topic, ask the team members to post one positive thing and one negative thing. For each negative comment, a plan for improvement needs to be included. If they encounter this situation on a future project, what would they do differently? Requiring a plan for improvement serves two purposes: it engages the team members in the review by making them part of a problem solving process, and it helps keeps those few team members who may only want to whine under control. This is not the time or place to complain about the pastry or lunch selection at a team meeting. After the team members have posted their sticky notes, you can moderate a group discussion of the items that have been posted. Seeing what others have posted may generate additional thoughts.
>
> When you have concluded the session, collect all the easel paper to use as input for your written report.

Positive Aspects of the Project

This is the easiest part of the written report; everyone wants to share successes. Talk about what went right with the project. Provide detail regarding specific tasks that you thought went exceptionally well and why. You may also include any positive comments that customers made about the project and its progress.

It would be a good political idea to also mention positive participation from people from other departments or teams that helped you get your job done. Mentioning other departments has two effects: It reinforces the opinions of people from those departments, putting it in the back of their minds that they'd like to work for you on another project. It also shows other departments that your team wasn't a force of one; you needed them to help you get your job done.

With respect to the constraints of any project, if something went particularly well, it's important to point it out at this time. If your project came in well under budget, ahead of schedule, or with an output whose quality is higher than expected, this should be mentioned in your closure document.

Negative Aspects of the Project

Project managers sometimes avoid writing anything negative about a project, but that really defeats the purpose of doing lessons learned. If you do not document what went wrong and what you would do to change the situation, other project managers are likely to make the same mistake. You have to be careful not to use this portion of the report to point fingers or assign blame. If you had communications difficulties with a particular department, stating ways you could improve the communications plan is more beneficial to future projects than stating "department X was not responsive."

If your relationship with a vendor did not go smoothly, list the areas that were problematic such as deliverables being off track, or poor quality and state what you would do differently—more frequent review sessions, more detailed acceptance testing, etc.

Describe any problems you ran into with software or hardware that you purchased—problems that surfaced time and again and weren't a one-time thing. For example, if you had trouble with some firmware updates, software that you had to apply across a lot of the same equipment, you would mention that here. You should also talk about hardware that consistently malfunctioned the same way, regardless of the number of units you deployed.

You should also mention limitations that you encountered simply based on the constraints of the project. You don't have to come across negatively when mentioning a constraint, but it's important that readers know that if you had had more time or budget, you could've brought in a better product.

It's important to stay away from blaming people directly, but also to not be shy about talking about processes that didn't work, promises that weren't kept, and fundamental operations that could've gone better. The point is to clearly state what went wrong and what you would do differently in that situation in the future.

As you are writing your project report, you will also need to be implementing project turnover.

Project Turnover

When a project ends, another work group will maintain the deliverable produced by the project. The project deliverable needs to be turned over to this new team. This is not something that just happens magically; it has to be coordinated between the project manager and the operational groups that will run and maintain the new system.

For an IT project, it may be easy to think about the groups who will operate the equipment and update the system. But your project turnover may be far more involved.

Many systems involve a help-desk function. Your project schedule should include activities for developing and delivering training to the help-desk staff. In addition to making sure the help-desk technicians are thoroughly trained, you need to coordinate when this group will start taking end user calls. Typically, a help desk takes over a new system as it is deployed to the users. If the system is being deployed on a staggered schedule across multiple end user locations, the help-desk management should be involved in the development of the schedule to ensure adequate help-desk coverage as each office comes online with the new application.

Although the development of supporting documentation is part of the project work, updating the documentation is the responsibility of the individual operations groups. You need to make sure that the technical documentation reflects any changes to the project scope or requirements. All documentation should be updated to include any changes as a result of testing or other quality control activities.

If your project was cross functional, there may be user related documentation that will require maintenance and updates as the system is enhanced. If project team members were responsible for development of user documentation, you will hand off the user documentation to the ongoing operations technical writing team. User training material needs to be moved to the training department for the client organization.

If additional technical staff is required to maintain your system or provide end user support, these people may have been brought on using money from the project budget. The length of time these people are charged against the project budget should have been negotiated up front. You need to make sure that you have a written agreement as to when salary dollars or any other ongoing operational expenses are transferred to the operation budget.

Case Study: Chaptal Wineries—Intranet and Email

Closeout of the Chaptal project is straightforward. You need to validate that all the email servers are up and running and that email is able to move back and forth between the sites. Also, you want to validate that the intranet is working and people are satisfied that the information they derive from the pages is useful and straightforward and that information that needs to be put onto the intranet by various stakeholders can be done so with a minimum of hassle.

Email You can use the Exchange Server administrator interface to validate that you see all of the sites in your organization. You pull up the administrator interface and see the California, Australia, France, and Chile sites just fine. You can also see the mailboxes that are associated with each site. Even though systems testing has validated that everything is working well, you send a couple of email items to various people throughout the organization. You include some emails with attachments to make sure that they're being transported well.

You adjust some Exchange routing metrics and are satisfied that email is moving well. While at the international sites, you visited user computers and installed the Outlook client so that users are ready to utilize their email. You now send out an email to the main contact at each site instructing them that the system is available for immediate use. You have already trained your international contacts on how Outlook works and how it interfaces with Exchange—you feel they are prepared to handle most end user problems.

You will now enter into maintenance mode with the email system. You note in your project closeout that you have successfully concluded this step and that the system is in production. From this point forward, new additions or enhancements will be considered a new project. You interview Kim Cox and the international stakeholders to see what input they can provide relative to ways that you could have done things better. This information will go into the lessons learned component of the project.

> **Intranet** The Chaptal intranet site pages have been developed and approved for usage. You're particularly pleased with a page that the contractor developed that allows the winemakers at the various sites to key in information pertinent to the wines being developed. Topics that are interesting to Kim will be the type of grapes used as well as the percentages of mixture of grape varieties (i.e., 40 percent cabernet sauvignon, 60 percent Shiraz, etc.). Also of interest is the specific gravity of the wine, sugar content, alcohol content, container aging (barrel and stainless steel), and bottling and labeling information. Additionally, Kim wants to keep track of the number of barrels made as well as shipping and reseller information. The application that your intranet Web page developer created elegantly handles all of these elements in a nicely built application interface.
>
> An additional application that Kim would like to have—one that was not included in the purview of the original project—would track the costs involved to maintain tasting rooms at each winery. Currently, French and Chilean wineries that provide tasting rooms for drive-up customers are rare. But Californian and Australian wineries commonly include this feature as a part of their operation. Kim would like to provide tasting opportunities at all Chaptal wineries and wants to track the costs (and revenue) of this side of the operation from site-specific levels. This will be a new project that's tied to the build-out of tasting rooms at the French and Chilean wineries.
>
> The Web page developer also created a financial tracking application that allows the various sites to report earnings and expense numbers for final accounting roll-up at the California main site. The next project you will undertake relative to Web development work will involve designing and building a full Internet site that details information about all of Chaptal's wineries from a single site. The lessons learned segment for the intranet site has a very short list. Overall Kim's quite pleased and only wishes that some expandability was built into the intranet interface so that as new wineries are acquired (she's looking at a lovely operation in the Piedmont area of Italy), they can be easily snapped into the existing infrastructure.
>
> You prepare an end user training manual that you'll post on the intranet as well as the lessons learned documentation. You send out notice that the project is officially closed.
>
> You begin work on your next projects: The Chaptal Internet site and the acquisition of Marcello Wineries of Piedmont.

Project turnover can sometimes be shortchanged because everyone on the project team is in a hurry to move on to the next assignment. It is your job as project manager to oversee this process and resolve any outstanding issues before you officially closeout the project.

Turnover of various aspects of the project to ongoing maintenance is also a signal to start releasing your team members.

Release of Team Members

The staffing management plan developed during project planning should have addressed any special procedures you are required to follow as part of releasing team members from the project. It is a good idea to review this document as the project starts to wind down to ensure you are in compliance with all human resource guidelines.

You should start communications with functional managers at least a month before the anticipated release date. The functional manager needs to know when staff members will be available to be assigned to a new project or functional work.

Team members may also become anxious about their status, especially if people are rolling off the project at different times. You should explain to team members that as various deliverables are completed, team members who have completed their assignments are released. Unless you are prevented from doing so by labor contract terms or human resource guidelines, provide your team members with as much information as you can on anticipated release dates.

Once all of the closure documents are complete, the project is turned over to maintenance, and the team members have been released, you can start the planning process all over again for your next project.

Summary

Although project closure involves many important activities, it often falls off the radar for many project managers. Anxious as you may be to move on to your next assignment, your current project should not just cease to exist before you complete project closure activities.

You need to complete the project closure processes whenever the project ends, whether it was successfully completed or canceled. If you are working with any vendors, you need to complete contract closure by confirming that the terms of the contract have been met and all deliverables have been accepted. Contract closure includes written notification to the vendor that the terms of the contract have been met.

Although you may find some of the tasks tedious at times, administrative closure involves several key elements. As project manager, you create a project archive in either paper or electronic format to store a copy of all project documentation. A final review session with the stakeholders is scheduled to obtain formal acceptance and sign-off on the project. The project manager also organizes and facilitates a review session with project team members to discuss all aspects of the project life cycle, both negative and positive. The output of this session is a formal lessons learned document that can be used to replicate your successes and avoid the pitfalls you encountered in your project. Project documentation such as user guides or systems manuals as well as all ongoing maintenance and support of the system need to be turned over to the appropriate operational staff. Finally, as their work is completed, you release the project team members to their respective functional organizations. Now you are ready to move on to your next project.

Perhaps the most important element of project closure is the lessons-learned element. It is here that you identify where things went wrong, how you fixed them and what you'd consider as alternatives in the future. Lessons learned isn't helpful in the here and now, but it's extremely useful for those who have a similar project and who will come back to yours to see what kinds of issues you ran into. If you're into protecting the future, lessons learned is an endeavor that will be very worthwhile for you.

Exam Essentials

Name the project phases included in a project closeout review. The phases included in project closeout document are planning, organizing, executing, directing, controlling, and budget.

Understand why it is important to document both the positive and negative aspects of the project. It is equally important for the success of future projects to capture both what worked on the project and what you would change.

Explain the purpose of obtaining formal customer or stakeholder sign-off. Formal sign-off documents that the customer accepts the project work and that the project meets the defined requirements.

Describe the purpose of a project archive. The project archive is the official copy of all of the project documentation, which can be referenced to answer future questions regarding the project or as a resource for other projects.

Understand the key elements of contract closeout. Contract closeout verifies that all the work described in the contract was completed satisfactorily per the contract terms and conditions. It includes written notification of contract completion to the vendor.

Know what groups are involved in project turnover. Project turnover includes any group that will be involved in the ongoing maintenance, update, or support of the system, and includes both technical and nontechnical teams.

Understand why lessons learned is such an important facet of project closeout. Often overlooked as a vital component of project closeout, a formal lessons learned endeavor can reveal much valuable information that can be used in future projects. There is no such thing as the perfect project—all projects could have benefited by something being done differently or better than it actually happened.

Realize that end user support is a part of your closeout efforts. Because you've introduced a new system, it's vital that you don't simply close out the project with a "There, it's all done!" statement. You have to be sure that the project has provided for things such as end user training, training manuals, help-desk preparations for support, and so forth.

Key Terms

Before you take the exam, be certain you are familiar with the following terms:

administrative closure

contract closeout

project closure

proof of concept

Review Questions

1. Your project is winding down and you are eager to get started on your next project, which is high visibility and could lead to a promotion. An outside company was responsible for completing several of your deliverables. There are acceptance test activities for each of these deliverables on the project schedule. The procurement manager has called you because the terms of the contract require notification to the vendor of acceptance or rejection of all deliverables be provided to the vendor in 4 days. What action should you take? Choose the best answer.

   A. You should forward the procurement manager's message to the person assigned to vendor acceptance test.

   B. You need more time to complete testing, so tell the procurement manager there are problems with some of the tests results.

   C. You should confirm that the vendor acceptance testing included all aspects of the vendor deliverables and that all testing has been completed with satisfactory results. If testing is ongoing, you need to take appropriate action to ensure it will complete before the contract deadline.

   D. You can ignore the procurement manager's message for now, as you should have the final test results with a week. Procurement always thinks they need an answer right away.

2. You have just left a meeting with the project sponsor where you were advised that your project has been canceled due to budget cuts. You have called the project team together to fill them in and to review the remaining activities to closeout the project. Several of your team members question the benefit of doing a lessons learned review on a project that has been canceled. What should your response be? Choose the best answer.

   A. Advise the team that part of the review time will be spent on deciding how to blame the project failure on the lack of clear client requirements.

   B. Tell the team they need to do this to be able to stay on the project payroll another week while they look for a new assignment.

   C. Inform the team that a final report is a requirement from the PMO, regardless of how the project ends.

   D. Explain that there is value both to the team and for future projects in analyzing the phases of the project that have been completed to date to document what went right, what went wrong, and what you would change.

3. Which of the following scenarios would NOT trigger the project closure processes?

   A. The project is behind schedule and over budget, but no additional resources will be provided and a request for additional funding has been denied.

   B. End user deployment is delayed due to conflicting demands on the user training staff.

   C. The sponsor advises you the project does not fit the vision of the new CEO.

   D. Your critical path resources are pulled off your project to work on a newly approved strategic in initiative

4. You are gathering documents to work on your comprehensive project review. What aspects of the project should you focus on?

   A. The review should focus on the technical aspects of the project.

   B. All phases of the project, from planning through execution should be included in the review.

   C. The review should focus on the project schedule with an emphasis on the accuracy of the original estimates.

   D. The review should be limited to the positive aspects of the project. This will help all the team members get better assignments in the future.

5. You have scheduled a session with your project team members to obtain their input for documentation of key learnings from your project. Which of the following is the most effective technique to get the information you need?

   A. An informal project team session with no guidelines will produce the most data. Encourage team members to assign responsibility for portions of the project that did not go well.

   B. Send a survey to all project team members asking them to document five successes and five failures during the life of the project. Compiling this data can produce the report.

   C. Facilitate a session with the project team members structured around the project phases. For each phase ask team members to identify the successes and failures. For any item that did not go well, ask for a recommendation of what to do differently in a similar scenario.

   D. As project manager, you have the best perspective on what went right and what went wrong on the project. A review is not needed to complete an accurate report.

6. What is the purpose of a formal sign-off at the conclusion of the project work?

   A. A sign-off allows the project manager to start a new assignment.

   B. The sign-off finalizes the client agreement that the project team is no longer accountable for this product.

   C. The sign-off is the trigger for releasing team members back to their functional organization.

   D. A formal sign-off indicates that the project meets the documented requirements and the client has accepted the project deliverables.

7. You are transitioning a project to maintenance/support mode when you discover that the training for the help-desk staff to support the end users has still not been done. During the project deployment, all questions were funneled through project team members. What is the best course of action to take at this point?

   A. You should work with the functional managers to retain the team members currently taking end user calls until the help-desk staff is trained to take the calls.

   B. This is an operations issue, not a project issue. The operations manager will have to deal with the impact of the decision to delay training.

   C. The client should be notified that until further notice, all questions regarding the new application should be routed through the local office supervisors. The supervisors should call the help desk only as a last resort.

   D. You should shut down the new application until the help desk is prepared to support the end users.

8. What is the focus of the written report resulting from the comprehensive project review session?

   A. The report should cover both the positive and negative aspects of the project, with suggestions for improvement.

   B. The report should summarize the results of the project schedule, the budget, and any approved scope changes.

   C. The report should focus on the IT deliverables and any issues that were created by the client

   D. The report should cover what went well during the project. If the project was canceled, blame for the failure needs to be established.

9. Your project is winding down, and some of your team members are anxious about their status. What is the best way to deal with their concerns?

   A. Explain to the team members that they will be released when the project is done.

   B. Let the team members know that you can only discuss their release date with the functional managers.

   C. Establish the same release date for all the team members, even if their work is completed. If some people start leaving, others may try to jump ship as well.

   D. Review the team member release plans from the staffing management plan. Keep team members and functional managers informed based on the status of the project schedule.

10. Your client has suddenly produced a list of items that he wants fixed prior to final sign-off on the project. You suspect that he is attempting to add functionality to the system that should be handled through operations as a potential enhancement. What is the best approach to deal with the client's request?

   A. Let the client know that this is too late in the process to be bringing these issues to your attention. Any user issues should have been formally documented during user acceptance testing.

   B. Advise the client you will forward the list to the operations manager to provide time and cost estimates for each item.

   C. Request that the client map the fixes to specific requirements in the project scope document and explain what the problem is. Review the results of acceptance testing to determine if any "bugs" were identified.

   D. Escalate this to the project sponsor, so he can tell the client to follow the proper procedures for requesting enhancements

11. Which element of project closure is most often overlooked by project managers creating finalized project documentation?

   A. Completing the project book
   B. Including all metrics comparisons
   C. Getting the signatures of all of the stakeholders
   D. Creating lessons learned documentation

12. Which aspects of the project will you review when preparing your final closure documents? (Select all that apply.)

   A. Unfulfilled
   B. Positive
   C. Negative
   D. Unrealistic

13. Which four situations indicate that the project is ready to be closed?

   A. Stakeholders approve final testing results.
   B. Completion metrics are achieved.
   C. Sponsor says it's time to use the project members on another project.
   D. Project is canceled.
   E. Project plan is rejected.
   F. Company priorities change.
   G. Project resources are exhausted.

14. Which of the following denote an *unsuccessful* conclusion to a project? (Select all that apply.)
    A. Resources exhausted.
    B. Project plan rejected.
    C. Project canceled.
    D. Project renamed.
    E. Project priority reduced.

15. From the list below, select those project phases in which you would expect successful project closure. (Select all that apply.)
    A. Initiating
    B. Planning
    C. Activating
    D. Executing
    E. Controlling
    F. Closing

16. You're a project manager for a large, complex IT project that's just begun. You're in the middle of the executing phase. The project sponsor has looked over your requirements definition plan and decided that the project is way too complicated for the minimal deliverables the customer has requested. She decides to cancel the project. What are your next steps? (Select all that apply.)
    A. Change vendors to obtain a lower bid for hardware and software components.
    B. Prepare project closure documents stipulating lessons learned.
    C. Release resources.
    D. Get the sponsor to let you redesign the project.
    E. Ask for a new sponsor.

17. Which projects should be required to have a closing phase? (Select all that apply.)
    A. Small projects
    B. Medium-sized projects
    C. Large projects
    D. All projects
    E. No projects

18. Which outflow of the closing phase stipulates that team members are free to go back to their departments?
    A. Release of resources
    B. Lessons learned
    C. Project book
    D. Sign-off

19. You are a project manager for a medium-sized project that's close to closure. You've worked through the majority of the UAT for the deliverables, but you have a few more tests to go. Your sponsor wants you to conclude the project now, because by doing so it will look as though the project came in a few days ahead of schedule. What do you tell the sponsor?

   A. OK, that's doable. The last few UAT tests weren't all that critical.

   B. No can do. We have to wait through the final UAT tests to make sure we're completely successful.

   C. You're the sponsor and can conclude the project any time you want, but for successful conclusion, we need to finish the UAT tests.

   D. I'm sorry, Dave, I can't do that right now.

20. Who is responsible for authorizing the closure of the project?

   A. Stakeholders

   B. Project manager

   C. Customers

   D. Sponsor

Answers to Review Questions

1. **C.** Acceptance of deliverables is a key part of the vendor contract. Failure to meet the terms of communicating acceptance could put your company in breach of contract. You should immediately confirm the status of vendor deliverable acceptance testing and ensure that all results are completed to meet the deadline. This is not something that should be pushed aside or handed off to someone else.

2. **D.** There is valuable information to be gained from a review of any project, even projects that do not complete. The assessment should focus on those phases of the project that did complete, as well as a look at whether anything could have been done differently to make the project a success. The purpose of a review is not to assign blame, even for projects that are canceled. Facilitating a review session for a canceled project may not be the easiest task, but you will not energize the project team with the attitude that you are being forced to do this.

3. **B.** A delay in project implementation is not a signal that the project should be closed out, as long as the project is still viable. You will have to do some re-planning and analyze the impacts of the delay on other aspects of the project plan. If you have exhausted your budget, lost your resources, or no longer have executive support, you should obtain sponsor approval to officially cancel the project and move into the closure phase.

4. **B.** A project review is most beneficial to future projects if it covers all aspects of the project and includes both the negative and the positive of each phase.

5. **C.** A project review session can quickly turn into "blamestorming" if it is not well structured and tightly managed. By setting the expectations at the start, team members will know that they must offer suggestions for improvement and not just complain about whatever they did not like. A survey can be used as a last resort, but it lacks the human interaction that triggers ideas and suggestions. A report written from just one point of view may miss key elements.

6. **D.** A sign-off is the formal acceptance of the project. It signifies client acceptance of the product. Team members are released according to the staffing management plan, and both the project manager and the project team members may continue to be involved in the project until all closure activities are complete.

7. **A.** Your goal should be to continue the momentum of the project by working to provide a temporary solution for user support. If you take the application away from the users, they may need to be retrained once the help desk is in place. Reducing client support or taking the attitude that this is not your problem could jeopardize the long-term success of your project.

8. **A.** There are key conclusions for the future from both the successes and failures of a project. Successes will provide blueprints to follow, and failures will alert teams on what to avoid. A good lessons learned document covers all aspects of the project and deliverables from all participants.

9. **D.** The procedures for releasing project team members should be documented in your staffing management plan. Both team members and functional managers need to know in advance when you think a team member will be released. Team members may roll off the project at different times, so you need to discuss release with each team member individually.

10. C. You need to determine whether there is a valid issue here. If the system does not perform according to the requirements, the client has every right to expect fixes to be made. By asking the client to map the fixes to specific requirements, you can both determine if you are dealing with a fix or an enhancement. Escalation to the project sponsor would be premature at this point, as would passing the list to operations before you have determined the appropriate category for each item on the list.

11. D. Lessons learned is a simple idea: You're pointing out the things that might've gone better on this project and then documenting them so that project managers in later projects have information they can refer back to. Neophyte project managers might like to avoid lessons learned because they somehow associate this element with at least a modicum of project failure. In reality, no project is perfectly implemented, and all projects can offer additional information in the form of lessons learned. The project book is completed when all documentation has been signed and completed. You don't need the signatures of all of the stakeholders, only the project sponsor.

12. B, C. You'll evaluate both the positive and the negative aspects of the project. Undoubtedly, acknowledging the negative aspects of the project will be much more difficult than the positive. Part of the reason for this is that you have to be careful to not name names of people in the company who might've had a less than positive effect on your project. The project's not complete if you have unfulfilled items. Unrealistic items should've been dealt with at requirements definition time.

13. B, D, E, G. The project is complete when the completion criteria say so, when the project is canceled, when the project plan has been rejected for whatever reason, or when the project resources have been consumed. The project isn't necessarily complete just because the stakeholders approve the final testing results, nor if the sponsor would like to free up team members for some other project.

14. B, C. Just because a project's resources are exhausted does not necessarily imply that the project's a failure; it may simply mean that the project utilized all of the resources allocated to it. If the project plan is rejected or the project is canceled, then one can assume there has been an unsuccessful conclusion to the project. Renaming, or even reduced priority, aren't reasons to conclude the project.

15. F. Successful projects can be closed out only at the closing phase. You have successfully completed the project's deliverables, met the success and completion criteria, and you're ready to finish up. You've entered the closing phase and can close out the project.

16. B, C. If you have a sponsor who opts to cancel the project, for whatever reason, you will still want to put the project into closing phase. During this phase, you'll assemble the correct closure documents, in this case indicating why the project was closed and the metrics that were formulated for the requirements, and you'll release any resources you've already set aside for the project.

17. D. All projects should recognize some sort of closing phase, even if it's informal with a quick little document that specifies the criteria that indicated successful project completion, associated sign-off by the sponsor, and, of course, lessons learned.

18. A. The completion of the closing phase results in the documents that conclude the project and authorizes the release of the project's resources, including team members.

19. C. The sponsor has the right to conclude the project any time he or she wants to. Remember that the sponsor is the one who can authorize the expenditure of resources in order to prepare the deliverables. However, you cannot call it a *successful* project until you've completed your testing and then have validated your success and completion metrics.

20. D. The sponsor is the one who signs off on the closure documents. As project manager, you create them, providing supporting documentation that illustrates that all deliverables have been successfully completed.

Appendix A

Systems Development Life Cycle

This book covered project management from the perspective of PMI approach. In this appendix, we discuss the Systems Development Life Cycle (SDLC) approach, which is commonly used in managing IT projects. The proclivity of project management methodologies and techniques today, while valuable, may have had an adverse effect on different people working together toward a common goal. Some have had standard systems analysis and design training, and have learned about the Systems Development Life Cycle (SDLC), a more-or-less standardized approach to how people technically trained in Information Technology handle systems development. There are different flavors of the SDLC, but all of them have at their root the elements discussed below.

Project managers with a certification or formal education in project management, as taught by the Project Management Institute (PMI), have a slightly different approach to how projects get done. For starters, the PMI approach, with its five process groups, is more homogeneous in nature—that is, the project at hand doesn't necessarily matter as long it is handled within the context of the methodologies that PMI espouses. On the other hand, SDLC isn't standardized and yet its base features are so fundamentally well known that IT professionals are accustomed to them.

Another camp—the agile development people—have a little different spin on project management, but we won't talk about that in this appendix as it's too far-reaching for the point we're trying to make here.

The differences, while subtle, are vast and could potentially lead to some infighting between your project managers and your technical team. If you know that there are those who "think SDLC" and those who "think PMI," then you've got some points to discuss. The purpose, of course, is to get people aligned down a common road toward successful completion of your project.

If you've had training in Information Technology you may have run across a common systems development methodology that has been worked out over many years of refining and building IT systems. This methodology was originally developed for software developers writing code for mainframe systems, but even in today's complex interaction of software applications with disparate server, network, and Web environments, the methodology still fits a variety of different IT systems.

The Systems Development Life Cycle (SDLC) is a way of thinking about developing and implementing IT systems. The SDLC is built around the notion that a corporate IT department (or departments) handles the job of maintaining the IT infrastructure and works with business entities to build and deploy new systems. The SDLC consists of five phases.

Planning

The planning phase begins with a request from a business unit for help in building a new IT system. The request could come from a variety of different people—the business unit manager, an executive in the corporation, some sort of planning committee, or even a consultant who has been working on a feasibility study. (Note that feasibility studies are actually a part of the SDLC planning phase. In some cases the business unit might've undertaken the study prior to coming to you with the work request. So even though they're unwitting participants, they're helping you fulfill a component of SDLC—the feasibility study.

The planning phase also includes the preparation of a formal business unit request. This work request sums up what it is that the business unit is after. Many different types of work might be requested. A business unit might want a completely new system to take the place of time-intensive manual processes. Or they might want a system that replaces an old antiquated system with one that uses current technology. Alternatively, the business unit might be looking for ways to augment its current operations and have ideas in which technology can assist. A request can be phrased in a variety of different ways. It is the system analyst's (SA) job to analyze the request and formalize it in such a way that the business unit and the IT group understand what is being requested.

In order to accomplish this work request, it will probably be required that you undertake a preliminary investigation in order to understand the type of work that is currently being done and how the business unit envisions technology enhancing that work. In the preliminary investigation, you delve into the nature of the problem or the opportunity before you. By coming to a 5,000-foot view of what's being asked, often you can determine that a new system or an upgrade to a previous system isn't in order, a simple business refinement may be the ticket.

In some cases, the project might be so large in scope that you have to perform a feasibility study. Generally you'll use outside sources in the form of consultants who are able to objectively look at what the problem is versus the proposed solution so that you can identify the proposed solution's viability and/or recommended alternatives. In some cases in government work, a feasibility study is *required* before a project can be undertaken. Executives with a fiduciary duty simply don't want to make a mistake undertaking a multimillion-dollar project before they understand the ramifications of what is being asked for. A feasibility study fleshes out the project's costs and associated outcomes, and recommends a path based on the various factors involved (such as political, financial, and technical capability among others).

The SDLC planning phase somewhat maps to the *Guide to the PMBOK*'s Initiation process group.

Analysis

The analysis phase is a continuation of the planning phase and goes more in-depth into what the actual project requirements are and what they involve. This phase involves the understanding of the business unit's process flows, a *very* critical element in bringing about high-quality systems.

Often, once an SA understands the work flows, he or she can recommend changes in those flows, apart from technology, so that the work effort is reduced. This is called *business process re-engineering (BPR)* and could potentially be a huge part of an SA's work.

An output of a preliminary investigation will be Data Flow Diagrams (DFD), drawings that highlight the way that the business flows are actually occurring today, along with proposed new flows. The DFDs will become the building blocks toward realizing a complete new system or a remodel of an old one.

> **TIP:** It is key to remember that you must always *first* understand the business work flows *before* you apply technology. Too often people get the cart before the horse and wind up with a poor product as a result.

In the Analysis phase you're going in-depth, trying to ascertain how the different users interact with the current system, what the current system documentation (if any) looks like, and so forth. You may even get into things like performing surveys to find out what people think about the different system requirements, or perhaps work on some sampling to get a flavor for how the current setup works. In short, you're trying to utilize any tool in your bag that might help you be certain that you've trapped in detail exactly what it is that is being asked for.

Getting Your Hands Dirty with SDLC—Planning and Analysis

Perhaps the best way to think about the SDLC process is to try to imagine a home fix-up project that you've undertaken—maybe a landscaping project, a room remodel, or finishing a basement.

Your husband or wife says: "Honey, we need to do something with that backyard!" This is the work request.

From this humble beginning you might've started out by drawing the layout of what you were going to work on. In the landscaping example, you'd have a rough sketch of the outline of the grounds, coupled with symbols for the trees, bushes, flowers, grasses, and accoutrements such as statuary that you planned on placing in the area. You could roughly analogize that this is your landscaping DFD. You have enough information to understand where things go, but probably not enough to completely understand how you'll fully go about doing your landscaping job.

If the job were big enough, you might actually hire a landscaping architect to develop plans for you before you go about doing your work. This would represent a feasibility study, in which you bring in an expert and ask them how they envision accomplishing what you have in mind. In this case, the landscaping architect provides you with the blueprints—your DFD—but you still have to go about doing the work. Note that this work is expensive and you'd probably *not* undertake it with a smaller project.

The outcome of this step is a document called the *Systems Requirements Document*—a thorough paper that details the requirements that the different parties (managers, end users, recipients of reports, etc.) stipulated, forecasted project costs, and positive takeaways as well as suggesting suitable alternatives to full-scale systems development.

This phase tracks closely to the *Guide to the PMBOK*'s Planning process group.

Design

The design phase represents the real nitty-gritty of the project. It is here that you fully formulate all the aspects of the system in such a way that each step is well understood and translatable to technology. This phase includes any current manual steps. For example, you might have identified in your earlier analysis a step in which a person keys several columns' worth of data from another computerized source into a separate tabular format for processing. The computerized version of this step might be to parse the data from the first source and then place it electronically into the second, saving an incredible amount of time.

It is important in the design phase that every element of the process has been identified, is well understood, and is now translated into the way that you see the new technology handling things. The end result of this effort is a document called the *Systems Design Specification* and will be used by system developers to create the new system.

The point is the same with the System Design Specification document. This doc is a blueprint, a set of lists, a how-to guide, and all of the other things that the folks developing the system will need to get started.

Getting Your Hands Dirty with SDLC—Design

In our little landscaping project, the landscape architect's blueprint would represent a part of your system design specification document, but you'd augment that documentation with things such as:

- The kind of soil you'd use to prep the grounds before you lay down grass, including how many yards of dirt you'll require and how you'll till it into the existing ground.

- The type of mulch you're going to use, where you'll put it, and how much you're going to need.

- The type of blocks you'll utilize for the walkways, the amount of sand that you'll require as a base for the blocks, and the pattern that you'll create with them.

And so forth. The point here is that by the time you've gotten to this stage, you know an awful lot about how you're going to do things.

Note that the System Design Specification is *not* line-for-line code. That stuff is done by the developers writing the application programs that the system will utilize. But you *could* use a type of software application called *Computer Aided Software Engineering (CASE) Tools* that would allow you to develop the basic shell of the system by keying in business rules then hitting a button to tell the CASE software to write the underlying components of the code. CASE Tools are not used heavily in smaller application development environments, but in larger environments they're still a part of the framework that project teams use to make the job go more quickly. Additionally, CASE Tools can be used to help you organize and understand the project's requirements.

The Analysis phase of the SDLC closely maps to the *Guide to the PMBOK's* Planning process group.

Implementation

The singular objective of the implementation phase is to bring to the customer a complete and fully functioning system that has been carefully and completely documented and thoroughly tested.

In the Implementation phase, project members write the software programs needed by the system, they set up the servers, install the database software, and get the schemas built and working, and so forth. If the system is going to utilize a COTS application, the application is installed and configured.

Testing occurs in the implementation phase. We've covered some of the testing phases (Unit, System, and User Acceptance) in previous chapters. In the Implementation phase, project members make very sure that the system is fully tested so that it is validated to work as expected. Larger systems may require several phases of testing.

> **NOTE** In a software development methodology known as *agile development*, testing techniques are utilized that allow for testing while the software modules are being created. In this way, programmers can discover problems earlier than at unit testing time and thus push code out the door faster. See www.agilealliance.com/home for more info on agile software development.

There are several other smaller elements involved with the Implementation phase. In this phase, data from old systems is converted and ported to the new system. Users of the system are trained in its functionality. Users are also actually migrated to the new system.

Additionally, system designers will go through a process called *Systems Evaluation*, in order to evaluate and report that the system does indeed meet the previously identified requirements.

The Implementation phase most closely maps to the *Guide to the PMBOK*'s Execution and Controlling process groups.

> **Getting Your Hands Dirty with SDLC—Implementation**
>
> Now that you know what your new landscape is going to look like, you've got a blueprint and all the associated documentation you need to make your yard look fantastic!
>
> You go to your local garden supply store and pick out all of the supplies that you need that you can directly transport home. You also order the delivery of the mulch, soil enhancer (sheep manure), turf, and stones you need—things you can't haul home in your personal vehicle. You also rent the specialized equipment you'll need, like the tiller.
>
> While awaiting the delivery, you go about doing all of the preparatory work you identified earlier—things that you can get done in preparation for the big stuff. You till the area where you're going to plant grass. You also dig out the flower beds and lay down the edging that will serve as the boundary for your stone paver patio and walkway. You run the sprinkler system from the grass and sprinkler hose (bubbler system to conserve water) for the plants. You plant the shrubs, flowers, and bushes. You place the statuary.
>
> When the delivery truck(s) arrives, full of big mounds of sand, soil enhancer, mulch, and paving stones, you begin the heavy work of hauling the soil enhancer to the grass beds, then tilling anew to make sure the soil is augmented and ready for the turf delivery folks. You apply the mulch to your garden beds and then lay down the sand in your paving stone areas so you have a nice even surface with which to lay down your pavers. The turf delivery people show up and lay down the sod.
>
> After weeks of work, you test the entire system by walking around in it to make sure you're happy with how it looks, then you plop down in your chaise lounge with a tall, cool drink and slip into a much-deserved nap!

Operations and Support

Unlike the *Guide to the PMBOK*'s Closing process group, where you close out the project and anything new is considered a brand-new project, in the Operations and Support phase you actually work on enhancements, training, and support. The idea behind the Operations and Support phase is solid—you've just deployed a system and now a group of people must actively support it. Whether you train new people or you've been asked to add some enhancements, or you need to pull routine maintenance (such as backups or security patches), all of these elements fall into the Operations and Support phase.

Elements of Operations and Support, such as help-desk operations, clearly fall into the *Guide to the PMBOK*'s Closing process group. In the Closing process group, you would've written and made available help-desk documentation for the new system but that's where you stop. In the SDLC, you go beyond that and see ongoing help-desk operations as a part of the system. We need to reiterate that when you've concluded the Closing process, the project's *over* and enhancements or additions are considered to be a new project. The *Guide to the PMBOK* doesn't talk about maintenance or enhancements. As far as *A Guide to the PMBOK* is concerned, technically, you would turn the project over to a support group. Remember that the definition of a project is an endeavor designed to produce a unique product or service and that has a definite beginning and end. However, SDLC accounts for this as the fifth phase of the life cycle and requires that you make accommodation.

> **Getting Your Hands Dirty with SDLC—Operations and Support**
>
> Several months into your new landscaping project, your sprinkler system clock goes out. Fortunately it's under warranty, but you have to make temporary provisions for it while you send the old one off to the factory for a replacement. You wind up purchasing a cheap little clock that doesn't have as many zones as you require, but at least enough to keep watering the grass. You simply go into the old drag-the-hose routine to make sure the flower beds are watered until you get the replacement clock.
>
> Also, you discover that some of the pavers in the walkway have sunk a half-inch or so and look unsightly. You have to pull them up, add some more sand, tamp it down thoroughly, and then reset the pavers.
>
> Additionally, you had one plant die (you wondered about it when you bought it at the garden supply store) and so you had to replace it.
>
> You've got a problem with an unusual new bug. You drive over to the local university extension office to ask them about it and get some helpful advice. Turns out the bug isn't harmful; in fact it's quite useful as it loves to eat aphids. However, this discovery points to the fact that the new trees you planted are *loved* by aphids—so much so that you've got to do something about it—they'll devour the tree bark in no time!

This is a subtle differentiation to make. Good project managers would, of course, realize that a new system requires ongoing maintenance and caretaking and see to it that steps were taken to accommodate the need. However, the project plan itself does not have any provision for this post-project work.

Comparing the *Guide to the PMBOK*'s Process Groups with the SDLC Phases

In Table A.1, we've provided you with a chart that may help you understand the close parallels between the *Guide to the PMBOK* process groups and the SDLC phases. IT projects have a unique character all their own—we're not building a battleship or a skyscraper—and so it's important to understand SDLC in order to help shape and bring about an excellent system deployment. However, *A Guide to the PMBOK*'s process groups provide a wonderful project management framework in which to work, so it's quite important to understand how the two juxtapose.

TABLE A.1 Project Life Cycle Key Elements with SDLC Phases

Project Process Group	Outputs or Key Activities	SDLC
Initiation	Project charter/Project request	Planning phase
		Create formal business unit request
		Provide preliminary investigation
		Complete feasibility study (if necessary)
Planning	Scope statement (Establish project goals and deliverables)	Design and analysis phase
	Critical success factors	Model requirements
	Work breakdown structure (WBS)	Document system requirements
	Resource plan (assignment of tasks)	
	Risk management plan	
	Communication plan	
	Quality plan	
	Change control plan	
	Project schedule	
	Project budget	
	Implementation plan	
	Support plan	

TABLE A.1 Project Life Cycle Key Elements with SDLC Phases *(continued)*

Project Process Group	Outputs or Key Activities	SDLC
Executing	Implement project team	Implementation phase
	Progress reporting	Development of system
	Take corrective action	
Controlling	Overall change control	Implementation phase
	Assess the impact of change	Development of system
	Testing and inspection	
	Write user guides	
	Write system administration guides	
	Provide training	
Closing	Obtain sign-off	Operation and support phase
	Document lessons learned	Training
	Evaluate the project	Maintenance
	Archive project information	Enhancement

Appendix B

Standard IT Project Documents

For this Appendix, we've created some project templates that you might find helpful during project execution. You can find these documents as Microsoft Word and Excel spreadsheets on the companion CD of this book.

Initial Project Proposal Analysis Template

This document gives you different questions you can ask in order to determine the basic nature of the project request before you. Use this at initial project assessment time. When presented with an initial project proposal, it may be helpful to ask a few basic questions of your clients in order to clarify what the project entails:

Customer Information

Ask yourself and your team specific questions about the nature of your customer and its needs.

- Who is my customer?
- What is the problem or issue that we're trying to solve?
- If we solve this problem, how will we benefit?
- If we can't solve this problem, what will happen? (Is there a penalty that we might incur if we don't solve this problem?)
- What does the solution to the problem look like?
- What are the primary deliverables?
- What do you think this project will cost and where will the project funding come from?
- How long do you think the project will take?
- What does my customer have to do to ensure the success of the project?

- Who will be the sponsor of this project?
- Who will be the project manager?

Success Information

You need to decide the criteria that will determine project success. Ask yourself and your team these specific questions about the project you are tackling.

- By what metrics will we be able to measure that we've successfully solved the problem or met the need?
- Will we increase sales? If so, what are current sales and what do we project future sales to be?
- Will we be lowering the costs of an operation? If so, what does the operation currently cost and what do we anticipate it will be after we've implemented our solution?
- Will the overall quality of our product or service be enhanced? If so, what is the measurement of product or service quality now and what will it be when we're finished?
- Will our performance be improved? If so, what is the current measure of performance that we use and what does the enhanced measure look like?

Business Impact

You need to record the projected impact the project will have on your business. Ask yourself and your team these questions to determine if the project is right for your organization at this time.

- Are there other projects vying for corporate time and resources?
- How will competing projects be impacted should this project go forward?
- Do the other projects depend on the successful outcome of this project?
- What is the impact to the business for these other projects?

Issue Notification

We've provided a document that you can use so that project team members or stakeholders can notify you of impending issues. The Issue Notification Worksheet, partially shown in the illustration below, would ideally be an email form or intranet document that utilizes workflow software in order to forward the document to key reviewers.

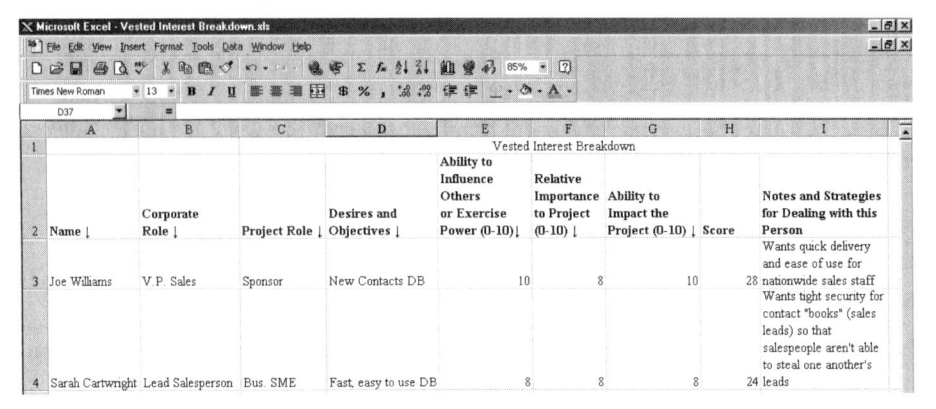

Name	Corporate Role	Project Role	Desires and Objectives	Ability to Influence Others or Exercise Power (0-10)	Relative Importance to Project (0-10)	Ability to Impact the Project (0-10)	Score	Notes and Strategies for Dealing with this Person
Joe Williams	V.P. Sales	Sponsor	New Contacts DB	10	8	10	28	Wants quick delivery and ease of use for nationwide sales staff
Sarah Cartwright	Lead Salesperson	Bus. SME	Fast, easy to use DB	8	8	8	24	Wants tight security for contact "books" (sales leads) so that salespeople aren't able to steal one another's leads

Risk Identification and Assessment

You would not begin a project without knowledge and understanding of the risks involved, therefore you must identify and assess these risks and keep them on record for the project team.

In the following table, we show a basic risk identification template that will be useful for you in your initial risk assessment efforts. Note that this is *not* an all-inclusive list! You'll want to add to the list as you work through your projects and identify more commonly held risks.

Basic Risk Identification Template

Use this template to identify basic risk assessment characteristics. Note that this template can be modified as you go forward in your project management work to account for other elements that you may encounter in your work.

In this table, in column 1, we've identified project categories that are of interest to you. In column 2, you should identify the risk as you see it: L = Low, M = Medium, and H = High. In the notes section, make comments about the category to describe your thoughts about this particular category's risk to the project.

Category	Risk (L/M/H)	Notes
Business Benefit	L	The project's benefit is well established.
Project Scope	L	The scope of the project is understood and well defined.

Risk Identification and Assessment

Category	Risk (L/M/H)	Notes
Sponsor	L	The sponsor has been identified and has accepted the responsibility.
Customer Commitment	L	The customer is committed to the project and wants to see it completed.
Project Manager	L	The project manager has worked on similar projects and understands the nature of what needs to be done.
Project Team Location	L	The project team is centered in one location. (Geographic disparity adds risk to the project.)
Project Methodologies and Processes	L	Project techniques, methodologies, procedures and processes are identified, well understood, and currently in practice corporate-wide. (Note: This does not necessarily imply that there's a PMO.)
Business Requirements	L	The project's requirements have been firmly identified and defined and are well understood.

Category	Risk (L/M/H)	Notes
System Availability	L	This risk identifies the amount of uptime that the system will actually be held to. Note that high-availability systems will naturally require more project planning and intervention. You should include system maintenance windows in your availability plans and note them in your risk assessment.
Technical Requirements	L	The requirements put forth in this project are similar to projects we've worked on before.
Data Requirements	L	The data needs are easily defined, built, and maintained.
Geography (deployment locations)	L	There is only one geographic location in which we'll be deploying this system.
Integrated System	L	There are no other systems with which this project will have to interface.
Business Units Affected	L	This project only affects one business unit.

Category	Risk (L/M/H)	Notes
Number of Person-Hours Required	L	This project will require less than 1,000 hours to complete. (Note: You should determine the number of person-hours that makes up a Low, Medium, or High risk.)
Subject Matter Expertise	L	The content of this project is well understood by the project team.
External Dependencies	L	There are no external dependencies (such as vendors) on which this project relies.
Process Engineering	L	Business processes do not have to change—processes are well-identified and are correct.
Organizational Structure Modifications	L	No modifications to the organization's structure are required in order to enact this project.
Technology	L	Current technologies (e.g., hardware, software, database, internetworking, etc.) can be used to bring about this project.
Data Quality	L	The data in the current system has been properly normalized and lacks any integrity issues. Indexes, triggers, stored procedures, and other database elements have been well defined in the previous system.

Category	Risk (L/M/H)	Notes
Project Costs	L	The costs of the project are accepted and not a problem.
RFP/RFI/RFQ (also Feasibility Study)	L	The various Requests for Input, Requests for Proposal, Requests for Quote, and Feasibility Studies have returned favorable, cost-effective information about the project.
Bleeding-Edge Quotient	L	This project is well within bounds of currently understood technologies
IT Team Communication	L	All the IT teams that will be affected by or working on this project are on board and prepared for its inception.
Infrastructure	L	The infrastructure is in place for the new system

Risk Assessment

Perhaps another useful document for you will be a scorecard that you can use in determining the severity, in decimal form, that a given risk presents. The Risk Assessment and Mitigation Scorecard, shown below, requires that you key in a given risk (see examples already included in the form) along with a number from 0–10 (1–10 for the mitigation element) for various facets of the risk. Add the numbers up and you have your score. Work on making sure that the high scorers have a solid mitigation plan because they're the ones you're most likely to encounter. Remember that risk assessment and mitigation strategies are a *team* effort, so the form should be worked on at a team meeting.

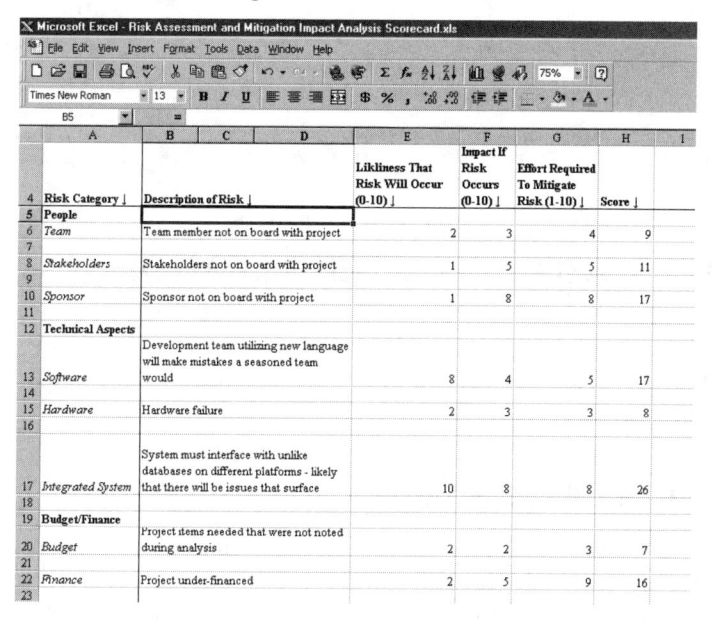

Risk Category	Description of Risk	Likliness That Risk Will Occur (0-10)	Impact If Risk Occurs (0-10)	Effort Required To Mitigate Risk (1-10)	Score
People					
Team	Team member not on board with project	2	3	4	9
Stakeholders	Stakeholders not on board with project	1	5	5	11
Sponsor	Sponsor not on board with project	1	8	8	17
Technical Aspects					
Software	Development team utilizing new language will make mistakes a seasoned team would	8	4	5	17
Hardware	Hardware failure	2	3	3	8
Integrated System	System must interface with unlike databases on different platforms - likely that there will be issues that surface	10	8	8	26
Budget/Finance					
Budget	Project items needed that were not noted during analysis	2	2	3	7
Finance	Project under-financed	2	5	9	16

Vested Interest Breakdown

Another useful document, the vested interest breakdown shown in here, allows you to assess numerically the relative "scores" of each of your stakeholders. This scoring mechanism allows you to get a more concrete feel for the strength of the players involved with the project. If you're new to the company and not as politically astute as your team members, it would be helpful to have them review this matrix with you.

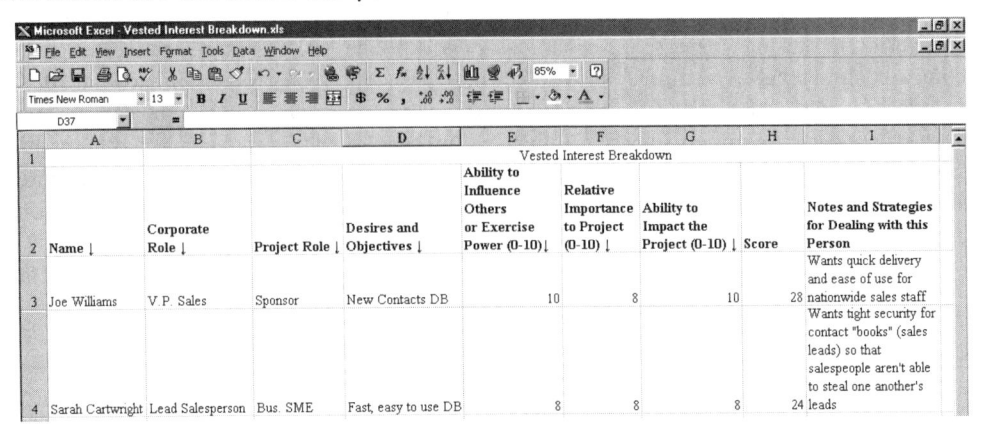

Name	Corporate Role	Project Role	Desires and Objectives	Ability to Influence Others or Exercise Power (0-10)	Relative Importance to Project (0-10)	Ability to Impact the Project (0-10)	Score	Notes and Strategies for Dealing with this Person
Joe Williams	V.P. Sales	Sponsor	New Contacts DB	10	8	10	28	Wants quick delivery and ease of use for nationwide sales staff
Sarah Cartwright	Lead Salesperson	Bus. SME	Fast, easy to use DB	8	8	8	24	Wants tight security for contact "books" (sales leads) so that salespeople aren't able to steal one another's leads

Human Resources Considerations

It's a good idea to keep records and charts regarding the people on a project team. You'll want to keep a Human Resources Assessment, a Skills Inventory worksheet, and a Responsibility Assignment document as well.

Human Resources Assessment

The Human Resources Assessment template, illustrated below, allows you to perform a basic assessment of each of your team members to identify their skills. You can use a scorecard rating of N = Neophyte, J = Junior, S = Senior for their experience level, or simply key in some text describing their experience. Note that you might have to fill out this matrix by visiting with the supervisors of the various team members on the matrix.

Human Resources Assessment

General Information

Project Name: Project Number:
Project Manager Name: Date:

Task ID	Description of Task	Skills Needed to Complete Task	Experience Level Required (N, J, S)	Team Member Assigned

Skills Inventory Worksheet

Similarly, the Skills Inventory worksheet, illustrated here, will allow you to assess the education, training, and certifications of your various team members.

Skills Inventory Worksheet

General Information

Project Name: Project Number:
Project Manager Name: Date:

Employee's Name	Job Title	Skills and Training	Years of Experience	Education, Certifications

Responsibility Assignment Document

The Responsibility Assignments document, allows you to note a task, and then fill in the team members that will be working on that task. The legend provides a way for you to describe the level of involvement in a percentage of his or her time for a particular person.

Responsibility Assignments

General Information

Project Name: Project Number: _____
Project Manager Name: Date:

Responsibility Assignment Matrix

Task	Resource	Resource	Resource

Legend:

Full (100%) △   Half (50-75%): ◯   Partial (0-50%): ▆

Glossary

A

***A Guide to the Project Management Body of Knowledge* (PMBOK)** The project management standard developed by the Project Management Institute.

Acceptance The decision to tolerate the defects that are found as a result of the quality testing. Also a tool for risk response planning.

Activity definition Identifying the activities of the project that need to be performed to produce the product or service of the project.

Activity duration estimating Assessing the number of work periods needed to complete the project activities. Work periods are usually expressed in hours or days. Large projects might express duration in weeks or months.

Activity sequencing Sequencing activities in logical order and determining whether dependencies exist among the activities.

Actual cost (AC) The cost of work to date including direct and indirect costs. Formerly known as actual cost of work performed (ACWP).

Actual cost of work performed (ACWP) See actual cost.

Administrative closure Gathering and disseminating information to formalize project closure. The completion of each project phase requires administrative closure also.

Analogous estimating An estimating technique that uses the actual duration of a similar, completed activity to determine the duration of the current activity. Also called top down estimating.

Appraisal costs Costs that cover the activities that keep the product defects from reaching the client, including inspection, testing, and formal quality audits.

Assumption An event or action believed to be true. Project assumptions should always be documented.

B

Backward pass Calculating a late start and late finish date by starting at the end of a network diagram and working back through each path until reaching the start of the network diagram. This is a part of CPM, which is a mathematical technique to develop the project schedule.

Benchmarking Compares previous similar activities to the current project activities to provide a standard to measure performance against. It's often used to derive ideas for quality improvements for the project.

Benefit measurement methods   A type of decision model that compares the benefits obtained from a variety of new project requests by evaluating them using the same criteria and comparing the results.

Bottom up estimating   Every activity or work item is individually estimated and then rolled up, or added together, to come up with a total project estimate. This is a very accurate means of estimating, provided the estimates at the work package level are accurate.

Budget analyst   A person in the department or organization who handles the budgetary elements of enterprise.

Budget at completion (BAC)   The total amount of the project budget as estimated during the planning phase.

Budgeted cost of work performed (BCWP)   See earned value.

Budgeted cost of work scheduled (BCWS)   See planned value.

Business analyst (BA)   Person in charge of understanding the business unit's needs when assessing a project request. The business analyst might be assigned directly from the business unit itself, or may be a part of the IT organization.

Business case   Formally documents components of the project assessment, including a description of the analysis method and the results.

Business process reengineering   Applying changes to an IT system and putting those elements into place based on a project request and a business analyst's examination of the work flow—how people handle their work relative to the request.

Business requirements   The big picture results of fulfilling a project.

C

Commercial off the shelf (COTS)   A software application that is purchased from a reseller, vendor, or manufacturer.

Communications management plan   Documents the types of information needs the stakeholders have, when the information should be distributed, and how the information will be delivered.

Communications planning   This Planning process determines the communication needs of the stakeholders, when and how the information will be received, and who will receive the information.

Comprehensive project plan   Integrates all planning data into one document that the project manager can be use as a guidebook to oversee the project work during the Execution and Controlling phases.

Configuration management Describes the characteristics of the product of the project and ensures the description is accurate and complete. Controls changes to the characteristics of an item, and tracks the changes made or requested and their status. It is usually a subset of the change control process in most organizations, or it may serve as the change control system.

Constrained optimization models Decision models that use complex principles of statistics and other mathematical concepts to assess a proposed project.

Constraint Anything that either restricts the actions of the project team or dictates the actions of the project team.

Contingency reserve An amount of money or time set aside and dedicated to the project to be used to cover unforeseen costs within the original scope of the project that were not identified as part of the planning process.

Contract A legal document that covers the work that will be done, how the work will be compensated, and any penalties for noncompliance.

Contract administration The process of monitoring vendor performance and ensuring all the requirements of the contract are met.

Contract closeout The process of completing and settling the terms of the contract and determining whether the work described in the contract was completed accurately and satisfactorily.

Control chart A graph of the variance of several samples of the same process over time based on a mean, an upper control limit, and a lower control limit.

Cost baseline The expected cost of the project from the planning phase. Used as a comparison to actual project expenses.

Cost-benefit analysis A commonly used benefit measurement method that calculates the cost, the projected savings, and projected revenue of a project.

Cost budgeting Assigning cost estimates to activities and creating the cost baseline, which measures the variance and performance of the project throughout the project's life.

Cost control Managing the changes to project costs using the cost change control system.

Cost estimating Developing an approximation of the cost of resources needed for each project activity.

Cost of quality The cost of all of the work required to assure the project meets the quality standards. The three costs associated with the cost of quality are prevention costs, appraisal costs, and failure costs.

Cost performance index (CPI) A project tracking mechanism that compares the budgeted cost to the actual cost using ratios. The formula is CPI = EV/AC.

Cost reimbursable contract Provides a seller with payment of all costs incurred to deliver the product and includes a fee to cover the seller's profit.

Cost variance   The difference between a task's estimated (budgeted) cost and its actual cost.

Crashing   Adding resources to a project to reduce the time it takes to complete the project.

Critical path (CP)   The longest path through the project's network diagram that's made up of activities with zero float.

Critical path method (CPM)   A schedule development method that determines a single early and late start date, early and late finish date, and float for each activity on the project.

Customer   The recipient of the product or service created by the project. In some organizations this stakeholder may also be referred to as the client.

D

Database administrators (DBAs)   People that handle the databases that systems use.

Database schema   The structure of a given database, which defines the tables in the database and their data elements (fields), as well as the relationships between the tables.

Data flow diagram (DFD)   A block diagram that describes how data is entered into a system resulting in useful information.

Datacenter   The primary room in an organization's building where the servers are housed. Often the routers, switches, and telephony gear are kept in the datacenter as well, in which case it may be called an MDF (see Main Data Facility).

Decision model   A formal method of project selection that helps managers make the best use of limited budgets and human resources. Includes benefit measurement methods and constrained optimization models.

Decomposition   The process of breaking project deliverables down into smaller, manageable components so that project tasks and activities can be planned and estimated.

Definitive estimate   An estimating technique that assigns a cost estimate to each work package in the project WBS. The most accurate of the cost estimating techniques.

Demarcation   The termination juncture where a telecommunications company provides the interface for wide area networking (WAN) services, such as T1 or ISDN.

Dependencies   The relationship between two project activities.

Dependency relationships   Identifying the type of dependency between two activities and the specific relationship between the activities.

Discounted cash flow (DCF)   Compares the value of the future cash flows of the project to today's dollars.

Discretionary dependency   Something that the project manager and project team choose to impose on the project schedule, such as the use of an established corporate practice.

Document control process   Defines how revisions are made, the version numbering system, and the placement of the version number and revision date.

Duration compression   The use of techniques such as fast tracking or crashing to shorten the planned duration of a project or to resolve schedule slippage.

E

Early finish   The earliest date an activity may finish as logically constrained by the network diagram.

Early start   The earliest date an activity may begin as logically constrained by the network diagram.

Earned value (EV)   A measurement of the project's progress to date or the value of the work completed to date.

Earned value analysis   Looks at schedule, cost, and scope project measurements and compares their progress as of the measurement date against what was expected. Three measurements needed to perform earned value analysis are planned value (PV), actual cost (AC), and earned value (EV).

Economic model   One of the benefit measurement methods. It is a series of financial calculations that provide data on the overall financials of the project.

End user   The person(s) who directly uses the product that is the end result of the project.

Enterprise   The computing basis of the organization as a whole.

Enterprise project   A project that will be used by users throughout the enterprise.

Enterprise resource planning   A business planning methodology that encompasses all facets of the business. ERP software handles such things as human resources, accounting, manufacturing, and so forth.

Entity relationship diagrams   A block-type diagram that shows the logic flow between various system entities.

Equipment   (a) Resources such as servers, specialized test equipment, or additional PCs that are required for a project.
   (b) One of the categories of project resources. It includes test tools, servers, PCs, or other related items required to complete the project.

Estimate at completion (EAC)   A forecast of the total cost of the project based on both current project performance and the remaining work. The formula is EAC = AC + ETC.

Estimate to complete (ETC) The cost estimate for the remaining project work.

Expert judgment A project selection method that relies on information provided by those with expertise on the requested product. Expert judgment can come from stakeholders, other departments, consultants, or industry groups.

External dependency A relationship between a project task and a factor outside of the project, such as weather conditions, that drives the scheduling of that task.

F

Failure costs Covers the cost of activities generated if the product fails including downtime, user support, rework, and scrapping the project.

Fast tracking A schedule compression technique where two activities that were previously scheduled to start sequentially start at the same time. Fast tracking reduces schedule duration.

Feasibility study Undertaken to determine whether the project is a viable project, the probability of project success, and the viability of the product of the project.

Finish to finish A project task relationship in which the finish of the successor task is dependent on the finish of the predecessor task.

Finish to start A project task relationship in which the successor task cannot begin until the predecessor task has completed.

Fixed price contracts A fixed fee for the work that the vendor will provide.

Float time The amount of time the early start of a task may be delayed without delaying the finish date of the project. Also known as slack time.

Flowchart A diagram that shows the logical steps that must be performed in order to accomplish an objective. It can also show how the individual elements of a system interrelate.

Formal communications Planned communications such as project kickoff meetings, team status meetings, written status reports, or team-building sessions.

Forward pass The process of working from the left to the right of a network diagram in order to calculate early start and early finish dates for each activity.

Functional organization A form of organizational structure. Functional organizations are traditional organizations with hierarchical reporting structures.

Functional requirements Define what the product of the project will do by focusing on how the end user will interact with the product.

H

High-level requirements Explain the major characteristics of the product and describe the relationship between the business need and the product requested. Also referred to as a product description.

Human resources The people with the background and skills to complete the tasks on the project schedule.

Human resources planning Defining team member roles and responsibilities, establishing an appropriate structure for team reporting, securing the right team members, and bringing them on the project as needed for the appropriate length of time.

I

Informal communications Unplanned or ad hoc communications including phone calls, emails, conversations in the hallway, or impromptu meetings.

Information distribution Providing stakeholders with information regarding the project in a timely manner via status reports, project meetings, review meetings, email, and so on. The communications management plan is put into action during this process.

Infrastructure The backbone of the organization's computing environment. Typically the infrastructure will include such elements as the network cabling, routers and switches, and termination points.

Interactive voice response (IVR) A system that uses telephony and allows users to connect to a database using a touch-tone telephone for the retrieval of information or to interact with the system in other ways.

Initiation The first process in a project life cycle. It is the formal acknowledgment that the project should begin using a charter.

Inspection A quality control technique that includes examining, measuring, or testing work results.

Integrated change control A process that influences the things that cause change, determines that change is needed or has happened, and manages change. All other change control processes are integrated with this process.

Integrated system A computing system that draws its data elements from various sources, such as an Oracle database and a SQL Server database.

Integration testing The process of testing several distinct software modules (called units) as one intact entity. Integration testing proves that the various unique software modules work together in harmony.

Intermediate data facility (IDF) A room that houses necessary infrastructure components and is connected by network cabling to the datacenter, but is not considered to be the datacenter. Typically, in large buildings there are several IDFs spread around so that it's easier and cheaper to run network cabling to user endpoints. Servers generally are *not* placed in the IDFs, but are kept at the datacenter, also called the Main Data Facility (see also Main Data Facility).

Internal rate of return (IRR) The discount rate when the present value of the cash inflows equals the original investment. Projects with higher IRR values are generally considered better than projects with lower IRR values. Assumes that cash inflows are reinvested at the IRR value.

Iterative process Any process that is repeated more than once. The five process groups are repeated throughout the project's life due to change requests, responses to change, corrective action, and so on.

L

Late finish The latest date an activity can complete without impacting the project end date.

Late start The latest date an activity can start without impacting the project end date.

Loaded rate A rate used for cost estimating of human resources that includes a percentage of the salary to cover employee benefits, such as medical, disability, or pension plans.

M

Main Data Facility (MDF) The primary location where the servers, telephony gear, routers, and demarcation points are kept. (Note that in some cases the demarcation points are at a separate place in the building, but cabling is run to the datacenter for purposes of connecting the computer and communications equipment.) Unless the servers are kept elsewhere, another name for the MDF is the datacenter.

Major deliverables Outputs that must be produced to bring the phase or project to completion. Deliverables are tangible and can be measured and easily proved.

Make or buy analysis Looking at the trade-offs between doing something in-house versus procuring it outside the organization.

Managerial reserve An amount set aside by upper management to cover future situations that cannot be predicted.

Mandatory dependency A relationship between two tasks that is created by the type of work the project requires.

Materials A catchall category of project resources that includes software, utility requirements such as electricity or water, any supplies needed for the project, or other consumable goods.

Mathematical analysis Calculating theoretical early and late start and finish dates for all project activities.

Matrix management Using people from different business entities in a project for at least a part of their time; team members report to both their functional manager and the project manager. Matrix management is common in IT projects.

Matrix organization An organizational structure where employees report to one functional manager and at least one project manager. Functional managers assign employees to projects and carry out administrative duties, while project managers assign tasks associated with the project to team members and execute the project.

Metric A standard of measurement that specifically defines how something will be measured.

Milestone A major deliverable or key event in the project used to measure project progress.

Multiple business unit project A project that is initiated by multiple business units.

N

Net present value (NPV) Evaluation of the cash inflows using the discounted cash flow technique, which is applied to each period the inflows are expected. The total present value of the cash flows is deducted from the initial investment; assumes that cash inflows are reinvested at the cost of capital. Similar to discounted cash flows.

Network diagram A depiction of project activities and the interrelationships between these activities.

Network operating system (NOS) Server software that allows the creation of network user accounts, and provides other functionality such as network printing, etc.

Normalization The process of reducing data elements in a database to their base elements so as to reduce redundancy. Typically many different tables will be needed in a database system to accommodate the various sections of data.

Normalizing The process of normalizing a database (see normalization).

O

Order of magnitude A high-level estimate of the time and cost of a project based on the actual cost and duration of a completed similar project.

Organizational planning The process of addressing interfaces that may impact how to manage a project team, define roles and responsibilities for project team members, identify how the project team will be organized, and document a staffing management plan.

P

Parametric modeling   A mathematical model that uses parameters, or project characteristics, to forecast project costs.

Pareto diagram   A quality control technique used to rank importance of a problem based on its frequency of occurrence over time. This diagram is based on the Pareto principle, more commonly referred to as the 80/20 rule, which says that the majority of defects are caused by a small set of problems.

Payback period   The length of time it takes a company to recover the initial cost of producing the product or service of the project.

Performance reporting   Collecting information regarding project progress and project accomplishments and reporting it to the stakeholders, project team members, management team, and other interested parties. It also makes predictions regarding future project performance.

Pilot test   Building and testing a proposed system in a small environment that includes a handful of users (also called *pilot mode*). The purpose of pilot testing is to develop a fully functioning system and then put it out for a small component of people to test to see if it meets the expectations of the project. From successful pilot testing it's easy to put the system into full production.

Planned value (PV)   The cost of work that's been budgeted for an activity during a certain time period. This was formerly referred to as budgeted cost of work scheduled (BCWS).

Precedence diagramming method (PDM)   A diagramming method that places activities on nodes, which connect to dependent activities using arrows. Also known as activity on node.

Predecessor   A task that exists on a path with another task and occurs before the other task.

Preliminary investigation   An investigation at project request time to determine the costs and benefits of the project, as well as examine alternatives to the proposed solution in order to determine the feasibility of carrying out the project.

Preventative action   The review of potential risks to determine if any steps can be taken to prevent the problem from occurring or reduce the probability that the problem will occur.

Prevention costs   Costs of the activities performed to avoid quality problems including quality planning, training, and any product or process testing.

Procurement planning   Identifying what goods or services will be purchased from outside of the organization. Also uses make or buy analysis to determine whether goods or services should be purchased or performed by the organization.

Product description   Explains the major characteristics of the product and describes the relationship between the business need and the product. Also referred to as high-level requirements.

Program   A grouping of related projects that are managed together. The individual projects are usually part of one bigger project.

Program evaluation and review technique (PERT) Uses expected value, or weighted average, of critical path tasks to determine project duration by establishing three estimates: most likely, pessimistic, and optimistic.

Progress reports Reports from project team members listing the tasks each team member is working on, the current progress of each task, and the work remaining.

Project A project is temporary in nature, has definite start and end dates, creates a unique product or service, and is completed when the goals and objectives of the project have been met and signed off on by the stakeholders.

Project champion This person, usually not the project sponsor, is one who fully understands, believes in, and espouses the benefits of the project.

Project charter An official, written acknowledgment and recognition that a project exists. It's issued by senior management and gives the project manager authority to assign organizational resources to the work of the project.

Project closure The formal acceptance of a project and the activities required to formally end the project work.

Project description Documents the key characteristics of the product or service that will be created by the project and the work required to deliver the product.

Project execution Carrying out the project plan. Activities are clarified, the work is authorized to begin, resources are committed and assigned to activities, and the product or service of the project is created. The largest portion of the project budget will be spent during this process.

Project justification Documentation in the project scope statement that includes the reason the project is being undertaken and the business need the project will address.

Project life cycle The grouping of project phases in a sequential order from the beginning of the project to the close.

Project management The process that's used to initiate, plan, execute, monitor, control, and close out projects by applying skills, knowledge, and project management tools and techniques to fulfill the project requirements.

Project Management Institute (PMI) The world's leading professional project management association.

Project management knowledge areas These nine project management groupings, or knowledge areas, bring together common or related processes. They are: Integration, Scope, Time, Cost, Quality, Human Resource, Communications, Risk, Procurement.

Project management office (PMO) Established by organizations to create and maintain procedures and standards for project management methodologies to be used throughout the organization.

Project manager The person responsible for applying the skills, knowledge, and project management tools and techniques to the project activities in order to successfully complete the project objectives.

Project performance indicators   Measures the project manager uses to determine whether the project is on track, such as any deviation from the baseline schedule or the baseline budget.

Project plan   A document, or assortment of documents, that constitutes what the project is, what the project will deliver, and how all the processes will be managed. Used as the guideline throughout the project Executing and Controlling phases to track and measure project performance and to make future project decisions. Also used as a communication and information tool for stakeholders, team members, and management.

Project review   A formal presentation by the project manager or project team members to the sponsor, the client, and other executive stakeholders.

Project schedule   Determines the start and finish dates for project activities and assigns resources to the activities.

Project selection   Used to determine which proposed projects are approved to move forward.

Projectized organization   An organizational structure focused on projects. Project managers generally have ultimate authority over the project, and, sometimes, supporting departments like human resources and accounting might report to the project manager. Project managers are responsible for making project decisions and acquiring and assigning resources.

Proof of concept   A project that undertakes to prove that a specific activity can be done or an idea can be accomplished.

Q

Qualitative risk analysis   Determining the impact of identified risks on the project and the probability they'll occur; puts the risks in priority order according to their effect on the project objectives.

Quality control   Monitoring work results to see whether they fulfill the quality standards set out in the quality management plan; determines whether the end product conforms to the requirements and product description defined during the planning processes.

Quality management plan   Describes how the project management team will enact the quality policy and documents the resources needed to carry out the quality plan, the responsibilities of the project team in implementing quality, and all the processes and procedures the project team and organization will use to satisfy quality requirements.

Quality planning   Identifying the quality standards applicable for the project and how to fulfill the standards.

Quantitative risk analysis   Assigning numeric probabilities to each identified risk and examining their potential impact to the project objectives.

Quantitatively based durations   A duration estimate obtained by applying a productivity rate of the resource performing the task.

R

Rebaselining Setting a new project baseline if there are substantial changes to the schedule or the budget.

Request for proposal (RFP) A document that is sent out to potential vendors requesting them to provide a proposal on a product or service.

Requirement The specifications of the goal or deliverable.

Resource planning Definition of all the resources needed and the quantity of resources needed to perform project activities.

Resource pool description A list of all job titles within a company or department with a brief description of the job. May identify the number of people currently employed in each job title.

Resource requirements A document containing a description of the resources needed from all three resource types for work package items from the WBS.

Responsibility Assignment Matrix (RAM) Ties roles and responsibilities with the WBS elements to ensure that each element has a resource assigned. Usually displayed in chart form.

Revision An update to the approved start or end date of the schedule baseline, typically a result of approved scope changes.

Rework Any action that is taken as a result of quality activities to correct a defect.

Risk An element of uncertainty that can have either negative or positive consequences.

Risk analysis The process used to identify and focus on those risks that are the most critical to the success of your project.

Risk identification Identifying the potential project risks and documents their characteristics.

Risk management plan Details how risk management processes will be implemented, monitored, and controlled throughout the life of the project. It does not define responses to individual risks.

Risk monitoring and control Process of responding to risks as they occur based on the risk management plan, which details how risks are managed, and the risk response plan, which details how risk response strategies are implemented in the event of an actual risk event.

Risk planning A process determining how areas of uncertainty will be managed for a project.

Risk response planning The plan for steps to reduce threats and take advantage of opportunities; assigns departments or individual staff members the responsibility of carrying out the risk response plans developed in this process.

Risk trigger An event that warns a risk is imminent and a contingency plan should be implemented.

S

Schedule baseline A copy of the schedule prior to the start of project work that is used during project execution to monitor project progress.

Schedule control Documenting and managing changes to the project schedule.

Schedule development Calculating and preparing the schedule of project activities, which becomes the schedule baseline. It determines activity start and finish dates, and finalizes activity sequences and durations; assigning resources to activities is done in resource planning, a cost management planning process.

Schedule performance index (SPI) The ratio of work completed to the work planned, measured over time. The SPI indicator acts as an efficiency rating. The formula is SPI = EV / PV.

Schedule update Any change that is made to the project schedule as part of the ongoing work involved with managing the project.

Schedule variance (SV) The difference between a task's progress as compared to its estimated progress represented in terms of cost. The formula is SV = EV – PV.

Scope The size of the work involved to complete the project. Can define both what is included in the project as well as what is excluded from the project.

Scope change control Documenting and managing changes to project scope. Any modification to the agreed on WBS is considered a scope change. Changes in product scope will require changes to project scope.

Scope creep The minor changes or small additions that are made to the project outside of a formal scope change process.

Scope definition *A Guide to the PMBOK* defines scope definition as the process of breaking down the major deliverables from the scope statement to create the WBS. For purposes of the CompTIA objectives and exam, scope definition is used in a much broader sense to cover several scope planning elements, including the scope statement and the scope management plan.

Scope management plan Analyzes the reliability and stability of the project scope. Documents the process that manages project scope and changes to project scope.

Scope planning The work of the project, culminating in the scope statement, which describes the project deliverables, objectives, and justification.

Scope statement Documents the project goals, deliverables, and requirements, which are used as a baseline for future project decisions. It also includes the project objectives and the business justification for the project.

Scope verification Formal acceptance of the project scope; primarily concerned with the acceptance of work results.

Scoring model One of the benefit measurement methods. It contains a predefined list of criteria against which each project is ranked. Each criterion has a scoring range and a weighting factor.

Sequencing Putting the project activities in the order in which they will take place.

Sidebar systems Systems that arise out of end-user frustration with the limitations of the primary system. End users may use a spreadsheet or database to help them work through some of the processing requirements of an ERP system. Sidebar systems often don't show up at requirements gathering time because people are afraid to reveal sidebar systems.

Slack time The amount of time allowed to delay the early start of a task without delaying the finish date of the project. Also known as float time.

Software development life cycle (SDLC) A methodology that describes five distinct phases involved in building any system. The five phases are Planning, Analysis, Design, Implementation and Operations, and Support. Also known as the systems development life cycle

Sole source A requirement that a product or service must be obtained from a single vendor in government work; also includes justification.

Solicitation Obtaining bids and proposals from vendors in response to RFPs and similar documents prepared during the solicitation planning process.

Sponsor An executive in the organization with authority to assign resources and enforce decisions regarding the project.

Staff acquisition Attaining human resources and assigning them to the project. Human resources may come from inside or outside the organization.

Staffing management plan Documents when and how human resources will be added to and released from the project team and what they will be working on while they are part of the team. Adding and releasing resources may be an informal or a formal process, depending on the organization.

Stakeholder A person or organization who has a vested interest in the project and stands to gain or lose something as a result of the project.

Start to finish A task relationship where the finish of the successor task is dependent on the start of its predecessor.

Start to start A project task relationship where the start of the successor task depends on the start of the predecessor task.

Statement of work (SOW) Contains the details of a procurement item in clear, concise terms and includes the project objectives, a description of the work of the project, concise specifications of the product or services required, and a project schedule.

Status date The date when the project manager measures how much has been spent on a specific task.

Storage area network (SAN)   A network of storage arrays, designed to provide the safekeeping of information. May be connected by fiber-optic cabling using the fiber channel protocol, but this doesn't have to be the case. May be connected by Ethernet, or other protocols.

Storage array   A device that houses multiple disks designed to provide a highly fault-tolerant and highly available place where information can be stored. At a minimum, provides a method of making the information available to users and a system for monitoring the health of the array.

Success criteria   A definition of the measurable business results the product is expected to produce.

Successor   A task that exists on a common path with another task and occurs after the other task.

System design specification   The final outcome of the design phase of SDLC; a document detailing what the system will do, how it will do it, and what it will cost. Used by systems developers who will actually build the new system.

System request   A request made by business unit stakeholders for a new system.

Systems analysis   Analyzing the details of a systems project request to determine how the current system (if any) flows and how the new system will change in its flows. Involves understanding the way that the business organization currently does its work and how that work translates into a new system. Also involves understanding how the various system components will connect physically and logically together. This is the second phase of an SDLC.

Systems analyst (SA)   Person specially trained in the analysis and design of a business request for a new system.

Systems design   Designing a new system after obtaining a request from a business unit for a new project and analyzing the flows of the system. This is the third phase of an SDLC.

Systems implementation   Deploying the new system. This is the fourth phase of an SDLC.

Systems operations and support   Maintaining, upgrading, and enhancing the released system. This is the fifth and final stage of an SDLC.

Systems planning   Receiving a request for a new project from a business unit, examining the requirements of that request, and formulating it into a working project document. This is the first phase of an SDLC.

T

Team development   Creating an open, encouraging environment for stakeholders to contribute, as well as developing the project team into an effective, functioning, coordinated group.

Time and materials contract   The buyer and the seller agree on a unit rate, such as the hourly rate for a programmer, but the total cost is unknown and will depend on the amount of time spent to produce the product.

To-complete performance index (TCPI) The performance that must be achieved in the remaining elements of the project in order to satisfy financial or schedule goals.

Top down estimating An estimating technique that uses actual durations from similar activities on a previous project. Also referred to as analogous estimating.

Trend analysis A mathematical technique that can be used to predict future defects based on historical results.

Triple constraint The link between impacts of the constraints put on a project by time, cost, and quality.

U

Unit testing The successful completion and testing of a single software module.

User acceptance testing (UAT) The final phase in a software development process during which the intended audience receives the software so they can test for functionality.

V

Variance analysis The comparison of planned project results with actual project results.

W

Work breakdown structure (WBS) A deliverables-oriented hierarchy that defines the total work of the project. Each level has more detailed information than the previous level.

Work effort The total time it would take for a person to complete the task if they did nothing else from the time they started until the task was complete.

Work package The lowest level in a WBS. Team assignments, time estimates, and cost estimates can be made when this level represents tasks or activities. On very large projects, this level is handed off to subproject managers who develop their own WBS to fulfill the requirements of the work package deliverable.

Index

Note to the reader: Throughout this index boldfaced page numbers indicate primary discussions of a topic. Italicized page numbers indicate illustrations.

A

acceptance
    of defects, 288
    of project, 324–325
accommodating style for conflict management, 237
accountability of team members, 174
activity definition in schedule planning, 104–105
activity duration estimates
    in network diagram, 110
    in schedule planning, 108–110
        estimating techniques, 109–110
activity sequence in schedule planning, 105–107
    dependency types, 106
    network diagram, 107, *107*
    task dependency relationships, 106–107
actual cost, 298
actual cost of work performed (ACWP), 299, 300
administrative closure, 323–332
    comprehensive review, 325–329
    formal acceptance, 324–325
    project archive, 324
    project turnover, 329–331
    release of team members, 331–332
administrative components in project plan, 210
agenda for team meeting, 248
agile development, 348
American National Standards Institute (ANSI), 291
analogous estimating
    of activity duration, 109
    of costs, 142
    potential inaccuracies, 146
analysis phase in SDLC, 345–347
appendix in project plan, 213
application developers, typical day, 118
appraisal costs, 179
approval of charter, 54–58
approval of project withheld, 322
archive of project, 324
assessment at project end, 325–329
assumptions
    documenting, 148
    in project plan, 211
        sample, 220
    in scope statement, 75
        case study, 92
        sample, 77
automated systems, 5–6
avoiding style for conflict management, 238

B

backward pass, in critical path determination, 112
baseline
    adjustments after scope change, 280
    for costs, 151
    display, 212
    documenting progress against, 246–247
    for schedule, 116
benchmarking, 177
benefit measurement methods in decision models, 42
benefits, in business case summary, 54
binder, for project documentation, 324
bottom up estimating, 144
boundaries of project. *See* scope of project
brainstorming, 81
    and cost estimates, 146
    on risks, 182
budget. *See also* cost planning
    comprehensive review of, 327
    crashing and, 114
    in project plan, 211
        sample, 221
    for team recognition, 147
budget analysts, 49
    IT project manager as, 7
    meeting with, 149
budget at completion, 298
budget constraint, 74
budgeted cost of work performed (BCWP), 298–299, 300
budgeted cost of work scheduled (BCWS), 299
business analysts, 6, 49
business case, in charter, 53–54
business customers. *See* client
business process, 8
business process re-engineering (BPR), 8, 346
business requirements of project, 36
business unit, negotiation with, 12

C

calendar days, vs. work days, 108
canceling project, 305, 322
Capability Maturity Model (CMM)
    analysis, 292
CASE (computer aided software engineering)
    tools, 348
case scenarios, 17
case study
    wineries e-mail and intranet systems, 57–58
        closeout, 330–331
        communications plan, 195
        cost planning, 152–154
        evaluating, 306
        finalized plan, 218–221
        procurement planning, 197
        project execution, 260–261
        quality plan, 196
        risk assessment, 196
        scope document, 91–94
        work breakdown structure (WBS), 120–121
CD-ROM, templates, 252, 354–362
champion. *See* sponsor
change control, 278–283, 325
    cost control, 281–282
    exam essentials, 307–308
    other changes, 282–283
    schedule control, 280–281
    scope change control, 279–280
        management plan for, 78
charter, 51–58
    business case, 53–54
    formal approval, 54–58
    goals and objectives, 53
    matching to project team, real world scenario, 50
    project description, 52
    team, 52–53
checklists
    in project plan, 213
    for quality, 180
checkpoints, 19
client, 45
    project plan review by, 216
    project review for, 251
    relationship management with, 241–242
    working with, 87
closeout
    of planning phase, 216–217
    of project. *See* project closure
closing processes, 15
CMM (Capability Maturity Model)
    analysis, 292
COCOMO (COnstructive COst MOdel), 143
collaborating style for conflict management, 238
collaboration, online, 167
Commercial Off The Shelf (COTS) program, 4

communications, 11–12, 248–252. *See also* documentation
    about cost estimates, 146
    among IT job roles, 9
    with client, 86, 241–242
    of milestones, 116
    of performance deviations, 302–303
    planning, 166, 185–189
        case study, 195
        example, 187
        with project team members, 188
        with stakeholders, 188–189
        strategy, 186–187
    in project plan, 212
        sample, 221
    project reviews, 250–252
    status reports, 250
    within team, 249
    team meetings, 248–250
    with vendor, 256, 257–260
        preparation before, 259
communicator, IT project manager as, 7
competing style for conflict management, 238
completion criteria, in scope statement, 74
comprehensive project plan. *See* project plan
compromising style for conflict management, 238
computer aided software engineering (CASE) tools, 348
confidence level for project estimates, 74
configuration, changes, 283
conflict, styles for dealing with, 237–238
consensus
    with client, 242
    for scope statement, 77
constrained optimization decision models, 43
constraints
    in project plan, 211
        sample, 220
    in scope statement, 75
        case study, 92
        sample, 77
COnstructive COst MOdel (COCOMO), 143
consultants, relationship with, 88–89
contingency action
    for risk, 185, 295
    and schedule control, 294
contingency fund, 149, 154
contract closeout, 323
contract workers, 175, 191
    for testing, 180
contracts, types, 191–192
control charts, 287, 287
controlling processes, 15. *See also* change control; quality control
    comprehensive review of, 327
    exam essentials, 307–308
corrective action
    for cost overruns, 282
    in schedule control, 280
    for scope creep, 279
cost baseline, 151

cost-benefit analysis, 42, 177
cost control, 278, 281–282
cost estimates, 141–148
   revised, 281
   in scope statement, 74
   techniques, 142–145
      analogous estimating, 142
      definitive estimates, 143–145
      parametric modeling, 142–143
   tips, 145–148
cost of quality, 178–179
cost performance index, 301
cost planning. *See also* cost estimates
   case study, 152–154
   cost budgeting, 148–155
      baseline, 151
      budget creation, 149–151
      budget targets, 151–152
   exam essentials, 155–156
   with project management software, 154–155
   real world scenario, 140
   resource planning, 134–141
      requirements definition, 137, 137–141
      types, 135–137
   trade-offs, 305
cost reimbursable contracts, 191–192
cost variances, 152, 301
costs
   in business case summary, 53–54
   data collection on, 246
   evaluating, 247
   vendor payment process, 256–257
COTS (Commercial Off The Shelf) program, 4
crashing, 114
critical path method (CPM), 111–114
   and schedule control, 280, 281
customer. *See* client

D

data collection
   progress reports, 244–245
   on spending, 246
data flow diagram (DFD), 12, 17, 177, 346
Data Transformation Services (DTS), 119
database administrators (DBAs), 48
   documentation for, 290
   typical day, 118
database design, configuration change, 283
database schema, 118
datacenter creation, 4
DCF (discounted cash flow), 42
decision making by client, 242
decision models for project selection, 41–43
decision tree analysis, 183
decomposing
   major deliverables, 79, 80–82, 82
   requirements of project, 39–40

defects
   frequency in Pareto diagram, 286
   rework to correct, 288
Defined operational level in CMM, 292
definitive estimates of costs, 143–145
deliverables, major
   completion as milestone, 116
   decomposing, 79, 80–82, 82
   defining, 83, 86–87
   in project plan, 211
      sample, 220–221
   in scope statement, 73
      case study, 91
      sample, 76
   sign-off, 247
   team members' disagreement over, 238
   testing, 285
   turnover of project to maintaining group, 329–331
   from vendors, 191
   written notice of acceptance, 323
demarcation location, 4
dependencies, 105
   relationships, 106–107
      network diagram to display, 107, 107
      predecessor/successor, 106
   types, 106
design phase in SDLC, 347–348
development environment, 139
DFD (data flow diagram), 12, 17, 177, 346
diminishing returns from resources, 114
directing process, comprehensive review of, 327
discounted cash flow (DCF), 42
discretionary dependency, 106
Distributed Management Task Force, 291
distribution of project plan, 215
document control process, 215
document information, in project plan, 210
documentation
   archiving, 324
   of assumptions, 148
   maintenance by operations group, 330
   on progress against baseline, 246–247
   project concept, 18–19
   with quality checklists, 180
   quality of, 288–290
   requirements of project, 38–39
   with risk management template, 185
   roles and responsibilities, 170–171
   scope change process, 78–79
   sole-source, 193
   for support groups, 289–290
drive-bys, 117
DTS (Data Transformation Services), 119
duration. *See also* activity duration estimates
   defining, 108
   estimating techniques, 109–110
   in network diagram, 110
duration compression, 114–115

E

early finish, 112
early start, 112
earned value, 298–302
    basics, 299–300
    indexes (ratios), 301–302
    variances, 301
economic model for project selection decision, 42
ego factor, 254
electricity, in resource planning, 140
end user, 45. *See also* users
enterprise project, stakeholders for, 47–48
Enterprise Resource Planning (ERP), 5
entity relationship diagrams (ERDs), 17
environmental processes, setup, 292–293
equipment
    hardware, 138
    make or buy analysis, 190
    resource planning for, 136
equipment descriptions, 138
estimate at completion, 298
executing processes, 15
    comprehensive review of, 326
execution of project
    communications with vendor, 257–260
    exam essentials, 262–263
    information distribution, 248–252
        project reviews, 250–252
        status reports, 250
        team meetings, 248–250
    performance according to plan, 244–247
        data collection, 244–246
        progress against baselines, 246–247
    stakeholder relationships, 241–244
        client, 241–242
        functional managers, 243–244
        wavering sponsor, 242–243
    team development, 233–241
        performance monitoring, 237–239
        project kickoff, 234–237
        rewards and recognition, 239–241
        training, 239
    vendor contract administration, 253–260
        delays, 256
        managing disagreements, 253–256
        payment process, 256–257
        progress reporting, 253
Executive Project Summary Worksheet, template, 252
executive summary in project plan, 210
    sample, 218
exempt employees, 153
exit criteria, 180
expectations of client, 242
expenditures. *See* costs

expert judgment
    in activity duration estimates, 109
    in project selection, 43
external dependency, 106

F

factory acceptance testing (FAT), 284
failure costs, 179
failures, frequency in Pareto diagram, 286
fast tracking, 16, 114–115, 281
feasibility study, 16, 41
    in SDLC, 345
feedback for team members, 237–238
finish to finish relationship, 107
finish to start relationship, 107
fixed price contracts, 191
float time, 111
    calculation, 113
flowcharting, 177, 178, 287
formal communications, 188
forming stage of team development, 234
forward pass, in critical path determination, 111–112
functional managers, 45
    negotiation with, 173–175
    relationships with, 243–244
functional organization, 19–20, 20
functional requirements of project, 35–36

G

Gartner Inc., 255
goals and objectives in charter, 53
government procurement policies, 193
guest speakers in kickoff meeting, 235
Guide to Project Management Body of Knowledge (PMBOK), 9–10
    as ANSI standard, 291
    on earned value, 298–299
    mathematical analysis definition, 111
    project turnover, 350
    risk response planning techniques, 184
    scope definition, 72
    vs. Systems Development Life Cycle (SDLC), 350–352
    work packages breakdown, 105

H

handout for project review, 251

handout, for project review, 251
hardware. *See* equipment
help-desk training, 289
hierarchy, frustrations of, 56–57
high-level requirements, documenting, 38–39
human resources assessment template, 360–361, 361
human resources planning, 135–136, 166–175
   organizational planning, 166–172
      project interfaces, 168
      project organization chart, 171, 172
      roles and responsibilities, 170–171
      staffing management plan, 171–172
   staff acquisition, 172–175
      interviewing potential team members, 173
      negotiation with functional managers, 173–175
   staff augmentation, 191

I

IDC Corporation, 255
IDF (Intermedia Data Facilities), 4
IEEE (Institute of Electronic and Electric Engineers), 291
implementation phase in SDLC, 348–349
implementation plan in project plan, 213
   sample, 221
Independent Validation and Verification (IV&V) companies, 180
indexes (ratios) in earned value, 300, 301
industry standards, impact assessment, 37
informal communications, 188
information distribution, 248–252
   project reviews, 250–252
   status reports, 250
   team meetings, 248–250
information gathering
   about project requirements, 36
   for project request, 33–34
Information Technology Infrastructure Library (ITIL), 291
infrastructure
   changes, 282–283
   as IT project, 4
Initial operational level in CMM, 292
initial project proposal analysis template, 354–355
initiation processes, 14–15
   charter, 51–58
      business case, 53–54
      formal approval, 54–58
      goals and objectives, 53
      project description, 52
      team, 52–53
   exam essentials, 59

project selection, 40–43
   expert judgment, 43
   selection criteria, 41–43
   techniques, 41
receiving project request, 33–39
   documenting requirements, 38–39
   high-level requirements, 34–36
   vendor bids, 37–38
stakeholders, 43–51
   for IT project, 46–50
   matrix, 51
   sponsor, 44
inspection (testing), 284–285
Institute of Electronic and Electric Engineers (IEEE), 291
integrated change control, 278. *See also* change control
integrated system, 4, 168–169
   disadvantages vs. advantages, 255
integration testing, 90
Interactive Voice Response (IVR), 49
interfaces for project, 168
Intermediate Data Facilities (IDF), 4
internal rate of return (IRR), 42
International Organization for Standardization (ISO), 291
internetworking specialists, 48
   typical day, 118
interpersonal interfaces, 168
interviews of potential team members, 173
introductions in kickoff meeting, 235
invitation to bid (IFB), 192–193
IRR (internal rate of return), 42
issue notification template, 356
issues
   monitoring resolution, 295–296
   notification template, 356
   in project plan, 212
      sample, 221
   tracking log, 245, 245–246
   updates in team meeting, 249
IT chain of command, 55
   frustrations of, 56
IT project
   definition. *See* project definition for IT project
   description, real world scenario, 52
   evaluating scope, 85–95
   team members as stakeholders, 48–50
   team time for, 116–117
IT project manager
   common job roles, 6–8
   communication, 9
IT quality control, 290–293
   environmental processes setup, 292–293
   standards, 290–291
IT research, websites for, 255
iterative process, for project plan updates, 215
ITIL (Information Technology Infrastructure Library), 291

J

job descriptions and titles, 138
justification for project, 72–73

K

kickoff for project, 234–237
    for remote team members, 236

L

labor negotiations, and schedule control, 294
late finish, 112
late start, 112
leadership, 11
    for team meeting, 248–249
legal analyst, IT project manager as, 7
lessons learned, 325–329
    from deviations from cost baseline, 282
    documenting, 329
    from schedule changes, 281
    team member involvement in, 328
level of confidence for project estimates, 74
licensing, impact assessment, 37
loaded rate, 146
log for issues tracking, 245, 245–246

M

Main Data Facility (MDF), 4
make or buy analysis, 190–191
Managed operational level in CMM, 292
management skills, 10–13
    communication, 11–12
    leadership, 11
    negotiation, 13
    organization and time management, 13
    problem solving, 12–13
managerial reserve, 150
mandatory dependency, 106
materials descriptions, 138
materials, resource planning for, 136–137
mathematical analysis, 111
matrix for stakeholders, 51
matrix management, 5
matrix organization, 20, 21
MDF (Main Data Facility), 4
measurable results, defining, 73
meetings. *See* team meetings
metrics, 179
Microsoft Access, 119
Microsoft Project, 154
Microsoft Systems Management Server (SMS), 291
Microsoft Web-Based Enterprise Management (WBEM) standard, 291
milestones, 19, 115–116
    and cost tracking, 305
    exit criteria, 180
    and scope statement, 247
minutes for team meeting, 249
module testing, 284
Monte Carlo technique, 183
multiple business unit project, stakeholders for, 46–47

N

NASA Parametric Cost Estimating Handbook, 143
negativity in team members, 238–239
negotiation, 13
    with business unit, 12
    with functional managers, 173–175
    with vendor, 259–260
negotiator, IT project manager as, 7
net present value (NPV), 42
network diagram, 107, 107
    with task duration, 110
network operating system (NOS), 48
non-exempt employees, 153
non-functional requirements of project, 36
normalizing database, 118, 119
norming stage of team development, 234
NPV (net present value), 42
numerical identifiers, in work breakdown structure (WBS), 84, 84

O

online collaboration, 167
operating systems, platform wars, 255–256
operations and support phase in SDLC, 349–351
Optimizing operational level in CMM, 292
order of magnitude estimates, 74, 142
organization management, 13
organizational interfaces, 168
organizational planning, 166–172
    comprehensive review of, 326
    project interfaces, 168
    project organization chart, 171, 172
    roles and responsibilities, 170–171
    staffing management plan, 171–172
organizational structure impacts, 19–22
    functional organization, 19–20, 20
    matrix organization, 20, 21
    projectized organization, 21, 21–22
organizing and writing project plan, 214–215
outsourcing, 86

P

paradigm shift, 254
parametric modeling of costs, 142–143
Pareto diagram, 285–286, 286
payback period in business case summary, 54
PC technicians, documentation for, 290
PDM (precedence diagramming method), 107
performance according to plan, 244–247
    data collection, 244–246
    progress against baselines, 246–247
performance feedback for team members, 237–238
performance indicators, 217, 280
performance monitoring, 237–239
performance reporting, 278, 296–307
    driving stakeholder action, 302–307
        canceling project, 305
        communicating performance deviations, 302–303
        trade-off management, 303–305
    earned value, 298–302
        basics, 299–300
        indexes (ratios), 301–302
        variances, 301
    estimate at completion, 298
    exam essentials, 307–308
    trend analysis, 297
    variance analysis, 297
performing stage of team development, 234
person-hour estimate, 144
pilot test, 6
planned value, 299
planning components
    comprehensive review of, 326
    in project plan, 210–213
planning phase in SDLC, 345
planning processes, 15. *See also* scope of project
    brainstorming, 81
    exam essentials, 197–198
    importance, 71
platform wars, 255–256
PMI (Project Management Institute), 9
PMO (project management office), 55, 55, 135
PMP (Project Management Professional) certification, 9
postponed project, 322
precedence diagramming method (PDM), 107
predecessor task, 106
preliminary investigation, 16
prevention costs, 178–179
preventive action to avoid risk, 184, 293
probability of risk, 183
problem solving, 12–13
    in team meetings, 250
process diagrams, 177, 178
processes, adjustments, 288
procurement planning, 166, 190–194
    case study, 197
    contract types, 191–192

make or buy analysis, 190–191
statement of work (SOW), 192
vendor selection criteria, 193–194
vendor solicitation, 192–193
product description in scope statement, 73
    case study, 91
    sample, 76
production environment, 139
program, defining, 2
program management office (PMO), 148
programmers
    junior-level, 174
    typical day, 118
programming language, platform wars, 255–256
progress reports, 244–245
project closure
    administrative closure, 323–332
        comprehensive review, 325–329
        formal acceptance, 324–325
        project archive, 324
        project turnover, 329–331
        release of team members, 331–332
    case study, 330–331
    contract closeout, 323
    exam essentials, 333
    types, 322–323
project concept documentation, 18–19
project definition, 2–9
    for IT project, 3–6
        automated systems, 5–6
        considerations, 6
        datacenter creation, 4
        Enterprise Resource Planning (ERP), 5
        infrastructure, 4
        server/system deployment, 4–5
        software development, 3
        storage area network (SAN), 5
project description
    in charter, 52
    for IT project, 52
project execution. *See* execution of project
project justification in scope statement, 72–73
    case study, 91
    sample, 76
project kickoff, 234–237
project life cycles, 16–19
project management, 9
    defining, 9–10
    exam essentials, 22–23
Project Management Institute (PMI), 9
Project Management Knowledge Areas, 10
project management office (PMO), 55, 55, 135
Project Management Professional (PMP) certification, 9
project management software, 115, 154
    cost planning with, 154–155
    training for, 155
project manager, 45. *See also* IT project manager
    caught between sponsor and vendor, 258–259

charter identification of, 52–53
communication
   of constraints impact, 74
   of schedule delays, 304
   with stakeholders, 217
expectations in kickoff meeting, 235
project organization chart, 171, 172
project overview in kickoff meeting, 235
project plan
   case study, 218–221
   components, 209–214
      administrative, 210
      appendix, 213
      planning, 210–213
      references, 213
      templates and checklists, 213
   consolidation
      organizing and writing, 214–215
      planning phase closeout, 216–217
      review, 216
      updates, 215–216
   development after-the-fact, 214
   purpose and benefits, 209
   what it is, 208–209
project processes, 14, 14–15
project reviews, 250–252
project team. *See* team
project turnover, 329–331
projectized organization, 21, 21–22
projects
   canceling, 305
   decision to move forward, 217
   distractions from, 117
   at risk of failure, 296
proof of concept, 322

Q

qualitative risk analysis, 182–183
quality control, 278, 283–290
   actions, 287–288
   for documentation, 288–290
   exam essentials, 307–308
   inspection (testing), 284–285
   IT, 290–293
   tools and techniques, 285–287
quality planning, 166, 176–180
   case study, 196
   quality management plan, 179–180
   tools and techniques, 176–179
      benchmarking, 177
      cost benefit analysis, 177
      cost of quality, 178–179
      flowcharting and process diagrams, 177, 178
quantitative risk analysis, 183
quantitatively based durations, 109–110
question and answer period in kickoff meeting, 235–236

R

RAM (responsibility assignment matrix), 139
rebaselining, 280
recognition for team members, 239–241
   budget for, 147
references, in project plan, 213
regulations, impact assessment, real world scenario, 37
regulatory noncompliance, 36
reimbursement of vendor personnel expenses, 257
release of team members, 331–332
remote team members, kickoff for, 236
Repeatable operational level in CMM, 292
request for project, 33–39
   documenting requirements, 38–39
   high-level requirements, 34–36
   vendor bids, 37–38
request for proposal (RFP), 38, 192–193
request for quotation (RFQ), 192–193
requirements of project, 35–36
   changes, 282
   decomposing, 39–40
   documenting, 38–39
   in project plan, 210
      sample, 218–219
resource loading, 146
   where to start, 147
resource planning, 134–141
   changes, 282
   requirements definition, 137, 137–141
      equipment and materials descriptions, 138
      job descriptions and titles, 138
      responsibility assignment matrix (RAM), 139
   types, 135–137
      equipment, 136
      human resources, 135–136
      materials, 136–137
resource pool description, 138
resources. *See also* procurement planning
   adding for duration compression, 114
   list in project plan, 211
      sample, 219–220
   unavailability, 322
responsibility assignment document template, 362, 362
responsibility assignment matrix (RAM), 139
restrictions. *See* constraints
review
   comprehensive, 325–329
      written assessment, 327–329
   final, by stakeholders, 324–325
   of project plan, 216
   of scope statement, 77
revision
   of cost estimates, 281
   to schedule, 280
rewards for team members, 239–241
   budget for, 147

rework, 288
RFP (Request for Proposal), 38, 192–193
risk
    contingency fund and, 149
    in fast tracking, 115
    monitoring and control, 278, 293–296
    in project plan, 212
        sample, 221
risk assessment and mitigation scorecard template, 359, 359
risk identification and assessment template, 356–359
risk planning, 166, 181–185
    analysis, 182–183
        case study, 196
    risk identification, 181–182
    risk response, 184–185
        contingency action, 185
        preventive action, 184
roles and responsibilities document, 170–171

S

SAN (storage area network), 5
schedule baseline, progress reporting against, 246–247
schedule control, 278, 280–281
schedule performance index, 301
schedule planning
    activity definition, 104–105
    activity duration estimates, 108–110
        estimating techniques, 109–110
    activity sequence, 105–107
        dependency types, 106
        network diagram, 107, 107
        task dependency relationships, 106–107
    exam essentials, 122–123
    need for, 104
    schedule development, 110–116
        baseline, 116
        critical path method (CPM), 111–114
        duration compression, 114–115
        milestones, 115–116
        project management software, 115
    time juggling in real world, 116–120
    trade-offs, 303–305
        phased delay, 304
schedule variance, 301
scope change control, 278, 279–280
scope creep, 78, 279
scope evaluation for IT project, 85–95
    definitions for testing elements, 90, 95
    deliverables, 86–87
    loss of senior project technician, 89–90
    mini-project consultant/vendor relationships, 88–89
    project crosses IT shops, 90
    sidebar systems and undisclosed process elements, 88
    size of IT shop, 85–86
    success criteria, 88
    working with business clients, 87
scope of project
    cost trade-offs and, 305
    exam essentials, 95–96
    management plan, 71, 77–79
    overview, 71–85
    planning, 71–72
    trade-offs, 303
    verification, 247
    wineries e-mail and intranet systems, case study, 91–94
scope statement, 71, 72–77
    assumptions, 75
    completion criteria, 74
    constraints, 75
    major deliverables, 73
    and milestones, 247
    product description, 73
    project justification, 72–73
    in project plan, 210–211
        sample, 219
    review and consensus, 77
    sample, 76–77
    success criteria, 73
    time and cost estimates, 74
scoring model for project selection decision, 42
SDLC. *See* Systems Development Life Cycle (SDLC)
SDS (system design specification), 17–18, 347–348
security analysts, 49
security for project documentation, 215
SEI (Software Engineering Institute), 292
selection of project, 40–43
    expert judgment, 43
    selection criteria, 41–43
    techniques, 41
sensitivity analysis, 183
sequence for activities in schedule planning, 82, 105–107
    dependency types, 106
    network diagram, 107, 107
    task dependency relationships, 106–107
server administrators, 48
    documentation for, 289
    typical day, 118
server/system deployment, 4–5
severity of risk, 183
sidebar systems, 88
    real world scenario, 89
sign-off on deliverables, 247
single business unit project, stakeholders for, 46
site acceptance testing, 284–285
Six Sigma, 176
    "belts", 292
skills inventory worksheet template, 361, 361
SMS (Systems Management Server), 291
social interaction in kickoff meeting, 236–237
software
    development, 3
        life cycle, 8, 16
    for project management, 115

software developer, 48
Software Engineering Institute (SEI), 292
sole-source documentation, 193
solicitation of vendors, 192–193
SOW. *See* statement of work (SOW)
spending, data collection on, 246
sponsor, 44
    changing commitment of, 242–243
    involvement in jeopardized project, 296
    project manager caught between vendor and, 258–259
    project plan review by, 216
    project review for, 251
    and vendor delays, 256
SQL Server, converting Access database to, 119
stability of scope, 78
staffing. *See* human resources planning
stakeholders
    buy-in to charter, 54
    communication with, 86, 188–189, 189
        on milestones, 116
    driving action, 43–51, 302–307
        canceling project, 305
        communicating performance deviations, 302–303
        trade-off management, 303–305
    final review by, 324–325
    for IT project, 46–50
    list in project plan, 211
        sample, 219
    matrix, 51
    plan review by, 217
    relationships, 241–244
        client, 241–242
        functional managers, 243–244
        sponsor, 44, 242–243
    and vendor delays, 256
standards
    for IT quality control, 290–291
    organizations for, 291
start to finish relationship, 107
start to start relationship, 107
statement of work (SOW), 38, 192, 257
    progress report from vendors in, 253
statistical analysis, monitoring quality outputs through, 292
statistical sampling, 287
status date for earned value, 299
status reports, 250
storage area network (SAN), 5
storming stage of team development, 234
strategist, IT project manager as, 7
success criteria, 88
    in scope statement, 73
        case study, 91–92
        sample, 76
successor task, 106
suppliers. *See* vendors
support plan in project plan, 213
    sample, 221
system architects, 49

system deployment, 4–5
system testing, 284
systems analysis, 8, 17
systems analysts, 6, 49
systems design, 17–18
systems design specification (SDS), 17–18, 347–348
Systems Development Life Cycle (SDLC), 344–352
    analysis phase, 345–347
    design phase, 347–348
    vs. Guide to the PMBOK, 350–352
    implementation phase, 348–349
    operations and support phase, 349–351
    planning phase, 345
systems evaluation, 18, 348
systems implementation phase, 18
Systems Management Server (SMS), 291
systems operation and support, 18
systems planning phase, 16
systems request, 16
systems requirements document, 17, 347

T

table of contents in project plan, 210
    sample, 218
target date for completion, 74
task dependency relationships, 106–107
team
    in charter, 52–53
    communication with, 188
    development, 233–241
        performance monitoring, 237–239
        project kickoff, 234–237
        rewards and recognition, 239–241
        training, 239
    geographically dispersed, 167
        and testing, 285
    interviewing potential members, 173
    IT project manager as builder, 7
    loss of critical member, 89–90
team meetings, 248–250
team members, 45
    disputes, 238
    ego factor, 254
    hours available and accountability, 174
    interaction between, 249
    lessons learned involvement, 328
    misunderstanding with vendors, 253
    negativity in, 238–239
    performance feedback for, 237–238
    release at project closure, 331–332
    remote, kickoff for project for, 236
technical interfaces, 168
technical issues
    project requirements, 36
    project review and, 252
technical writers, 49

technologist, IT project manager as, 7
telecommunication specialists, typical day, 118
telephony specialists, 49
templates
　　on CD-ROM, 252, 354–362
　　for cost estimating, 146
　　Executive Project Summary Worksheet, 252
　　human resources assessment, 360–361, 361
　　initial project proposal analysis, 354–355
　　issue notification, 355–356, 356
　　in project plan, 213
　　for project review, 251
　　responsibility assignment document, 362
　　risk assessment and mitigation scorecard, 359, 359
　　risk identification and assessment, 356–359
　　skills inventory worksheet, 361, 361
　　vested interest breakdown, 359–360, 360
test environment, 139
testing, 90, 284–285
　　elements, 95
　　in SDLC implementation phase, 348
time and materials contracts, 192
time constraint, 74
time estimates in scope statement, 74
　　sample, 77
time management, 13. *See also* schedule planning
time manager, IT project manager as, 7
to-complete performance index, 301–302
To Do list, 83
top down estimating, 109, 142, 154
total quality management (TQM), 176
tracking project expenses, 148
trade-off management, 303–305
training
　　contracting for, 191
　　plan in project plan, 213
　　　　sample, 221
　　in project management, 240
　　of team members, 239
　　for users, 289
transference of risk, 184
trend analysis, 287, 297
trigger for risk, 295
triple constraint, 74
turnover of project, 329–331

U

UAT. *See* user acceptance testing (UAT)
uniqueness in product description, 73
unit testing, 90, 284
updates
　　to project plan, 215–216
　　to schedule, 280

user acceptance testing (UAT), 95, 284
user documentation
　　quality of, 289
　　updates, 330
users, 45
　　failure of process elements disclosure, 88
　　training for, 289

V

variance analysis, 297
variances in earned value, 300
vendor, bids, 37–38
vendor contract administration, 253–260
　　delays, 256
　　managing disagreements, 253–256
　　payment process, 256–257
　　progress reporting, 253
vendors
　　communications with, 256, 257
　　　　preparation before, 259
　　misunderstanding with, 253–254
　　project manager caught between sponsor and, 258–259
　　relationship with, 88–89
　　selection criteria, 193–194
　　solicitation, 192–193
　　testing deliverables, 285
vested interest breakdown template, 359–360, 360
visionary, IT project manager as, 7

W

WBS. *See* work breakdown structure (WBS)
Web-Based Enterprise Management (WBEM) standard, 291
websites
　　for IT research, 255
　　for standards organizations, 291
weekends, in activity duration estimates, 108
wineries e-mail and intranet systems case study, 57–58
　　closeout, 330–331
　　communications plan, 195
　　cost planning, 152–154
　　evaluating, 306
　　finalized plan, 218–221
　　procurement planning, 197
　　project execution, 260–261
　　quality plan, 196
　　risk assessment, 196
　　scope document, 91–94
　　work breakdown structure (WBS), 120–121

work breakdown structure (WBS), 71, 79–85, 84
   benefits, 85
   case study, 92–94, 120–121
   creation guidelines, 82–84
   decomposing major deliverables, 80–82, 82
   organizing, 80
   starting, 81
   template, 80
work days, vs. calendar days, 108
work effort, 144
work package, 82
writing project plan, 214–215
written assessment of project, 327–329
written commitments from vendor, 260

Sybex Covers CompTIA
CERTIFICATION PROGRAMS

Sybex publishes self-study materials for the following CompTIA certifications:

- A+
- i-Net+
- IT Project+
- Linux+
- Network+
- Security+
- Server+

STUDY GUIDES

- Practical, in-depth coverage of all exam objectives
- Includes hands-on exercises and hundreds of review questions
- CD includes a test engine, electronic flashcards for PCs, Pocket PCs, and Palm devices and a PDF version of the entire book

ISBN 0-7821-4244-3

VIRTUAL LABS™

- Realistic, interactive simulations of key network features, such as router and switch functionality
- Step-by-step labs covering critical certification skills
- Customizable labs to meet your needs

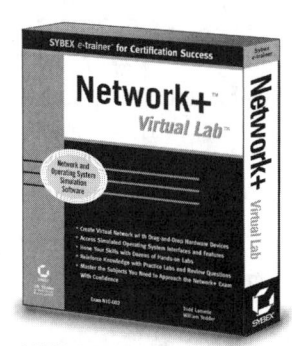

ISBN 0-7821-4098-X

In addition to being CAQC approved, Sybex is a cornerstone member of both the Security+ and Server+ Cornerstone Committee.

ISBN 0-7821-3026-7

Go to **certification.sybex.com** for a complete listing of certification products

CompTIA. One Industry. One Voice.

SYBEX®
www.sybex.com

Sybex—The Leader in Certification

Project Management Skills for all Levels

Project Management JumpStart™

by Kim Heldman, PMP • ISBN: 0-7821-4214-1 • US $24.99

For those interested in beginning or exploring a career in project management, coverage include

- The basic skills of a project manager
- Creating project schedules and determining project budgets
- Communication and negotiation skills

PMP®: Project Management Professional Study Guide, 2nd Edition

by Kim Heldman, PMP • ISBN: 0-7821-4323-7 • US $59.99

A comprehensive package to prepare for the PMP certification exam, this Study Guide provides

- Detailed coverage of all PMP Exam Process Groups
- Refreshed content that make project management concepts clearer and easier to comprehend
- Companion CD with Testing Software, Flashcards for PCs, Pocket PCs, and Palm Handhelds, Two Bonus Practice Exams, and the Entire Book in PDF

PMP®: Project Management Professional Workbook

by Claudia Baca, PMP; Patti Jansen, PMP • ISBN: 0-7821-4240-0 • US $34.9

A one-of-a-kind book that will give you hands-on experience as you prepare for the PMP exam, this workbook provides:

- Clear introductions that put the exercises in context and explain the importance of key project management skills
- Dozens of exercises designed by two veteran project managers to correlate directly with PMP objectives
- Cross references to the PMP Study Guide for additional instructional content

PMP®: Final Exam Review

by Kim Heldman, PMP • ISBN: 0-7821-4324-5 • US $29.99

To ensure you're truly prepared for the exam, this book contains:

- Four complete practice tests
- Complex scenario questions with detailed explanations
- Companion CD with testing software and flashcards for PCs, Pocket PCs, and Palm Handhelds

PMP®: Project Management Professional Certification Kit

by Kim Heldman, PMP; Claudia Baca, PMP; Patti Jansen, PMP
ISBN: 0-7821-4325-3 • US $109.97

A 3-in-one product, this kit includes:

- PMP®: Project Management Professional Study Guide, 2nd Edition
- PMP®: Project Management Professional Workbook
- PMP®: Final Exam Review

$124.97 Value Save $15!

SYBEX
www.sybex.com